MW01275586

Wrestling with Dem
Voting Systems as Politics in the Twentieth-Century West

Though sharing broadly similar processes of economic and political development from the mid- to late nineteenth century onward, western
countries have diverged greatly in their choice of voting systems:
most of Europe shifted to proportional voting around the First World
War, while Anglo-American countries have stuck with relative majority or majority voting rules. Using a comparative historical approach,
Wrestling with Democracy examines why voting systems have (or have
not) changed in western industrialized countries over the past century.

In this first single-volume study of voting system reform covering all
western industrialized countries, Dennis Pilon reviews national efforts
in this area over four time spans: the nineteenth century, the period
around the First World War, the Cold War, and the 1990s. Pilon pro-
vocatively argues that voting system reform has been a part of larger
struggles over defining democracy itself, highlighting previously overlooked episodes of reform and challenging widely held assumptions
about institutional change. In doing so, he underlines the key importance of social class, disputes between left and right, and the messy and
unpredictable impact of historical events.

(Studies in Comparative Political Economy and Public Policy)

DENNIS PILON is an associate professor in the Department of Political
Science at York University.

Studies in Comparative Political Economy and Public Policy

Editors: MICHAEL HOWLETT, DAVID LAYCOCK (Simon Fraser University), and STEPHEN MCBRIDE (McMaster University)

Studies in Comparative Political Economy and Public Policy is designed to showcase innovative approaches to political economy and public policy from a comparative perspective. While originating in Canada, the series will provide attractive offerings to a wide international audience, featuring studies with local, subnational, cross-national, and international empirical bases and theoretical frameworks.

Editorial Advisory Board

For a list of books published in the series, see page 393.

Wrestling with Democracy

Voting Systems as Politics in the Twentieth-Century West

DENNIS PILON

UNIVERSITY OF TORONTO PRESS
Toronto Buffalo London

© University of Toronto Press 2013
Toronto Buffalo London
www.utppublishing.com
Printed in Canada

ISBN 978-1-4426-4541-7 (cloth)
ISBN 978-1-4426-1350-8 (paper)

Library and Archives Canada Cataloguing in Publication

Pilon, Dennis, 1965–
Wrestling with democracy: voting systems as politics in the twentieth-century West / Dennis Pilon.

(Studies in comparative political economy and public policy)
Includes bibliographical references and index.
ISBN 978-1-4426-4541-7 (bound). – ISBN 978-1-4426-1350-8 (pbk.)

1. Democracy – Western countries – History – 20th century. 2. Western countries – Politics and government – 20th century. 3. Voting – Western countries – History – 20th century. 4. Political parties – Western countries – History – 20th century. I. Title. II. Series: Studies in comparative political economy and public policy

JC421.P55 2013   321.809182'10904   C2012-908360-7

This book has been published with the help of a grant from the Canadian Federation for the Humanities and Social Sciences, through the Awards to Scholarly Publications Program, using funds provided by the Social Sciences and Humanities Research Council of Canada.

University of Toronto Press acknowledges the financial assistance to its publishing program of the Canada Council for the Arts and the Ontario Arts Council.

University of Toronto Press acknowledges the financial support of the Government of Canada through the Canada Book Fund for its publishing activities.

To Dann and Ryann

Contents

Acknowledgments

This book has a history. It began with my introduction to the topic while living in the United Kingdom in 1987. Upon returning to Canada I became fascinated with uncovering the largely forgotten historical episodes of voting system reform in various Canadian municipalities and provinces. So began my decades-long engagement with this topic, one I continue to find interesting. Over the years I have come at the issue in different ways. I have written fine-grained, archive-based historical studies of Canadian voting system reform, focusing on the national, provincial, and municipal levels. At the same time, I have produced more synthetic and comparative accounts of voting system change across Western countries, like the 2002 study I prepared for the Law Commission of Canada. This book is cast in the latter approach and is based on my PhD dissertation. However, the present book represents a major revision of the original study, with a completely reworked introductory chapter, a wholly new chapter on democracy, as well as significant changes to the empirical chapters.

Not surprisingly, given its long gestation, I have many people and institutions to acknowledge for their support of this project. Given its origins in my dissertation research, I must first thank the committee who helped direct and shape the work: Leo Panitch, Fred Fletcher, and Bob MacDermid, as well as my external examiner, Frances Fox Piven. As the book has transitioned from a dissertation to a book, I have benefited from the advice of numerous academics: Mark Leier, Henry Milner, Graham White, Rob Walker, Miriam Smith, Bryan Palmer, Joan Sangster, David Marsh, Joyce Green, Greg Albo, James Curran, the members of the Law Commission of Canada, and my colleagues in the Political Science Departments at University of Victoria and York.

A number of scholars read all or part of the manuscript and offered excellent suggestions to improve it: Stephen Hellman, Jim Tully, and Stephen McBride. The participants in the European Consortium on Political Research meetings in Lisbon read what would comprise a significant part of my revised introduction and gave me helpful feedback: Pippa Norris, Alan Renwick, Amel Ahmed, Jorg Elklit, and David Farrell. I must also thank the three anonymous reviewers for the University of Toronto Press for their attentive and detailed comments. Of course, any remaining errors in the book or problems with the analysis are solely my responsibility.

This book has been published with the help of a grant from the Canadian Federation for the Humanities and Social Sciences, through the Awards to Scholarly Publications Program, using funds provided by the Social Sciences and Humanities Research Council of Canada. It has also benefited from research funds provided by York University, the Frost Centre at Trent University, and the University of Victoria.

In researching this book, I have benefited from libraries and librarians in many places: the University of Toronto Robarts Library, the York University Library, Columbia University Special Collections, and the University of Victoria Library. I would also like to thank Pia Russell at the University of Victoria Library for securing me space to work on revisions to the manuscript. A number of scholars sent me materials – thanks to Michael Bernhard for sending me his book on German institutional reform, and Alan Renwick for sending me a number of his articles on European and New Zealand voting system reform. Two research assistants at the University of Victoria also laboured to find different sources for me and clean up my bibliography – my thanks to Shawn Courtney and Stephan Fortin. The index for this book would not have been produced without the patient instruction and generous labour of my colleague at York, Jacqueline Krikorian, who kindly offered to teach me how it was done.

At the University of Toronto Press, I would like to thank to Virgil Duff for expressing an initial interest in the book and Daniel Quinlan for pursuing it and getting it through the approval process. Additionally, thanks to Wayne Herrington on the production side, and Ian MacKenzie for his detailed editorial work on the manuscript. Thanks to Stephen McBride for suggesting I bring the project to UTP.

Over the years many friends have discussed and debated voting system reform with me and had a strong influence on my thinking: William Chadwick, Howard Cherniak, Larry Gordon, Alan Alvare, Bob Webster, Rick Slye, Geoff Kennedy, Charles Smith, and Dennis Soron.

Finally, I should acknowledge my family – parents, grandparents, brothers, and sisters – who have been very supportive of my obsession over the years. But the man who has done the most heavy lifting throughout the long process of making this book has been my husband Dann, with support from our daughter Ryann. In recognition, I dedicate this book to them.

Let me end with a few words about the cover of the book. The photomontage was created by the late Toronto artist Richard Slye, a jazz drummer, Faulkner scholar, cineaste, poet, and social critic, particularly on questions of class. The cover is meant to capture the clash of social visions I argue is at the heart of twentieth-century struggles over democracy, particularly at the level of perceptions and propaganda. The right often promoted the left's agenda as if there were little difference between social democrats and Leninist communists. Some believed it, but many more opportunistically blurred the differences for political gain. So too on the left, critics complained that the right were merely apologists for American influence and a democratic process reduced to consumerism. Behind these representations were, in fact, real differences in terms of what left and right thought democracy should amount to. But, as the book makes clear, sometimes decisions were based as much on struggles over these perceived differences as the substantive ones.

Wrestling with Democracy

Voting Systems as Politics in the Twentieth-Century West

Chapter 1

Introduction

Introduction

For most of political science, *democracy* is a word that seems to engender a degree of uneasiness, similar to the way economists respond to the word *capitalism*. Economists, it is said, prefer to talk about "market societies" rather than capitalist ones. The former term seems neutral and universal, whereas the latter seems historical, vaguely normative, and freighted with political connotations. In a similar way, and for arguably similar reasons, political scientists will often briefly mention democracy but spend most of their time talking about elections. In practice, most simply reduce democracy to elections. While there may be practical reasons for such shorthand, the convention can have the effect of obscuring important lines of enquiry. For instance, Alan Renwick's recent book *The Politics of Electoral Reform* begins by suggesting, "Elections lie at the heart of modern democracy."[1] For that reason, he argues, we should understand where election rules come from and how they change. But after reading the book one might be forgiven for thinking that, for Renwick, elections are not merely the heart of democracy but the entire body. Indeed, he says at one point, "Belief in democracy amounts to belief in the value of following certain processes."[2] Democracy then seems little more than the rules concerned with carrying out elections. Such a narrow casting of the scope of democracy has the effect of presuming the very thing that should be examined – what did people think they were doing when they engaged in efforts to change democracy's rules? The "democracy equals elections" shorthand obscures this question before any investigation can begin.

This book is also interested in where democratic rules come from and why they change or stay the same. But it seeks to displace the electoralist focus of the current political science work on this topic with an interdisciplinary one that puts democracy at the centre of the study. Renwick's claim must then be reversed. If we want to know where election rules come from, we need to recognize that democracy, and more specifically democratic struggle, is at the heart of elections, particularly when the rules come under critical scrutiny. Such an approach would recognize that democracy is not merely this or that institution, nor is it amenable to a neat ideal-type definition or categorization, but is instead a messy historical accomplishment with no fixed boundaries or content. Despite a recent spate of books with *politics* in the title, much work on democratic structures and their reform seems unaware of these struggles, or that such struggles may have influenced what they are studying.[3] In fact, most are devoid of any engagement with the issues and movements that defined politics and democratic struggle in the twentieth century, such as battles between left and right, historic campaigns around social citizenship and the welfare state, etc. This reflects the peculiar penchant in political science for dealing with such institutions in isolation, divorced from the larger social environment.[4] An interdisciplinary approach, by contrast, brings the social back in, recasting the story into a narrative where the very shape of democracy is recognized to be constantly under pressure from competing and conflicting political interests and campaigns. Here democratic struggle is the story, and fights over election rules are just one locale for the brawl.

Of course, that modern democracy appears to be all about elections should not really be surprising. As the key interface between citizens and government in western societies, elections are where politics is seen largely to occur. As a result, political science has examined many aspects of the electoral process: voter behaviour, political party activity, the role of the media, etc. Yet, until recently, one key aspect of elections was largely overlooked: the origin of the electoral rules themselves. Modern representative elections are governed by a complex body of rules generally known as an "electoral system." These rules cover everything from who can vote and how to mark a ballot paper, to how much money aspirants to office may spend to get elected, and much else. While scholars have expended much effort cataloguing and comparing these various rules across western democracies, they have spent less time enquiring about their origins or why particular countries use the rules that they do. This has been particularly true of one specific set of election rules: the voting system. Yet, since the 1990s, voting systems have elicited considerable interest, with academics and some members of the public and media wanting to know where particular western voting systems come from, why different countries use the ones they do, and what factors may contribute to keeping them in place or replacing them with something else.

Just to be clear, the voting system is understood here as the subset of electoral laws that set out how votes cast in an election will be converted into representation. Throughout the twentieth century, western industrialized countries typically used one of three major voting systems – plurality, majority, or proportional – for national elections.[5] Historically, political scientists devoted considerable attention to analysing how these different voting systems work, and an enormous scholarly literature emerged debating how different voting rules may condition different political effects.[6] But less attention was paid to why a voting system may change at any given time in any given country. The lack of interest might be explained by the long-term stability of voting system arrangements in most western industrialized countries – from 1920 to 1993, France was the only western democracy to change from one system to another. For the most part, then, political scientists tended to assume that the choice of voting system somehow reflected the needs of its particular polity, the desires of its citizens, or the ability of existing, self-interested political party elites to prevent consideration of change from emerging as a serious issue. Widespread public indifference towards the voting system, and a general ignorance of its workings or the existence of alternatives, only further convinced political scientists that the origin or alteration of these voting rules was not a terribly important object of study.

But a host of developments in the 1990s forced political scientists to revisit the question of voting system change, including the rapid institutional renewal of the former Soviet bloc countries in Eastern Europe, the end of the apartheid regime in South Africa, and the return to civilian and democratic rule throughout Latin America. Voting system reform came even to the more established western democracies – something political scientists had long declared nearly impossible – with change effected for national elections in Italy, New Zealand, and Japan, and at the sub-national level in the United Kingdom. Observers quickly noted that political science apparently had little to offer in explaining these recent developments.[7] Since then, scholars appear to be making up for lost time. Fortunately, at a more general level, the discipline had already been in the process of expanding its focus to include questions of institutional development.[8] The revival of interest in the state in the 1970s and 1980s helped fuel new research into the historical origins and development of state institutions and the factors that caused them to change.[9] As political scientists turned their attention to voting system reform, they discovered that voting rules were neither as stable nor as uncontested historically as past literature had suggested.

Since the 1990s, a considerable body of work has emerged addressing voting system change, some of it building on past work, some moving in new directions. Despite this increased attention, no consensus has emerged about why or how voting systems either change or stay the same in western industrialized countries. The literature can be divided into three broad, sometimes overlapping, streams: cultural modernization, rational choice, and historical institutionalism. Current cultural modernization work builds on traditional modernization approaches, arguing that voting systems change in line with the shifting values and needs of the particular polity undergoing reform. While offering plausible accounts of change, cultural modernization approaches struggle to provide any concrete links between the claimed social changes and the specific voting system reforms. By contrast, current rational choice accounts of voting system reform address this shortcoming directly, identifying the actors interested in change and the contexts that influence their decisions. But rational choice work says little about just *why* various actors are interested in voting system change and tend to operate with a thin version of context, one that seldom ventures into the specific details of any actual historical or comparative context. Indeed, both cultural modernization and rational choice accounts largely eschew any engagement with historical or contextual detail by design, favouring more variable-driven cross-national quantitative studies. This latter absence is addressed by work grounded in the emerging historical institutionalism tradition. These scholars do map the details of the historical context, paying particular attention to the path dependencies that emerge from the adoption of various institutions. But such work, while a dramatic advance on the rest of the canon, seems to have little to say about the expressly political issues and disputes driving reform. Given such results, it is not surprising that one recent overview declared a theory of voting system change to be still elusive while another suggested it may never be found.[10]

Such pessimistic observations seem curious when one plots the actual episodes of change comparatively and across time in western countries. Attending to comparable western industrialized countries – in other words, countries with similar economic and political development – it is striking both how little voting system reform there has been over the past century and how often the rare episodes of reform have tended to ripple across borders, encompassing many countries at the same time. For instance, voting system reform emerged as an issue across many western countries in the late nineteenth century but was introduced nowhere. Then most western European countries switched to proportional voting around the First World War. Another lesser-known wave of voting system reform occurred in Europe after the Second World War. And then the issue re-emerged in multiple arenas again in the 1990s. The fact that reform has risen and fallen so dramatically over time, and simultaneously across national borders, would seem to suggest that there is something consistent going on, that there is something about voting system reform in western countries that is systematic and particular, something waiting to be found by social scientists. Yet so far, they have failed to grasp what it might be.

In a bid to grasp that elusive something that is fuelling voting system reform in western countries, this book will build on and depart from existing work in a number of ways. It agrees with cultural modernization that larger social changes are important in understanding voting system changes but seeks to define the "social" more clearly and identify how actors link the social with campaigns for institutional change. It agrees with rational choice that actors and contexts matter but seeks to identify in more detail just what actors are trying to accomplish in fighting over voting systems and how specific contexts influence their decisions. The book has the most in common with historical institutional approaches, though it seeks to take up historical analysis more critically and comparatively, with an eye to underlining the role of political conflict in fuelling these events. To accomplish all this, it will draw from an interdisciplinary tradition of comparative historical method to develop a "critical institutionalist" approach. In doing so, it will challenge the bias in political science against a deep knowledge of contexts and actor motivations in pursuing and formulating causal explanations.[11] In fact, it will argue that such bias is the major barrier in advancing the study of comparative voting system change. Instead, it is precisely by analysing the "deep politics" of societies – that is, the issues that polarize and divide modern political societies – and how they influence political struggle that we may come to understand why anyone cared enough to fight over voting systems in the first place.[12]

Why Study Voting System Change?

As a rule, voting systems are not well known by the public, and even many political scientists are hazy on the basic details that distinguish one from another. Some would argue that this is for good reason. They might argue that voting systems are not terribly important, that they are simply an administrative detail, or that institutions do not affect politics in any significant way. Whether voting systems have any real impact on politics is a huge debate and not one that we need to settle here. It is a sufficient response to note that politicians with the power to alter voting systems have acted as if they are important, and it is their motivations for acting thus that concern us, not whether they are ultimately correct in their beliefs. Of course, many political scientists today would agree that the choice of voting system has potentially important effects on any given polity. As Sartori once noted, many analysts consider voting systems "the most specific manipulative instrument in politics," primarily because they are seen to control access to the political system itself.[13] For these reasons alone, there would appear to be ample reasons to study voting systems.

Yet there are other reasons that make the study of voting system change important to contemporary political analysis. Attention to the historical and contemporary struggles over voting system reform fit with the renewed interest in institutions and institutional change fuelled by the emerging sub-field in historical institutionalism, thus potentially contributing to our understanding of processes of institutional reform more generally. Debate over voting system origins and reform may also offer important insights into contemporary concerns about the "democratic deficit" and potential measures to address it. For instance, recent citizens' assemblies in two Canadian provinces approached the question of voting system reform by focusing participants on linking what they perceived to be the broad democratic values held by the public to choices over different institutional designs, assuming that fitting the two would lead to successful reform.[14] Yet both initiatives failed for reasons that appear to have little to do with public values about democracy. The designers assumed there was a link between the public and their democratic institutions, yet such a link failed to materialize as their reform process played out.[15] This is where examining what the links really are would be helpful. Existing work on institutions is too uncritical – it is generally too willing to accept the conventional reasons offered about why various institutions exist or operate as they do. By contrast, the *critical* institutionalist approach to be developed here operates on the assumption that discovering where institutions *actually* come from may help to understand why they are still being used, why they seem difficult to change, and what might be required to change them.

Finally, as will be noted in more detail below, the study of voting system change offers us a chance to bring more interdisciplinary approaches into the study of politics, particularly the value of historical comparison, and questions about how we frame the exploration of institutional origins and their reform. As will be explained below, this study will explore voting systems in a context very different from that of much existing work, bringing it into dialogue with critical work on democratic struggle and democratization.

Sketching the Research Project

This book will examine every instance of national voting system reform in western countries throughout the twentieth century. It will examine both successful and failed attempts at reform. Let me define a little more clearly the parameters of the project by delimiting the meaning of various terms used here.

By *voting system* I mean the institutional rules that convert votes into seats in a national election for a country's main legislative body (typically, the lower house). Some may complain, why limit the institutional scrutiny to voting systems? After all, there are many aspects of electoral systems that could be explored: America's unique primary system, comparative regimes of campaign finance, districting issues in single and multi-member ridings, etc. As already noted, the historical attention to and struggle over voting systems distinct from other electoral institutions is more than enough to justify giving it sole attention in a study like this one. However, there are also methodological reasons to limit the focus, precisely so as to make comparison as straightforward as possible and to narrow the claims made about institutional change.

By *reform* I refer to a major reform of a voting system, that is, changes from one family of voting system to another (e.g., from plurality to a proportional system), excluding more minor reforms (like ones that may only affect degrees of proportionality, e.g., post–Second World War reforms in Sweden).

By *western* I refer to the countries typically associated with the pattern of political and economic development of western industrialized countries throughout the twentieth century, specifically the countries of northwestern Europe and the Anglo-American countries of North America and Australasia. The countries defined as *western* change over time, thus Japan is included in "the west" by the 1990s but not in prior periods. Though non-western countries also witnessed efforts at voting system reform throughout this period, their general political and economic development has been markedly different from that in western countries.[16] While useful comparisons may be made at some point between western and non-western patterns of reform, too often indiscriminate comparison amongst widely different countries only confuses matters.[17] As this study seeks to uncover why voting systems change in many different countries, limiting our study to countries with a broadly similar history of economic and political development will allow us to more effectively isolate the key factors contributing to change.[18]

The main point of the research is to explain *why* voting systems did or did not change in the different countries. In large part, the book operates on a simple premise: if we want to know why different actors have pursued voting system reform at different times and in different places, we should examine the episodes in some detail. Then we can use what we find to establish some generalizations about the reform process. Of course, the *way* we choose to explore these episodes may influence what we find. Existing work tends to be stuck offering rather superficial generalizations about reform motives (e.g., self-interest) or weak connections between social change and institutional reform. This, in part, results from an overweening reliance on quantitative studies that tend to slice and dice the complexity of historical events into neatly measurable variables that can be compared across countries and across time, but at a cost of explanatory depth and power. However, even more historical work in political science tends to offer merely descriptive distinctions between different reform contexts, with little insight into the larger political disputes that might be animating the struggle. Indeed, there is a curiously apolitical quality to most existing work on voting system change that seems devoid of the great political divisions that animated the twentieth century, specifically battles between left and right for control of the state or the public's shifting sense of the acceptable parameters of democratic activity. Instead, they offer rather bloodless accounts that highlight interests (parties, politicians) or functional needs, with seemingly little curiosity about what historical, social, or political factors might be influencing these "interests" or defining "public needs."

The analytic framework to be employed here seeks to take the "why" questions deeper than the work to date, beyond vague allusions to politician self-interest or changing social values, to the larger political objectives that actors have sought in maintaining or changing an institution like a voting system. As such, the actors must be understood within their own historical contexts to critically assess their motives and actions. Specifically, we need to know more about how they understood the contexts they were operating within (rather than imposing ideal type definitions on various contexts), how they were affected by them, and how they strategized to act within them or change them. To understand the possible impact of such contexts, the study will pay particular attention to the order of historical events as an important factor in influencing the decisions actors make.

Baldly stated, this book will provide considerable evidence for the classic explanations of voting system change from history and political sociology (e.g., Braunias, Duverger, Rokkan, Boix), namely, that class factors have been the key influence on voting system choices throughout the twentieth century in western industrialized countries. But it will resurrect these claims in a way somewhat different from that of past practitioners, using both different methods and different definitions of key concepts. Over the course of the book, through a detailed and comparative exploration of the different cases across time and space, it will be shown how voting system reforms have repeatedly become a strategic site of struggle between opposing forces with dramatically different visions of political society and antagonistic social and economic interests. Whether in struggles for or against democracy itself circa the First World War, or amid the superpower confrontations animating the Cold War, or the more recent campaigns to neoliberalize western states, it will be argued that struggles to change voting systems were really struggles over the substance of democracy itself, what it might do and for whom. In all these, the strategic position of left political parties and the threat they did or did not pose to conventional political elites was crucial.

In what follows, the existing work on voting system reform will be reviewed, followed by a more detailed breakdown of the new framework that will be employed in this study, followed by the plan for the book as whole.

What's Been Done: A Review of the Literature

Early scholars tended to explain voting system choices normatively, either as the choices of enlightened democrats or corrupt party hacks.[19] Later scholars turned to modernization theory and the role of cleavages in influencing franchise reforms, the shape of party systems, and, by extension, voting systems.[20] These scholars did suggest that class was an important factor in voting system choice, particularly the fear of how a mass working class suffrage might negatively affect traditional political and economic elites. But, for the most part, many scholars simply assumed the reasons that different voting systems were used. Reading back from the political results of their own time, most scholars asserted that voting systems somehow reflected the political culture of the society that used them, claiming, for instance, that European usages of proportional representation (PR) reflected a consensus orientation to politics while Anglo-American preferences for relative majority systems reflected an adversarial political culture.[21] By the 1970s, the long use of most western voting systems was proof enough for most researchers that the choices were functional to the societies using them. After all, the logic went, the fact that people used the various systems with little complaint was evidence of their compliance. Still, alongside these views were crypto-rational choice observations that voting systems were unlikely to be reformed because those who benefited from them were unlikely to change them.[22] With such views, political scientists had a rationale for both the origins of voting systems and their long-term stability.

The events surrounding the dramatic voting system reforms of the early 1990s, specifically the replacement of long-entrenched national voting systems in New Zealand, Italy, and Japan, quickly demonstrated the poverty of existing generalizations about voting system change. As analysts tried to make sense of the developments, they found they had to discard one truism after another. Pippa Norris suggested that typical political science characterizations of voting system reform as involving a "judicious and careful calculation about the most appropriate means to achieve certain ends" did not square with recent events. More realistically, she claimed, new systems were "born kicking and screaming into the world out of a messy, incremental compromise between contending factions battling for survival, determined by power politics."[23] Researchers began to question whether institutional reform required a "crisis" to emerge, suggesting instead that reform might be seen as continuous and ongoing, a part of "normal" politics as well, while others even challenged the long-accepted wisdom that voting systems were particularly stable institutions and resistant to change.[24] But why voting systems *specifically* had become such popular vehicles for reform produced less consensus.

Recent work on voting system change is rooted in what Pippa Norris might call cultural modernization theories and/or actor-centred models.[25] Cultural modernization approaches include behavioural models that use surveys to highlight changing public attitudes and political party organization amidst a shift from an industrial to post-industrial form of society, or seemingly functionalist models that employ variable-based measures of voting system performance. By contrast, actor-centred models are primarily logic-driven rational choice approaches that use quantitative or historical data to generate testable propositions about when and how voting systems might change. Some practitioners combine both approaches. Only the traditional cleavage models appear to have been abandoned, as fewer and fewer analysts accept that a post-industrial polity still produces anchored political preferences.

The most common cultural modernization approach has focused on how the transition from industrial to post-industrial society has contributed to a shift in social values from material to post-material concerns, leading to a decline in organized cleavages and a de-alignment of traditional party systems.[26] For some, the continuing de-alignment of western party systems was potentially the most important factor contributing to voting system reform in all the affected countries.[27] Across western countries, the traditionally dominant parties witnessed a drop in their combined support between 1960 and 1990, with third parties rising from insignificant levels to around 20–25 per cent of the national vote.[28] But de-alignment on its own hardly indicates when or where reform will occur, if at all. In fact, de-alignment is occurring just about everywhere, but voting system reform is not. A number of analysts try to get around this by explaining change as the product of long-term factors (de-alignment) and short-term factors (scandal, corruption).[29] Unfortunately, this hardly improves things, as the short-term factors most often cited (for instance, corruption and scandal in Italy and Japan) have long been recognized and decried by just about everyone, without being eliminated. It is not clear why they should suddenly contribute to institutional reform now.

Another approach recognizes the importance of de-alignment but also highlights how parties themselves have changed. Contemporary political parties tend to have fewer members and more streamlined internal democracy. The parties also campaign differently, eschewing volunteer door-to-door voter contact in favour of professional telephone contact, paid polling, copious amounts of radio and television advertising, and leader-oriented appeals. But, again, as this trend is happening nearly everywhere, it is not clear how these changes contribute to voting system reform in particular countries. Margetts and Dunleavy argue that these changes signal a larger global convergence on how politics is done. They point out that all the voting system changes moved in a similar mixed-system direction, which they credit to an increasingly globalized public sphere. Basically, they suggest that today's general public is better educated and informed, more aware than ever about how other countries do politics and what potential reforms could be taken up. The end of the Cold War has allowed greater criticism to emerge about the workings of liberal democracies, and a process of international "policy learning" has affected both public and party views. Margetts and Dunleavy's "globalization" thesis offers some provocative but largely ad hoc assertions about our increasingly small world that leaves much unexplained. Specifically, they fail to identify how voters influence the process, why parties seemingly cannot maintain control over it, or why current public dissatisfaction should move in an institutional rather than policy direction. To suggest, as they do in other work, that a new process of modernization and convergence is underway with the decline of the Cold War is hardly more illuminating.[30]

Another cultural modernization approach relies less on behavioural data to make its case than an exploration of the internal dynamic of the voting systems themselves. Matthew Shugart has designed a model that claims to differentiate between "efficient" and "extreme" voting systems as a first step towards explaining why some systems change. He suggests that "electoral systems that are 'extreme' ... contain within themselves the pre-existing conditions that generate reformist pressures." However, being "inherently prone to reform" does not guarantee that any system will be reformed. Reform requires the existence of both these inherent "extreme" tendencies and some "triggering event," a contingency. In examining the recent examples of voting system reform, Shugart holds that all were "extreme" voting systems that finally succumbed to reform under pressure of different contingencies: corruption, voter dissatisfaction, scandal, etc. He then proceeds to categorize different voting systems as either "efficient" or "extreme" by measuring their performance against a number of indicators divided along two dimensions, inter-party and intra-party. The inter-party dimension establishes a continuum ranging from single party majority governments elected with well under a majority of votes at one end, to coalition governments formed amongst many parties at the other. The intra-party dimension does the same for the question of how individual legislators secure election – through highly personalistic networks at one extreme to complete reliance on party lists at the other. The mid-point on each dimension then represents the most "efficient" spot.[31]

Shugart's model discovers pre-reform Japan, New Zealand, and Italy to be using "extreme" voting systems. Their "extreme" features, according to Shugart, meant that they failed to "connect government formation to policy-based electoral majorities," leading to low levels of "electoral efficiency" for voters. Mixed-systems then became a popular solution because they helped reconnect government performance with voter preferences by balancing the need for clearly accountable govern-ing coalitions with a degree of direct politician accountability via single member ridings. Shugart essentially combines a pluralist understand-ing of what drives the polity – citizens – with a functionalist under-standing of political systems and their need to establish and maintain "equilibrium."[32]

The problem is that Shugart's model produces unconvincing re-sults, despite matching its "extreme" categorization with the reform-ing countries. For instance, one of his "extreme" voting systems, New Zealand, apparently "prone to reformist pressures," lasted 140 years with only one break (a four-year trial with the majoritarian second bal-lot between 1908 and 1912). Even if we limit ourselves to that coun-try's most "extreme" phase, the period after the abolition of the upper house in 1950, we still have four decades of largely uncontroversial use of the traditional voting system.[33] Voting rules were more regu-larly criticized in Italy and Japan but, again, both persisted with their systems for almost half a century, nearly the whole of democratic ex-perience for both nations. It is hard to agree with Shugart that various systems are "prone to change" when they have, in fact, survived most of the modern democratic era. Nor do Shugart's "trigger" contingen-cies save the analysis – most were longstanding problems, well known and seemingly intractable. In addition, Shugart assumes that voters ultimately judge the "efficiency" of any arrangement and thus fuel any change but nowhere provides any evidence of where or how this oc-curs. Given these difficulties, the predictive capacity of Shugart's model would appear to be very weak.

Cultural modernization approaches assume that larger social and economic changes affect how people view politics and the efficacy of the political system, yet they tend to provide largely actor-less accounts of change. Rational choice work on institutional change remedies this problem by linking it directly to the interests of political actors, spe-cifically political parties. Taking off particularly in the 1990s, various authors have used rational choice assumptions to explain why political parties would be interested in or agree to change the rules of the electoral game, with various and sometimes conflicting results. Some have claimed that voting system change occurs to maximize the legislative representation of a particular party, or protect and enhance individual political careers, or respond to trade imperatives, or even save the political system as a whole from ruin.[34] There is less agreement about just why institutions, the voting system specifically, become the target of such efforts. In fact, there is considerable debate within rational choice about whether institutional rules are "sticky" and should be considered either less or equally likely to be challenged than other political terrain (i.e., specific policies).[35] Some, like Colomer, argue that politicians and political parties want to keep institutional rules in place that benefit them and will agree to change rules only when they fear that maintaining them will cause them to lose out perpetually. Specifically he cites the rise of a multi-party situation as the key factor driving most historical shifts to PR worldwide (though he qualifies this generalization with a host of historical caveats). Boix is more historically and ideologically specific, citing the threat of strong left-wing parties in Europe in the early twentieth century as fuelling voting system change.[36]

Rational choice approaches succeed admirably in designating the agents of voting system change – political parties – but offer rather meagre explanations for their actions, or the larger social, political, or economic forces that might be influencing their efforts. Colomer suggests that parties are the driving force for change, but we get no sense of what forces are driving the parties. It is as if these rational actors exist in a kind of social or historical vacuum. However, one sub-theme in rational choice does address this, linking the structure of the economy and patterns of labour market regulation to the use of different voting systems. Cusack, Iversen, and Soskice argue that countries that rely on employer–employee cooperation are more likely to use PR, while ones that do not will use plurality voting systems. The addition of context here is helpful but the analysis is wholly deductive – they do not demonstrate how or why the specific actors made these decisions. Arguably the most sophisticated rational choice work on the subject comes from Boix, who identifies both the actors and the contexts that contribute to reform or stasis. Boix argues that socialist parties are the key competitive threat motivating reform around the time of the First World War because of the class-oriented policies they would enact if they gained state power. Boix's conclusions tend to mirror those from the existing historical work but do so in a way that verges close to determinism, leaving little room to chance, judgment, and uncertainty. Meanwhile others have taken this potential uncertainty to mean that nothing of substance can be said about actor motivations or strategy, which seems equally unsatisfying.[37]

The missing dynamic of context and agency in both rational choice and cultural modernization approaches could obviously be addressed by a more historically focused approach. The relatively new field of historical institutionalism would, on the surface, appear to be a natural approach to studying the use of different electoral institutions over time.[38] Indeed, both Renwick and Kreuzer argue that history can effectively fill in the gaps produced by more quantitative work.[39] Elements of this approach do appear in some recent work, particularly rational choice accounts, but, on the whole, historical institutionalist explorations of voting system reform remain rare.[40] Meanwhile, there have been a few context-rich accounts of voting system change[41] but, as Renwick notes, they have tended to lack a comparative focus and thus offer little insight into change over time or across countries.[42]

Here Renwick's own work is certainly the most promising, examining voting system change in New Zealand, France, Italy, and Japan from 1945 on in a way that explicitly compares the different reform processes across time and space. Renwick's work offers a helpful corrective to those seeking a "one-size-fits-all" approach to voting system reform by arguing that we must distinguish various reform processes as characterized by either an elite imposition or mass–elite interaction. In fact, Renwick offers a dizzying array of potential influences on the reform processes in terms of the range of potential actors (politicians, judges, experts, external actors, citizens) and the mechanisms or "building blocks" that combine to contribute to the various reform processes. First he sets out what he sees as the possible motivations for reform (power, values, and interests) and then he painstaking maps both the potential exogenous (history, changing ideas, party system, state institutions, events, individual actors) and endogenous factors (leadership, path dependence) that may contribute to reform actually occurring. Then he explores the concrete episodes of reform, identifying just which mechanisms he thinks are in play in the different cases.[43] The results are often referred to as "process tracing," an increasingly popular approach to studying institutional change.[44]

Renwick's effort marks a considerable advance on previous work by engaging with the different political contexts in some detail. But somehow his work still manages to miss the "politics" of the eras he is studying. His study suffers from a seeming inability to name the "whole" that has resulted from the "parts" he has identified, an all-too-common problem in contemporary political science that might be best described as "all trees, no forest." In the end, Renwick's careful parsing of the mechanisms contributing to reform tends to occur without engaging the actual political disputes dividing the polities. While he is attentive to what different political actors are doing and the broad contours of the competitive context within which they are doing it, we get little sense about the explicitly political motives behind their actions and decisions. With little insight into the "deep politics" of the contexts, Renwick's efforts remain largely descriptive, offering us an interesting typology of change processes but little insight into why reform is occurring in the first place.

For instance, to take up just one of his examples, Renwick claims that the 1985 reform of France's voting system emerged as a result of the Socialist party's response to flagging polls, poor local election results, and a desire to break the bipolar logic of the second ballot that linked the party to the more left-wing Communists.[45] While this description captures the logic of the decisions, it provides no insight into the social and political factors influencing why they are being taken. In this case, the historic victory of the French left in 1981 had been premised on turning back the neoliberal reorganization of the European economy, which the government actively pursued for two-and-a-half years with limited success. It was only when the Socialists abandoned that goal that the left coalition broke down, and changing the voting system became a priority.[46] The point here is that party self-interest alone does not tell us enough about where the impetus for institutional reform is coming from. In the French case, debates on the left about neoliberalism and the national and international power of capital must be factored in somewhere, as we can easily find reference to them amongst the players at the time.

Renwick's difficulties may reflect some broader problems in the approach he is using. For instance, historical institutionalists were long accused of privileging stasis over change and only weakly theorizing the social. Indeed, their failure to address questions of change was once a staple of critiques of the method.[47] But a new second wave of historical institutionalism has taken up this challenge, now offering a number of novel arguments about why institutions might change and how coalition dynamics or conflict might influence institutional stability.[48]

Renwick's work and its careful attention to the mechanisms contributing to change are a part of this. Yet despite this progress, some argue that the approach still has little to say about conflict and power inequalities. Jenson and Merand argue that this is surprising, given that the roots of historical institutionalism can be found in such seminal volumes as *Bringing the State Back In*, which they claim argued "that institutions 'matter,' but so too do social relations." For historical institutionalists, "this lack of concern with power is a departure from the analysis of structured power relations that was at the heart of historical institutionalism's original agenda."[49]

Jenson and Merand's call to rediscover the sociological roots of historical institutionalism is timely and overdue. Specifically, they urge them to rediscover from the likes of Marx and Weber that "power relations are institutionalized in the state, public policy and symbolic representations."[50] Of course, an older tradition of comparative historical analysis has arguably retained a more open-ended and sociological approach to questions of change and continues to draw on a broader range of theories in attempting to understand social change, highlighting social conflict specifically.[51] A small body of work examining voting system reform has opted for this broader approach, with encouraging results. Amel Ahmed (looking at Belgium, France, the United Kingdom, and the United States), Sunil Bastian (Sri Lanka), David Pottie and Shireen Hassim (South Africa) and I (Canada) have all explored voting system reforms in terms of class and social conflict, using an episodic approach to historical analysis to capture the back-and-forth of actions and reactions between different actors, events, and contexts to explain how voting system were challenged and sometimes changed.[52] This book will further this project by dramatically expanding the scope of the comparisons.

A great deal of modern work on voting system change appears to be at an impasse, offering either thin descriptions of rationality (i.e., the self-interest of parties and politicians) or a host of possible, competing variables (i.e., party de-alignment, "trigger" events, etc.) as the factors motivating reform. In both cases, the results are less than satisfying. To say that party self-interest motivates change sounds like common sense, as few commentators offer up examples of parties consciously committing electoral suicide with voting system reform. On the other hand, party de-alignment, the impact of trigger events, public unhappiness with the status quo – none of these factors are new or consistent in their impact on the various political systems. Disappointingly, the more context-rich work that has emerged recently has not improved things much, producing, at best, more finely grained description and typological breakdowns rather than better explanations. Nor can the problem be addressed through some creative combination of the existing approaches, as advocated by Leyenaar and Hazan.[53] Something is clearly missing from most explorations of voting system reform that needs to be incorporated into our analysis if we are to make any progress. That something, captured in the few recent comparative historical works noted above, is worth exploring in more detail.

What Will Be Done Differently Here: The Framework

Doing Social Science Differently

At some point, every voting system across western countries had a beginning. In every country, at one time or another, a particular group of people in a particular place with a particular purpose in mind chose a specific set of voting rules. What interests us is *why* they made the choice that they did. If they were still alive we could ask them about their choice, and they might tell us, but we have no way of knowing whether their claimed reasons are really the ones that motivated their decision. Nor can we read back from the results that emerged from their chosen voting system as a means of eliciting their reasons, as sometimes even the best-laid plans do not work out as intended. Some researchers try to address these limits by looking for the consistent presence or absence of different variables as a way of establishing what factors may have caused a decision to be made. But this won't work either, because the choosers always exercise judgment about how to proceed. Even when facing exactly the same set of variables, choosers could decide to make a different choice, or reflect on the previous experience with them in a way that could alter their choice, or fail to recognize that the variables they face are the same ones they faced before, or simply exercise poor judgment about how to respond to them.[54]

This, then, is one of the key problems with the work on voting system change: an often rather mechanical view of how to approach studying the question. The choice of a particular voting system at any given historical moment is not really amenable to "covering laws" or "one-size-fits-all" deductive calculations, the apparent goals of much of the existing work. The explanatory strength that can be gained with quantifying doesn't really apply in situations where a study involves just a handful of cases of what are essentially non-repeatable historical events. In other words, there is a radical openness to the choosing process, one that prevents any law-like predictions from being made or ahistorical rationalities from being discovered. Humans have agency. They can learn from past choices, whether they are their own or others. At the moment of choosing, they are influenced by their own objectives but also those of others. What this means is that their "preferences" are never entirely their own; they are also shaped by the contexts they find themselves in, something they may or may not be aware of. As such, we require a deep knowledge of those contexts if we are to sort out why this or that choice of voting systems emerged, as opposed to any other. Instead of searching for consistent mechanisms that provoke change, or the combination of variables that would allow us to predict institutional choice, social science should focus on a retrospective critical analysis of competing possible explanations of complex social phenomena in a bid to ascertain the best one.[55]

For many social scientists this is disappointing. They yearn for an overarching explanation that will help predict when things may happen or at least apply consistently to all cases. They hope to find the constant conjunction of factors that will produce x or y voting system. But such hopes are misplaced. A great deal of work on voting system reform operates on an assumption of causation that is inappropriate to the study of societies. The dominant positivist models assume causal laws of constant conjunction, so that wherever A happens, B happens. The problem is that studied social phenomena do not exist independently of the contexts we find them in or the actors participating in them. In other words, when actors witness A causing B in one scenario, they might intervene next time in a way that prevents A from causing B, even though the variables remain the same. Unlike the observed regularities in natural science, human beings are reflexive and can respond to and shape the environment they find themselves in.[56] But this doesn't mean that nothing is "caused" in social reality. As the influential social historian E.P. Thompson once argued, "History is not rule governed, and it knows no sufficient causes." It appears we can learn "how things turned out ... not why they had to turn out that way."[57] What we tend to think of as "cause" then must take a very different form. Again, Thompson is instructive: "The historians of the future, who will know *how* things turned out will have a powerful aid to understanding, not why they *had* to turn out in that way, but why in fact they did: that is they will observe in the laboratory of events the evidence of determination, not in its sense as rule governed law but in its sense of the 'setting of limits' and the 'exerting of pressures.'"[58]

Thompson's view captures the human agency that must be at the heart of causation in social science. It also underlines the contextual web of influences – the "setting of limits" or the "exerting of pressures" – that actors find themselves in. Theories of causation in social settings must come to grips with agency and structure, a perennial debate in sociology but less so in comparative politics.[59] This means we need know a lot about the different actors' motivations, what they are trying to accomplish and why, as well the contexts they find themselves in.

Applying a Comparative Historical Method

To capture this complexity, this book will explore these questions using a comparative historical method. Mahoney and Rueschemeyer describe this as "historically grounded explanations of large-scale and substantively important outcomes" that are "defined by a concern with causal analysis, an emphasis on processes over time, and the use of systematic and contextualized comparison" and the "importance of temporal sequences and the unfolding of events over time."[60] As Hay notes, the point here is to "proceed by way of dialogue between theory and evidence as the analyst ... pieces together a rich and theoretically informed historical narrative," one that can "preserve and capture the complexity and specificity of the process of change under consideration, examining the interplay of actors, ideas and institutions."[61] To capture this interplay between actors against shifting historical contexts is crucially important in crafting explanations with any depth. As Thelen and Steinmo argue, goals, strategies, and preferences are to be explained rather than assumed: "Unless something is known about the context, broad assumptions about 'self interested' behavior are empty." For them, explanation requires a "historically based analysis to tell us what they are trying to maximize and why they emphasize certain goals over others."[62] Capoccia and Ziblatt call this "reading history forward" where, they argue, it is

> crucial to reconstruct what actors were actually fighting about and assess the respective causal force of structural and conjunctural factors in creating democratic institutions. Episode analysis identifies the key political actors fighting over institutional change, highlights the terms of the debate and the full range of options that they perceived, reconstructs the

extent of political and social support behind these options, and analyzes, as much as possible with the eyes of the contemporaries, the political interactions that led to the institutional outcome. In this sense, the assessment of how much an observable institutional outcome can be explained by more contingent political decisions rather than by earlier antecedents or later developments is above all a matter of empirical investigation and of comparing the "criticalness" of different episodes in the chain leading to that outcome.[63]

Clearly the comparative historical method as set out by these scholars aligns better with Thompson's notion of "causation" outlined above.[64] Now let's assess how this approach can fill the gaps left by the more conventional approaches to voting system reform specifically.

If we return to the problems identified with the existing approaches above, we can see what the comparative historical method offers that is so distinctive. Cultural modernization work suggested that changes in society influenced institutional change but were rather vague on the nature of the social change or just how it directly affected choices over institutions. Meanwhile, rational choice work specified the actors and their motivations but offered a thin and unspecified notion of just what the motivations were (e.g., self-interest). The comparative historical method will help us address both problems. First, it will allow us to investigate the "social" in more depth. What were the big events, debates, and changes in different historical periods and across different countries? Who were the actors, how did they understand the historical moments and opportunities, and what actions did they take? Second, by attending to the temporal order of events and the sequence of actions taken by different actors, we can more effectively link changes in the social terrain to changes in institutions. Concretely, this means we'll have to sketch out the broad outlines of the "social" in different historical periods and how this connected to politics. Obviously, what might be construed as "the social" is potentially infinite, and how to approach addressing that challenge will be dealt with more concretely below. For the moment, we could simply admit that any process of narrative construction will involve choices and a certain degree of creativity. Of course, similar observations have been made about the choice of variables and defining them in cross-national quantitative work.[65] In the end, the choices will be subject to scrutiny and critique and will either be found to be even handed and convincing, or not. But, as noted above, this is really not different from the kind of critical scrutiny applied to other methods as well.

Employing this comparative historical framework will involve a number of steps: selecting and defending the choice of countries, formulating a periodization of the different voting system reform eras, an elaboration of the "social" in these different periods, and then constructing an explanatory and comparative narrative of the actors and events pertaining to voting system reform in different times and places. Let's deal with each in turn.

As noted earlier, the study examines all struggles over major voting system reform in western industrialized countries throughout the twentieth century. This is in keeping with the comparative historical approach to case selection where cases are chosen of "sufficient similarity to be meaningfully compared with one another," as well as J.S. Mill's well-established "most similar" principle. As G.K. Roberts notes, "The advantage of using a 'most similar' approach is that, where the problem is one of identifying and accounting for specific differences, selection of units for analysis which possess many similarities in terms of relevant variables makes easier the identification of variables which *do* differ, and which may thus be considered as the first candidates for investigation as causal or explanatory variables."[66]

Beyond methodological concerns, there are simply good academic reasons to want to know more about specifically western voting system reforms. First, as Renwick notes, there has been a surprising inattention to processes of voting system reform in western countries, particularly studies that are comparative in approach.[67] Many contemporary works on voting system reform still draw on Carstairs's account of western European voting system origins and change for historical insight, a volume that is now decades old and actually contains no footnotes![68] Second, given the west's self-proclaimed leadership in all things democratic, some theoretically informed and reflexive insight into its own processes of democratic institutional change would appear to be long overdue.

Questions of periodization are always tricky, as the borders between one period or another may be difficult to draw and can easily appear arbitrary. For instance, post-war German voting system reform efforts stretch from 1944 to the late 1960s, whereas the Netherlands began their discussions of the issue only in the 1960s and 1970s. Again, some investigation of the social must inform where and how to draw these lines. As it stands, there are many precedents to consult here. For instance, a considerable body of research marks off different eras by the beginning and end of the century's major wars or economic realignments: the First

World War, the Great Depression, the Second World War, 1970s oil shocks, etc. Luckily, when we consult the cases of voting system reform, they tend to cluster in different historical periods: pre–First World War, First World War and after, post–Second World War, and post-1980s. This will become more apparent in the chapters dealing with different periods. Where borderline cases are involved, like the 1960s discussions in Germany and Netherlands, again, the particular context will help in deciding which period to assign them to. For instance, the 1960s represent the end of Germany's post-war discussions of voting system reform, while the same decade represents something new in the Netherlands.

Elaborating the social is obviously one of the most challenging tasks for this study, though, again, there are plenty of examples of comparative historical work that do this effectively. For instance, Charles Mair examines how social conditions influenced the post-war stabilization of Western Europe after the First World War, arguing that struggle between different classes ultimately produced different forms of corporatist accommodation. How do we know if his social factors were the right ones for such an explanation? Mair himself recognizes the immense challenges in such broad comparative historical undertakings: "In the last analysis, there can be no *a priori* validity or lack of validity in historical comparison. The researcher can group together any range of phenomena under some common rubric. The issue is whether the exercise suggests relationships that would otherwise remain unilluminated. Some comparative approaches are more fruitful than others."[69]

Mair argues that it is responsibility of the researcher to make judgments about which aspects of the social are more or less important: "Comparative history remains superficial if it merely plucks out elites in different societies – or working-class organizations, or party systems, or revolutionary disturbances. Flower arranging is not botany. A bouquet of historical parallels provides little knowledge about society unless we dissect and analyse the component parts. What is important to learn is what functions were served by supposedly comparable historical phenomena in establishing and contesting power and values."[70]

Mair's point here is that certain social factors may be quite important in one episode and not in another. For instance, he argues that organized political parties were key to developments in Germany in his study but not France or Italy. Or he points out how nationalization of French railways was intensely political in 1920 but hardly contested when accomplished in 1937. Sorting these factors out is complicated by the fact that historical actors themselves may describe what is at stake in the conflict in misleading terms, sometimes using imagery of social and political conflict from previous eras. Indeed, sometimes those caught up in the struggles cannot really see what is going on or how things are changing. For all these reasons, Mair argues that we cannot simply "borrow the terminology of the era, but must impose our own unifying concept."[71] At the same time, that concept cannot *simply* be imposed as some kind of ideal-type definition, it must be constructed in dialogue with the context under study.

No better example of this confusion around concepts can be found in the conventional voting system literature's understanding of *democracy*. On the whole, most conflate the term with regular elections featuring multiparty competition and an independent media. But a considerable body of work highlights that what democracy is or could be is not nearly so fixed, particularly when we consider the entire breadth of the twentieth century. For instance, one recent contribution to the debate declared that voting systems changed in Europe after the First World War largely because traditional elites were now committed to "democracy."[72] Yet most of these same elites would quickly repudiate democracy in the years that followed, raising questions about just how deep their commitment ever was. An analysis that explored the contemporary debates over just what different social forces thought of democracy would have been better equipped to interpret just what elites were doing in this period, instead of imposing a clearly inadequate concept ahistorically.[73]

Critical Institutionalism

The comparative historical method set out above provides a very different way of examining how institutional arrangements like voting systems come into being, what keeps them in place, or what leads to their reform. Crucially, this approach facilitates the development of a *critical* study of these institutions and the processes of change. By "critical" I mean drawing on various strands of critical theory about how the dialectical interplay of the institutional structures and social dynamics in western societies may fuel political disputes, some of which may spill over into institutional reform.[74] Of course, many researchers have underlined how institutions may bear the marks of political struggle or be held in place as a stand-off between competing and conflictual political forces. But it is the characterization of these struggles that is often superficial or insufficiently theorized. Indeed, the struggle itself seems to disappear, replaced by actorless cultural modernization or the decisions of individual rational actors. By contrast, a critical institutionalism takes the historical moment of choosing seriously, examining the social context and political disputes for clues about what may be animating the reform process. Jenson and Merand capture what is required to make this dynamic work effectively:

> We see then that it is possible to pay attention to social relations, agency and power without ignoring formal institutional developments. But the institutions need to be seen as being built through social processes rather than merely by rational intention or mechanical reproduction. Secondly, they must be treated as products of action through time, and not simply as constraints or payoff matrices. An institution can be a set of formal rules and informal norms that persists through time, but it is also always a pattern of social relations, which can be competitive, oppositional and characterized by unequal power relations.[75]

Though the prescription above is aimed at historical institutionalism, I marshal it here in aid of yet another variant of "institutionalism" – this time under the rubric of "critical." By dubbing this critical institutionalism, we put the concern over the social up front. In some ways this brand of institutionalism is hardly new. Recently Dan Krier has argued that a distinct sub-field in economics employed a "critical institutionalist" approach in the early twentieth century that sounds very similar to what is being described here:

> The institutionalists of the early 20th century placed "society," institutions and habits of thought at the center of their economic analysis. The individual enters into the economy not as an individual, but primarily as a carrier and enactor of group interests and concerns. The society was seen to be an organic whole, evolutionary in development (adaptation to the environment), composed not of an aggregate of atomistic individuals but rather of a complex web of networks, interaction and patterns of thought. Actors creatively "tackled" the environment around them rather than passively soaked up the pleasures about them. Finally, the conflict of interests between groups and associations was something to be analyzed in the foreground of analysis.[76]

Other examples of a kind of critical institutionalism across different fields all have in common this concern for the impact of the larger social context, particularly the impact and contradictions of the ruling social relations that structure the society and fuel political disputes. As Bastian and Luckham note in their volume on democratic struggle in the global south, "Democratic institutions are never introduced in a political, economic or social vacuum. They come into being within specific historical contexts, national societies and cultures."[77] Later in the same volume, Luckham, Goetz, and Kaldor argue that too many studies of democratization focus on the "high politics of state rather than the deep politics of society."[78] In other words, by ignoring what is going on beyond the elite negotiations around institutions, researchers fail to appreciate how myriad forms of political organizing within civil society may impinge on decisions about democratic structures.[79] Other examples of this critical institutionalism could include Ran Hirschl's study of constitutional politics as a practice of hegemonic preservation by political and economic elites, or Stephen Gill's analysis of how capitalists and state actors have struggled over institutions to create a disciplinary neoliberalism in global politics.[80]

However, the main body of work that we could link to critical institutionalism that will prove useful in this study is the critical literature on democratization. As a field, democratization is inherently interdisciplinary, drawing from sociology, history, law, political science, etc. But political scientists, particularly those associated with electoral studies, usually cite only the contributions from political science (e.g., Lipset, Huntingdon, Diamond), work that is typically neither interdisciplinary nor critical. In fact, it suffers from many of the same problems as the voting system reform literature: actorless change, context-free rationality, and under-theorized historical narrative.[81] The critical work (e.g., Moore, Therborn, Rueschemeyer et al.), by contrast, analyses democratization struggles by examining the deep politics of any given context to make the links between social disputes, organized political forces, and institutional choices.[82] This research makes clear that the struggle over democracy was never simply about establishing certain institutional arrangements – regular elections, for instance. There was a struggle in the first place because different social forces had very different ideas about what a democracy would amount to, how it might alter existing social dynamics, or, put more bluntly, whom it might help and whom it might hurt. In such a context, institutional choices like voting systems are unlikely to be technical or administrative decisions. Instead, they are likely to be steeped in politics, even when rationalized with a rhetoric of the public good.

The critical democratization literature then offers keen insights into the study of voting system reform, though much of the work focuses only on the initial struggle for democratic institutions.[83] This study will borrow and extend this analysis, examining voting system reforms as key episodes in democratization struggles. In doing so, it will build on a small body of work (e.g., Amel, Bastian, Pilon, etc., noted above) that has already linked voting system reform to social conflict and historical events, though often focusing on just one country or a small group of countries.[84] By exploring a large group of cases in some detail and comparing them across space and time, this study will be able to isolate commonalities and differences. Specifically, it will demonstrate how voting system reforms have been intimately linked to fundamental disputes about the nature of democracy itself in the twentieth century. When we examine the deep politics of the societies under study here, we will find that the different actors are initially resisting or agitating for some kind of democracy, and subsequent battles are also about just how democracy will function, what it will do, and whom it may affect. Of course, many factors will be seen to contribute to processes of voting system reform, but the point here is simply that an awareness of this larger context and set of struggles is crucial to explaining what is going on. And, as Charles Mair suggests, it may turn out that very different combinations of social factors influence the process in different places and times:

One final word at this point about sources: the book will draw primarily on secondary sources in developing its explanation. Though challenging for a host of methodological reasons, comparative work of the scope set forth here would be impossible any other way.[85] As Theda Skocpol has noted, "A dogmatic insistence on redoing primary research for every investigation ... would rule out most comparative-historical research."[86] With careful attention to changing historiographical conventions and a critical reading of the theory and evidence provided, secondary sources can be used effectively for historical comparative reinterpretations.[87] As Katznelson suggests, we must "interrogate less systematic evidence methodically."[88] In the end, the trade-offs between historically rich case studies and broad comparative work can balance out in a kind of dialectical influence on one another. This study hopes to raise some new ways of interpreting voting system change through a broad comparison across countries and across time, obviously something single case studies cannot do. Any conclusions drawn here will have to be tested subsequently in more fine-grained historical enquiry, thus letting the process of interaction begin again.

The Plan of the Book

The book is divided into eight chapters, including this introduction and a conclusion. Chapter 2 begins the process of elaborating the social in more detail by focusing on what will be argued here is the key concept being fought over in the various contexts: the parameters of democracy itself. The chapter will begin by noting the academic debates involved in defining democracy and then set out a working, albeit limited, definition of what conventional western "democracies" have amounted to institutionally, focusing primarily on the franchise, parliamentary sovereignty, and conditions of political competition. Then the chapter will shift to more substantive debates about democracy, specifically concerns or claims about what democracy normatively should be concerned with. The chapter will review the different periods, noting how this debate has shifted and remained contested throughout. With this insight into the fluidity and essentially contested nature of democracy as a concept and concrete aspiration, we then turn to the various episodes of reform over time as set out in chapters 3 though 7.

Chapter 3 investigates how key developments in the nineteenth century – struggles over the franchise and responsible government, changes in class structures and the coercive capacity of the state – laid the basis for the democratic struggles in the twentieth. Chapters 4 and 5 explore voting system reform efforts alongside struggles for minimally democratic regimes in western countries from 1899 to 1939. Chapter 4 covers the period stretching from the turn of the century up to and including the war. This includes both conservative, clearly non-democratic countries (Finland, Sweden, Norway, the Netherlands, Belgium, and Germany) and quasi-democratic jurisdictions (Denmark, France, Switzerland) in Europe, as well as the Anglo-American countries (Britain, the United States, Canada, New Zealand, and Australia). Chapter 5, beginning with the end of the war and extending through the revolutionary tumult of the early post-war years to the more reactionary turbulence of the interwar period, includes most of these same countries (except the Netherlands) and adds Italy. It should be noted that political parties, their names, and organization could be extremely fluid in some of the countries covered in this period, particularly in Germany and France. To avoid cluttering the text, I have tended to refer to ideological groupings where appropriate (e.g., in imperial Germany, *conservative* refers to a number of different parties that identified as conservative). In some cases, where a coherent group can be identified along a spectrum of choices at a particular time, I have capitalized them (e.g., *Radical* refers to the group of politicians associated with various parties in pre–First World War France utilizing *radical* in their name). But in most instances, I have capitalized group names only when they have officially organized as a party (thus Sweden's liberals become Liberals only in 1894, the year they organized themselves into a more formal party). However, there are a number of borderline cases. For instance, Sweden's conservatives created a Conservative party only in 1904 but had been acting as a fairly coherent party group since the mid-1890s. Similarly Denmark's conservatives, despite a number of splits and fissures after 1901, also appeared coherently party-like after the turn of the century. In these cases, I have adopted the practice in evidence in the relevant country-specific literatures.

Chapters 6 and 7 take up reform politics in the post-1945 era. Chapter 6 focuses on the wave of voting system reforms after the Second World War, stretching from the radical politics of the immediate post-war period through to the entrenchment of the Cold War in the 1950s. Countries examined include France, Germany, and Italy. Chapter 7 looks at the most recent reforms in New Zealand, Japan, Italy, and the United Kingdom, linking them to earlier debates in the Netherlands, Canada, and France, against a backdrop of economic change, declining democratic legitimacy, and party de-alignment. Chapter 8 concludes by drawing together the insights gathered from the explorations of the different periods.

Chapter 2

Contextualizing Democracy

Introduction

For historians, sociologists, political theorists, and many others, democracy is recognized as a fundamentally contested concept.[1] Political scientists, by contrast, tend to treat democracy as fixed and unproblematic, equating it with regular elections, multiparty competition, and the existence of commercial media.[2] This is particularly true of academics studying voting systems.[3] All this is surprising, given that elections themselves predate modern democracy, however defined, by many centuries.[4] Indeed, for some, elections are less a means to democracy than a method to "delimit mass political activity, popular influence and access to power."[5] Beyond ignoring these larger debates, the pragmatic acceptance of elections as democracy by political science is a problem because it obscures what C.B. Macpherson once called "the muddle about democracy": "At bottom, the muddle … is due to a genuine confusion as to what democracy is supposed to be about. The word democracy has changed its meaning more than once, and in more than one direction."[6]

The explanatory weakness of much of the work on voting system change can be linked to the problematic characterizations of democracy and democratization used more generally in political science. As noted above, political scientists tend to assume what democracy is or offer up ideal-type definitions that focus on decision-making processes. This offers us little insight into where "actually existing democracies" have come from or what factors may have conditioned processes of democratic reform. This is not surprising, as the actual historical emergence and struggle over modern western democracies is largely ignored. The problem is compounded for scholars grappling with voting system reform. They want to understand how a key component of modern democracies – the voting system – is changed, but lack any sense of how this fits into larger patterns of democratic struggle. Thus we must return to debates about democracy to improve our analysis of voting system reform.

Debates over democracy tend to take one of two forms. One focuses on democracy as a process. To the extent that political science is willing to countenance a debate over democracy, it tends to be one that focuses on the proper form of democracy, such as representative or participatory, elite versus mass, mediated as opposed to direct, etc. The content of politics is largely ignored as unimportant.[7] The other approach is less concerned with "democracy as a process" than democracy as a historical accomplishment. Here the stuff of politics – what people are disputing or fighting over – must be recovered to make sense of what democracy means in any given time or place.[8] In the former approach, debate may be normative or analytical, focusing on defining what is "right" or "realistic" for democracy. But in the latter approach, debate focuses on discovering what democracy has been understood to be by different social actors, how the dominant social meaning of democracy may change over time, and what factors contribute to democracy remaining a site of political struggle. The argument that will be pursued here is that this latter historical approach is crucial to making sense of voting system reform in the twentieth-century west.

This chapter will proceed through three stages. First, we will review how political science generally has taken up debate over democracy, underlining the limits of its ideal-typical approach. Second, we will contrast this with the historical approach to debates over democracy, exploring how and why various dominant ideas about democracy gave way in different periods, yet also how such dominant views remained contested by some, even when they were largely accepted by many. Finally, we'll make the case for a link between various eras of voting system reform and these shifting historical struggles over democracy, setting the stage for a further elaboration of this theme throughout the book.[9]

Political Science and Defining Democracy

Political science, particularly the American version, tends to take up democracy as a question of normative philosophy (i.e., "What is the nature of humanity and how should its affairs be organized?"), or as a practical problem of mass organizational behaviour (i.e., "How can we realistically organize a mass of people into politics?").[10] In either case, political science produces prescriptive models – what Max Weber termed "ideal types" – of democracy. Such ideal types are then compared with the "real world" to either criticize the latter or modify the former.[11] While useful as a heuristic device or in simplifying the complexity of the world, such models may obscure more than they reveal, particularly when research is interested in questions of change. This penchant for ideal-type explanation is a major problem for those studying voting system reform because the models tend to strip away the messy complexity that may provide the clues about why things are happening. As we shall see, political science has been dominated largely by one model of democracy, though some debate has emerged by those offering rival models.

As a discipline, political science is a very twentieth-century field. Capturing the modernist faith in humanity's ability to control its own affairs, political science sought out the "science" of governing, first by mapping institutional details, then tracking public behaviour through surveys, and more recently by modelling complex political events mathematically.[12] But early political science was rather vague about just what democracy was, where it existed, or what it should apply to. In the American context, the United States was simply assumed to be a democracy.[13] Of course, some early scholars still argued that democracy was what the ancient Greeks had practised and, as such, democracy was an unattainable ideal. And there were a few still vocally opposed to democracy. For many, these contradictions between declarations of democracy and the lack of specifics about just what democracy was were simply left unexplored or uncommented upon. In the United Kingdom, scholars avoided the problem by referring to "popular" government (i.e., responsible government) rather than democracy.[14] Only in Europe did the line between democracy and non-democracy seem somewhat clear, undoubtedly because few European countries could be characterized as democratic, even by the most generous standards.

Yet there were scholars who recognized these gaps between affirmations of democracy and actual democratic practice. Reformers like U.S. academic John R. Commons produced early work that echoed populist themes of disenchantment with the practice of American democracy, arguing for institutional reforms to "empower the people."[15] So while some assumed that the United States already was a democracy, a consistent theme emerging from the late nineteenth century argued that democracy was an ideal that had not yet been met in America.[16] The lack of clarity about just what democracy was or should be allowed these criticisms to move in a number of directions at once. Indeed, a great deal of public debate was confused, because supporters and opponents of "democracy" often had very different understanding of what it might entail.[17] Here, political science was not much help.

The end of the First World War contributed to a change in discourse about democracy, as political scientists increasingly elided the representation and governing practices of western countries with democracy tout court. As western countries began appearing more uniform in using elections, a mass franchise, and party competition for governing office, this set of processes increasingly became referred to as "democracy."[18] But publicly debate continued about just how democratic this form really was. In the American context, the populist critique that pitched "the people" versus the "interests" continued, while in Europe, and to a lesser extent the United Kingdom and its colonies, the debate was between a procedural view of democracy and a more substantive social democracy that would extend to social and economic rights. Political science struggled to grapple with these popular critiques. In 1934 the president of the American Political Science Association defended the procedural view, arguing that democracy was primarily about "political liberty and economic individualism." While he was prepared to accept the need for expanded government services in response to the Depression, he suggested "democracy" might have to give way to a franchise restricted to the more educated members of society.[19] Some, like American Charles Beard or Britain's Harold Laski, argued that economic power was an important influence on and problem for democracy, but they were the exception.[20] For the most part, particularly in American political science, democracy remained an undefined "muddle."

All this would change after the Second World War. Here the expanding and now dominant American field of political science finally produced clear and unequivocal definitions of what was and was not democracy. Early post-war work began by weakening claims about majority rule and popular sovereignty, highlighting the importance of constitutional limits to power.[21] Then in the 1950s American democratic theory settled on two key elements: a Schumpeterian notion of restricted competition for government and the pluralist group-based theory of interest group aggregation. From Schumpeter, American political science took the view that the people in a democracy do not rule directly. Instead, their prime democratic role is simply to choose between competing slates of elites who will rule in their name. Sometimes referred to as the "elite theory" of democracy, its implications were softened somewhat by the addition of pluralist theories of political action. Pluralists argued that "the people" had no unified vision to be represented. Instead, people joined or responded to group appeals in a bid to influence each other and the political class. Democracy then involved competition for influence where competing slates of political elites responded to plural interest groups in their bid for state power.[22]

This new consensus dominated thinking about democracy in political science during the 1950s and 1960s, though it increasingly came under challenge near the end of the latter decade. In line with the rise of civil rights campaigns, national liberation movements, and activist student politics, some political scientists challenged the reigning elite theory of democracy with more participatory versions of a democratic polity, ones where citizens would not simply vote but actively participate in policy development and implementation.[23] By the 1970s, this debate had polarized between those that felt the dominant version of democracy didn't go far enough and those that felt it had gone too far. On the one side, theorists of participatory democracy called for an opening up of democratic processes to more substantive engagement by citizens. On the other, groups like the Trilateral Commission argued that democratic demands from the public were threatening to overload western democracies and that public expectations should be dampened.[24]

While the 1950s consensus remains dominant, aspects of the two 1970s critiques continue to be taken up. One influential strand develops the Trilateral Commission's "overload thesis" in arguing for reduced expectations of democratic process. Though with roots in the 1950s, rational choice work on democracy became very influential in political science from the 1980s on. Rational choice scholars support the minimal democracy approaches by casting doubt on the efficacy of democratic procedures, specifically the meaning and effectiveness of voting or group action. Some argue that the logical conclusion of rational choice work actually goes much further than the minimal democracy school to undermine claims for democratic practice altogether.[25] Another strand supporting the minimal democracy approach adds market independence to the list of minimal democratic practices. Here, particularly in democratic development literature, democracy must not interfere with the workings of the free market.[26] The other side of the 1970s critique – participatory democracy – has been less influential in political science but lingers on, continuing to explore how more substantive democratic experiences could be designed.[27] But, as noted, working political scientists spend little time defining democracy and instead simply assume that where we can find regular elections, the existence of competing claimants for office, and a functioning commercial media, we have also found democracy.[28]

The political science penchant for debating these ideal-type definitions of democracy, justified either normatively or pragmatically, has produced many nuanced arguments for the different models. But it has largely failed to provide an effective guide for exploring questions of democratic origins or change. Those keen to explain voting system reform need to look elsewhere.

From Definition to Context: Historical Struggles over Democracy

In a series of publications, Lawrence Whitehead has encapsulated the enduring problems associated with trying to "define" democracy: the concept is both historical and political. As he points out, attempts to "fix" what democracy means procedurally usually lead to absurd or meagre results. For instance, defining democracy as full suffrage, a common shorthand approach to the problem, would arguably discount Switzerland as a democracy until 1971 (when women were enfranchised nationally) and the United States until 1965 (when the federal Voting Rights Act assured the voting rights of Blacks in the South), results that hardly seem satisfactory. This focus on an inventory of "what democracy is" also ignores the more substantive aspects of democracy, like whether all citizens enjoy the social rights to participate effectively or even protect their civil and political rights. For Whitehead and others, concerns over the *substance* of democracy, rather than simply its procedures, explains the shifting parameters of the concept at different times and in different places.[29] As Cammack notes, "Liberal democracy is a conjunctural historical phenomenon, explicable in terms of its structural conditions of emergence and reproduction, and their interaction with its own institutional dynamics. As such it can be understood theoretically only if the social context in which it emerges and is reproduced can be theorized."[30]

Cammack is highlighting that democracy emerges from particular social contexts, and it is those contexts that fuel the debates for and against democracy, as well as inform struggles over just what the substance of democracy should be. Working from anthropology, Paley sums this up nicely, arguing that "meanings of the term 'democracy' are hotly contested among groups with interests in different outcomes, all of whom are linked to each other in unequal relations of power."[31] What this means is that defining what democracy is or could be is often, itself, a political project. As Whitehead notes, this is why we often speak of "democratic struggle": "This reference to 'struggle' highlights the fact that democracy is such a desirable label, that control over its meaning necessarily becomes an object of political contestation. This 'essential contestability' is a distinctive feature of our key political concepts, both because of the good and bad consequences for particular interests that will flow from adopting one meaning rather than another, and because although the concept has real substance, its meaning is not fixed by some extra-political authority (logic, incontestable evidence) to which ultimate appeals can be made."[32]

And this struggle continues, even when some dominant view of "what democracy is" has been established in a particular place and time. Indeed, it is precisely this ongoing process of contestation rooted in the social that eventually gives rise to challenges to the reigning view, as historical conditions and opportunities change.[33]

C.B. Macpherson was one of the first political scientists to call the discipline's attention back to history as concerns democracy, noting how it had continued to be considered a bad thing long after the establishment of most western nation states. In fact, his point was to highlight how seamlessly and almost imperceptibly "democracy" had shifted from being a clearly bad thing in the late nineteenth century to an unquestionably good thing after the First World War, at least for political commentators.[34] Macpherson was interested in just why and how this had occurred. Essentially, he argued that nineteenth-century governing elites feared democracy would amount to "class rule by the poor." For instance, he cited liberal political philosopher J.S. Mill, who worried that democracy would allow the working class to pass "class" legislation that might violate the "laws of political economy" as he saw them, thus threatening the economic system that workers ultimately relied on. Mill's proposed solution was to give the wealthy and middle classes more votes until workers could be educated to work within acceptable parameters.[35]

Prior to Macpherson, a number of scholars had highlighted how democracy seemed to align with particular conditions (like modern industrial economies), but they offered little insight into the precise relationship between the two.[36] Since then, an entire literature has emerged that has debated just how democracy happens, where it comes from, and why it is subject to change. The historical strand of this research essentially furthers Macpherson's analysis, attempting to uncover the political disputes underlying the historical struggles over democracy.[37] While differentiated in important ways, this literature approaches a kind of consensus in underlining the important economic dimensions of these democratic disputes. In every period under study, they suggest, the struggle over democracy is really a struggle over what that democracy might do.[38] We can see this dynamic at work by examining four key periods in the twentieth century: the period up to and including the First World War, the interwar period, the Cold War, and the neoliberal era.

1900 to the First World War

In 1900, democracy was rare or deeply flawed in its operation. Few countries satisfied even the most minimal procedural requirements – full male suffrage, legislative control over the executive, and free and fair elections. Countries like the Netherlands, Belgium, and Italy had powerful legislatures but severely restricted access to them via a narrow franchise. Others like Germany allowed full male suffrage but lacked legislative control over the executive. The United States, France, and Switzerland had both broad male suffrage and a degree of legislative independence, but their democratic credentials were marred by electoral corruption and inconsistent democratic practices. Britain operated very much as if it were democratic by 1900, though Britain's franchise and voter registration laws kept as many as a third of male – primarily working-class – voters out, as well as all women, while the hereditary House of Lords acted as a brake on the elected House of Commons.[39] Arguably Britain's colonies – Canada, Australia, and New Zealand – best satisfied all three conditions, but they were not politically independent countries. Indeed, their "democratic" decisions could be overturned by the British government or legally challenged in the British Judicial Committee of the Privy Council.[40] Similarly, Norway and Finland operated with a degree of local autonomy within larger imperial systems of power. Yet by 1920 all these countries would satisfy the minimum conditions defining democratic rule. The process would involve intense social struggle, heightened political mobilization, and myriad institutional reforms, all fuelled by concerns about the content of democracy, rather than its form.

Central to these social struggles were class disputes, largely animated by the dramatic economic and social changes of the late nineteenth century (i.e., industrialization, urbanization) and the political organizing that emerged from them.[41] In suggesting that class was central, the point is not to reject all other factors – religion, region, party competition, etc. – as unimportant. But these factors were not decisive on their own in pushing all these countries towards great democratization. By contrast, after 1900, support for working-class political parties grew rapidly, restrained only by restrictive suffrage laws and lopsided, rurally biased distributions of legislative seats. Increasing urbanization and industrialization across western countries in effect "mobilized" people into more exclusively working-class neighbourhoods and workplaces, facilitating the rise of group identity, patterns of culture, and political organization. Such mobilization also contributed to the development of new political demands for social rights like housing, education, better wages, and shorter working hours. Working-class parties organized and defended working-class institutions like unions and self-help societies by facilitating mass electoral participation and introducing a more disciplined party behaviour into legislatures.[42] Whether they were explicitly socialist or reformist, all left parties rallied public support behind demands for universal male suffrage and democratically accountable government, sometimes with support from liberal or farmer parties.[43] Their opponents – traditional elites and bourgeois forces – responded to this mobilization with a mixture of repression, obfuscation, and partial reforms, particularly before the First World War.[44] But the anti-democratic forces were hardly united, and sometimes the intensity of their own disagreements forced them to cooperate with more working-class parties.

It is important to note the character of the two main themes that comprised the demands coming from the left. On the one hand, the demands centred on inclusion: voting rights, an end to restrictions on candidacies and parties, and the freedom of elected governments to be able to act on public demands, unencumbered by unelected courts, regents, or upper houses. On the other hand, the demands exhibited a different democratic imaginary, one that would see the democratic state use its considerable power to protect and advance the welfare of all its citizens. This latter point is important to underline, given the reigning economic ideas of this period legitimized laissez-faire, small government, and free markets. One should also note intermediary positions, as when protectionist economic forces made common cause with the economic nationalism of labour and socialist parties. Colonial societies like New Zealand, Australia, and Canada, for pragmatic reasons, could not deny the key role for the state in economic development, though opponents railed against what they saw as violation of the natural laws of the market. As one critic complained "To the Australian, the State means collective power at the service of individualistic 'rights.' These rights include 'the right to work, the right to fair and reasonable conditions of living, the right to be happy.' Australians see the state as the 'instrument of self-realisation' with regard to these rights. They do not want to claim these rights against a potentially despotic state but view the state as the source of their rights. In using the state as the realisation of democracy, Australians consider their quest for justice to involve essentially protecting themselves from forces that they see as harmful."[45] It was precisely this vision of the state as a possibly democratically directed economic leveller that worried the right and fuelled their resistance to democracy.

Still, despite considerable divisions across the centre-right, the left's opponents were largely successful, as democracy was still a rare form of government in 1914. But war, though it initially buttressed conservative politics, eventually undermined traditional rule and the resistance to democratic reform by further aiding the mobilization of working-class demands. The emergence of "total warfare" required substantial public and industrial commitment to the war effort, spawning overlapping networks of social organization through which political demands could be formed and articulated, eventually increasing the leverage of left parties and strengthening organized labour.[46] Combined with pervasive domestic and international instability at the war's end, all western countries were forced to concede at least minimally democratic rule between 1915 and 1920. But what these democracies were understood to be was unclear. Left political forces believed that a more substantive social democracy was at hand, one that would alter the dramatic economic inequalities of their societies, but their myriad political opponents were just as keen to resist any interference with key conservative or liberal political objectives.[47]

The Interwar Period

As the war ended, the real battle to define democracy began. At a glance, the degree and scope of formal changes to governing structures across the west was striking. Between 1917 and 1921 Germany, Finland,

and Sweden would gain legislative control of the executive, Belgium, the Netherlands, Italy, and Britain would expand voting to full male suffrage, and France and Switzerland would address election improprieties. But it is important to underline that these accomplishments were not merely responses to new public demands, as these specific changes had been long sought after. Instead, the shift to a minimal form of democracy was defensive, designed to head off and limit the more thoroughgoing social, economic, and political demands that emerged from the war. The war had altered the fundamental trajectory of the left and started to shift public thinking more generally, away from a bias for local provision of services to a more national orientation. Some thought this would require revolution to see through, but for many others democracy would suffice. Of the many voices scrambling to be heard above the tumult there were numerous, sometimes conflicting, proposals for social change, most reformist in nature. But as Geoff Eley notes, it was the undercurrent of rebellion at home along with the spectre of revolution from abroad (e.g., Russia) that ultimately forced democratic concessions from the political status quo in most countries at this historical juncture.[48]

However, after an initial burst of labour militancy and social upheaval in the two years following the First World War, more traditional political forces began to find their footing in the new electoral environment, particularly in mobilizing their own supporters, while worsening economic conditions weakened the new democratic challengers from the left. The bold proposals for a kind of economic democracy from the left now met unyielding resistance. In some countries, this required abandoning democracy altogether, as in Germany, Italy, and regions like Central and Eastern Europe. But most western countries muddled through the interwar period, maintaining mass suffrage, legislative supremacy, and regular elections. The threat of democracy that elites feared proved manageable by a host of means: institutional reforms, the rise of mass parties of the centre and right, and the liberal application of money to the electoral process. The right was learning how to respond to the new era of mass politics and counter some of the organizational advantages of the left.[49] By the mid-1920s, the initial post-war crisis had passed and, much to the surprise of traditional and business elites, the sizeable working-class electorate in most countries did not translate into leftist majorities at the polls. Except where the left remained on the brink of power, the more social concessions of the democratic bargain struck in the immediate post-war period were either forgotten or whittled away by the late 1920s.

The battle was renewed in earnest in the 1930s as the Depression offered the left considerable ammunition about the failings of the prevailing economic order. Left ideas about constraining and redistributing wealth and using government to make economic results more fair gained more adherents and pushed traditional elites to either make concessions or find new ways to resist their popularity. Meanwhile, economic planning as a strategy to democratize the economy became popular with socialists and non-socialists alike.[50] In some countries, like Belgium and the Netherlands, it opened new avenues for left cooperation with other political forces.[51] In the United States these conditions pushed the Democratic party to the left, facilitating the introduction of Roosevelt's New Deal and a dramatic increase in American government spending. But in others, even left victory at the polls was met with considerable – often successful – opposition from the centre-right and powerful forces in civil society (e.g., Sweden, France).[52] Academics were not unaffected by these real world battles, and left proposals for an economic democracy influenced Dewey's thinking about democratic process, Keynes's proposals for economic reform, and Shumpeter's later calls for a restrained, elite driven electoral democracy.[53] As war again intervened directly in political affairs in 1939, the conflict over these competing views of democracy was temporarily sidelined but not resolved.

The Cold War

The period after the Second World War witnessed the battle over defining democracy re-emerge, though the terrain of struggle took a number of twists and turns. Two factors would prove most influential: a surge in public support for traditional left ideas about economic security and social programs within western countries, and the playing out of super-power influence across national borders, particularly as it solidified into what would become known as the Cold War. The first influence seemed to suggest that left aims – to democratize economic decision-making, socialize risk, and dramatically expand the space for democratic involvement beyond just elections – were going to be implemented, particularly in the period between 1945 and 1947. But the second influence effectively checked a great deal of the first, though some left influence remained with the adoption of welfare states and full employment as ways of managing risk for the masses. Of course, the strength of these two influences varied across countries, which in part explains the different patterns of welfare state developments and levels of entitlement, as well as the character of debate that continued in each country throughout this period.[54]

The slow drift of left ideas into the mainstream tended to reflect the facts on the ground in warring nations. Long before the war ended, it was clear to observers both within and outside Europe that public sentiment had shifted strongly towards the left. Nazi rule had wreaked havoc on local civil society, destroying pre-war alliances and balances of power. In most locales the pre-war political elite – in effect, most of the centre-right of the political spectrum – actively collaborated with the Germans. When the war began to turn against the Axis powers in 1943, these collaborators were utterly discredited, leaving the field open to the left. As populations bore witness to mounting death tolls and the destruction of great swathes of urban Europe, this combined with lingering memories of the Depression and the appeasement policies that ultimately led to war, leading to a greater appreciation for left themes like economic security, peace, and internationalism. As a more active resistance to Nazi rule sprang up across Europe in the last two years of war, new alliances were forged that transcended traditional divisions between left and right, and a public consensus emerged in favour of social security, full employment, state intervention in the economy, and punishment for those responsible for war and collaborating with the enemy.[55] Even beyond continental Europe, plans for what would become known as the welfare state emerged about halfway through the war, largely in response to domestic social pressures related to maintaining the war effort (e.g., the U.K. Beveridge Report or Canada's Marsh Report). T.H. Marshall would later argue that the addition of these "social rights" completed a trinity of rights (i.e., legal, political, social) that were essential to the functioning of modern democracies.[56] For some, these developments promised to finally deliver on the left's twin historic goals of economic (not just political) democracy and substantive (rather than merely nominal) participation.

But this seeming consensus was quickly undermined by the emergence of the Cold War in 1947. Though often billed somewhat hysterically in patriotic terms by both sides, the struggle was mainly about giving shape to the post-war geopolitical and economic order, one that pitted an American design for a new world economy on the one hand against Soviet interests for border security and economic compensation for wartime losses on the other. Between 1945 and 1947 both countries worked at keeping up the appearance of playing nice, as long as they could reasonably hope to secure their objectives. But there appeared to be little basis for genuine compromise. The United States seemed to be stalling for time, hoping that the colossal scale of the economic and social problems would eventually push Europe towards market-led solutions and away from its dalliances with socialism, and convince the Soviets to accept much less than they were promised at Yalta.[57] Meanwhile the Soviets did use their influence to dampen leftist expectations across Western Europe after the war but not surprisingly used their occupying position in the east to their advantage. Still, American political elites interpreted the Western European left's victories as proof of Soviet interference in their zone of influence.[58] As left fortunes appeared only to be improving between 1945 and 1947, American strategists embarked on a bold effort to marginalize them and the economic and security claims of the Soviet Union by formulating a controversial economic stimulus package, the Marshall Plan, and by forcing the pace of German state renewal in the western-occupied zones. American efforts were, not surprisingly, strenuously opposed by the Soviet Union, sparking a new phase of international hostilities, eventually dubbed the "Cold War."[59]

Democracy itself would become an important part of the ideological battle between the United States and the USSR in the Cold War. In this the U.S. government gained considerable aid from the intellectual classes, particularly American academe.[60] A perceptible shift in democratic theory witnessed the replacement of the traditional democratic imaginary of "the people" ranged against various oppressors (government, plutocrats, etc.) with one where a differentiated mass public, divided into separate but equally powerful plural groups, competed for power and influence. Traditional themes associated with democratic struggles like problems of social injustice and inequality, tropes that fuelled European socialism and American populism alike, made little sense in this new market-style understanding of democratic competition gaining ground with elites.[61] In addition, in the face of potential left-wing democratic majorities, intellectual elites began to repudiate many generally accepted views about democracy like majority rule, executive accountability, and an active role for the public in political affairs. Some questioned whether a left majority at the polls was really enough for a democratic majority, or whether individual choices could be aggregated into collective decisions at all, while others argued that public levels of democratic participation should amount to little more than voting for or against a government.[62] The emerging polling industry was converted into a full-blown behavioural science that "discovered" voters to be poorly informed and largely irrational, further justifying a normative bias in political science away from democratic participation as potentially extremist.[63]

Despite these efforts to narrow the scope of democratic participation, at the same time a kind of consensus emerged across the west that endorsed social rights in the form of the welfare state and referred to the existence of a "mixed economy" that would now avoid the excesses of old-style capitalism. These developments did represent major concessions when compared to the debates about democracy in earlier periods. And these concessions did remain contested by some throughout the consensus era of the 1950s and 1960s, most notably by various right-wing societies, smaller political parties in Europe, a few high-profile economists, and the Republican Goldwater presidential campaign in 1964. Still, a kind of consensus did solidify in this period about what democracy was and how it should operate.

The Neoliberal Era

The breakdown of the post-war consensus around western democracy moved in two stages: one motivated primarily by political issues, the other by economic concerns. The initial political stage focused on opportunities for democratic participation. The limited nature of conventional electoral democracy came under increasing challenge in the mid-to-late 1960s by a host of actors in western civil society – youth, women, people of colour, the poor, etc. – who demanded more meaningful and substantive opportunities to participate democratically than simply casting a ballot every few years.[64] Governments responded in a host of ways: lowering the voting age, reforming and expanding social entitlements, increasing opportunities for higher education and training, etc. Some political parties embraced the calls for more substantive citizen engagement by expanding the opportunities to participate in policy development, both within their parties and more broadly in civil society. Reforms aimed at increasing bureaucratic responsiveness like ombudservices and community consultation mechanisms were widely discussed and occasionally introduced.[65] A few academics echoed these critical views, challenging the dominant pluralist notions that western democratic competition was relatively equal and fair, or that voting in elections could be equated with democracy tout court.[66] A considerable body of thinking emerged, both popular and academic, exploring more participatory forms of democratic engagement and governance.[67]

But arguably the crucial stage in challenging the post-war consensus on democracy coincided with the more economic challenges of the 1970s. The post-war combination of limited democratic participation and social welfare entitlements mirrored an economic golden age. The simultaneous rise of inflation and unemployment in the 1970s brought key aspects of this western post-war compromise under scrutiny, particularly government economic policies focused on full employment, import substitution, and increasing social welfare. The economic crisis opened space for critics on the right to argue that the key problem facing western democracies involved too much citizen influence on politics, not too little, as the participatory critics had argued. The political scientists who authored the influential Trilateral Commission Report, issued at the height of the crisis in 1975, argued that the "democratic spirit is egalitarian, individualistic, populist, and impatient with distinctions of class and rank" and that the spread of this spirit may pose an "intrinsic threat" to western democracies.[68] They called for governments to seek ways to lower public expectations of what government could or should do. At the same time, early critics of the post-war compromise like economists Milton Friedman and Friedrich Hayek weighed in, arguing that present activist government economic policies violated the "laws" of the market and needed to be scaled back.[69]

For a time it seemed unclear which direction western governments would move. On the left were many calling for participatory governance and even more government direction of economic activity. A long-time goal of the historic left had been the extension of democratic influence to the economy itself. Some saw the 1970s crisis of political Keynesianism as an opportunity to forward a more substantive vision of economic and social democracy. In various countries, proposals were formulated to carry this out: the Alternative Economic Strategy from the U.K. Labour party's left wing, the Left Programme of France's Communist/Socialist party coalition, and the Meidner plan of Sweden's Social Democrats.[70] On the right, the proposals seemed just the opposite: to weaken the influence of public demands for government programs and weaken the state's role in regulating the economy. Right-wing think tanks like the Fraser Institute emerged to provide concrete policy prescriptions linked to the economic ideas like balanced budgets, privatization, and free trade.[71] In between were many, including most politicians, who simply tried to carry on with the post-war settlement, hoping it would correct itself over time. From the vantage point of the period itself, say from 1974 to 1983, which side was winning or losing in this emerging struggle over democracy was far from clear.

Unlike the crises that followed the First or Second World Wars, the 1970s economic crisis and how it contributed to reshaping western democratic practices played out much more slowly. In the end, a right-wing vision of neoliberal democracy – one animated by smaller welfare states, less secure employment, and more international free trade – ultimately triumphed.[72] But the political process contributing to this shift has been obscured by rather determinist readings of how economies work and influence politics. Part of this can be attributed to the enormous influence of the leading economists used to legitimize these new policies and their use of language that suggested their prescriptions were merely objective assessments of the workings of economic laws and market logics. Such views have been reinforced by both popular and academic work that has argued that economic realities – globalization, greater competition, increasingly sophisticated technology – have forced states to abandon government direction of the economy and social welfare as the result of market pressure.[73] In political science, the rising influence of techniques and assumptions from economics departments has helped obscure what might be some of the more explicitly political factors contributing to these changes.[74] However, even at the level of the claims themselves, the evidence is hardly conclusive. A considerable body of research raises questions about the direction of the causal arrows in economics and politics, with many reversing the flow of "economics forcing political choices" to "politics shaping economics policies."[75]

A political reading of the responses to the 1970s economic crisis moves us away from determinism to an assessment of the political interests and contexts that may have influenced the decisions that were ultimately made. Thus the economic crisis, which on one hand produced genuine problems and puzzles for policymakers and political analysts, was at the same time also an opportunity for critics from both the left and right to advance and struggle for their new vision of democracy.[76] What is important here is to avoid reading back from the results of the political struggles in a way that makes various choices seem obvious or inevitable. For instance, recent work on the financial crisis in the United Kingdom in 1976 counters the conventional view that the British Labour government had little choice but agree to demands of the International Monetary Fund to cut program spending in return for loans to stabilize the value of the pound. Instead, researchers argue that the crisis became a political opportunity for different forces both within and outside the Labour party to change the direction of the government.[77] More broadly, part of the victory of the right-wing neoliberal vision of democracy over the 1980s and 1990s involved politicizing issues like bureaucratic accountability, crime and delinquency, and taxes and government spending, among others.[78] At the same time, powerful lobbyists and funders also influenced governments on issues like trade, industry, and union regulation.[79] In addition, the decline of mass parties as forces for mobilizing public participation in politics and the rise of television as the key site of political information and conflict were also important factors in this change.[80]

Yet, as with previous eras, the neoliberal democratic realignment that has emerged as the dominant view has remained contested by a host of forces across western civil society. Some critics argue the neoliberal vision ignores concentrated economic power and distorts the nature of state power, particularly its role in regulating modern economies. Others claim that neoliberalism unduly individualizes what are really social problems, forcing the less fortunate to scramble to cope with changes ultimately designed and implemented by and for those with considerably more social and economic power. A range of oppositional voices, all claiming the mantle of democracy, continue to contest this most recent sedimentation of "what democracy looks like."[81] As such, the neoliberal democratic realignment represents a shift in the balance of forces trying to influence how we understand democracy, rather than a new or triumphant vision of what democracy really is or should be. Instead, with this long view of democratic debate and struggle, we can see that the basic tension animating the struggles over democracy throughout the twentieth century – freedom versus equality, individual versus collective power, social rights versus corporate rights – appear to be as central as ever.

Voting System Reform and Democracy: Making the Links

The basic argument of this book is that most major voting system reforms in the twentieth-century west have been intimately linked with larger social struggles over the parameters of democracy itself, specifically just what any democratic state should do with its power. As sketched out above, both left and right have recognizable core views on what they think democracy should be, which have then been affected by the actions of their opponents and historical contingency. On the right, the vision has largely been one that sees the state defend liberal property rights with minimal democratic interference. On the left, the democratic imaginary adds social rights to civil and political ones, using the state to redress the economic and social inequalities in civil society. Depending on which side of the spectrum appeared to have the upper hand in any given historical period, the centre line dividing these two political forces would shift in one direction or another. Thus the post–Second World War right reacted to an ascendant left by agreeing to some form of welfare state, in part to forestall more radical demands. In the neoliberal era, with the right gaining advantage, we see the left fighting a rearguard action to protect certain aspects of the welfare state by surrendering other parts of it. But political struggle is not always limited to a clearly stated exchange of views. Sometimes politics can occur "by other means," including struggles over the institutions themselves as means of defeating or limiting opponents. As Charles Mair noted about post–Second World War Europe, "significant institutional transformation" and "new institutional arrangements and distributions of power" were a key part of the political strategies of both left and right political forces in this period. This section will sketch out how the voting system reforms in the twentieth-century west illustrate this kind of "politics by other means."

In the study of voting system change there have been many attempts to link historical reforms with specific factors or variables. Some have studied increases or decreases in the number of parties, the size of left-wing parties, the relationship of left-wing parties to organized labour, and so on. But none of the factors links neatly with all the cases. In this study, we will map the links between periods of democratic instability, or contestation over the substance of democracy itself, and episodes of voting system change. On the face of it, there is a striking level of congruence between the two. For instance, the upheaval during and after the First World War coincided with nine of the twelve Western European countries studied here changing their voting system. It is not surprising then that many scholars have studied this period in an attempt to isolate the variables that contributed to this degree of consistency. But in seeking a variable or combination of variables to explain this phenomenon, such approaches have tended to miss the forest for the trees. A variable or clutch of variables in isolation does not cause anything. Such variables make sense only when cast against the larger social tensions and dynamics influencing change. This is why a particular variable may appear to be dominant in one case but not in another. In this period, this broader dynamic would be the larger struggles for and against legislative control of the executive and for or against democratic control of the legislature. This is also why a deep understanding of the specific contexts is crucial to link broad social struggles with specific instances of reform.

In addition, to understand why voting system reform may be related to these larger social struggles, we also need to attend to the order of historical events and the perceptions of the actors at the point of choosing. For instance, many scholars have dismissed the threat of the left as influencing a change of voting system in this period in countries like Belgium, Switzerland, and the Netherlands by pointing to what appear to be consistently underwhelming results for left-wing parties after the First World War.[82] But this is reading back from historical results, rather than taking seriously the historical moment under study. In the case of all three countries mentioned above, at the moment they switched voting systems around the time of the First World War, there is considerable evidence of elite fears of a surge of support for the left. The fact that such a threat did not ultimately materialize in these cases is irrelevant – we are interested in why elites made their decision, not whether their fears were justified by later historical results. But such insight can get lost when the historical moment is sliced and diced into variables like electoral statistics. So too can earlier reforms in Germany, Finland, and Sweden be understood if we try to get at what was at the root of the struggle, rather than the presence or absence of this or that variable. Before the First World War, all three were conservative-dominated regimes that resisted both legislative control of the executive and democratic influence over the legislature. By investigating the details surrounding the adoption of new voting systems in all three, we can try to unravel the conflicting statements and motives of the actors and assess why the reforms were carried through. As will be explored in more detail in chapter 3, all three regimes appeared to using institutional reform as a strategy to divide their opponents and block demands for both legislative and democratic power.

Broadly speaking, there appear to be five key eras of voting system reform. The first occurs between 1900 and 1914, and successful voting system reforms are limited to the conservative regimes noted above (and Belgium in 1899). But campaigns for and consideration of new voting systems occurred in most other western countries as well during this period, though only occasionally did a political challenge force conventional elites to seriously consider reform (e.g., New Zealand in

1908). This changed under the pressure of wartime mobilization and the perception of increasing support for labour and socialist parties. In some cases, countries near the fighting did opt for reform during the war (Netherlands, Denmark), while others quickly adopted reforms amid the political uncertainty following the cessation of hostilities (Belgium, France, Germany, Switzerland, Norway, Italy, Austria). As noted above, the situation was not merely one of transitional uncertainty (what would democratic rule look like?) but fear of what democratic rule might mean for different groups of people, particularly traditional ruling elites and the affluent. This is why the interwar period also offers interesting insights on this topic, despite the lack of much voting system reform, as left and right both discovered the depth and limits of their electoral support and responded accordingly. In some cases, this led to reversals of prior reforms (France in 1928) while in others it solidified a stasis where the left was represented but appeared to lack the electoral strength to further their more robust notions of social democracy. And there were a number of locales that considered reforms in this period, even if they did not introduce them. Again, these failures, as explored in chapter 4, had less to do with this or that variable than the perceptions of the different actors about their opponents' strengths and the impact of events (like specific election results).

What should be clear at this point is that researching voting systems and voting system reform appears to be less about these institutions per se than their relationship to this larger struggle over democracy. That is why the search for constant variables affecting choices over voting systems fails to capture what is really going on. The real battle is over what democracy will be, with voting systems and their reform taken up as one of many possible terrains. This is readily apparent in examining voting system reform in the Cold War era. As noted above, western politics shifted to the left after the Second World War, a trend countered partly by the emerging Cold War after 1947, leading to a kind of left-right consensus in favour of social rights and a welfare state. But the extent of those social rights depended on the balance of forces in the polity. Where the left was particularly strong, as in Scandinavia, social rights were extensive. Where it was weak, as in North America, welfare state entitlements were meagre. And in a few key locales, like Germany, France, and Italy, the state of left-right political competition was unstable, and, for various reasons, voting system reform became a key space to seek advantage, influenced by both internal (i.e., left-right) and external (i.e., Cold War) political dynamics. This episodic appearance of voting system reform was also the case in the neoliberal era where, despite the fact that all western countries underwent political battles to restrict democratic spaces, only a few resorted to voting system reform as part of the process. As we shall see in chapter 7, neoliberalism succeeds to varying degrees everywhere but through various means. In countries like Canada, the United States, and the United Kingdom, conservative political forces gained enough electoral power to simply introduce it. But in others, like Japan and Italy, existing political coalitions could block its progress, and under these conditions the institutional reform of voting systems became more attractive. Of course, in other locales, like New Zealand, voting system reform was sought by the forces opposing neoliberalism.

Conclusion

What democracy is or should be in the west has never been settled. Though political scientists often carry on as if democracy were obvious and can be equated with a shorthand of elections, party competition, and the existence of a commercial media, the historical experience of the twentieth century would suggest that grasping the substance of democracy is much more complicated. Political scientists have tended to avoid investigating democratic complications concretely by opting for ideal-type definitions instead. But scholars interested in where democracy comes from and the factors that give it shape have discovered that democracy is a site of struggle, that it remains a fundamentally contested concept, and that throughout the twentieth century forces of the right and left have attempted to redefine democracy to fit their own preferred values. Depending on their efforts, their reactions to one another, the impact of historical events, and the sense of which side was gaining advantage, both left and right have adjusted their take on just what democracy is.

Voting system reform is also about democratic struggle, what shape it will take, and who will benefit from its workings. Too much of the study on this question, and the mainstream political science work from which it stems, takes for granted the very things that we need to know more about to understand these specific reforms, namely what democracy is understood to mean in various shifting historical epochs. Specific voting system reforms cannot be understood without tracking how different actors understand what democracy should be, how they are affected by those mobilized against them, and the impact of historical events and shifting public and elite perceptions of whose version of democracy has more influence at any given moment. Really, democratic struggle is the topic, while voting system reform is sometimes part of its story. With this larger context of the battle of competing visions of democracy as the backdrop, this book can now effectively explore the many episodes of voting system reform in the twentieth-century west.

Chapter 3

Prologue to the Democratic Era

Introduction

Historical studies of voting system reform invariably begin in the nineteenth century. Most start by reviewing the contributions of political theorists and voting system designers like Condorcet, Hare, Mill, and others, then shift attention to the emergence of organizations dedicated to electoral reform in the particular country or region under study, and finally recount important debates and campaigns.[1] Denmark's short-lived experiment with a partially proportional voting system in 1856, the adoption of PR in a few Swiss cantons in the 1890s, and Belgium's introduction of PR for national elections are all typically highlighted as the key examples of this early "minority representation" phase of voting system reform.[2] But these historical accounts are misleading, because pro-reform political theorists, voting system designers, and reform organizations had little influence with governments or politicians in the nineteenth century, and nowhere did minority interests alone secure a new voting system.[3] In fact, excepting Belgium's adoption of PR in literally the last days of 1899, the century can hardly be characterized as a voting system reform era at all, especially when compared to the more dynamic reform periods associated with the First World War, after the Second World War, and the 1990s. But possibly of more importance, conventional historical work also is misleading, because its focus on minority representation obscures the real dynamic fuelling voting system reform in the nineteenth century and later. Far from being merely a method of minority elite inclusion or, later, a reaction to electoral competition from new parties, voting system reform was part of a larger struggle for democratically elected, accountable government.

The problems start with conventional understandings of the origins of democratic government or, as it is often called, the "process of democratization." Put simply, most work assumes too much. Either democracy is assumed to have been accomplished sometime in the nineteenth century, to which voting system reform is merely the last significant detail, or various reforms passed at different times – male suffrage, the secret ballot, etc. – are stitched together to form an ineluctable process of democratization, with voting system reform comprising merely the last stage.[4] Either way, the specific significance of changing the voting system is lost, both in terms of what makes voting system reform distinct from other institutional reforms, and what makes it consistent with previous struggles over institutions.

For all these reasons we must return to the nineteenth century to reorient our exploration of voting system reform. First, we need to recognize that the nineteenth century involved primarily the accomplishment of representative, not democratic, government.[5] Using even the most minimal standards of democracy – a significant degree of mass suffrage, government accountable to an elected legislature, and free and fair elections – only the United States, France, and Switzerland might be considered democratic by the late nineteenth century, and then only with significant qualifications.[6] Second, we must acknowledge that the achievement of even minimally democratic government was a historical accomplishment, not the result of some inexorable democratization process. It is only with hindsight that early suffrage or parliamentary reforms can be characterized unproblematically as the first steps towards democracy. For instance, Britain's First Great Reform Act of 1832 gained the name only in light of later events; at the time, its authors understood it as the end, not the beginning, of reform.[7]

The nineteenth century, then, was not the era of democratic consolidation, but rather the one where the idea of democracy as a potential system of government emerged for the first time as a serious proposal, fuelling great debate, hope, fear, and struggle. Traditional elites, typically royalty, the aristocracy, and landowners, feared democracy and opposed it at every turn. But so did the newly emerging elites of merchants and industrialists, even while they sought greater power and influence for themselves.[8] Only the lower classes – displaced artisans, tradesmen, and an emergent, largely unskilled working class – consistently demanded and defended proposals for democratic government.[9] It was out of this crucible of conflict that early institutional reforms emerged. However, contrary to democratization proponents, these reforms were specifically designed to strengthen the governing system against pressures for more democracy. Thus manipulations of the franchise, the introduction of voter registration laws, plural voting, etc. were explicitly intended to broaden access to the government to politically acceptable groups, while keeping the increasing majority of the citizenry, the urban working class, far distant from decision-making.[10]

In this light, voting system reform can also be seen as part of a long tradition of institutional change aimed at bolstering anti-democratic forces. For instance, in both the nineteenth and twentieth century, proportional voting systems received considerable attention for how well they might diminish the strength of the working-class vote. Yet at the same time, most of the emerging left parties also endorsed PR, no doubt contributing to some of the academic confusion about what role the reform really played. Some minor voting system reforms were introduced in the nineteenth century in Denmark, Britain, Illinois, and Ontario, but they were typically short-lived.[11] Public debate and minority advocacy were no more successful in getting serious voting system reform than they were gaining democratic government. Discussion tended to give way to action only where the pressures for democracy could no longer be resisted. And the key to achieving democratic government, particularly in Europe, was the rise of ideologically disciplined, organizationally sophisticated political parties of the left, parties that were clearly politically mobilizing and directing the masses.

Voting System Reform in the Nineteenth Century

In the nineteenth century, European countries used either plurality or majority voting rules.[12] Countries with any degree of Catholic influence used majority systems (a legacy traced by many to the long tradition of majority voting for elections in the church hierarchy), while Protestant countries all used plurality rules, typically a holdover from estate schemes of representation.[13] The modern era of debate begins with French discussions of representation and voting in the late eighteenth century, culminating in a number of proposals for proportional voting systems during the French Revolution.[14]

The emergence of debate over voting systems reflected the increasing importance of elections. Jenifer Hart suggests that reconsideration of Britain's voting system did not emerge until the late eighteenth century, because elections before then were seldom competitive. Traditionally, representation had been worked out informally amongst leading members of the community, a group who often comprised the total electorate.[15] The experience of greatly expanded suffrage during the French Revolution demonstrated the inadequacy of these traditional methods of social and political control under such circumstances. More generally, voting system reforms emerged as one response to the increasing consolidation of national states as the sole repositories of political power and legitimacy.

Interest in voting systems paled in comparison to the more general campaign for parliamentary reform, a sometimes century-long struggle to expand the suffrage, specifically to include men of property, and to subordinate the executive, or the effective control of the government, to parliament. Historically, franchise reforms, involving a shift from estate representation to property qualifications, came well before parliamentary control of the executive.[16] By the mid-nineteenth century, nearly all of Europe had opened up representation to the wealthy or those with sufficient property. Yet voting rights did not lead to dramatic changes in the composition of European parliaments (most remained decidedly aristocratic) or assure bourgeois influence. In fact, frustration with monarchial and/or aristocratic control of government in the early to mid-nineteenth century even contributed to bourgeois support for revolutionary outbursts in 1820, 1831, and 1848. As it turned out, subordinating control of the government to parliament would prove a formidable battle. The "parliamentarization" of political power was often a piecemeal affair, involving myriad legal, electoral, and political party strategies that could stretch over decades.[17] Yet all this occurred without any serious challenges arising to traditional voting systems. There were repeated calls for proportional voting from French advocates of voting reform – in the 1790s, the 1830s, and just before the revolution of 1848 – to address all manner of political instability, and some brief discussion of semi-proportional systems in Britain in the 1830s.[18] But the nature of the competition in this early period, still very much competing elites amongst small electorates in most places, was such that discussion of voting system reform remained marginal to the key political debates and movements.

The Rise of a New Class

Interest in voting system reform had mushroomed by the end of the nineteenth century, with a number of Swiss cantons adopting PR in the 1890s and a dramatic, last-minute conversion to a mild form of PR nationally in Belgium in 1899. These accomplishments cannot be explained by either the actions of reformers or the representational deficiencies of their majority voting systems. Both countries had witnessed long periods of dogged advocacy for reform and longstanding problems with representation.[19] What was distinctive in the 1890s was the rise nearly everywhere in the western world of an organized working class and working-class parties. The perception of the threat this new class posed and its relative strength vis-à-vis other classes would prove decisive in voting system reforms in the 1890s and beyond.

Of course, working-class pressure for political reform had been influential throughout the nineteenth century. While scholars generally recognize the key working-class role in specifically revolutionary upheavals, particularly on the European continent, they have failed to appreciate its influence on what appear today as more mundane institutional reforms like suffrage.[20] For instance, much work contrasts the violent nature of political change in Europe with an allegedly more peaceful approach in Britain. But British elites were just as uneasy with the social changes wrought by capitalist industrialization as their European counterparts.[21] Some contemporaries in 1815 described Britain as the most politically disturbed locale in Europe, with widespread elite fears of insurrection. Attempts to organize publicly were met with police repression, and a number of participants were killed.[22] One commentator described the British system as "aristocratic government tempered by rioting."[23] The revolutionary outbursts on the European continent in the 1830s resonated in Britain as well, leading to mounting public demonstrations and the "Captain Swing" riots in rural areas.[24] By 1832, an organized public meeting for franchise reform attracted two hundred thousand people, a key influence on the First Great Reform Act passed later that year.[25] Mass meetings and public demonstrations would also play a key role in pushing British reforms in 1867 and 1884.[26]

The revolutionary insurrections of the 1820s, 1830s, and 1848 were examples of working-class power and influence that fuelled a dialectic of repression and reform by increasing elite fears of the urban "mob."[27] But elite responses were not limited to these; strategic concessions were accompanied by the development of new military and police power. In the face of what appeared to be revolution elites sometimes responded with strategic concessions to the coalition of interests, or particular members of the coalition like the middle class, leading to franchise reforms, relaxation of press restrictions or limits on political organizing, and, in 1848, even a short-lived capitulation to liberal government. But at the same time, governments invested considerable resources in developing a permanent military and police infrastructure, one that could more effectively respond to social upheaval.[28] On the other side, dissenting elements found it difficult to hold or expand on these concessions for long after the events themselves. Even the remarkable revolutions of 1848, which established liberal regimes across Europe, proved hard to sustain after the immediate revolutionary conditions had receded.[29] With the violent suppression of the Paris Commune in 1871, traditional insurrectionary politics faced new, frighteningly lethal limits.

Rioting was essentially a holdover from a pre-capitalist era when peasants would intervene directly to reassert a customary price on the market or force the sale of local goods to local buyers. As E.P. Thompson points out, "riot" was often a misnomer for what actually occurred. In most cases, the whole process was conducted in an orderly fashion, with even the offending merchant ultimately getting the "just" price for his wares.[30] But the shift to an increasingly urban society meant that an urban "riot" was potentially much larger. Demonstrations ranging from ten thousand to one hundred thousand people emerged across Europe at different times, frightening the middle and upper classes. For their part, early working-class activists did not envision creating a new society by these actions, as much as forcing a return to the better parts of the old one. Artisans and tradesmen sought a return of their privileged positions in controlling production, while others sought land enough to assure economic independence for their families through a locally controlled economy. The permanence of the new capitalist economy and the national and international direction of the reforms it inspired were not immediately clear, and for most of the early nineteenth century resistance to it harkened back to an idyllic localism where the height of progress was a plot of land for every family.[31]

By the 1830s Britain was both the most advanced industrialized country and the first to see a shift in the direction of working-class agitation. The rise of Chartism, the first working-class movement for democratic government, was a direct response to the repression of early trade unions in Britain.[32] As organizers witnessed employers use their influence with the state to crush unions, they recognized that workers would need that influence as well to further their efforts.[33] The Chartists demanded full male suffrage, a secret ballot, and government accountable to the voters, and they organized thousands of working people to demand it with petitions and public meetings, and by putting pressure on the political class. These Chartist demands would eventually form the standard program for the left everywhere, though many decades would pass before the working classes of Europe or Anglo-American countries posed the kind of threat that would inspire significant institutional and democratic concessions from political elites. This is a key point. The debate over working-class strategy was also linked to working-class strength. The pre-1860s working class was often powerful enough to sponsor serious revolts but was too small and structurally weak to maintain them. Only with the take-off of capitalist economies in the 1850s and 1860s was the basis laid for a new organization of the working class.

From the 1860s to the 1890s, working-class organizations multiplied and took on a more permanent form. The improved economic conditions of the 1850s and 1860s created more space for union organizing and also witnessed the emergence of the first working-class political parties.[34] States initially responded to these developments with repression, outlawing strikes and union organizing.[35] Germany's anti-socialist law barred its emerging Social Democratic Party from organizing publicly, though it continued to contest elections. But the economic downturn of the 1870s and 1880s altered the balance of power within European countries. As countries moved away from free trade and towards various kinds of protectionism, the pressures of nation-building and state consolidation forced elites to ease repressive laws against unions and working-class politics.[36] In fact, in this national context of capitalist development, unions were better placed strategically to finally wield enough power to force recognition from the state, or at the very least a greater degree of tolerance.[37] In some cases like Germany, social welfare measures were introduced in a deliberate attempt to win working-class support away from radical politics, even while restrictions on unions and left party activity remained.[38]

The period was also characterized by much debate in working-class circles about appropriate political strategy. In Britain, working men who could vote were pursued by both Liberal and Conservative parties, though the first "labour men" elected worked exclusively with the Liberals, while a significant minority agitated for a separate labour party.[39] In Europe, debate divided between anarchists who called for direct action against employers and the state, and Marx's First International, which argued for the organization of a mass party that would mobilize working people and focus their strength. Subsequent developments would demonstrate the deep influence of both approaches, though the mass party model would clearly dominate. But these debates were no more important than the deep, structural changes that were remaking the working class itself, changing how and where it lived, how it interacted amongst its members, and its orientation to the national state.[40] Eric Hobsbawm argues that by the 1890s, distinctive national working classes had emerged across Europe, reflecting the particular historical struggles over capitalism and the governing institutions in each country. But more importantly, the refocusing of formerly locally identified working people to a national identity and state project, particularly when it was embodied in a mass party, dramatically increased the power and threat of the working class.[41]

The 1890s were the turning point. The Second International was formed in Paris in 1889 and largely set the agenda for left political parties in western industrialized countries for the century to come. Though participants were committed to replacing capitalism with a socialist organization of society, their immediate goals included the establishment of democratic government, a peaceful approach towards capturing political power, regulation of the labour market, the introduction of a variety of social programs, and a host of other objectives that would eventually come to pass.[42] Despite their focus on peaceful methods and democratic objectives, the founding of the Second International and their designation of the first of May as a workers' holiday aroused widespread fears of revolution. Some elites were convinced that the first May Day scheduled for 1890 was really an effort to mobilize working people to insurrection and revolt.[43] More shrewd observers understood the real threat behind what was emerging – that a mass party drawing resources from an emergent national union movement might seriously erode the traditional financial and organizational advantages of the old liberal and conservative cadre parties, perhaps eliminating the need for insurrection at all.

Of course the idea of a mass party was not enough to change anything; its emergence depended on many factors. Class structure clearly mattered, with Germany and Britain's urban-based proletariat more easily organized than France's more decentralized workers.[44] The structure, organization, and location of national industry was influential for how it contributed to the remaking of working-class life and consciousness along the lines set out by Hobsbawm, facilitating the emergence of a national class consciousness, as in Germany and Britain, or the survival of strong traditions of localism, as in France and Switzerland. Yet class structures themselves emerged historically, and timing – or the sequence of historical development – would also prove an important factor in the formation of working-class parties.[45]

In addition to class structure, the historical interplay of the various classes was also an important factor fuelling working-class party formation. In Britain, class compromise between Liberals and Conservatives, between urban industrialists and the landed class, was smoothed by the predominantly capitalist nature of both activities in that country by the nineteenth century.[46] The political victory of free trade in 1846 essentially settled the question of how government policies vis-à-vis the economy would be changed, a problem that would bedevil most of Europe for another half century. The recognition of these parameters, then, led both Liberals and Conservatives to seek working-class support electorally, though neither acknowledged that this was anything akin to democracy.[47] These overtures delayed the emergence of independent working-class representation in Britain for some decades, while the most privileged strata of the workforce explored what they could get from the status quo parties.[48] Wherever a certain stratum of the working class had gained political rights by the mid- to late nineteenth century – Switzerland, Australia, Canada, the United States – their participation in elections affected both how they understood their own political options and how political elites understood them. Opposition to working-class participation in politics could be heard in elite circles in these countries too, but experience, particularly the rather modest form of lib-labism that emerged in Britain and her colonies, tended to counter much of the criticism.[49]

On the Continent, Germany and France entertained very different class relations. Germany's rapid industrialization was premised on steel production, initially for railways but with a view for export. Britain's control of overseas trade, however, particularly steel markets, threatened to limit Germany's growth and helped push development towards military spending and shipbuilding.[50] This contributed to a strong state and a weak liberal bourgeoisie, while the landed class was split between the national state–building project and a defence of state power, particularly the dominance of Prussia.[51] Bismarck's enfranchisement of all working men in 1871 was part of his struggle to strengthen the German central state against the German states, but neither conservatives nor liberals offered much to workers.[52] In fact, Germany's rapid industrialization and military capitalism brutally destroyed artisan and tradesmen power bases, effectively proletarianizing them. Forced into urban areas under desperate conditions, they turned their experience to political organizing with socialist parties.[53] France, on the other hand, never completely broke with the property settlement arising out of the French Revolution. With a large, somewhat viable rural peasantry, a good measure of rural and local economic regulation survived, limiting capitalist expansion and urban growth.[54] Meanwhile, the urban working class were often militant but weak, at times pushing change to the point of revolution, only to see reaction restored by the superior numbers and power of rural areas. The experience of the Paris Commune in 1871 was a particularly powerful and long-lasting lesson. After the killing of over twenty thousand Parisian participants in the Commune by French and German soldiers, French workers remained keenly aware of their minority position in the state. They spent the rest of the nineteenth century either helping to secure Republican victories against the Conservatives, despite the indifference of Republican leaders to working-class issues, or avoiding formal politics altogether in favour of direct action.[55]

Though not all countries produced working-class parties in the 1890s, increased working-class participation in elections did make political contests more competitive, even under restricted franchises. In both France and Britain the number of uncontested constituencies plummeted in the late nineteenth century, despite the lack of a left party.[56] In Germany, the rise of the Social Democratic Party (SPD) forced many more contests to a second ballot to determine a winner.[57] This sudden spike in working-class participation caused alarm everywhere it registered, though the "perception" of threat posed was magnified wherever left parties were making gains. The SPD's first election after Bismarck's anti-socialist laws were lifted witnessed it dramatically increase its support: by 1898 it was the most popular party in Germany in terms of the popular vote.[58] In the 1890s socialist parties elected members in Sweden, Belgium, Holland, Switzerland, and Italy, while labour members were elected in the Australian colonies and Britain.

The success of the left was due primarily to its innovative organization.[59] As a rule, nineteenth-century political parties had no permanent existence; they came together only at election time or as loose agglomerations of political interest within parliament. But left parties of the 1890s, and even earlier in the case of Germany, embarked on the political organization of the masses through permanent, hierarchical party structures.[60] Left parties did not just fight elections, they attempted to provide organization and leadership in all aspects of working-class life on an ongoing basis. Germany's Social Democrats organized myriad cultural, educational, and social services in working-class neighbourhoods and through affiliated trade unions. As early as 1877 the SPD had 40,000 party members, published forty newspapers with a combined circulation of 150,000, and had links to unions with 50,000 members. By the 1890s, socialist union membership swelled to 900,000.[61] Though less powerful than Germany's left, socialist parties across Europe served similar functions and increased in popularity during this period, particularly in Belgium and Sweden.

But the threat of left parties in the 1890s cannot be measured simply by counting party members or elected officials. The threat of the left was also by the example its set both within and outside party ranks. Left parties were the first essentially democratic political organizations. As mass organizations, they opened up political parties to their supporters by allowing anyone membership.[62] Members were key to party policy formation, the recruitment of candidates, and the development of leadership cadres within the party.[63] Through the use of extensive democratic procedures within their organizations, left parties exhibited the kind of democratic accountability they would champion for society as a whole.[64] Their increasing ability to use a democratic organization to mobilize the working class electorally eventually created a "contagion from the left" as other political forces had to reckon with their efforts. Later, confessional and minority parties would mimic the left's mass organization, with conventional liberal and conservative forces following.[65] Left parties also forced greater discipline on all other political competitors because they typically voted as a bloc in parliament. Their tight party discipline gave them an advantage against the "loose fish" and independents who populated late nineteenth-century legislatures. As the left increased its electoral strength, other parties were forced to tighten party discipline, and fewer independents were elected.[66]

The perceived threat of left parties in the 1890s was also heightened by the diversity of their political tactics. The lively debate within socialist circles between anarchists and political party adherents produced support in some locales for direct action in the form of a political mass strike.[67] The party influence here was to focus these efforts on state-level reforms, particularly demands for democratic government, including at a minimum full male suffrage, the abolition of upper houses, full executive accountability to the elected legislature, payment for members, and an end to the state harassment of dissidents.[68] Though eschewed by the large and influential German socialists, political strikes eventually took place in Belgium, the Netherlands, Sweden, Finland, and Russia, with varying degrees of success.

The idea of a political strike first emerged out of riots in Belgium and the Netherlands in 1886. Though these were initially not political, socialist influence eventually gave shape to a host of working-class grievances. Socialists continued to organize protests in Belgium to demand male suffrage every year thereafter, culminating in massive, country-wide general strikes in 1892 and 1893, involving upwards of two hundred thousand people. In the face of these paralysing strikes, Belgian political elites finally granted male suffrage in 1893 but added enough plural voting for the rich that governing power remained safely in their hands, despite the reform.[69] In Sweden, socialists and liberals organized a "people's parliament" in 1893 and 1896 that brought out more voters than the actual state elections, demonstrating a groundswell of public support for democratic government.[70] Though neither Belgian nor Swedish efforts produced democratic government, they did demonstrate the power of the left to organize significant levels of public participation and in doing so influence public debate. Traditional political elites, increasingly resigned to the fact that political repression was no longer viable, scrambled for ways to respond.

The Link between Class Politics and Voting System Reform: Sweden, Germany, and Belgium

One consequence of the emergence of all these conditions was that voting system reform finally became a serious issue. For instance, various proposals for proportional voting had circulated in Sweden ever since Denmark adopted a quasi-PR system in the 1850s, but it was only in the face of left organizing in the 1890s that the discussion turned serious.[71] Bishop Gottfrid Billing, described by some contemporaries as the "father-confessor" to conservative political forces, was an early promoter of PR as a kind of insurance against democratic politics.[72] In 1891 he told the Reichstag that if suffrage was extended, "guarantees ought to be established in order that political power will not, in the future, belong to only one class of citizens." Billing proved quite creative in fashioning guarantees. His list included not just PR, but plural voting scaled to income, military service as a precondition for voting, a raised age for voting, and the elimination of pay for lower house members.[73] In 1896 the government sponsored a bill that promised (but largely failed to deliver) suffrage extension and the introduction of proportional voting. However, PR was to be used only in urban areas, the main source of liberal and socialist strength, a move clearly designed to weaken them.

In the end, even these reforms proved too challenging for Sweden's conservative elites, though PR continued to arouse interest.[74]

Debate over voting system reform also increased markedly in Germany in the 1890s. Though long advocated by the Social Democrats, PR became a serious issue only in response to the SPD's rising electoral strength after the end of the anti-socialist prohibition in 1890. Attempts by conservatives to return to repressive methods of dealing with the left were dealt a blow in 1894 when the legislature failed to pass a rather ambiguous anti-revolution bill that would have outlawed attempts to "subvert the existing social order."[75] Increasingly, middle-class opposition to the left eschewed violent means and focused on institutional reforms and manipulations to minimize their influence.[76] Principle had little to do with the rising interest in PR outside of SPD circles. As Ziegler notes, "In almost every case [in Germany] P.R. was used to combat the socialist movement, appearing chiefly where the latter threatened the interests of dominant social and political groups."[77] This anti-left reform effort made its first appearance in the 1890s just where SPD forces had made their most serious advance: the industrial courts. Kaiser Wilhelm II thought he could weaken the appeal of the socialists if he established some means by which workers could settle disputes with employers. The industrial courts, with members chosen half by workers and half by employers, were supposed to undercut the need and appeal of socialist representation. Just the opposite occurred, and SPD members routinely won all the worker-elected seats. To help fragment the working-class vote, the city of Frankfurt attempted to switch the voting method for the courts from the traditional German majority system to a proportional system in 1895. Though German courts struck down the change in 1898 as a violation of federal law, government amendments in 1901 opened the way for just this sort of reform.[78] From the turn of the century to the start of the First World War in Germany, the conversion to PR voting would advance rapidly at the sub-national level wherever left voting support appeared headed for a majority.[79]

But the most dramatic example of the dynamic that would fuel voting system reform well into the twentieth century occurred in Belgium in late 1899 when, under pressure from the left both electorally and in the streets, the government passed legislation making its small country the first to adopt proportional voting for national elections.[80] The 1899 reform had been preceded by a considerable amount of social organizing by the left and important changes to the party system. In 1890 seventy-five thousand people demonstrated in Brussels demanding universal suffrage. Then in 1893 the Socialists organized a country-wide general strike that eventually moved the government to widen the franchise, though with the addition of plural voting to strengthen the influence of non-Socialist voters. Still, despite this limit, the Socialists made an impressive breakthrough electorally in the first election under the new rules, electing twenty-eight deputies and surpassing the Liberals as the second-largest party. As the Socialists, in the words of their leader Émile Vandervelde, "entered, almost as if we were burglars, into the most bourgeois Parliament of Europe," their victory caused a sensation throughout Europe, inspiring the left and frightening traditional power brokers.[81]

The franchise reforms of 1893 had increased the electorate tenfold, a factor that pushed the Socialists into second place ahead of the Liberals when the first election was held a year later, despite the impact of plural voting. The rise of a strong third party only magnified the anomalous results produced by the country's traditional majority bloc voting system in multi-member ridings, leading to one-sided, all-or-nothing results nearly everywhere.[82]

Not surprisingly, agitation for electoral reform soon recommenced with Liberals anxious to change the voting system in the face of declining support, and Socialists keen to end plural voting to better represent their voting strength.[83] Even the Catholic government, despite controlling a large majority of the seats, was also unhappy with the status quo, worried that if politics polarized between itself and the Socialists, the left would be in a good position to come to power at some point.[84] Yet it was divided about how to respond, with some arguing for the "British solution" of applying plurality in single-member ridings while others promoted PR.[85] In 1899 the Catholics introduced a bill very similar to the Swedish one of 1896, proposing PR for those areas where Liberals and Socialists were strong, and a continuation of the multi-member majority system where the government was strong. The opposition balked and Socialists organized mass demonstrations against the government initiative, culminating in a general strike in late fall 1899. In the face of what appeared to be an increasingly chaotic situation, what one historian described as the "most dangerous moment in the history of Belgium in this period," the prime minister finally relented, then resigned.[86] The demonstrated strength of the left swept away that last Catholic opposition to proportional voting, and a new PM quickly introduced a party list PR system that would cover the whole country.[87] The Liberals achieved their aim, but the Socialist demands for an end to plural voting were studiously ignored.[88] Belgium was still far from achieving the minimum conditions for democratic rule at the turn of the century, and PR had proven instrumental in keeping the clamour for democracy at bay.

In all three countries – Sweden, Germany, and Belgium – the rise of left parties, and the organizational and ideological threat they were perceived to pose by traditional political elites, was key to raising PR as a reform worthy of serious consideration. The perception of the threat was key.[89] Both Britain and France had extensive working-class participation in politics, but neither perceived it as a threat worthy of considering voting system reform in the 1890s, because in both cases left forces were institutionally and organizationally weak.[90] Neither produced a mass party of the left or harnessed the power and organizational strength of the trade union movement to political action in an independent way. Attempts to raise PR during the British reform debates of 1884–5 on the basis of "fairness" or "progress" were treated with disdain and dismissed.[91] Voting reform made even less progress in Italy, the Netherlands, Denmark, and Norway in this period for similar reasons — the left was simply too weak. When the left did become an electoral threat in those countries, as it would over the next two decades, voting system reform also moved up the agenda.

Where voting system reform did move forward, the strategic context informing its adoption has often been obscured by the seeming cross-party consensus for change.[92] While right and centre parties shifted their views about voting systems in the face of political competition from the left, socialist and labour parties tended to support PR fairly consistently in the nineteenth and early twentieth centuries. Left support for PR was not terribly surprising, as it fit well with a larger set of essentially democratic demands that were animated by rhetorical appeals to notions of justice and fairness. PR would lend "mathematical clarity" to election results and end the distortions of voter preferences created by plurality and majority voting rules. Unions and socialist societies were some of the first organizations to experiment with proportional voting.[93] Certainly most left parties could see that they would be one of the first beneficiaries of such a reform – socialist and labour parties were chronically under-represented before the First World War.[94] While some agitated for voting system reform for just such reasons, others thought that "self-interest" was less important, convinced that the left would eventually benefit from a perceived working-class majority, regardless of the voting system, once other barriers to full and equal electoral participation were overcome. Here local conditions help explain the relative strength of different left party commitments to PR, fuelling strong support in Germany, and more moderate support everywhere else, typically well behind questions of suffrage and executive accountability.

Conclusion

In the century-long struggles to remake western government to better respond to and further the interests of an emergent capitalism, voting system reforms arose amid struggles for power and influence. Far from representing an evolutionary step towards greater democracy or a political recognition of minority rights as set out in conventional accounts, the story of voting system reform in the nineteenth century is one of pedantry, indifference, naivete, opportunism, and fear. Reformers were often well-meaning but naive, and their largely pedantic efforts were marginal in the handful of adoptions that were accomplished. Long-standing minority concerns about religion, language, region, and ethnicity produced no rush by political elites to embrace proportional voting, despite repeated pleas to consider it. Political parties and powerful interest sometimes dabbled with minor voting system reforms, but shied away from them if they appeared to grant room for other, less savoury political forces (like socialists and organized labour) to participate. In fact, though there were forces, particularly on the left, that argued that proportional voting systems were key to shifting to democratic government, the reform really gained impetus only from anti-democratic forces, and its introduction in the nineteenth century was mainly about frustrating moves towards even minimally democratic accountability.

By attending to the historical sequence of events leading to various voting system reforms, we can see that the key catalyst shifting consideration of proportional voting from the earnest meeting rooms of reformers to the halls of power was the rise of disciplined, organized mass parties of the left in the 1890s. Throughout the mid- to late nineteenth century, the expansion of capitalist social relations was altering the class structures of western societies, giving rise to a new working class and working-class organizations. Where distinctive left parties emerged, appearing strong and set to expand their influence, traditional political elites began to seriously consider voting system reforms. Though few judged the threat from the left worthy of such a drastic change of practice in the 1890s, a pattern clearly emerges from the historical record in Germany, Sweden, and Belgium. Where the left was strong, proportional voting reforms were readied for possible deployment; where the left was weak, as in Italy, or divided, as in France, or loyal to existing parties, as in Britain, the voting system hardly mattered (though it occasionally might be manipulated for partisan gain where class factors were wholly absent from the political scene). But into the twentieth century, as the left continued to build on its organizational strength and threat to existing political elites, interest in voting system reform would also rise in seemingly proportional intensity.

Chapter 4

Facing the Democratic Challenge, 1900–1918

Introduction

The period from 1900 to 1920 witnessed the inauguration of modern democratic government throughout all western countries. It was also the single most dynamic era of voting system reform. From the perspective of 1900, however, it was not at all clear that the democratic era was dawning. Conservatives throughout Europe were keen to resist democratic demands and appeared to be securely in power in most locales. In some places they conceded a mass franchise but denied the elected legislature any control over the government (e.g., Germany), while in others the legislature was in control but few were allowed to vote for it (e.g., Netherlands, Italy). Often a combination of rules was employed to keep power in the appropriate hands (e.g., plural voting, rural over-representation, unelected upper chambers, etc.). Even the allegedly democratic countries of the era – the United States, France, and Switzerland – were dogged with election irregularities and accusations of corruption. Yet by 1920, all western countries would be deemed at least minimally democratic in terms of a mass franchise, parliamentary control over the government, and somewhat fair electoral practices. The process would involve intense social struggle, heightened political mobilization, and myriad institutional reforms.

The shift to democracy would be mirrored by a shift towards new proportional voting systems. The scale of voting system change across western countries between 1900 and 1920 was unprecedented. In 1900 nearly all used plurality or majority voting systems. Only Belgium stood out as a late convert to PR in literally the last days of 1899. Yet by 1920 all of continental Europe had switched to proportional or semi-proportional voting systems, leaving just the five English-speaking democracies using plurality or majority approaches. Even these English-speaking countries witnessed considerable agitation over voting systems in this period, leading to serious consideration of reform in Britain, and actual (albeit modest and sometimes temporary) reforms in New Zealand, Australia, and Canada. This distinct wave of voting system reform did not merely coincide with the struggle for democratic government, they were intimately related. As pressure mounted everywhere for greater government accountability to the emergent mass publics, voting systems specifically came under scrutiny, often playing a key role in struggles both for and against democracy. The key factor animating consideration of voting system reforms throughout this period was the character and competitive position of left political parties and the democratic imaginary they promoted.

Events were also important, particularly the social and political impact of the First World War. Though it initially appeared to strengthen conservative political forces against their liberal and socialist challengers, the war eventually undermined traditional rulers and ruling institutions. The emergence of "total warfare" ended up aiding the mobilization of working-class demands through overlapping networks established to support the war effort. As the war ended, the degree of domestic and international instability forced all western countries to concede at least minimally democratic rule at various points between 1915 and 1920. Again, voting system reforms figured prominently in the struggle to resist, establish, and limit democratic rule.

The next two chapters will set out the relationship between these democratic struggles and voting system reform, demonstrating how successive waves of mobilization involving economic restructuring, population migration and resettlement, the efforts of left political parties, and the socially integrative and destructive effects of war all drove consideration of the issue by the left and right, contributing to the sweeping reforms of 1918–19. However, though both left and right called for voting system reforms at various times, the right was much more the decisive force in securing it, either to avoid democracy or to fashion a form of "conservative insurance" within it. The left's role was more indirect. Where the left was strong and appeared to be getting stronger, voting system reform became attractive to the right. Where the left was weak, reforms were more modest, temporary, or failed to make the political agenda. Only by tracing this historical sequence of the events can we sort out why voting system reform became a means of "condensing" class forces in the institutions of the state in some places and not others, despite the common tension inherent in all these emergent forms of capitalist democracy. This dynamic will be sketched over the next two chapters, examining first pre-war and wartime Europe, then the same period for Anglo-American countries, and then shifting to the immediate post-war period and the 1920s.

Conservative Resistance to Democracy in Europe, 1900–1918

From 1900 to the First World War, voting system reform emerged across Europe to serve many purposes. In some locales it buttressed conservatives against calls for responsible government or was designed to blunt the impact of the electoral left or simply offered solace to the critics of the rising power of "the party." New voting systems were sought to divide the opponents of conservative rule in Finland and Sweden, stem the rise of the socialists in Germany and France, and limit the drift of democratizing pressures in Norway, Denmark, Belgium, and the Netherlands. In each case, the distinctive strategy and organization of working-class parties was an important factor. While there had been political parties with considerable organizational capacities in the nineteenth century, particularly in the United States and Britain, the scope of their activities paled in comparison to the new labour and socialist versions.[1] Left parties did not merely organize people to vote, they mobilized burgeoning urban populations into demonstrations, cultural and educational events, and the democratic processes of unions and the party itself. Out of the multiple experiences and demands of the new working class, they helped shape a distinct political identity and sense of purpose.[2] This contributed to a new discipline in electoral politics, for both voters and politicians. Increasingly, left supporters would not give their support to non-left candidates, whether in run-off votes or multi-member ridings. And the discipline of left representatives in caucusing and voting as a bloc put less-coordinated, cadre-style politicians on the defensive. These efforts eventually created a "contagion from the left" that forced more conventional political players to respond.

The coming of war in 1914 initially appeared to buttress the political right and place severe constraints on the drive for democratic government. The left was quickly overwhelmed by the rise of popular support for war, dissent of all kinds was marginalized or criminalized, and the mounting pre-war pressures for more democracy gave way to a tacit public acceptance that strong government was needed to respond to the crisis.[3] Throughout Europe, formerly internationalist, anti-war socialists felt compelled to join the "patriotic consensus" supporting the war effort, sometimes with promises of democratic reform later (as in Germany), but often simply to retain political credibility in the face of rising nationalist sentiment.[4] Needless to say, ongoing democratic reform projects like the negotiations for more proportional voting that were underway in France and Belgium, or plans to expand the franchise elsewhere, were quickly shelved. For conservatives, war offered, among other things, a way out of the seemingly uncontrollable spiral of strikes, demonstrations, and unpalatable political results gaining ground across Europe from 1910 on. Even a short war, what most in fact were predicting, might help shift the balance of social and political power in their favour.

But "the great war" turned out to be a conflagration like no other. The first modern, technologically sophisticated war to take place in what was now a densely populated Europe inaugurated the twentieth-century phenomenon of "total war," a condition that quickly began to undermine the authoritarian basis of conservative rule. War production gave rise to increasing levels of industrialization, while the conditions of wartime facilitated the recognition of unions, bargaining rights, and corporatist negotiations between workers, employers, and government.[5] The need to make society-wide sacrifices to further the war effort required widespread controls and rationing, greatly expanding the scope of government, and fuelling the creation of elaborate networks throughout civil society to monitor these efforts and in turn channel new demands back to the state. The "patriotic consensus" turned out to be a double-edged sword, as those making the sacrifices came to expect a greater say in just how they were to be spread across society. More so than earlier efforts, war brought masses of people into an explicitly political realm, opening up questions for debate and resolution.[6] Rather quickly, these links gave rise to more explicitly oppositional politics on both sides of the war, fuelling food protests in Berlin and rent strikes in Britain as early as 1915, and more generally across Europe by 1916.[7] The war that initially stifled dissent and democratic agitation would eventually spawn a more dynamic and thorough-going democratic agenda across Europe, one more threatening than traditional elites had thought possible, and one that would dramatically increase interest in voting system reforms.

These tensions can be readily observed in the most conservative countries in Europe between 1900 and 1918: Germany, Finland, and

Sweden. All three resisted pressures for parliamentary control of the government, using divisions between liberal and socialist reformers to their advantage and instituting reforms like PR as means of maintaining those divisions.

Germany

German politics would prove influential to both the right and the left throughout Europe in the pre-war period. On the right, Germany's stolid defence of conservative rule meant that even liberal reforms like "responsible government" – never mind democracy – were viewed as radical and dangerous. Such intransigence towards political reform and unabashed celebration of conservative government from continental Europe's largest, arguably most powerful country heartened the nobility and traditional ruling classes from Moscow to Lisbon. For the right, Germany was proof that neither liberal reform nor democracy was an inevitable development accompanying modernity.[8] However, on the left Germany's large and socially powerful Social Democratic Party established the pattern for left-wing organization and set the trends for political action across the Continent. The SPD's unwavering commitment to socialism *and* democratic action steered the Continent's left away from "adventurism" towards electoral political action through working-class organization and mobilization. Early on, the SPD committed to a host of democratic reforms, including proportional voting. Socialist programs in other European countries were often cribbed directly from the SPD. Thus what happened politically in Germany reverberated throughout Europe, repeating like echoes amongst different peoples and places.

Germany's approach to political representation was decisively shaped by the complications of state-building in the 1860s. As with Italy and France, Germany was put together at that time by unifying many disparate territories. However, the German states were stronger, more developed, and more independent than comparable territories were in France or Italy. They insisted on a federal system of government and were quick to defend their interests against perceived encroachments by the new federal power, particularly the most powerful and dominant state, Prussia.[9] As a counterbalance Bismarck introduced a radical full male suffrage in 1871 to create a national constituency, while most states retained much more restrictive suffrages. He hoped that by opening political space to the masses, he could mobilize their support into his battle against the states to strengthen federal power, a battle that also pitted Bismarckian conservatives against liberals.[10] But from the 1870s on, German society would undergo profound economic and social change, and this newly opened political space would be used for purposes very different from what Bismarck intended.

The 1860s marked the take-off of the German economy, from a late developer in the early nineteenth century to arguably the most dynamic capitalist economy in the world by 1900. Economic growth decisively reshaped German society, spurring a dramatic population increase and a shift of that population from rural to urban locales.[11] The breakneck speed of German development, combined with an autocratic form of rule despite male suffrage, aided the rise of the first modern, mass socialist party.[12] The SPD organized the new urban masses politically, socially, culturally, and economically. By 1878 Bismarck found these developments so threatening that, together with support from conservative and liberal forces in the Reichstag, he banned socialist activities.[13] Socialist political and economic associations were suppressed, including the party's many newspapers, journals and printing presses, and any meetings, marches, or celebrations (though, curiously, the party could still run in elections).[14] But suppression did not work, as socialists kept meeting surreptitiously under the guise of bowling clubs and singing groups. When the ban ended in 1890, the SPD emerged stronger than ever. With the failure of suppression, conservatives tried cooptation, introducing nascent welfare state reforms like social and health insurance, and systems of employment arbitration.[15] But reform measures did not wean working-class voters from the socialist party either. Instead, socialists came to dominate the elections for insurance and arbitration boards. Critics soon complained that public boards had become the "third prop" of socialist power after the party organization and the trade unions.[16]

The continued rise of the socialists by the turn of the century raised grave concerns amongst other political forces despite an apparently firm conservative control of the polity. As Fairbairn notes, "Contemporaries, unlike present-day historians, had no idea where this would all end. The perception of a boundlessly growing and unstoppable socialist movement was fundamental to the attitudes of anti-socialists and deeply conditioned their gloom about democratic suffrages, parliamentarism, and the future."[17]

Though blocked from taking power by the lack of parliamentary control over the executive, the SPD was arguably the most significant political force in the country, becoming the most popular party in the national house after 1890, and making headway in state and municipal elections despite more restrictive franchises. In analysing the strength of the SPD's hold over working-class voters, some contemporary observers blamed the voting system. This seemed curious in that, on the whole, Germany's traditional run-off form of majority voting had discriminated against the socialists.[18] Wherever the party failed to win a majority on the first ballot, it usually lost on the second for lack of allies amongst other parties. In 1903 the SPD won just 21 of 117 run-off contests in the national election.[19] But where a working-class party could win, the majority system tended to reinforce SPD dominance on the left, because it was clearly the dominant party. Most workers voting left, socialist or not, would support it or risk splitting the vote. German liberals and conservatives soon discovered that PR might be used to divide working-class politics and cut into socialist support.[20] For conservatives, weakening the socialists might allow working-class votes to be mobilized for other purposes, like the struggle between state and national power. For liberals, weakening the socialists offered the only hope of attaining some measure of executive accountability to the legislature.

From 1900 on, voting system reform was pursued in Germany for all representational bodies (labour arbitration, health insurance, municipal councils, state legislatures, even the national Reich) wherever the left formed or threatened to form a majority. The first effort focused on the industrial courts. The German courts dealing with labour conflict originated in the period of Napoleonic rule. Employers financed them and held the majority of seats, workers with a prescribed income could vote, and local government sometimes intervened to act as a mediator. In 1845 Prussia authorized local councils to create labour courts, which was extended to the North German Federation in 1869. The strike wave of 1889 convinced traditional elites to strengthen the mediating function of labour courts, and in 1890 labour representation on industrial courts was increased to half, and secret voting was introduced.[21] However, as the SPD quickly came to dominate all the representation accorded to workers, its opponents began exploring electoral reform to limit its influence. Initially, these efforts arose at the local level. Though regulated by federal law, the industrial courts were under the control of local authorities. In 1895 Frankfurt city council changed the voting system for its local industrial court from the traditional majority system to PR in an attempt to weaken the SPD monopoly over worker-designated seats. State courts quickly struck down the change as a violation of federal law, but the incident brought the issue to federal attention. In 1901 the federal law was amended to allow any municipality the option of adopting PR for industrial court elections.[22] The fact that the new law was optional was important. It meant that where the socialists were weak, the traditional majority voting system could be maintained to discriminate against them, but where the socialists were strong, PR could be brought in to help fragment their support amongst weaker working-class competitors.

The tactic worked so well that its application quickly spread wherever SPD representation approached a majority. When the Prussian government created special mining councils in 1904–5 it made the use of PR a mandatory provision in an explicit effort to limit the SPD.[23] Local and state governments also turned to PR as the sheer number of working-class voters threatened to overwhelm traditional methods of limiting their influence, like three-class franchises and plural voting. For instance, Hamburg's lower chamber used a three-class franchise allocating forty seats to traditional elites, forty seats to property owners, and eighty seats to residents with a specified minimum taxed income. Between 1896 and 1904 the number of voters in the last category rose from 16,000 to 54,000, with 73 per cent voting SPD. These trends, combined with the effects of majority voting, seemed destined to deliver all eighty lower-tier seats – or half the council – to the SPD in the coming 1906 contest. To forestall this surge, Hamburg switched from majority to proportional voting for most of these seats, thus allowing SPD competitors to gain some representation at their expense.[24] Similar reforms were introduced in a number of states (Wurttemberg, Oldenburg, Lubceck, Bavaria, Baden) between 1906 and 1910, and applied to all municipal elections where population exceeded a prescribed amount, typically between two and four thousand residents. Increasing urbanization meant that such laws led to sweeping changes. In Bavaria alone, 85 of the state's 115 municipalities exceeded the threshold and thus switched from majority voting to PR. In 1906 Wurttemberg also reformed the voting system used for elections to the state legislature, designating PR for use in urban areas like Stuttgart where the SPD was strong, and maintaining majority voting everywhere the SPD was weaker.[25]

Perhaps the most crippling use of voting system reform against the SPD involved the introduction of PR for elections to local social insurance boards in 1911. The introduction of mandatory, state-regulated

social insurance in the 1880s had been a conservative strategy to undermine a key source of socialist power, the independent, socialist-controlled
insurance funds.[26] But the plan backfired. Instead of weakening socialist
influence, the SPD came to dominate these new state-sanctioned boards
through the seats apportioned to workers. Given that the locals were
funded one-third by the employers and two-thirds by the employees,
and representation on the local boards followed suit, SPD representatives often held a majority, even if they did not win all the working-class
seats. The reforms of 1911 essentially ended SPD control in two ways:
by reducing working-class representation in social insurance boards
from two-thirds to one-half, and by switching from majority to proportional voting, thus easing the entry of competitors for SPD voters. The
higher-level appeal boards for local social insurance cases witnessed
even more blatant bias, with PR applying only to the election of the
worker representatives.[27]

That PR was introduced in Germany before the First World War primarily to thwart the left can be seen in the asymmetrical state responses
to its advocates. Where coalitions of the centre-right wanted the reform,
it was readily introduced. But where the left or centre, or even a PR-
specific coalition of the left and centre, called for it, as they did in Baden
in 1894 or Alsace Lorraine in 1908 or Saxony in 1909, they were not successful.[28] The bias can also be seen in the different rules established for
the use of PR in the SPD-dominated industrial courts and the more
middle-class mercantile courts. The latter were established in 1904 to
help settle disputes between merchants and shopkeepers and their assistants and apprentices. For the industrial courts, PR was optional, so
that local city councils could introduce it to limit SPD gains where they
were strong or ignore it and let the majority system keep them weak.
But for the mercantile courts, where the SPD had no real presence, the
centre-right were prepared to make PR mandatory as a means of dis-
couraging divisions from emerging within their own ranks by assuring
all views were represented.[29]

The opportunistic use of voting system reforms against the SPD in
the pre-war era put the party in an awkward position. Though PR was
clearly introduced to weaken them, the party would not condemn the
reform, though it grumbled about the manner in which it was introduced or that it did not go far enough, because the socialists had been
firmly committed to PR for decades. Party founder Wilhelm Liebknecht
had advocated it as far back as 1849, and extensive positive discussion
of the issue in the party journal *Die Zukunft* in the 1870s appeared to

settle the question. By 1891, the demand for PR was article one in the party's Efurt program, alongside universal suffrage.[30] The SPD then went on to capture the largest popular vote of any party in 1890, and more seats than any other party in 1912, results that often moved other left parties to waver in their support for PR.[31] But the SPD commitment to PR never wavered. Critics have since argued that the party's adherence to PR was a strategic blunder, especially in light of Weimar experience, and that if it had stuck with the majority system it would eventually have been awarded majority government.[32] Some suggest that the party's views were shaped by abstract notions of democratic justice, or a preference to "count heads" of socialist supporters rather than struggle for government within the constraints of a bourgeois system.[33] But the SPD had very concrete reasons for sticking with PR. Apart from a general belief that PR was a more fair democratic system, party activists and elites believed the majority voting system was rigged against them, as no parties would cooperate with them when a run-off ballot was required. Moreover, they were not content to wait until a working-class majority formed in each constituency, despite believing that this would eventually come to pass, because they rejected constituency-based voting. Instead, socialists wanted to replace voting based on geographic areas with voting for "communities of interest" that could be pooled across the nation as a whole. To stick with constituency voting would leave some SPD voters "orphaned" where the party was weak, while PR would assure they too would be counted.[34]

The SPD aversion to constituency voting, and by extension its strong support for PR, was a direct result of the party's discriminatory treatment under the grossly unequal allocation of districts in imperial Germany. While the districts were somewhat equal in 1871, they remained unchanged throughout the imperial period, despite dramatic increases in population and a shift of the majority of Germans from rural to urban locales. Over time, rural areas became dramatically over-represented, a fact that benefited the ruling conservatives.[35] As SPD support was primarily urban, the party was constantly under-represented. Thus despite dramatic increases in SPD support from the 1890s up to the First World War, the party's parliamentary strength lagged behind. And the more popular the socialists became, the more conservatives refused to sanction any change to the district boundaries. However, this did not stop the SPD from agitating for changes.[36] Again and again the party called for the introduction of PR for federal and state elections and, failing that, at least a boundary revision that would allocate more representatives to urban areas. The appeals fell mostly on deaf ears, as the ruling conservatives knew that any changes would come at their expense, and the centrist liberal forces feared the socialists much more than they wanted change. The socialists were so frustrated that even some of their most moderate members called for a general strike to gain suffrage and voting system reforms.[37]

Before the First World War, voting system reforms in Germany were discussed by political activists from the right to the left. Though much fine talk referred to notions of justice, fairness, and equality, reforms were actually introduced only when the centre-right wished to wrong-foot the socialists by splitting their vote. Whenever the left made an appeal for proportional voting, the request failed. However, things began to shift just before the start of the war. In the election of 1912 the Social Democrats became the largest single party in the Reichstag. Unlike in previous contests, part of their success came at the expense of a number of centre parties who now suffered under-representation for the first time and an overall decline in seats. It appeared that the SPD was approaching the point at which even the majority system would not limit its success.[38] At the same time, the cumulative effect of conservative economic, social, and military policies began to move some centrist forces away from the status quo and towards considering an alliance with the SPD, which, after all, had demonstrated its commitment to parliamentary and non-revolutionary politics.[39] Evidence of this new political flux could be seen when the 1913 SPD-sponsored bill to introduce PR for national elections failed by just one vote.[40] Though conservatives remained staunchly opposed to changing an electoral system that privileged their concentrated rural support, centre parties with urban support now believed that PR would serve them better than the majority voting system, especially as SPD support appeared on the rise. Unfortunately, the potential for an anti-conservative alliance was quickly dashed by the start of war.

The war effectively called to a halt the campaigns for democratic and voting system reform in Germany by narrowing the space for political disputes and party realignment. Hard decisions had to be taken from the outset of the conflict, commitments had to be made, and there was with little room for debate or reconsideration amid the fighting. For the left, the only organized social force that had been pressing for democratic and accountable government in Europe, commitment to the war effort meant supporting the status quo with promises of reform later. Germany's chancellor in 1914 promised the SPD that after the war he would see through democratic reforms, specifically the elimination of Prussia's biased three-class state voting system.[41] The socialists ultimately fell in line, fearing political marginalization at the hands of a pro-war working class, though many members of the party grumbled that the promises would never be fulfilled.[42] Party unity started to break down in 1916 as members increasingly pressed the government on their democratic commitments, with some voting against the war budget in protest.[43] The kaiser continued to promise that reforms would be forthcoming after the war, but as the strain of the war gave rise to social protest and demonstrations, the SPD and an increasing number of liberals began pressing for more immediate changes. Meanwhile, conservatives and the military high command resisted all efforts at reform, both publicly and behind the scenes.[44]

In March 1917 the SPD and various centre parties succeeded in establishing a constitutional reform committee. Sensing a shift in political support, both in the Reichstag and in the streets, Chancellor Bethmann-Hollweg convinced the kaiser to publicly support the immediate reform of the Prussian franchise. However, pressure from the military and Prussian political elites led the kaiser to reverse his position. The committee deliberations did not fare much better. When the committee reported in July 1917 with a rather modest set of reforms, including the use of PR in urban areas and an end to the Prussian three-class voting system, the chancellor and the kaiser initially agreed. But the military leadership threatened to resign and forced the dismissal of the chancellor instead.[45] The new chancellor shunted the committee report off for expert scrutiny and then, when it was approved, suppressed it altogether.[46] Despite promises of reform to come, conservatives doggedly resisted any attempts to democratize the national or Prussian governments. In fact, the only successful voting system reform of the period was the introduction of PR for war industry employee councils, a change specifically aimed to reduce the SPD's leading position amongst workers.[47]

From the fall of 1917 the SPD began increasingly moving into a kind of unofficial opposition, while by early 1918 the political centre also began shifting away from the government's conservative power base.[48] The partial-PR plan was reconsidered in February 1918 and, despite strenuous conservative opposition at the committee stage in May, became law in July.[49] A great deal had changed in a year's time. German efforts to sue for peace had failed and the war seemed deadlocked, despite the collapse of the Russian front. But a key factor shifting centre opinion in Germany was undoubtedly the Russian Revolution and its influence in fuelling nationalist aspirations in Eastern Europe. For their part, German conservatives embraced reform only when it was clear the war was lost in August, but then only to better position themselves in negotiating with the Allies. The last imperial chancellor tried to hurry along the reform process in October 1918, granting responsible government among other reforms, but it was too late.[50] As the war finally ground to halt, the traditional power system crumbled, replaced by a fragile declaration of a republic and near social chaos. At the sidelines the old political class were now united in calling for proportional representation.[51]

Finland

In 1906 Finland was the first country anywhere to adopt a fully proportional voting system. It seemed an unlikely innovator. Dominated by a local Swedish-speaking elite and a Russian imperial power, Finland was an overwhelmingly rural and agricultural country that up to that point had maintained the last feudal Estates-General in Europe.[52] Representation was restricted to the nobility, the clergy, burgesses, and farmers, with only the wealthiest of the latter two groups allowed to vote. In 1900, the electorate comprised just 124,000 people out of a population of nearly three million.[53] Yet in one flurry of reform the country appeared to move from the Middle Ages to the modern age, from a narrow franchise to full male and female suffrage, from plurality voting to proportional representation. The impetus for these reforms was revolution. Though ultimately a failure, the Russian Revolution of 1905 demonstrated convincingly the potential power of the masses, and its influence quickly spilled over into Eastern Europe, fuelling public demonstrations, revolutionary movements, and reform initiatives throughout the Russian and Austro-Hungarian empires. Ten days after the outbreak of a general strike in St Petersburg in October 1905, Finland was also facing a revolutionary situation, orchestrated largely by the Social Democratic Party (SDP). Faced with revolt at home and abroad, the Russian imperial authorities capitulated to SDP demands for full suffrage and a unicameral legislature. PR was not a key demand, but it emerged from the subsequent negotiations between divided local elites and imperial representatives.

The backdrop to the Finnish reforms involved a changing rural and urban class structure, an emergent cross-class nationalism, language politics, and an encroaching, centralizing imperial authority. Despite a seemingly rural and agricultural economy, the late nineteenth century witnessed Finland's integration into an emerging capitalist market for food and raw materials in Europe, an increasing proletarianization of the rural workforce, and the rise of rural manufacturing.[54] This is why Finland's socialists would eventually make solid inroads into rural areas.[55] However, initially working-class organization emerged in the late nineteenth century under cover of other activities – consumer cooperatives, sports, fire brigades. These efforts gained their greatest power in the temperance movement, often described as the "political arm of the working class" after the successful political strikes for the abolition of drink and a slight opening of the suffrage in 1898.[56] The Finnish Labour party was formed the following year, changing its name to the SDP in 1903.

Opposition to working-class organization was initially muted by elite support for Finnish nationalism and its hopes to mobilize workers behind a project of national independence when the time was right.[57] Nationalist sentiment had intensified from the 1890s on, fuelled by the modernizing efforts of the Russian Crown that led St Petersburg to increasingly interfere in Finnish internal affairs as well as the dominant role of Swedish-speaking elites in education and government.[58] These efforts to streamline the empire and make the Russian imperial state more efficient came at the expense of Finnish elites accustomed to near-autonomy in internal government decision-making. As capitalist development further integrated economic activity between Finland and Russia, and the Russian empire and Europe, the question of who would exercise decisive political sovereignty over trade and state decisions could no longer be avoided.[59] Nascent workers associations and early unions were active participants in a series of nationalist demonstrations from 1899 to 1901 and continued to support a "nationalist movement of the working class" as they struggled to form their own countrywide organization before 1905.[60]

But with the outbreak of the 1905 Russian Revolution, bourgeois demands for nationalist autonomy were quickly outstripped by more far-reaching left demands for democracy and the fact that only the SDP had the political organization and mobilizing capacities to turn opposition to imperial power into more than just talk.[61] As the socialist-launched general strike proved an effective tool in challenging imperial authority, Finnish elites joined reluctantly, torn between nationalist aspirations and a strong opposition to democracy.[62] For the first week of November the country ground to a halt, with effective power in the hands of local strike committees and the SDP. They quickly adopted a "Red Manifesto" demanding national rights and democracy. Faced with revolt throughout their empire, Russian imperial authorities and their local supporters in Finland quickly agreed to a number of longstanding demands, specifically full suffrage and the establishment of a unicameral legislature.[63] In the negotiations following the revolt, PR also emerged for a number of reasons related to these divisions amongst traditional ruling elites.[64] For opponents of democracy, PR emerged as a fallback position when it became clear that last-ditch efforts to restrict the franchise had failed. PR would also assure divisions amongst elites could be represented: the Swedish-speaking elite, rural and urban elites, etc.[65] But the imperial authorities also welcomed PR as a means of dividing the bourgeois forces amongst different parties, thus hoping to weaken their political independence project. In fact, imperial negotiators looked kindly on the rise of a left party for precisely this reason, clearly unaware of the organizational strength of the left.[66] As the left also supported the introduction of proportional voting, the change had the appearance of transcending political divisions.[67] But as it turned out, PR proved unnecessary as a bulwark against democracy, because after the revolutionary tumult had passed, the Russian imperial authorities refused to cede much decision-making power to the new assembly. Neither democracy nor local autonomy made much headway in Finland before the First World War.

Sweden

Just one year after the passage of Finland's ill-fated reforms in 1906, Sweden also adopted PR. Though, in a general sense, the reasons were the same – to insulate conservative political control from the threat of liberal rivals and "democracy" – the process and the social conditions fuelling the reform were very different. As an imperial power with sovereignty over Norway, Sweden had more in common with Russia than Finland. And like Finland's imperial master, Sweden maintained an oligarchic governing system with a highly restrictive franchise, one of the narrowest in Europe.[68] The constitutional settlement of 1866 had replaced a feudal four-estate system with a bicameral parliament, but essentially shifted power from traditional elites to a plutocracy, though the king still nominally "ruled." The commercial, bureaucratic, and aristocratic elements of society dominated the upper house, while farm-owners and some commercial interests controlled the lower house (urban over-representation limited farmer influence, despite their numbers).[69] Politics in the late nineteenth century centred on free trade versus protection, with various coalitions of commercial interests and farmers vying for power, depending on their position in the economy (e.g., domestic producers versus exporters). A high property and income franchise kept most Swedes from the polls for the lower house, while widespread plural voting by the wealthy weakened the impact of lower-class voting for the upper house. Membership in the upper house was also limited by a number of factors: indirect voting, high property/income thresholds, and a lack of any remuneration for those elected.[70] By the 1880s demands for suffrage reform emerged, with a few candidates supporting the initiative gaining election to the lower house. By the 1890s, increasing industrialization had fuelled a rise in urban population and a new middle class – both factors that furthered calls for suffrage reform and new political organizing.[71] Reform forces led by political liberals and some socialists organized successful "people's parliaments" in 1893 and 1896 demanding more open suffrage, and the conservative government finally offered up some reforms that same year, the first since 1866.[72]

Voting system reform emerged out of the suffrage battle. By the 1890s the rising public agitation for political and social reform worried conservatives and farmers, moving some to suggest that the adoption of PR or some other majority-limiting reforms must accompany any suffrage extension as a kind of guarantee against what was assumed would be a working-class majority. The conservative government even worked a measure of PR into its mild suffrage reform bill of 1896, applying it only in urban areas where conservative support was weakening and the rising liberal reform forces were already starting to face competition from the left. But the conservatives and farmers who dominated both houses of parliament were not prepared to alter the status quo, and the government's initiative failed.[73] As neither faction could be sure whether the recent political upheaval was permanent or temporary, each stuck with Sweden's traditional plurality voting system as the best means of limiting new political competition.

Meanwhile the reformers behind the "people's parliaments" faced internal divisions over strategy, with liberals arguing for a mass petition in favour of suffrage, and socialists supporting a general strike (a strategy that had gained political concessions recently in Belgium). Both approaches were eventually attempted and in different ways fuelled the rise of modern party organization.[74] The socialists had founded the Social Democratic Party (SDP) in 1889, very much influenced by the structure and program of the German SPD. But in 1898 the party deepened its organizational structure, making strong links with organized labour for increased membership, consistent financial support, and coordinated action.[75] A Liberal party had been founded in 1894 but held the allegiance of few of the many independent parliamentarians elected in 1896. However, the organization and funds raised through the suffrage petition formed a jumping off point for a new Liberal party organization, and in 1900 a drive to attract independent MPs into a loose liberal caucus gained over eighty members in the lower house.[76] Social Democrats used their new organizational muscle to stage a country-wide general strike for three days in 1902. This breakthrough in political organization by the opposition put suffrage back on the agenda, and forced conservatives to operate more like a coherent Conservative party. The next few years witnessed a flurry of competing reform proposals as both Liberals and Conservatives tried to out-manoeuvre one another.[77] In the process, PR moved from a marginal to central issue.

Though a number of prominent conservatives promoted PR at the turn of the century, they failed to convince all conservative forces. When the Conservative government finally introduced its suffrage reform package in 1902, PR was not included. Liberals and Social Democrats were more receptive to PR initially, though the issue fell well below the expansion of the suffrage, their over-riding concern.[78] Yet in just two years political opinion on the question would reverse itself, with the Conservatives coming out strongly for PR, while the centre-left tried to organize public opinion against it. For conservatives, the chief concern in the suffrage struggle was to effect change in such a way that different groups could be represented but not interfere with property, taxes, and economic decision-making by the state.[79] The 1866 bicameral settlement had accomplished this nicely. The combination of a plutocratic franchise and indirect elections typically assured a solid bloc of loosely defined "conservatives" (industrialists, bureaucrats, nobility) in the upper house. In the lower house, the slightly more open franchise allowed farmers and others to gain election, though urban over-representation gave these conservative forces considerable representation there as well. Thus when it came to budget decisions, which required a joint vote of both houses, conservatives could effect much more political unity than anyone else and, as such, retained control of the purse. But these political distinctions were fluid, divided between government and opposition, defined by issues of protection versus free trade, more than party versus party. By the 1890s, a large group of farmers was often the key component of any conservative government. The rise of coherent opposition in the lower house would erode this fluid yet practical conservative dominance and threaten a potential political stalemate between the two constitutionally equal houses.[80] Not surprisingly, the Conservative government's first serious proposal for suffrage reform in 1902 tried to reduce urban over-representation in the lower house, previously so effective in limiting a farmer-based opposition, while only modestly opening the franchise. But neither rank-and-file Conservatives nor Liberals liked the bill and it failed to pass either house.[81] This failure created an opening for PR advocates.

With the failure of the government's bill, a compromise plan was quickly put to the lower house calling for the extension of full male suffrage, to be combined with the adoption of PR, which passed with both conservative and Liberal support. Meanwhile, at the same time, long-time Conservative PR advocate Bishop Billing convinced the upper house to study the possibility of using PR for elections to the lower house.[82] Billing and many other Conservatives could see the effect that increasing industrialization was having on electoral outcomes as they increasingly lost seats to Liberals and Social Democrats.[83] In response to Billing's proposal, the Liberals later called for PR to be applied not just to the more popularly elected lower house but to both upper and lower chambers.[84] Thus all political forces entered the 1902 election advocating full male suffrage, though there was some disagreement about the nature of the "guarantees" that would accompany it. The temporary consensus broke down a year later when the Conservative government's reform committee reported in favour of full suffrage and PR, but for the second house only. Liberals and Social Democrats complained that the plan was designed to reassert Conservative control over the political realm by turning the second house into an "annex" of the first. Both declared they might still support PR but only for a single-chamber parliament.[85]

The 1902 election proved to be a turning point in Liberal strategy. Though prominent Liberals, including then Liberal leader Sixten von Friesen, continued to declare public support for PR, subtle changes in the party's standing and organization moved the party in another direction. First, the 1902 contest improved Liberal standing in the lower house, moving them past the Conservatives as the largest coherent group in parliament. With the aid of the four Social Democrats and twenty independents, the Liberals could deny any Conservative coalition a majority and used their strength to gain control of nearly all committees.[86] As the Liberals began to see that they might soon form a majority in the lower house, their reform strategy shifted. Much influenced by developments in Britain, the Liberals decided to marginalize rather than reform the upper house, arguing for the parliamentary supremacy of the lower chamber.[87] Second, the Liberals had developed a permanent party organization to aid the 1902 election campaign. Realizing that the Social Democrats were increasingly their main competitors in the party's urban areas of strength, the party organization argued for the separation of the suffrage and PR issues. Liberals were divided on the question but a new leadership group justified the shift on tactical grounds. The new leader, Karl Staff, argued that because the Conservatives were using PR to prevent real reform, their proposal had to be defeated. Liberals were not against PR, he said, they were for suffrage. Yet at the same time the Liberal party organization was researching arguments to discredit the use of PR.[88] For their part, the Social Democrats remained committed to PR but opposed the Conservative proposals to introduce it in the existing bicameral parliament. As a result they opted to work with the Liberals to resist the introduction of PR between 1903 and 1907, but only because it did not apply to a single chamber house. SDP leader Branting repeatedly underlined through four separate campaigns that his party would support PR if used in a unicameral or lower chamber-dominated parliament.[89] Meanwhile, in the face of so much organized opposition, the traditional ruling politicians finally organized themselves into a more formal Conservative party in 1904.

The Conservative government presented its combination suffrage/PR bill to parliament early in 1904. The Liberals responded by spending much of the spring organizing hundreds of anti-PR rallies to discredit the Conservative initiative and promote their own suffrage/plurality alternative. When both proposals finally came up for a vote in May, the result was, not surprisingly, a stalemate between the Conservative-dominated upper house and the Liberal-controlled lower house. Now Liberal leaders and the Liberal party organization moved decisively against PR, shedding the ambiguity of their previous stand. They continued to organize public meetings to denounce PR. When the Conservatives tried to reintroduce their reform package in 1905 essentially unchanged, it failed again.[90] The 1905 election proved a decisive victory for the anti-PR forces, as the Liberals and Social Democrats gained an outright majority in the lower house for the first time. Karl Staff was now asked to form the first non-Conservative ministry in Swedish history. He made achieving suffrage reform and gaining recognition for the parliamentary supremacy of the lower house his chief objectives.[91]

Staff and his Liberal party organization interpreted the election results and the king's recognition of their victory in calling them to govern as signs that Sweden was moving towards a British-style constitutional settlement, where the lower house was supreme, and an essentially two-party system acted as government and opposition. Certainly party lines were becoming clearer. In the 1905 contest the remnants of the disorganized farmers continued to lose ground while Conservatives benefited from the formal party organization they had set up in 1904. Parties and formal organization were becoming central to politics while the number of independents in parliaments dropped to its lowest level ever.[92] Staff moved quickly to introduce the Liberals' reform package in 1906, modified in a number of ways, including the replacement of plurality with run-off majority voting.[93] When the upper house refused to pass it, Staff requested a dissolution from the king to force the issue to a public vote, one he felt confident he would win. Staff had two objectives: to win his reform package and establish the supremacy of the more broadly and directly elected lower house. But Staff's strategy failed. The king refused to dissolve the house, and when Staff resigned, a new Conservative ministry took up his old suggestion to apply PR to both houses.[94] To his surprise, the "double-PR" bill passed in 1907, primarily because a considerable number of his Liberals voted for it.[95]

The victory for PR in 1907 exposed deep rifts in the Liberal party and the still-shifting nature of the party system. While Staff and his Liberal party organization focused on achieving an ideal British model of two-party competition and steady constitutional evolution, the real state of Swedish politics was more fluid. The backdrop to the period involving negotiations over and implementation of PR was a dynamic increase in labour organization and strikes, culminating in a crippling general strike in 1909.[96] Sweden's rapid industrialization was dramatically altering the country's class structure, reducing the rural labour force and the economic importance of agriculture and increasing the urban ranks of the working class.[97] Liberals themselves were torn between a historic attachment to the struggle for the suffrage and a shared concern with Conservatives about the rising power of organized labour and the SDP.[98] Throughout the reform period Liberals could not agree over what restrictions, if any, should be placed on full male suffrage. And suffrage was an issue that probably most unified Liberals; other policy areas produced little party discipline amongst members.[99] In the not-so-distant future, those Liberals who sided with the Conservatives on PR would appear more clear-sighted than Staff and most of the Liberal party organization. In the 1908 elections SDP support jumped from thirteen to thirty-four seats, and by 1914 they had surpassed the Liberals.[100] As in Finland, the adoption of PR was designed to buttress Conservative rule and avoid the "democratic avalanche" that full male suffrage implied. The democratic threat ultimately moved many Liberals to make common cause with Conservatives, despite their reform inclinations. Though Staff returned with a minority government in 1911, his power was hemmed in by an upper house still elected on a restricted franchise, a king who retained a sovereign's right to interfere in government, and divisions within his own party.[101] "Democracy" would have to wait for the social upheaval flowing out of the coming world war.

The introduction of proportional representation in Finland and Sweden allowed conservatives to simultaneously deflect both liberal demands for responsible government and socialist demands for democracy by exploiting key divisions in the reform coalition. Liberals had made tactical alliances with the left in both countries, to challenge Russian rule in Finland and conservative intransigence over suffrage in Sweden, but it was always an uneasy alliance, especially as left parties became organizationally stronger and more militant. Conservatives skilfully exploited these fears, shifting the direction of reform towards PR and away from threats to their continued rule. Thus in these Scandinavian countries PR allowed the right to defeat or contain both the centre and the left. But the balance of political forces was not the same in all conservative-dominated regimes. In Germany, the conditions of conservative rule in this period were much more secure. The existence of full-male suffrage and the world's most successful left party dampened bourgeois enthusiasm for responsible government and limited the space for centre-left reform alliances against conservative rule. Instead, the centre and right were frank that their objective with electoral reforms like plural voting, three-class suffrages and proportional representation was to limit or suppress the left.

Negotiating the Limits of Democracy in Europe, 1900–1918

The adoption of PR in Finland, Sweden, and Germany (at the subnational level) helped conservative regimes resist both liberal demands for parliamentary control of government and the more radical left demand for democracy. Elsewhere in Europe – in Denmark, the Netherlands, and Belgium – conservative dominance had given way to various power-sharing arrangements between liberals and conservatives by the late nineteenth and early twentieth centuries that initially blunted the strategic threat from the left (though this began to give way in the years just prior to the First World War). Meanwhile, in the countries of southern and eastern Europe the left proved too weak to exact much reform before the war, and these countries remained essentially elite-governed. Where some degree of mass suffrage and responsible government did exist, the question of voting system reform did emerge in the pre-war era but took a turn very different in form from that of the conservative regimes. In Norway, France, Switzerland, and the Anglo-American countries, the emergence of a mass franchise and a kind of "responsible government" was gradual, tentative, and backed up by many avenues of conservative retreat, lest things become too "democratic" for the powerful. Nevertheless, the left organized and made its presence felt on the political scene to the extent that conventional politicians worried about its impact. In these cases, voting system reform was informed by the relationship between left parties and their nearest competitor. Unlike the conservative regimes, dominant parties in a competitive political system were not interested in PR, as that would only increase the leverage of left parties and possibly end the practice of single-party majority government. Many assumed that left party efforts were temporary and could be eventually absorbed into the existing parties. Instead, the party most affected by competition from the left paid particular attention to majority voting systems as means to both tactically ally with them and hopefully marginalize them. Again, the strength of the left was a key factor in just how far these reform efforts developed.

Switzerland and Norway

The impact of the left could take many forms. In Switzerland, left influence at the cantonal level was magnified by the existence of other divisions like religion, language, and the need for some degree of local unity in the struggle against what was seen as encroaching federal power. In a number of cantons, PR became a means to elite unity in the face of challenges from both the left and those supporting a stronger national government. Nine of Switzerland's twenty-two cantons had adopted PR by 1914. But the political balance at the federal level did not create the same tension, and agitation by Socialists for proportional voting was hindered by their weakness and isolation. Initiative referendums aimed at securing PR for national elections failed in 1900 and 1910, though support increased each time.[102] Yet conditions were changing rapidly in the years before the First World War, and in 1913 a Socialist-led coalition again gained enough signatures to hold another referendum on the issue. Only the outbreak of war allowed the government to put off the vote.[103]

In Norway the left was stronger, but the pressure for national unity to wrest independence from Sweden meant that, as in Finland, bourgeois parties were initially willing to tolerate them as political allies. Male voting rights had expanded slowly in the nineteenth century, culminating in universal manhood suffrage by 1897 (though voting would remain indirect until 1905).[104] At the same time, a kind of local autonomy, again similar to Finland's relationship to Russia, allowed local elites to run the country internally. But just as in the east, Norway's integration into the worldwide capitalist economy, particularly in terms of shipping, increasingly brought it into political conflict with its Swedish imperial master. A nationalist coalition came to power in 1884, giving rise to an early party system divided between independence-oriented Liberals and somewhat pro-Swedish Conservatives. In the period up to 1900 the Liberals pulled together a broad majority coalition in favour of independence, including peasants and workers.[105] By the time a vote on the question was extracted from the Swedish government in 1905, the majority had become a national consensus – 368,208 voted for independence, while just 184 voted against.[106] But just as the left-liberal national coalition approached victory it began to break down. The Labour party elected its first member to the Storting in 1903, pushing Liberals to form an anti-socialist coalition with Conservatives between 1903 and 1905.[107] Independence brought further pressure for reform, including an end to indirect voting that often produced anomalous results and was seen to disproportionately benefit Conservatives.[108] Furthermore, indirect voting allowed intermediaries to influence the choice of representatives, a process that worked against Labour. In the late nineteenth century, Conservatives had floated a number of schemes for proportional voting at the national level, but with Liberal support on the rise, the party remained uninterested.[109] By 1905, however, the competitive situation looked a bit different. Unsure about how much direct elections would benefit or hurt them, the government replaced plurality with majority voting to limit the impact of vote-splitting from the left and any vote shifts resulting from the end of the nationalist consensus.[110]

France

Unlike conservative regimes, where voting system reforms acted as a last anti-democratic rally, Switzerland and Norway anticipated the major trends to come. In the near future, countries would see either intractable elite divisions make PR the best response to a rising left, as in most of northern Europe, or fairly confident major parties try to use plurality or majority voting to stymie political labour, as in Anglo-American countries. The major exception was France. While in most locales voting system reform was an unusual and episodic event, the French seemed always willing to consider something new. From 1871 to 1990 there were no fewer than sixteen attempts to change the voting system, with at least one campaign mounted between every election between 1909 and 1932 and 1945 and 1958.[111] In the nineteenth century, reform had centred on the choice between plurality versus majority voting, and single versus multi-member constituencies. The key divisions in the late nineteenth century involved religion and the state, with political competition evenly divided between a monarchist right and republican centre-left. As each group came to power, it experimented with different voting systems and constituency arrangements as a means of entrenching itself in power. But most of these initiatives backfired, usually aiding their opponents. The fluid nature of electoral institutions reflected the instability of the republican regime, with conservatives keen to topple it, and left-liberal forces determined that it survive.[112] Electoral system manipulation stood alongside widespread electoral corruption as the favoured means of institutional political struggle.

By the turn of the century, increasing industrialization and repressive government responses to labour contributed to a shift in electoral alliances, fuelling left politics that would break out of the republican orbit, while moving liberals and conservatives to more explicit anti-socialist-inspired cooperation, ultimately forcing the latter to abandon their objections to the regime.[113] In some ways all that changed were the names of the political forces. The late nineteenth-century republic had witnessed the republicans marry left-liberal concerns for a kind of quasi-democratic government (even if it was corrupt and uneven in practice) with conservative concerns for fiscal prudence. But the rise of socialist organizations forced these deals out into the open.[114] Into the twentieth century the party system shifted, breaking down along four broad lines: socialists on the left, reformist radicals on the centre-left, economic liberals or "moderates" on the centre-right, and religious and monarchist supporters on the right.[115] These four groups in turn tended to coalesce into three broad blocs: socialist, radical, and conservative, with considerable movement across the boundaries. Yet, perhaps not surprisingly, the parties that emerged from these divisions tended to be weak, both in terms of voting in a disciplined way in the Chamber and organizationally at the constituency level.[116] Indeed, one contemporary commentator called them "tendencies" rather than parties, mere "factions which combine or dissolve when it suits their interest."[117]

The emergence of an electorally competitive and somewhat cohesive socialist party (SFIO) in 1905 altered the dynamic of the political system, pushing the Radicals to the left. As the party began to benefit from the transfer of socialist voting support on the second ballot of France's majority voting system, Radical ministries responded with some tentative social reform legislation. The right, on the other hand, was hard pressed to respond to this new alliance and spent much of the pre-war period searching for an effective alternative that might produce a majority.[118]

Not surprisingly, interest in voting system reform after the turn of the century shifted as well, from a debate between plurality or majority, to one defending majority or calling for PR. The Radicals preferred the majority system, as it allowed the party to broker election deals with the SFIO, Moderates, and even Conservatives, depending on the constituency.[119] As the centre party, the Radicals were well placed to exploit their strategic position, gaining left support on anti-clerical issues and right support for economic concerns.[120] But Radicals proved to be unreliable allies, often opportunistically attacking those who had supported them.[121] As with their nineteenth-century republican party forbears, the Radicals talked left but tended to govern from the right in terms of fiscal policy and responses to industrial disputes. But their attacks on the church also offended the right. Some members of the SFIO and Conservatives deplored the "immoral bargains" fostered by the run-off elections and promoted PR to end them, occasionally forming tactical electoral coalitions against the Radicals to further their agenda.[122] Moderates also sought reform to limit the local influence in politics and strengthen parties, hoping to contribute to more disciplined behaviour in parliament.[123]

France's first vote on PR occurred in 1902, animated by many of the usual themes that had dominated prior efforts at electoral reform – excessive localism, the problems of patronage, and corruption, etc. – but added to them this time a strong theme focused on rising socialist influence. Belgium's then recent conversion to PR in 1899 was cited approvingly as an effective check on the emerging left by many French deputies. The narrow failure of the motion indicated just how much interest there was in PR: 222 to 292.[124] This fear was reinforced with amalgamation of the various socialist deputies into the SFIO in 1905. Previously opposed forces shifted gears, claiming that the rise of the socialist party required a new approach to representation, one that would allow the left to be marginalized. This was the argument of Deputy Charles Benoist, a former critic of PR and author of the parliamentary commission report endorsing its adoption in 1907. Despite the fact that a considerable number of socialists continued to support the adoption of PR, the anti-left character of the campaign for it became more readily apparent after 1907.[125]

The fall of Clemenceau's Radical-dominated coalition opened some space for centre-right Moderates to try to reorient the political centre away from a Radical-SFIO axis and towards a Radical-Moderate basis, a strategy that would marginalize both the socialist left and the religious right. Particularly after the 1910 election, a contest that appeared to reinforce centrist opinion, former leftist Briand and Moderate elder statesman Poincairé made voting system reform a key part of their centre-right strategy between 1909 and 1913.[126] Briand had first raised the issue as part of the Radical government in 1909, convincing quite a number of Radicals to support the change before opponents within the party killed the initiative.[127] The 1910 election also returned a majority committed to some kind of electoral reform. When Moderate leader Poincairé became prime minister in 1912 he successfully steered passage of PR through the lower house, only to see it voted down by the Radical-dominated Senate.[128] Another majority of deputies favouring voting system reform was elected in 1914, but war precluded any action on the issue.[129]

Voting system reform, specifically a move to PR, was twice strongly endorsed by French deputies between 1909 and 1912, but both votes failed to effect change because of the electoral concerns of different political actors. A host of issues had fuelled interest in the reform: corruption, excessive localism, seemingly perverse election results, and, increasingly, concerns about the political strength of the left.[130] But

Radical indifference and rural Conservative opposition to reform were the key barriers. More urban Conservatives thought PR an urgent necessity to limit the rise of the SFIO, but their centrist and rural allies remained unconvinced. The weakness of the left electorally and organizationally also encouraged this indifference. The SFIO was not a mass party like the German SDP or the U.K. Labour party and additionally found itself challenged by the strength of syndicalist forces in the French labour movement, who rejected state-oriented political action altogether.[131] And unlike the rest of Western Europe, the potential shift to a predominantly urban, working-class majority in France was also limited by the continuing viability of an economically independent rural peasantry, still amounting to 46 per cent of the workforce as late as 1906.[132]

Denmark

Like the rest of Europe, Denmark and the Netherlands had witnessed rapid industrialization and urbanization since the turn of the century, giving rise to significant left parties and increased political competition. But when the First World War began, unlike in the countries at war, the left in these countries did not have to renounce its internationalism or its agitation for more democracy.[133] For reasons particular to the cleavage structures in each country, wartime-inspired social and political instability fuelled elite fears of the left and its superior organization, speeding the pace of domestic democratic reforms, including negotiations over proportional voting.[134] The pressures of war did not fall only on the combatants. Neutral countries like Denmark and the Netherlands were caught between the belligerents and faced economic ruin, as war cut them off from their trade routes and trade partners.[135] These conditions only intensified the political divisions that had emerged before the war and heightened centre-right fears about an expanding left.

The first wartime voting system reform came with the adoption of a semi-proportional hybrid system in Denmark in 1915. The Danes had been early innovators, briefly entertaining full male suffrage (though with "open" balloting), essentially responsible government, and some experimentation with proportional representation between 1849 and 1866. The devastating military loss to Germany in 1864, however, resulting in a loss of 40 per cent of Danish territory, led to a reassertion of conservative control over government, though male suffrage with some restrictions was retained for the lower house.[136] Throughout the latter part of the nineteenth century, Danish farmers struggled against conservative rule, aided near the end by an emerging urban-based labour movement and its socialist party (SDP).[137] In 1901 the Crown and the conservatives relented, granting responsible government to the lower house but keeping the upper house as a preserve of conservative influence and legislative delay.[138] The fairly rapid marriage of responsible government and nearly full male suffrage in Denmark was surprising, especially when compared to the rest of Europe, but in many ways it was encouraged by the geographic breakdown of political competition. Unlike in the rest of Scandinavia, Danish farming consisted of tight networks of small family farms, with little in the way of a rural proletariat that might respond to labour or socialist appeals.[139] Danish farmers also tended to support the Venstre, or Liberal party, as they relied on free trade to export to Britain and across Europe and had spent considerable energy fighting for the political power to protect it. The absence of the kind of rural socialist organizing present in Norway, Sweden, and Finland, combined with their liberal sentiments towards responsible government and the franchise, meant that Denmark's farmers were less concerned about the rise of an urban left.[140] However, conditions changed rapidly in the new century, with the more urban Liberals facing strong competition from the left SDP. By 1905, a breakaway faction of the Liberals, the Radical party, made an electoral pact with the left, one component of which involved seeking far-reaching electoral reforms.[141]

The fracturing of the Liberal party along urban/rural lines created an opening for voting reforms by destabilizing the party system.[142] Competition from the SDP had pushed the more urban members of the party towards reform liberalism, translating into support for social issues and a strong opposition to imperialism and Danish rearmament.[143] This eventually fuelled their formation of a new party. But competition from the dominant Liberal party and Conservatives forced them into an electoral pact with the left.[144] Though somewhat effective, neither the SDP nor the minority Liberals were pleased with the arrangement, and as such both sought electoral reforms as a way out. The Conservatives were also interested in reform, driven by concerns about the strength of the left and the manner in which the plurality system was eroding their support in the lower house. Perhaps recognizing that they could not hold their privileged position in the upper house indefinitely, and fearing being pushed out of the lower house altogether, the Conservatives were desperate for some form of proportional representation.[145] Not surprisingly, the majority Liberals, over-represented by the plurality system and usually in power, were uninterested in reform.[146] But when the 1909 election did not produce a majority for any party, allowing the Radicals to form a brief minority government with support from the SDP, the opening sparked inter-party negotiations over several electoral reforms. However, it was only when the same "progressive" coalition won a majority government in 1913 – with the Social Democrats jumping from 21 to 28 per cent of the seats – that negotiations became more serious.[147]

The problem with reform stemmed from a lack of consensus about just what needed reforming most urgently. The Liberals wanted to reform the franchise and constitutional status of the upper house but opposed the introduction of PR as a threat to their dominance in the lower house. The Social Democrats sought redress of the bias in favour of rural representation and called for a redistribution of riding boundaries, as well as reforms to the upper house. They were somewhat indifferent to PR, recognizing that their increasing strength would now see plurality's distorting effects work in their favour. The Conservatives focused on PR as means to better their representation and limit the SDP, but they also wanted to resist reform of the upper house, where indirect voting and a more exclusive franchise allowed them to dominate.[148] Negotiations over reform in the past had stumbled on just this triangular impasse.[149] But developments from 1910 to 1913, particularly the rise in labour militancy, the electoral success of the SDP, and efforts to remake the Liberal coalition, started to shift the reform ground. Though SDP support hovered around 30 per cent by the First World War, national figures tended to understate its threat to other parties. Specifically in urban areas like Copenhagen, SDP support in the 1913 election exceeded 50 per cent, forcing the problem of vote-splitting onto the Liberals and Conservatives.[150]

By 1913, the Liberals, Radicals, and Social Democrats had worked out an agreement on constitutional change that passed the lower house but was voted down by the Conservative-dominated upper chamber. Efforts to cooperate against the Conservatives in an election that year failed, as the Liberals despised the Radicals and feared the SDP. Liberal and Conservative intransigence backfired when the Radicals and Social Democrats won a majority of seats in the lower house for the first time.[151] Influenced by these new political conditions and the end of the Conservative majority in the upper house in 1914, a compromise emerged in 1915 that partially reformed the upper house and the electoral system. Out of the complicated negotiations, the single-member plurality system traditionally used for the lower house was replaced with a hybrid, semi-proportional alternative. Urban areas were grouped into multi-member constituencies and elected by PR, while rural areas combined single-member plurality with a top-up list. Conservatives could count on better representation in urban areas, while the Liberals protected their advantage in the countryside.[152] But more to the point, the new system would place limits on the left, eliminating the problem of vote-splitting for bourgeois parties and a potential over-representation of the left in urban areas.

The Netherlands

The only other country in Europe to reform its voting system during the war was the Netherlands. Like Denmark, the Netherlands was pitched between the combatants, dangerously close to the battlefields, and alert to defend its precarious neutrality throughout the war.[153] While the situation undoubtedly called for a kind of social solidarity and change in the character of political competition, the conditions of neutrality could not disarm or defer the pro-democratic agenda of the electoral left as effectively as the pro-war, cross-class "patriotic consensus" had in the belligerent states. As a result, the dramatic increase in support for the Dutch left that had been registered in the election just before the war could not be ignored. Instead, as the sacrifices of wartime deepened, traditional elites felt compelled to respond to left demands for a more open franchise while seeking institutional ways to guarantee their own continuing political influence.[154] The settlement of 1917, dubbed the "great pacification" by scholars, extended the vote to all men, changed the voting system to a highly proportional form of PR, and entrenched in the constitution the distinctive "pillarization" system that would assure religious elites an ongoing influence in social affairs.[155] But this was less about a recognition of "multiple cleavages" than the palpable fear from Liberals and religious elites that the left was on the verge of a dramatic expansion into their political constituencies.[156]

Though an organized labour movement and political left emerged as early as the 1870s in the Netherlands, it remained divided and weak for most of the nineteenth century and well into the first decade of the twentieth. Unlike neighbouring Belgium, the Dutch lacked large-scale industrial development, forcing their unions to build up from more small-scale capitalist enterprises, while the organization of rural agriculture, premised on small family farms, limited the left's expansion out of urban areas. As such, attempts to mimic the Belgian left's success with political strikes to further economic and democratic initiatives were miserable failures in the 1880s and in 1903. Meanwhile, electoral success for the left was limited by property restrictions on the franchise that excluded a great deal of the working class.[157] In the same period, the country's religious divisions manifested themselves in political representation for both Catholics and Protestants, who vied for civil rights guarantees and state funding for church-run schools. The religious parties also responded to the emergence of the left and union organizing by establishing labour organizations of their own.[158] Though hardly a match for the secular unions, these religious versions helped maintain a working-class constituency for the religious parties and gave them an interest in an expanded franchise as well.[159]

However, despite the rise of politically competitive religious parties, the key issue dividing Dutch politics at the turn of the century was not religion. Though government funding for religious schools was finally entrenched only as part of the multifaceted reform negotiations in 1917, the issue had ceased to be a point of debate in the nineteenth century. The Liberal government agreed that state funding for confessional schools did not violate the constitution in 1885 and provided the first subsidies to that end in 1889. Increases to the subsidies were agreed to in 1903 and 1905, along with state recognition of confessional university degrees and the admission of religious teachers to the state pension fund. The Liberal government was at the point of recognizing the full equality of confessional schooling with public schooling when its term ran out in 1913.[160] Nor was the SDP antagonistic to confessional schooling; the party had agreed to support the extension of full state subsidies at their 1902 Congress.[161]

The truly divisive issue at the start of the new century was the extension of the franchise, leading to splits in both Liberal and confessional ranks.[162] The steady increase in urban population, union density, and left political representation only reinforced prejudices amongst elites against change. The SDP tried to buttress pro-reform forces amongst Liberals by encouraging left voters to support them wherever SDP candidates did not make it to the second ballot. It also discussed supporting reform Catholic candidates, though the party never formally endorsed the strategy.[163] By 1910, the overarching economic changes remaking Europe were felt in the Netherlands as well, bolstering the left. The SDP had slowly improved its representation in parliament from three members in 1897, to between six and seven in the elections of 1901, 1905, and 1909, despite the restricted franchise.[164] Having resolved some of the disputes that divided the party and organized labour, it stepped up its public reform campaign, coordinating petitions and large-scale demonstrations calling for manhood suffrage. By 1913 the party and the union central had established strong links for electoral purposes.[165] The year 1913 also witnessed a breakthrough for the left electorally, jumping up to sixteen members of parliament, gaining 19 per cent of the national vote. Meanwhile, Liberal and confessional support dropped, moving the Liberal government to offer the SDP three cabinet posts in a coalition government. Though the SDP declined to join the government, it had clearly emerged as a threat to the status quo, even without suffrage reform.[166]

Up to the SDP breakthrough in 1913, Liberal support for some measure of franchise reform had increased, though the party wanted to apply literacy requirements and limit the extension to urban areas, thus granting little to its religious competitors. The confessional parties were split, with the aristocratic ones against reform, while those with working-class support were in favour.[167] The 1913 election results created a political stalemate in terms of who would govern (the Crown appointed an extra-parliamentary administration), but it broke the deadlock over reform.[168] As the war dragged on, left support grew and union membership and strikes increased dramatically, moving the bourgeois and religious parties to the realization that reform could not be postponed.[169] In the negotiations that followed, both Liberals and confessional parties were keen to limit the left and counter the organizational advantage they enjoyed. Class had become the key issue, as all the non-left parties attempted to fashion institutional safeguards that would prevent further socialist encroachment on their political constituencies. Constitutionalizing the rights of confessional schools in the 1917 agreement was meant as insurance against any further drop in confessional voting support.[170] PR was adopted both to limit the left to its numeric support and stem the impact of non-socialist competition between and amongst Liberal and confessional parties. Compulsory voting was added to help centre-right parties counter the organizational capacities of the left in mobilizing their voters by compelling non-socialist voters to go to the polls.[171] For its part, the SDP went along with the package to assure the passage of full male suffrage, a change it assumed would produce an absolute electoral majority for the left, despite the "safeguards."[172]

The adoption of proportional voting in the Netherlands has been characterized as a sop to the Liberals for agreeing to full male suffrage and confessional school funding, an issue of "natural justice" arising from the state of party competition, and the result of a emerging consociational approach to politics characterized by corporatist inclusion and accommodation.[173] But PR was not merely a gift to the Liberals: all the non-socialist parties were keen on it, both to limit the SDP and protect their own political viability and turf. Nor was religion or confessional school funding a divisive political issue by 1917. An arguably multiparty system had emerged in the late nineteenth century, but claims for "natural justice" in representation were not heard then from the non-socialist parties. And the 1917 negotiations hardly invoked a new era of inclusion and accommodation, as subsequent historical developments witnessed the socialists excluded from governing coalitions for the entire interwar period.[174] What moved the adoption of the reform in 1917 was the rise the political left amid tense social conditions – war, minority government, the seeming inevitability of franchise reform – where non-socialist political forces were unsure of their standing vis-à-vis the left and each other. Though the Dutch left hardly improved its standing for most of the interwar period, traditional elites had seen a slow, steady improvement of left fortunes, punctuated by a sudden rise before the war, a trend that hardly appeared promising. Attention to this specific historical sequence of events leading up to adoption of PR demonstrated the class factors fuelling the shift, not religion or culture or consensus.[175] As both left and right assumed that full male suffrage would mostly benefit the left, and by extension the radical economic project they proposed, voting system reform, among other institutional arrangements, emerged as a centre-right class response.

Anglo-American Voting System Reform, 1900–1918

Pre-war and wartime European considerations of voting system reform suggest the urgency attached to the issue had much to do with the size of the emerging threat from the left. But the nature of that threat was also important. Continental Europe witnessed the rise of socialist parties whose very raison d'être was the eventual destruction of the old order. Anglo-American countries tended to produce labour parties rather than socialist ones, and their discourse, though often nominally socialist, was more animated by reformism and inclusion of working people in the existing polity. Though patterns of political inclusion for the working classes in the U.S. and British dominions were as varied as those of Europe, the responses of traditional political elites to the challenge of labour politics were less hysterical. Anglo-American experience in competitive elections and an opportunistic approach to securing working-class political support by the traditional parties conditioned elite responses to an emerging challenge from the left, influencing debate and consideration of voting system reforms.

Frustrated with state actions against union organizations and strikes, independent labour candidates appeared with increased frequency in the 1890s in Britain, Australia, New Zealand, and Canada. While certainly perceived as threatening and undesirable by conventional political forces, electoral forays by organized labour were generally seen as tactical and temporary. Previous efforts by farmers in the United States and Canada, or Irish nationalists in Britain, had been co-opted, absorbed, managed, or marginalized without recourse to voting system reform. There was little to suggest that labour would pose any more serious political threat.[176] In fact, in the United States, Canada, Britain, and New Zealand, the dominant political parties had all made some efforts to marshal working-class support, contributing to considerable debate in labour circles about the advisability of independent political action. Even in the face of state suppression of union organizing and strikes, there were unions and left intellectuals who opposed the formation of a labour party, arguing that more influence could be brought to bear within existing parties.[177] Given the tentative nature of such a challenge, existing political elites were more concerned about how labour candidacies might hurt them competitively rather than how to replace them altogether. As such, most counted on the plurality system to discourage independent political action by labour candidates or parties, or they began to consider some form of majority system to marginalize these competitors, depending on the strength of the challenge. However, when labour parties did appear likely to capture state power, PR became a serious topic of discussion in Anglo-American countries, just as in Europe.

The challenge from political labour was the weakest in the United States and Canada.[178] A determined group of early progressive reformers pushed a series of campaigns for proportional voting in Oregon between 1908 and 1914, but it failed to pass in either the legislature or repeated initiative referendums. Organized labour, though involved in the campaign, was not strong enough to become an important factor.[179]

Some discussion of voting system reform could be heard in the Canadian House of Commons in 1909, eventually giving rise to an ad hoc committee to explore the question, but the driving force was not labour but a rump of Conservative MPs from Quebec who drew support from the minority English-speaking community. Language proved a weak incentive to reform: the committee met only once.[180] Political labour was stronger in Australia, Britain, and New Zealand, giving rise to independent labour parties in all three well before the First World War, as well as much higher levels of interest in voting system reform.[181] The latter registered with the establishment of independent voting reform associations in all three countries before the war, eliciting interest from politicians and parties.[182] But the most telling link between labour and voting system reform was the fact that reform moved furthest and most quickly where political labour was strongest.

Though the onset of war altered the balance of political forces in most countries involved in the conflict, it did not represent a decisive break with pre-war developments. The organizational and ideological power of the left, developed in the first decade of the twentieth century and aided by the increasing urbanization and industrialization occurring in western countries, was idle and muted but remained in place. The reform themes of various liberal reformers, particularly in Anglo-American countries, shifted gears amid the patriotic consensus but continued to adumbrate a politics of purity, anti-corruption, and party-less democracy. The changing circumstances required to fuel the war effort created both limits to conventional political activity and new opportunities to speak to social and political ills. In many countries the pressures of war production allowed unions to achieve significant concessions and recognition from the state, but as a consequence they were expected to keep their members from striking or making excessive demands.[183] The need to get behind the war effort muted conventional political competition, making room for all-party government, anti-party sentiment, and calls for a kind of functional representation (of women, workers, farmers, etc.).[184] These developments would also produce calls for voting system reform.

United Kingdom

Like Europe, Britain had witnessed dramatic economic and social changes in the nineteenth century. By 1900, Britain was further than most in becoming a modern urban industrialized society, rivalled perhaps only by Germany and the United States. But the process of change had occurred very differently from elsewhere. Unlike the break-neck shift to capitalist production that occurred in Germany in the last four decades of the nineteenth century, British capitalism emerged gradually over two centuries. Perhaps more importantly, British economic and political elites were fairly united, without the divisions between industry and the landed classes, or religious, ethnic, or regional divisions that plagued European elites.[185] As a result, British elites were more confident in responding to the upheavals of the new mass society and more open to competing for mass support.[186] Incremental advances in the franchise allowed the two major parties to divide and capture sections of the emergent working class by mobilizing them into the national polity and through attempts to socialize them about the "acceptable" limits of political activity. Both parties occasionally ran labour-identified candidates in predominantly working-class districts and assumed that the emergence of an independent Labour party in 1900 was merely a temporary phenomenon. Though consideration of voting system reform emerged in Britain for many of the same reasons it did elsewhere, it did not elicit the same response. British Labour appeared weaker than left-labour forces elsewhere, while British elites were more confident that they could manage the challenge.

Pre-war consideration of voting system reform in Britain mirrored developments elsewhere, particularly concerns over the rise of party discipline and independent labour politics. The Proportional Representation Society, established in 1885 but largely moribund thereafter, revived in 1905, fuelled by politician and reformer complaints about the power of modern parties and the decline of Parliament and the independent member.[187] Yet as familiar as this will sound to reform elsewhere in the British Empire, there were striking differences. In Britain, the challenge of political labour was met by much better organized Liberal and Conservative parties than in either Australia or New Zealand. Franchise reforms in 1867 and 1884 brought the most affluent members of the working class into the electorate, and both of the two main parties vied for their support, fuelling the rise of permanent political party structures and organization.[188] By 1900, when the forerunner to the official Labour party finally emerged, the Liberals and Conservatives already had considerable experience mobilizing mass electorates and had worked through the party nomination problems that bedevilled their colonial equivalents. The entry of labour into political competition did fuel consideration of voting system reform, but its impact was

mitigated by the strength of existing parties and franchise and registration restrictions that limited the potential working class electorate.
However, as elsewhere, the strategic location of labour in the political
system determined whether interest in voting systems rose or fell.

That organized labour might succeed in sending its own representatives to Parliament was suggested to many contemporary observers by
the rise of separate Irish nationalist representation in the latter half of
the nineteenth century.[189] Labour and socialist organizers did in fact
elect a number of representatives to local government, beginning in the
1880s, reflecting the predominant left bias of the time towards defending local rights and actions.[190] But a series of court decisions against
labour organizing and strikes in the mid- to late 1890s suggested the
need for a more national political strategy. In response, the Labour
Representation Committee (LRC), the precursor to the British Labour
party, was founded in 1900.[191] Though both Liberals and Conservatives
could claim working-class support, the Liberals enjoyed considerable
support in mining and manufacturing districts, just the ridings where
an independent Labour party would be most competitive. By 1903 the
pragmatic Liberals, out of power for eighteen years, had worked out
an electoral pact with the LRC guaranteeing them a free hand in at
least thirty seats, thus reducing the threat of vote-splitting.[192] In the
1906 general election the Liberals swept to power, with Labour candidates capturing twenty-nine seats. Initially, the pact had obviated the
need for voting system innovations by eliminating the immediate
threat of vote-splitting to the Liberals and by easing the entry of independent Labour representatives into Parliament. But very quickly the
Lib-Lab pact generated considerable debate about its political effects,
contributing to a renewed interest in alternative voting rules.

Between 1906 and 1914, elements within all parties agitated for voting system reform. A considerable number of labour activists were
convinced that the Lib-Lab pact was holding Labour back, effectively
limiting the party's growth.[193] They called for the adoption of the majoritarian alternative vote (AV) to end the pact but also reduce the risk
of vote-splitting between Labour and Liberal candidates.[194] There were
also those in the Liberal party who supported AV for similar reasons.
Parliamentary Labour Leader Ramsay Macdonald supported AV, but
others in the party feared it would widen the conflict between Liberal
and Labour activists. Other members did not see Labour increasing its
electoral support in the near future and instead proposed the adoption
of PR to better reflect their support.[195] But here too the party was split,

with Macdonald and the other leaders fearing that PR would weaken the "progressive alliance" Labour had established with the Liberals and limit Labour's influence on government policy. At the same time, the leadership worried that in allowing the various elements of Labour's coalition separate representation, PR might destroy the basis for party unity.[196] Liberal leaders had similar concerns. There were Liberals also promoting PR as a means of reconciling religious and nationalist differences in Ireland, particularly after the escalation of hostilities there from 1910 on. Conservative interest in voting system reform was limited initially to the minority of members defending free trade, though eventually interest spread to include those concerned that the Lib-Lab pact might keep their party from power indefinitely.[197]

The debates over voting systems within all parties were influenced by considerations of political advantage and party strength. But there has been little consensus then or since about the dynamic of the Edwardian party system in Britain.[198] A number of academic commentators have suggested that Labour was weak in this period, essentially dependent on the Liberals for representation.[199] Critics point out that Labour rarely beat the Liberals in a three-way fight.[200] Others argue that class voting preceded the rise of the Labour party and that the Liberals were the beneficiary, largely as a result of their progressive policies.[201] Yet the Liberals were concerned enough about the Labour challenge to strike a royal commission on voting systems in 1909. The royal commission looked into proportional and majority voting systems, examining Belgium's recent conversion to PR, continental experience with various majority systems, and previous British experiments with the limited and cumulative vote. In 1910, the commission recommended the adoption of AV for elections to the House of Commons, a proposal the Liberal Cabinet apparently seriously entertained. But the report was overshadowed by the constitutional crisis over the budget between the government and the House of Lords and only briefly debated in the House of Commons.[202] As it happened, the Lib-Lab pact held through the two 1910 elections, with many viewing Labour's only modest increase in representation as a sign of the party's decline.[203] Liberals may have viewed Labour as a containable threat, one unworthy of voting system reform.[204]

But another view sees the rise of Labour as the key political force moving the Liberals left, fuelling their progressive initiatives, with the potential threat of Labour's unique party structure and organization held in check only by the pact. In power, the Liberals proved much less

progressive than their platform suggested, delivering on some important union legislation and social measures but backing off when proposals elicited too much business criticism.[205] Despite a veneer of "social
democracy," social liberals in the party found themselves trumped by
the fact that the Liberals were as much a party of business in Britain as
the Conservatives, maybe more so.[206] As George Dangerfield so floridly
described them, the Liberals of the period were "an irrational mixture
of whig aristocrats, industrialists, dissenters, reformers, trade unionists, quacks and Mr Lloyd George" held together only by an "almost
mystical communion with the doctrine of laissez-faire." But as he
quickly added, "Asquith's cabinet was very far from being the democratic group which its radical supporters might have wished for."
Instead, aside from a few self-made men like Lloyd George, they were
as much part of the "ruling class" as the Conservatives.[207] As such they
might be better compared to the French Radicals of the period rather
than continental social democrats. Deal-making with Labour, then, was
less about a policy consensus between the two than an effort to exploit
the Liberals' strategic position in the centre of the political spectrum.
For instance, not long after the Liberals were secretly conducting pact
negotiations with Labour they were also trying to effect a centre-right
coalition deal with disaffected Conservatives, a strategy they kept in
reserve throughout the Lib-Lab pact era and put into effect a few years
after it expired.[208]

Ultimately the policy debates between Liberals and Labour were
less important to Liberal party strategists than the structural barriers
blocking Labour's advance. Despite improvements to the franchise in
1867 and 1884, Britain was far from entertaining full male suffrage. In
1911 seven different franchises were in operation under a host of specific qualifications. The 1911 census reported that nearly eight million
voters were on the electoral register, corresponding to 17.5 per cent of
the population, 29.7 per cent of the adult population, and 63.3 per cent
of adult male population. However, half a million of these names represented plural votes. Subtracting these multiple votes, it appears that
only 59 per cent of adult males could vote in 1911.[209] The 41 per cent
missing from the list – nearly five million potential voters – were not a
random cross-section of British society, they were primarily working-
class males. Put in these class terms, even the 59 per cent figure is misleading, as there was a great deal of regional variation, with heavily
working-class districts showing even lower levels of enfranchisement.[210] But the franchise was not the only barrier to working-class

participation. Britain's complex voter registration system made it difficult for working men to get on and stay on the electoral register, as it discriminated against those who had to move for work.[211] Meanwhile, the shift to single-member ridings in 1885 inflated the number of plural votes available to the affluent and, particularly in urban areas, greatly facilitated their being cast.[212]

The institutional barriers to an expansion of Labour's electorate, however, did not preclude it from creating problems for the Liberal party, a fact that kept voting system debate alive. Strong Labour candidacies contributed to a series of Liberal by-election losses in 1912 and helped reanimate interest in AV within the party.[213] Indeed, a first draft of the abortive 1912 franchise bill provided for its adoption.[214] In addition, Liberals grew concerned about the dramatic increase in strikes and labour militancy after 1910, especially as a key region of support for the party was the industrial north.[215] For their part, the Conservatives strongly opposed AV, seeing it as a means of sustaining the successful Lib-Lab pact and keeping the Tories from power, while a minority in the party expressed interest in PR as an alternative. Labour remained divided on voting system reform, with some members advocating AV while others called for PR. However, when separate resolutions calling for the party to endorse AV or PR hit the floor of the Labour party convention in 1914, both were defeated, despite considerable support.[216]

The state of the debate over voting system reform in Britain before the First World War reflected the uncertainty that the parties felt about their electoral prospects and those of their competitors. Liberal concerns about Labour focused on vote-splitting. As long as the electoral pact held, a pact that kept Labour in a decidedly junior position, voting system reform appeared unnecessary. When Labour appeared to be considering a more independent path or improved its representation in by-elections or local elections, Liberal interest in voting systems increased dramatically. However, before the First World War, the threat from Labour was never enough to make reform a government priority. For their part, Labour leaders held conservative views about the party's potential electoral advance, with some calling for PR to better reflect their limited support, while others argued for the status quo to maintain the "progressive alliance" with the Liberals.[217] Some Labour activists thought the party could improve its standing and advocated the majoritarian AV to prevent Lib-Lab vote-splitting but, in the end, they could not convince their party. In the Conservative party, interest in voting systems, specifically PR, emerged initially from internal battles over free trade. However, after two defeats in the back-to-back elections of 1910, Conservatives found PR more compelling.[218] The royal commission report of 1910 had set out three scenarios that might move the adoption of PR in Britain: an extension of the franchise, the emergence of three or more evenly matched political parties, or an increase in political competition driven by religious interests.[219] While on the radar, none of these predictions had come to pass before the First World War. Only with regard to Ireland did British legislators appear ready to embrace PR, incorporating it into the 1914 home rule bill that was passed by Parliament but, due to fierce opposition from Ulster and the outbreak of war in Europe, never proclaimed.[220]

Initially, the war did little to alter the seeming consensus on the voting system. Some debate over voting rules did emerge from a special all-party electoral reform committee established in 1916, before the break in the party system. Given the fact that the current Parliament had extended its own term because of the war, Asquith responded to calls for reform to the franchise, constituency boundaries, and voter registration by establishing a special Speaker's Conference that would include representatives from all parties. However, when Asquith's Liberal-led all-party coalition administration was replaced with Lloyd George's Conservative-dominated, all-party government, the scope of the conference broadened considerably.[221] Before the war, the dominant opinion about the voting system in all parties was for the status quo.[222] Now that all the parties were internally divided to a greater or lesser extent, with some supporting the war administration while others opposed it, the status quo no longer appeared as attractive. Even the Conservative members of the government, easily the most supportive of the war effort, were suspicious of Lloyd George's long-term intentions and how supporting him might affect their party.[223] Lloyd George himself entertained many ideas about how Britain's party system might be renewed after the war, sometimes leaning towards reconstituting the Liberal party, but also considering the formation of a new centre party that would take votes from Labour, Liberals, and free trade Conservatives.[224] The Irish question was also on the mind of politicians, as the violent Easter weekend uprising in 1916 and the emergence of Sinn Fein as political competition for the Irish Nationalists made voting reform an issue.[225] As the committee's work spilled into 1917, increases in labour militancy highlighted the potential future gains of Labour.[226] Amid such pervasive uncertainty, the Speaker's Conference surprised Parliament with a sophisticated set of electoral reforms, addressing a whole range of what had been considered longstanding and seemingly intractable problems. They also called for the introduction of a measure of PR.

The recommendations that emerged from the Speaker's Conference represented a finely balanced set of trade-offs on divisive issues like the franchise, voter registration, plural voting, majority and proportional voting, and others. For instance, the conference members understood the introduction of PR into urban areas as a concession to Conservatives in return for extending the vote to the remaining unenfranchised working men. Though most assumed that the expansion of the electorate would primarily benefit the Liberal and Labour parties, PR would allow the Conservatives some "minority" representation in urban areas where they were typically shut out.[227] However, right from the start of the deliberations over the Reform Bill in the House of Commons, the PR component came under attack from Conservative members. Before the war there had been noises amongst Conservatives about voting system reform, particularly after the two back-to-back election defeats in 1910. Many on the right blamed the Lib-Lab pact for their losses and feared their party might never return to power. Divisions within the party also generated some support for PR from free traders and other minority factions. But, on the whole, Tories were opposed to or uninterested in voting system reform. The 1917 proposals did little to further the cause on the right, at least in the Commons. The Reform Bill would introduce PR in some urban areas but see the majoritarian AV put in place everywhere else. Conservatives had two objections to the plan. First, AV was seen as an anti-Tory reform, as it would primarily ease the threat of Liberal and Labour vote-splitting. Second, PR would limit the number of plural votes that could be cast by introducing multi-member districts, a reform that would mostly hurt the Tories.[228] Early in the discussions the Conservatives narrowly passed an amendment effectively deleting PR from the bill. In successive votes, Conservative opposition to PR only grew larger. Ironically, Tory machinations only furthered the cause of AV in the bill, extending its proposed use to all single-member ridings.[229]

Tory opposition to PR in the House of Commons might have ended the debate quickly but for Tory support for PR in the House of Lords. Having just lost an extended battle with the Commons for supremacy, the Conservative-dominated Lords was concerned about the future of the chamber and the moves towards democracy emanating from below. When the Reform Bill reached the Lords, it reintroduced PR, deleting the Commons's preference for AV in all ridings.[230] The Lords reasoned that a PR House of Commons would be far less majoritarian and less open to radical vote swings. Agricultural interests were also concerned about an expansion of urban voting power and sought PR as a means of diluting it.[231] The Lords' championing of PR opened a tug of war between the two houses, as the Commons insisted on AV and the Lords kept inserting PR. Despite their recent loss, the Lords reckoned that stalling the Reform Bill might prevent it being put in place before the next election, a result the Commons politicians wanted desperately to avoid, and the Lords used this threat as leverage. Finally a compromise was struck that would eliminate AV and see PR applied to a select number of constituencies, to be decided upon by a committee of the Commons.[232] However, after the Reform Bill was dutifully passed and proclaimed, the subsequent report setting out the constituencies for PR was voted down.[233] Despite the deep divisions in all parties and the uncertain political conditions that might accompany a post-war election, Britain's status quo politicians were not worried enough to countenance a switch to PR.[234]

Australia

Earlier than elsewhere in the Commonwealth, political labour in Australia emerged as a competitive and potentially governing force.[235] Starting in the 1890s as a response to the state attacks on union-organizing and strikes, labour politicians were elected in most of the colonial territorial legislatures, holding the balance of power in New South Wales, the largest Australian colony, in 1891, and the first federal government in 1901.[236] The strength of political labour played a decisive role in the drive for Australian unity, assuring the process was much more democratic than it had been in Canada in the 1860s. Labour would also prove decisive in debates over voting system reform, especially as it organized itself into a more formal party.[237]

One of the first tasks taken up by the new Australian federal government in 1901 was the selection of voting systems for the lower House of Representatives and the Senate. Much of the public and political debate echoed the familiar themes of nineteenth-century reformers: the defence of a supposedly traditional British two-party system, the need for effective representation to limit party rule, etc.[238] But the choices were arguably more influenced by the nature of the party system that had emerged in the struggle over the new federation, coalescing in broad coalitions for protection or free trade, characterized by varying degrees of party discipline. The link between a reformer discourse concerned about the power of parties and the political pragmatism of potential governing parties was the emerging Australian Labor party's organization in the constituencies and discipline in the house. Party-like behaviour had long been developing amongst the leading politicians to finance political campaigns and expedite the management of government business through the house, giving rise to the occasional lament of backbench MPs and newspaper editors about the "decline of Parliament." But Labor's superior cohesion as a party became quickly evident, reinforcing reformer criticisms about party behaviour and signalling a serious competitive threat to the dominant political players.[239]

Australia's first national government comprised a liberal protectionist party with Labor support arrayed against a conservative opposition committed to free trade. The voting system debate essentially revolved around the future of political labour. The protectionist government proposed the majoritarian AV for the lower house and the proportional single transferable vote (STV) for Senate elections, reasoning that both systems would help it in working with Labor against free trade supporters.[240] The protectionists also lacked the Labor party's discipline and could not prevent multiple candidacies in single-member ridings between competing protectionist hopefuls, leading to vote splits and party dissension. Transferable balloting would lessen this problem too.[241] But the official opposition was not prepared to agree to a voting system that would primarily help the government manage its disparate coalition at election time and argued for the maintenance of plurality voting. Free traders believed that Labor would eventually fold into the protectionist party, leading to their preferred two-party system. And in the interim, vote-splitting amongst protectionist forces would aid the cause of free trade. Amongst protectionists themselves, opinion was divided, with some government and some Labor members also opposed to the reforms. Though the Labor party initially supported the government's initiative and was prepared to help it pass in the lower house, the issue went to the Senate first. There, under intense opposition grilling, the protectionist party split on the issue and the reform failed. The government then tried to introduce a version of the limited vote for Senate elections, but that failed too. Subsequently, when the lower house debated AV, Labor changed its mind and withdrew support for the government bill.[242] As a result, plurality voting was adopted for both houses.

The free trade forces' predictions about the future of the party system were not borne out. Instead of disappearing, Labor grew stronger and formed its first, albeit minority and short-lived, national government in 1905. By contrast, support for the protectionist party collapsed, slipping from 46 per cent in 1901, to 28 per cent in 1903, to just 23 per cent in 1906.[243] The waning protectionist party tried to interest Labor in AV in 1906, but political conditions had changed and reform sentiments had shifted accordingly.[244] Working from the state to the federal level, the continuing rise of Labor fuelled a realignment of Australia's party system, shifting the axis from protection versus free trade to Labor versus anti-Labor forces. Now that the brunt of vote-splitting had shifted to candidates opposed to them, and the party could foresee capturing power on its own, Labor was less interested in reform. Meanwhile, those opposed to Labor tried to "fuse" themselves into a single opposition party, with varying degrees of success.[245] The difficulty of this process would contribute to a resurrection of proposals for voting system reform at both the state and federal level.

The first reform to emerge involved the readoption of proportional STV in Tasmania in 1907. Tasmania had used STV for elections to its lower house from its two main urban centres in 1897 and 1900 but abandoned the practice under pressure from its upper house and because the complicated counting appeared to make little difference in the results. The 1900 election was also shrouded in controversy, as a disgraced politician regained election in one of the PR constituencies, leading some to condemn the voting system as open to abuse.[246] At the turn of the century, the economic development of Tasmania, Australia's smallest state, was primarily rural, and its politics remained personal, with little organized party activity.[247] Labour representatives were first elected only in 1903, promoted by a number of different ad hoc organizations. However, with three seats and 10 per cent of the statewide vote, a formal Labor party was soon established. By the 1906 election, Labor support had risen to 27 per cent and eight seats in the Tasmanian lower house. Labor's rise put pressure on non-labour politicians to found some party organization of their own or risk splitting the non-Labor vote. But creating a formal party out of disparate, personalistic political forces proved slow and difficult. Nor did the scale or type of economic development in Tasmania lead to the sorts of political divisions that had reinforced the trend towards more formal party organization amongst non-Labor forces elsewhere in Australia. In the end, the return to the proportional STV system in 1907 (this time extended across the state as whole) reflected the keen desire of anti-Labor politicians to avoid having to embrace the party model, with its extensive electoral organization and legislative discipline.[248] STV allowed a personalistic form of politics to survive, because it permitted anti-Labor politicians to run separately without risking vote-splitting while at the same time limiting Labor representation to its proportional vote.

The Tasmanian reforms represented a repudiation of the general trend towards greater party organization and discipline that characterized political change across western countries, particularly in larger, more economically complex societies. In doing so, they echoed a strong reform criticism emerging nearly everywhere in the west about the "evils" of party domination. Yet anti-party arguments could take many forms. Voting reform associations underlined how PR would weaken boss and party rule in favour of a better quality of political candidate. But mainstream politicians also complained about the encroaching power of parties, as they were subject to competitive nomination contests, increasing demands for campaign funds, and pressures for disciplined voting in the house. Labor and farmer politicians had their own "anti-party" arguments, claiming that old-style party representation should be replaced by more direct representation of different groups in society – workers, farmers, women, etc.[249] Yet all these complaints could not reverse the direction of party development. While small, economically undeveloped Tasmania could resist the pull of the party form, at least temporarily, most locales in western industrialized countries could not. Parties represented a collective action strategy aimed at the state, largely given shape by zero-sum economic disputes that required decisive government action so that development could move in one direction or another. Labour parties sharpened these disputes, forced political responses, and heavily influenced party organization and form, but they were not the only influence bringing parties into being. As could be seen in Britain, Canada, and the United States, parties of a sort were already coming into being before labour parties arrived.

Outside of Tasmania, the political differences between non-Labor forces could not be settled within a framework of personalistic politics. But creating a party out the disparate collection of free traders and protectionists, farmers and merchants, and liberals and conservatives, basically all the groups opposed to Labor, was not much easier. When the fusion initiated in 1909 eventually produced federal and state Liberal parties after 1910, the new parties remained unstable, faction-ridden, and prone to very public disputes over their many disagreements.[250]

Anti-Labor forces in New South Wales, now Australia's largest state, responded to the problems engendered by the need for centre-right political unity by adopting the majoritarian second ballot in 1910. The second ballot allowed all centre-right politicians to campaign on their particular issue for their first vote, but regroup behind a single anti-Labor candidate on the second. From 1911 on, most states adopted the majoritarian AV, which basically facilitated the same process.[251] But voting system reform alone proved inadequate in blocking Labor. Despite the introduction of the second ballot, Labor won the 1910 state election in New South Wales, its first majority government victory in what was arguably Australia's most important state. The problem of party discipline would need to be worked out for the anti-Labor forces, even with the added flexibility provided by majority voting systems.

Voting system reform moved more slowly at the federal level, despite a political dynamic similar to that of the state contests. In 1909 the remnants of the dwindling Protectionist party joined forces with free traders to form the Fusion party, later renamed the Liberal party, in a bid to prevent Labor from coming to power. But Labor won its first majority government in 1910, leaving the Fusion/Liberal forces to work out what went wrong. From 1910 to 1913 the party focused on building up its local and organizational strength. As for the voting system, Liberal leaders appeared to assume that the threat of Labor and the constraints of all-or-nothing plurality voting would be enough to produce party solidarity and discipline. They exhibited little interest in voting system reform after their defeat and did not support a private member's bill for preferential majority voting in 1911. Eventually state-level reforms would prove influential, convincing federal Liberal leaders that majoritarian voting systems might offer the best way for them to manage their divided coalition, because it could facilitate a more decentralized, flexible party structure than the Labor model. The Liberals returned to power with a bare majority government in 1913 and established a royal commission to examine voting system reform. Later they endorsed the commission recommendations in favour of AV for the lower house and STV for the Senate. When the government fell in 1914, the Liberals campaigned promising voting system reform if re-elected. However, Labor won the election and the report was shelved.[252]

Labor was enjoying its third tilt at federal government, its second with a majority of seats, when the war and conscription split the party and its administration.[253] Labor's misfortune became an opportunity for reformers to revive their campaign for new voting systems. Pro-war

Labor and Liberal MPs combined into a new National party, an amalgamation that promised to be competitive with Labor, if it could hold together beyond the crisis of war.[254] But no sooner had National formed than it faced a new threat from the country's farmers. Farmers had long been unhappy members of the Liberal coalition. Hurt by protectionist policies and marginalized politically since the demise of the free trade party, they had worked to a position of influence within the Liberal party by 1913, eliciting promises of voting system reforms that would assure farmers better representation within the party and Parliament.[255] The Liberal government campaigned to bring in voting system reforms in 1914 but lost the election to Labor, who dropped the issue. The sudden return to power of Liberals with pro-war Labor members in the election of 1917 seemed to offer farmers some hope that their concerns would be heard.[256]

Though the new government had a healthy majority, it felt very vulnerable, unsure whether the labour component of its vote would stick or drift back to the Labor party in subsequent by-elections and general elections.[257] It also faced increasingly strident demands from its farmer allies. Even before the May 1917 victory for National, members of the government suggested voting system reform would be a priority, a promise reiterated a year later.[258] In the meantime the farmers had not been idle. From 1914 they had begun forming their own separate political organizations that then agreed to lend support to "friendly" Liberal candidates.[259] By 1916, more militant farmers were pushing for independent political action to further their goals, including placing their own candidates to run for office.[260] Clearly National government promises about voting system reform were related to these developments. In January 1918 the farmers stepped up the pressure, informing the government of their plans to run their own candidates, regardless of how it might split the vote. In a letter to the prime minister they spelled out the consequences, noting explicitly that "without … reform your party will be in serious jeopardy at the next election."[261] A few months later, with no reform forthcoming, the farmers put up their own candidate in a by-election, refusing to withdraw until the government explicitly promised reform just two days before the poll. But when a series of fall by-elections were called, and the government had still not delivered on its promise, the farmers launched their own political campaign. The results were Labor victories in both cases, primarily as a result of vote-splitting by non-Labor candidates. With Labor support on the rise and the farmers clearly serious about independent political action, the government finally relented and rushed through legislation introducing AV for the lower house just before another by-election was due.[262] The reform served its purpose. Though Labor topped the poll in the first count, the subsequent transfer of votes allowed the farmers' candidate to win the seat.[263] Granting farmers their own political space was the price paid to defeat Labor.[264] Anti-Labor sentiment also fuelled the adoption of STV in New South Wales in 1918.[265] Later the federal Parliament introduced a block-voting version of AV for the Senate as well.[266]

New Zealand

In neighbouring New Zealand, voting system reform became a political issue in the pre-war period for many of the same reasons it did in Australia: problems of party discipline and the emergence of independent labour politics. As a remote settler country keen to attract and keep immigrants, New Zealand had moved quickly to enfranchise both women and men before the turn of the century. This early mass politics increased the saliency of working-class issues, leading to the introduction of arguably pro-labour legislation like compulsory arbitration for contract disputes in the 1890s, even though unions themselves were small and weak.[267] As in Britain, unofficial lib-lab candidacies were accommodated by the reform-oriented Liberals in government. In fact, the early Liberal party was officially known as the Liberal and Labour Federation.[268] This was a very loose form of party government, and it was not uncommon for rival candidates supporting the government to square off at election time.[269] As a result, government supporters, including the prime minister, repeatedly called for consideration of majority voting systems that would act as a kind of primary, alleviating the party of the divisive problem of choosing from a number of potential standard bearers.[270]

In just about every year from 1890 to 1908, proposals were made in the lower house for a new, usually majoritarian, voting system, but most failed to gain much support.[271] However, the situation began to change just after the turn of the century, as the constituent components of the government coalition became increasingly antagonistic to one another.[272] The Liberals' compulsory arbitration laws had helped fuel unionization rates, but as unions grew stronger they became impatient with the arbitration system and more militant in their demands to employers, especially as the cost of living kept rising.[273] From 1905 various efforts were made to launch a labour party that would be independent of the Liberal government.[274] Meanwhile, farmers who relied on rural workers grew alarmed by the rise of organized labour and increasingly joined a new political effort known simply as Reform.[275] Thus labour's militancy and independent political action finally pushed the government to seriously consider voting system reforms.[276] Faced with increased political competition, a string of by-election losses in 1907, and the faction-ridden nature of their own Liberal party, the government adopted the second ballot majority system in 1908. Reasoning that the new Labour party's voters and rival factions within the Liberal party would all lend their support on the second ballot to the strongest candidate, most likely a Liberal, the reform answered problems of party discipline and the challenge from their political competitors.[277]

The second ballot was used in the 1908 and 1911 elections but it did not work out as the Liberal government had planned. Some Liberals proved unwilling to support other government candidates after their preferred choice was eliminated, and the opposition parties demonstrated a keen tactical appreciation of the opportunities afforded by the new system.[278] In the 1911 contest, Reform even went so far as to encourage its supporters to choose Labour over the Liberals where a Reform candidate had been eliminated, with hopes of defeating the government.[279] Despite the use of majority voting, the 1911 election did not return a majority government. The Liberals now turned against the second ballot system and intended to replace it with AV but were defeated in the house before any action could be taken. Though Reform had proved adept in using the second ballot to its advantage in the 1911 contest, it gauged the system's ultimate impact to be in swinging the Liberals left and effecting some rapprochement between the government and its estranged Labour allies.[280] Besides, the strategic voting required by the second ballot system put a strain on the new party's fragile coalition. Not surprisingly, even though it was committed to some form of majority voting, Reform repealed the second ballot in favour of a return to the plurality system. The fact that Labour had been the most consistent, if minor, beneficiary of the majority experiment might also have been influential.[281] But opinion remained evenly divided on the question. Reform had committed to introducing STV for the upper Legislative Council as part of changing it from an appointed to elected chamber. When a Liberal member seized on this commitment to propose STV for use in the lower house as well, the measure nearly passed, failing by just one vote. Perhaps as compensation to those keen on reform both inside and outside the house, the government did pass a bill allowing municipalities to adopt PR if they wished.[282]

Canada and the United States

As the war got underway, political reformers in North America seized on the consensual mood to step up their campaign to rid government of corruption and special interests. The American Proportional Representation League, founded in 1893 but operating at a low level of activity since 1896, re-established its offices and quarterly journal in 1914. Failure to capture the attention of federal or state politicians moved the League to focus on municipal reform by advocating the adoption of PR by city councils. In 1915, the League enjoyed its first victory when its executive director convinced the council in Ashtabula, Ohio (population 22,082) to adopt proportional voting. Further north, Canadian activists secured and won a plebiscite on PR for the Ottawa city council in 1916, and later that year established a Canadian PR Society.[283] Very quickly, voting system reform was added to a host of progressive initiatives that had roots in the North American farmer-based populist movement of the late nineteenth century and the more recent urban-based liberal progressive movement. In the United States PR became part of a package of civic reforms focused on introducing city managers and smaller councils to make city government more professional and efficient.[284] In Canada, PR was taken up by the emerging farmers movement, organized labour, and reform Liberals in the west.[285] Under these circumstances, PR generated support for all sorts of reasons, some contradictory. Some claimed PR would better represent parties while others claimed it would eliminate parties, some argued it would give representation to the "working man," while others claimed it would make government more "business-like," and so on. But despite considerable effort, the reform initiative quickly stalled. Though activists in Canada could convince reform-minded Liberal provincial governments to pass enabling legislation for municipal uses of PR, those same politicians refused to consider introducing it for their own provincial elections.[286] In the United States, state-level politicians were even more hostile, as municipal politics was often run on party lines, unlike in Canada, where local contests were typically officially non-partisan.[287]

A more critical factor in raising the question of voting system reform at the time, particularly in Britain and its English-speaking dominions, was the political realignment brought on by debate about conducting the war, specifically the role of conscription. For the belligerent continental European countries, the patriotic consensus had

had to be developed quickly from the outset of the war. But for those more distant from the actual fighting (Australia, Canada, even Britain), many key issues were deferred, especially if they might be politically costly. Compulsory enlistment for war purposes was one such issue, dividing members of the Labor government in Australia, the Conservative and Liberal parties in Canada, and the Liberal government in Britain.[288] However, by 1916 the war in Europe was at an impasse. In the absence of decisive leadership, and under the strain of wartime privations, anti-war sentiments began to re-emerge in public debate and demonstrations. There was even talk in British Prime Minister Asquith's Cabinet about suing for peace. The idea of peace with Germany infuriated pro-war forces and led to a polarization of politics around the conduct of the war, including the policy of introducing conscription.[289] The debate nearly led to a split in the Liberal-led coalition government in Britain and fractured the Labor government in Australia, leading to the establishment of a new government there that comprised pro-war members from different parties.[290] In Canada, the governing Conservatives wooed pro-war Liberals from the opposition benches into a new Union government in 1917, then promptly called an election, essentially on the conscription issue, and won a decisive victory. For both winners and losers, the changes were unsettling and unclear in their long-term implications. From committee rooms and party conventions, discussion of voting system reforms would become gradually more prominent in response to this instability in the various party systems.

In Canada and Australia, voting system reform emerged out of debates within parties, as opposed to Parliament. The Canadian Liberal party had split on the conscription issue, with most English-speaking MPs joining the Conservative-dominated Union government. The rump that remained were mostly Quebec members, reflecting that province's opposition to involvement in foreign wars, and a few sympathetic English members like the future leader W.L. Mackenzie King.[291] The Liberals had explored the question of PR internally in 1916 just as the conscription question was rising to prominence, but little came of it. After the split, the Liberals who remained loyal to the party, specifically in English Canada, began considering PR as a means of maintaining their presence outside of Quebec.[292] For its part, the Union government showed little interest in voting system reform. With no left party to worry about, and its main adversary hopelessly divided, the government foresaw little danger in sticking with the status quo.[293]

Conclusion

Pre-war considerations of voting system reform throughout the west were informed by the strength and character of the left, related increases in industrialization, urbanization, the emergence of distinct working-class communities, and the organizational capacities of unions and left political parties, regardless of regime type. By contrast, concerns over minority representation did not secure any voting system reforms, despite a long history of advocacy. In conservative countries, the emergence of distinct left political parties fuelled the adoption of proportional voting systems either to limit their influence, as in Germany, or to help fragment opposition to conservative rule, as in Finland and Sweden. Even where the left was weaker in Europe – France, the Benelux countries, Switzerland – its emergence still sparked considerable discussion of voting system reform. The 1913 electoral breakthrough of the left in Denmark and the Netherlands, and the left's influential mobilization for democratic reform in Belgium in the same year, increased the tempo of discussion for voting system change.

In Britain and its colonies, discussion of voting system reform had everything to do with the strength of independent labour politics, and various partial or temporary reforms were introduced in Australia, New Zealand, and Canada. But the recourse to voting system reforms was not automatic. In Britain, where traditional elites had more experience in mobilizing a mass electorate and creating party discipline, the left challenge was initially answered by maintaining a highly exclusionary set of franchise and registration laws and effecting an electoral pact between Labour and the Liberal party that largely precluded the need for voting system reform, despite considerable interest in the topic. Still, in Britain as elsewhere, the increase in labour militancy and strikes in the period immediately preceding the world war kept voting system reform on the agenda. Only the onset of war decisively quelled reform efforts, though it would prove a temporary reprieve.

The fate of voting system reform in western countries during wartime also depended on the strength of the left, the nature of its involvement with the war, and the legacy of pre-war political developments. Countries in Europe faced taut political conditions that highlighted the need for social solidarity or at least a suppression of dissent. Even neutral countries faced tremendous pressures as war ravaged their economies and threatened to spill over into their territory. However, where countries were neutral, the left did not face the same limits in agitating for democracy as left parties in belligerent nations, and pre-war campaigns continued to have effect into the war, leading to reforms in Denmark and the Netherlands. By contrast, the German left's support for the war effort limited its mobilizing efforts and seemed to strengthen conservative resolve to resist reforms.

In Anglo-American countries, the war effort opened more space for some of the pre-war reform issues like municipal reform, the critique of parties, and the grievances of farmers, all of which fuelled interest in voting system reform (though without much success). However, when politically difficult issues like conscription had to be faced, leading to a dramatic realignment of party systems, voting system reform became a much more serious issue, especially where the left was strong. Still, reforms were not undertaken lightly. Though British and Canadian parliamentary committees called for plurality to be replaced by the majoritarian AV, the recommendations were ultimately rejected. In New Zealand and Canada, the class cleavage would prove too weak to inspire voting system reform. In Britain, both Conservatives and Liberals were divided internally about the threat posed by political labour, and a realignment of the party system that could absorb Labour or more effectively marginalize it still seemed likely well into the war. Only Australia moved to enact reforms, and then only because the government faced clearly suicidal competition from both Labor and an emerging independent farmers' movement.

The gradual emergence of Anglo-American mass government, even in the United States, informed elite responses to the rise of labour and socialist politics. A kind of quasi-democracy had emerged out of the nineteenth century in most and appeared to be capable of managing the contradictions related to their specifically capitalist character. The ambiguity of political labour when compared to European socialism also divided elite opinion, with some making no distinctions while others viewed them as lost sheep that would soon be reabsorbed back into the fold. Yet Anglo-American elites also kept voting system reform at hand, just in case political labour appeared close to gaining power or moving in a more radical direction.

Chapter 5

Struggling with Democracy, 1919–1939

Introduction

The period immediately following the First World War offers a concentrated view of the conditions fuelling the consideration and adoption of new voting systems in western countries. All of Europe and most of the Anglo-American countries either changed their voting system or debated adopting a new one in the tumultuous years that followed the peace, offering an excellent opportunity for comparison. As will become clear, contrary to conventional accounts, voting system reform was not driven by consensus but by conflict. The war had altered the class composition of western countries and mobilized their populations to demand not just political inclusion and greater government accountability but a more expansive form of government, a kind of social democracy. The resulting political and social struggles forced the concession of minimally democratic government across the west, but the fine print accompanying the negotiations often included a shift to proportional voting as one means of furthering or containing the new democratic polity. The sense of threat and the experience of existing political elites would condition the degree to which these struggles would shift to more institutional locales like voting systems.

The post-war period contains two distinct thrusts in voting system reform, one well-known but rather brief period involving the ascendancy of PR as the norm for voting in European democracies, and another less well-documented period of decline of interest in voting system change and reversal of the reform process in some cases. This chapter divides these developments into two sections, one a comparative recounting of PR's rapid rise across western countries, and another showcasing its slow decline, with attention to the conditions fuelling both processes.

The Sudden Rise of Proportional Representation, 1918–1921

From the end of 1918 to 1921 voting system reform became a key concern in western industrialized countries. In Europe, a wave of change swept the Continent. This included newly independent countries like Finland, Poland, and Czechoslovakia, defeated nations like Germany and Austria, war victors France and Italy, and neutral countries like Switzerland, Norway, and Denmark. In fact, by 1920 every country on the Continent used some form of PR. Britain continued to debate voting system reform and introduced PR for Irish local elections in 1919. PR became a key part of the settlement establishing a quasi-independent Ireland in 1920. The New Zealand and Canadian Parliaments considered the question, and two Canadian provinces adopted PR for urban areas. The sudden conversion to proportional voting has been explained as a trend, the victory of pro-democratic sentiments at the war's end, and an effort at greater social inclusion.[1] But the key reason for the dramatic surge of voting system reform was fear. Across Europe and the British dominions, the war's end provoked a social upheaval that traditional elites had never seen before. The makings of revolution suddenly appeared evident in locales as different as Stockholm, Berlin, Turin, and Winnipeg. A delicate dialectic of reform and revolution pushed change in the immediate post-war period as various social forces tried to find their footing amid dramatically changed circumstances. Voting reform would become part of the strategy on all sides.

The end of the war brought disaster to the losers and, after an initial wave of euphoria, uncertainty everywhere else. Throughout Eastern and Central Europe conservative regimes collapsed, sparking civil war, declarations of independence, or simply chaos. Stretched beyond limits both socially and economically by the needs of war, Germany appeared on the brink of revolution, while the Austro-Hungarian Empire simply ceased to exist.[2] Newly minted nations like Austria and Poland immediately faced dire food and energy shortages. In Western Europe, officially neutral Belgium was seriously damaged in the fighting, with 80 per cent of its workforce unemployed by the war's end.[3] Even victorious nations were uncertain about the future, particularly those under wartime coalition government. Political realignments effected to prosecute the war had divided parties and created new ones, but whether these shifts would hold or return to previous patterns under conditions of peace was unclear. Political elites also faced a more organized and articulate civil society, as the process of "total war" had mobilized citizens into claims-making networks and strengthened organized labour and farming interests. Everywhere, public expectations began to rise with the end of hostilities, not just for peace and prosperity, but for more democratic government as well.

Throughout the winter and spring of 1919, western countries witnessed a rising level of social revolt, ranging from sporadic strikes and demonstrations to general strikes and revolutionary insurgency. Pent-up demands from organized labour, returning soldiers, and the general public spilled out once the discourse of wartime unity could no longer be invoked, giving rise to volatile, sometimes violent, situations. These patterns of post-war upheaval could be traced to wartime conflicts like the European food riots and rent strikes of 1915–16, and the significant increase in union militancy and strikes from 1917 on. The patriotic consensus of 1914 had clearly frayed by 1916. Governments tried to shore up working-class support by legally recognizing unions and compelling employers to bargain collectively, but the effects were often temporary as union leaders had difficulty constraining their members. Debate on the left re-emerged in 1915–16 with two conferences aimed at re-establishing an international anti-war front, though the effect was initially more symbolic and organizational than influential. Yet, by 1917, socialist parties everywhere were increasingly debating their war commitments, while in Germany a considerable number of SPD members were forced out of the party for voting against war credits. In most locales, the patriotic consensus had effectively ended by September 1917.[4] Mass actions increased, becoming a way of registering discontent over war policies and, more indirectly, the war itself. The use of such tactics only increased after the war.[5]

However, arguably the most influential event fuelling social upheaval near the end of the war and after was the Russian Revolution of October 1917. As Geoff Eley notes, the Russian Bolsheviks struck at the fatalism of European socialism, demonstrating that a revolution could be forged by people rather than the ineluctable laws of capitalism.[6] Strikes increased dramatically in Europe in 1918, confirming, for some, Bolshevik predictions of a coming European-wide revolution.[7] But Bolshevik influence was not restricted to organizations of the working class; they also set a powerful example for nationalist movements in

Eastern Europe and Ireland. More broadly, the Russian Revolution and its egalitarian ideals (if not always its practice) stood in stark contrast to the lingering conservative rule of most of Europe, signalling that a new order, different from the corrupt regimes responsible for the war, was possible. Initially conservatives reacted with horror, resisting even more fiercely efforts for more democracy. Germany's ruling conservatives continued to block democratic initiatives at home and abroad. In fact, German support was crucial in giving conservatives in the newly independent Finland (temporary) victory over their more democratic opponents in the 1918 civil war.[8]

But Germany's defeat by the fall of 1918 shattered what was left of anti-democratic conservative forces in Europe, eventually contributing to democratic capitulations in Belgium, Sweden, Finland, and most of the former Austro-Hungarian Empire. Meanwhile, the survival of the revolutionary regime in Russia continued to inspire great swathes of the European left, fuelling an increasing radicalization in their ranks from the war's end well into 1920. Spring 1919 was probably the most revolutionary moment in twentieth-century European history, with Soviet-style regimes (briefly) established in Hungary, Bavaria, and Slovakia, while the left appeared dominant in Germany and Czechoslovakia and on the rise elsewhere. Factory council movements established during the war took on a quasi-governing role in some countries, threatening to morph into a soviet dual-power system.[9] The left re-established its international organizations with a meeting of both allied and entente socialists in February 1919, while the Russian Soviets established a Communist International a month later.[10] And regular strikes, occupations, and demonstrations emerged in all western countries. Capitulations to democracy and these militant, sometimes revolutionary, outbursts were clearly related. Even fairly conservative commentators on the events allow that the "Bolshevik revolution helped work a miraculous change of attitude among the Western ruling classes," as they worried just how far down the path of revolution their subjects might go.[11] The timing of the reforms clearly responded to apparent shifts in radical strength and activity, both at home and abroad (particularly in Europe). Though the shape of a country's party system and its experience with mass elections were mitigating factors, all countries were concerned about this rise of revolutionary fervour. Wherever the left appeared strong and conservatives were weak or divided, the democratic settlement was accompanied by "guarantees" like voting system reform.

Germany

Germany was the first country to switch voting systems in the post-war period. With the ink barely dry on the kaiser's resignation letter, the last imperial chancellor hurriedly turned power over the SPD's parliamentary leader, Friederich Ebert, on 9 November 1918, thus saddling the left with the role of brokering the peace. Ebert quickly formed a provisional government in coalition with the independent socialists and issued two decrees on 12 November, one establishing Germany as a democracy, and another introducing full PR for all elections.[12] Ebert's decree was hardly surprising. PR had long been popular with the SPD, and its introduction had been party policy since the Efurt program of 1891. Moreover, a majority of German deputies had endorsed a more limited version of PR for Reich elections as recently as July 1918. If anything was surprising, it was the absence of any opposition to the measure at all. Conservatives, formerly intransigent opponents of PR for the Reich, now demanded it. Liberals, who had sought to limit the proportionality of the wartime proposals, now supported a maximal form of PR. Even the SPD, though long supportive of PR, might have been expected to produce some proponents of plurality now that the party could clearly benefit from it – but it did not.[13] Everyone was now for PR, though not for the same reasons. When the new Reich election law, including PR, was formally announced on 30 November, there were no objections.[14]

The consensus for PR was produced in part by the lack of consensus on much else. From the start, competing visions of a new Germany struggled for pre-eminence, with the independent socialists and factory councils favouring a soviet-style revolutionary regime, the SPD and the trade unions for a democratic socialist republic, the centre and liberal parties calling for a limited democracy, and the conservatives (privately) still preferring no democracy at all.[15] Divisions on the left were particularly acute. The SPD, fearful of the army's loyalty to the new regime, spent the first months after the war suppressing soviet-style insurrections.[16] The trade unions were also threatened by the factory council movement and tended to support the SPD over the independent socialists.[17] But despite these divisions there was broad support on the left for economic – not just political – democracy, either in factory councils or some other form or through the extension of a host of social rights and services.[18] PR allowed for a basis of unity on the left to emerge, despite their differences. Though opposed to the left's economic democracy proposals, the centre-right parties were more fearful of revolution, and they quickly embraced a more thoroughgoing democratic agenda, offering strategic support to the SPD as the best bulwark against insurrection. Employers moved quickly in October 1918 to recognize trade unions and the eight-hour day as a kind of "inoculation" against radicalism.[19] At the party level, centre-right support for PR was meant to convey a commitment to democracy, thus heading off revolution with reform, and represent a concession to a longtime aspiration of the Social Democrats. Of course, they were aware that PR would also conveniently serve to deny the left the kind of over-representation that had been common for traditional parties under the majority system.[20] Thus both left and right had good reasons to favour reform. In debates over the provisional constitution in January 1919 and a more permanent version six months later, only one speaker raised concerns about PR.[21] When an even more highly proportional version of PR was introduced in 1920, it passed unanimously.[22]

The Neutral Countries in Europe

Europe's neutral countries also faced increasing economic and social instability towards the end of the war. In Norway and Switzerland, these conditions were accentuated by wartime election results that were skewed against the left. Norway's Labour party gained 32 per cent of the vote in both the 1915 and 1918 elections but captured around 15 per cent of the seats in both cases.[23] Meanwhile, the long-dominant Liberal party captured 40 per cent of the seats in the 1918 contest with just 28 per cent of the vote. Labour was outraged and demanded the immediate introduction of proportional representation amid threats to boycott future elections.[24] When the war ended, amid increasing labour militancy, the influence of revolutionary conditions wafting west from Russia, Finland, and even Sweden, and a strong sense that rules of the game were rigged against them, the Labour party moved left, eventually joining the Soviet-led Communist International.[25] Like other European countries, the mainstream parties responded to the undercurrent of revolution with reform, finally offering to switch from majority to proportional voting. It helped that Norway's Conservative party had long called for PR to shore up its support and that the dominant Liberals could now discern a clear pattern of decline in their dominance.[26] In Switzerland, the bias against the left was more extreme. In the 1917 national election the Social Democrats gained 31 per cent of the vote, but just 12 per cent of the seats. Though they had the second-highest percentage of support, they gained fewer seats than the third-place Catholic Conservatives, a party with just 17 per cent of the popular vote. This echoed similar results for the left in national elections in 1908 and 1911.[27] The left had gained enough signatures just before the war for another referendum on PR, but the governing Radicals, the key beneficiaries of the current system, stalled the process, using questionably legal practices to do so.[28] Demonstrations and strikes increased from 1917, fuelled mostly by labour and war concerns, but the increase in "direct action" was also informed by a sense that the political system was effectively rigged against the left.[29] This culminated in a general strike in the fall of 1918, where PR was a key demand. Fearing that left support was on the rise, perhaps heading for a majority after the war, the federal government responded to the upheaval by promising a referendum on PR for national elections (previous referendums had been initiated by citizens through the initiative process). This time a two-to-one majority of citizens and cantons voted in favour of the switch.[30]

In Denmark, another neutral country, the switch from a semi-proportional to fully proportional voting system in 1920 was, according to one Danish scholar, the result of "fairly violent and bitter struggles between political parties," while another expert credits the larger social upheaval of the period in fuelling reform.[31] Between 1917 and 1920 Denmark was gripped by the same social and labour revolt sweeping most of Europe, propelled by deteriorating social conditions since 1916. The moderate Social Democrats, who had participated in or supported Radical governments since 1913, now faced an unprecedented challenge from their members and voters to break with their policy of supporting a "civic truce" between the parties during the war.[32] Meanwhile, the right resented both the maintenance of wartime government intervention in the economy after the war and the 1918 re-election of the coalition Radical–Social Democratic government responsible for these nascent welfare state policies.[33] As post-war conditions worsened in 1919 and 1920, and reactionary nationalist and bourgeois forces attempted to reverse the democratic gains of earlier decades, the Social Democrats shifted gears, sponsoring a general strike.[34] In the face of considerable unity on the left in defence of the democratic parliamentary regime, the bourgeois forces retreated and sought institutional reforms instead. At this point, the Liberals dropped their objections to full PR, which since 1916 had the support of the Conservatives, Radicals, and the formerly indifferent Social Democrats as well.[35] However, the

Conservatives and Liberals insisted that the new voting system be entrenched constitutionally, making it very hard to change, even if the left were to gain a majority of the popular vote.[36]

The other two neutral countries in Western Europe, Sweden and Belgium, were also affected by the continental left revolt, though with different results. Both had previously introduced PR as a means of dividing the opponents to conservative rule and limiting the emergent left, while maintaining limited or plural suffrages or powerful upper houses to stem the push for democracy. But as the post-war labour upheaval swept Europe, they too were forced to concede reform, though tellingly no effort was made to remove PR. Sweden introduced PR in 1909 but did not grant complete parliamentary control of the executive, particularly when a Liberal administration was in power. An increasingly assertive king had installed a Conservative regime shortly after the start of the war, but the continuing agitation for democracy and the economic privations caused by the wartime interruption of shipping (particularly from 1916 on) fuelled social and labour radicalism. Conditions had deteriorated so much by 1917 that the Conservatives were forced to resign. The resulting election returned a Liberal-Socialist majority, and the king was forced to accept them, though he still refused to recognize parliamentary supremacy. It was only when news came that the monarchy could not be saved in Germany, and a near-revolutionary situation had emerged in the Swedish streets, that the king relented and renounced his power to actively interfere with policy, allowing the SDP-Liberal coalition government to assume full control.[37]

Belgium also already had a form of limited PR, passed at the end of the last century under pressure from the left.[38] The new rules allowed for some breaks in the party system, with the more socially minded Catholics breaking away from the government to work with the Socialists on reform issues.[39] Still, the maintenance of plural voting and a less-than-proportional design of the electoral system had led to highly undemocratic results. Before the war, the left had returned to direct action as a means of forcing the pace of democratic reform, marshalling a general strike in 1913 that elicited a government promise to improve the franchise.[40] But the arrival of German troops cut short further developments. The four-year German occupation devastated the country economically and fuelled pre-existing grievances based on language and territory. At the war's end, 80 per cent of the labour force was unemployed and most of the nation's resources were either destroyed or carted off to Germany. Such widespread social and economic carnage forced a caretaker Catholic-led government to grant democratic reforms, conceding full male suffrage in the spring of 1919.[41] Furthermore, the sheer scale of the destruction forced the government to actively intervene in rebuilding the country and the economy, facilitating further union recognition and the adoption of social programs.[42] As it became clear that Belgium would get far less for its wartime suffering out of the Paris Peace Conference negotiations than it had anticipated, the traditional elites began to worry about their future electoral standing with a mass electorate.[43] In October 1919 they decided to hedge their bets by shifting from a semi-proportional to a fully proportional voting system, which was later inscribed in the constitution.[44] In the end, the left in Belgium would make only modest gains in the interwar period, but for a time in 1919, elites there feared they were set to roll over the country.[45] Thus Belgium and Sweden conform to larger European trends where social revolt aided democratization, though the combination of institutional reforms differed because PR had come earlier.

Italy and France

Reaction to the international social upheaval emerging from the war took different forms in the victorious countries. Italy emerged a victor from the war amid deep divisions about its participation in the conflict and the country's political future.[46] Alone amongst warring western powers in Europe, Italy's left had refused to join the patriotic consensus and managed to continue opposing it throughout, with little discernible political cost.[47] It emerged from the war militant in its desire to overthrow capitalism and the Liberal elites that controlled Italian politics.[48] On the right, the war stoked imperial ambitions, encouraging a romantic revival of dreams for a greater Italy that would be gained mostly at the territorial expense of Yugoslavia, Austria, and Albania.[49] In the middle, various centrist members of the ruling Liberals attempted to pull together some kind of compromise between a rising working class, rural militants, Catholics, more right-wing Liberals, nationalists, and others, but with little success, especially given the party's strong connections to business. Franchise reform emerged as one response to the social challenges coming from both left and right as the government essentially extended the 1912 reforms to full male suffrage.[50] But later, after a particularly unstable month of strikes and work occupations, and amid disagreement amongst ruling Liberals, the government adopted PR in August 1919.

The pattern of reform in Italy was influenced by its distinctive party system and economic development, as well as the post-war upheaval. Divided between a rural, quasi-feudal south and an emerging industrial north, the dominant Liberal party typically enjoyed a super-majority because it controlled most southern seats through patronage and clientelist practices and could also win seats in the more competitive north. Landlords essentially ran their rural domains like independent fiefdoms while the Liberals operated at the national level, furthering business, trade, and urban development in the north.[51] At the start of the twentieth century the Liberals debated opening the franchise to the burgeoning working class, and some argued that the party could capture these new voters just as Liberals had in Britain.[52] But others worried that franchise reform would only fuel the left and in a bill under consideration in 1910 called for the inclusion of PR to apply to urban areas of the north, where labour was strong.[53] However, when the franchise was finally opened somewhat to working men in 1912, all mention of PR had been omitted, reflecting what would become lingering divisions within the Liberal party about the reform.

Before the war, Socialists and the emerging Catholic political forces had called for a host of democratic reforms, including full suffrage, an end to corruption in elections (particularly in the south), and PR. Liberals were less concerned, as the prime beneficiaries of the status quo.[54] But as left fortunes rose during the war, various factions within the Liberals began to reconsider.[55] Union strength jumped in Italy from 350,000 in 1914 to over 800,000 in 1919, while rural organizing by the left was also very successful.[56] By the end of the war, Italy bordered on a near-revolutionary situation across the north, as the left was strong in both rural and urban locales. Unions and the Socialist party organized strikes, demonstrations, and direct action interventions against increases in food prices in urban areas, and land occupations, marches, and rallies in rural areas. Rural landlords felt they were under a state of siege, while urban elites thought revolution was imminent.[57] But Liberals were still split on how to respond, depending on whether their base of power was in the north or south. Northern Liberals feared competition from such an energized and organized left and thought PR might be an appeasing reform. But Liberals from the south worried that any change to the voting system might interfere with their clientelist networks, the source of their power.[58] Events soon overtook the last resistance. By June 1919 the country was paralysed by strikes and occupations protesting cost-of-living increases.[59] Anti-socialist gangs trucked in from the south raised the level of violence and left/right street-fighting became common. At the same time, Italy suffered a serious setback at the Paris Peace Conference when the great powers refused its territorial claims, leading to the resignation of Liberal Prime Minister Orlando.[60] The old prime minister had disliked PR and though he promised to introduce it under pressure from the Socialists, left-liberals, and Catholics, he stalled repeatedly. The new Liberal prime minister was more closely tied to the Catholic political forces for support, and he moved quickly to introduce it just two months after taking over.[61] However, when the Catholics and Socialists made remarkable headway in the snap election called a month later, mostly at the expense of the Liberals, critics of PR within the dominant party began complaining again. Yet, given the new electoral strength of the centre-left, repeal of the new voting system appeared unlikely.[62]

On the surface, France appeared much like the rest of Europe in the aftermath of war. As the initial sense of relief at the end of hostilities gave way, social and labour demands mounted, giving rise to demonstrations, occupations, and strikes. Throughout the spring of 1919, French leaders worried about the influence of Bolshevism and events in neighbouring countries.[63] As elsewhere, French socialists in the SFIO had made an impressive breakthrough just prior to the war, jumping from 68 members of the lower house in 1910 to 103 in 1914. As the first post-war election approached, centre-right opinion focused on the threat from the left.[64] But the underlying social and political structure of France would prove more resilient to challenge from the left and organized labour and more quickly recover than Italy or the smaller European nations. Compared to the rest of the Continent, French elites, particularly business, were more united (despite the party fragmentation spanning the centre-right), while France's left, its unions, and its parties, were more divided (despite their apparent unity in the SFIO). The post-war upheaval would see some concessions made (the eight-hour day, a new voting system), but the shift back to the right would come earlier than elsewhere on the Continent.[65]

Since before the war, the SFIO, Conservatives, and Moderates had all called for a switch from France's double-ballot majority system to PR.[66] Ever since the rise of organized labour and Socialist parties in the 1890s began shifting the party system away from its republican/monarchist axis towards religious and economic questions, one party, the Radicals, tended to dominate politics, making deals with both the left and right.[67] Essentially, the centrist Radicals would make alliances for second-ballot support with socialists on anti-clerical grounds in regions where the latter were strong, and with right-wingers and more religious conservatives on an anti-socialist basis where conservatives had strength.[68] Not surprisingly, neither left nor right was happy with the situation, and occasionally their frustration with the Radicals led them to work together electorally to defeat Radical candidates, despite their hostility to one another.[69] The continued need for these kinds of "immoral bargains" fuelled support for PR. But party deal-making was not the only issue pushing reform. Conservatives wanted PR to slow the growth of the socialists and buttress religious forces in the lower house. The SFIO and Moderates wanted PR to bolster their representation and aid party-building.[70] More generally, the majority system was held responsible for a host of problems including government instability, corruption, and a locally dominated political culture.[71] Certainly the period just preceding the war appeared damning. Between 1910 and 1914, ten different administrations attempted to govern the country.[72] On two occasions before the war a legislative majority backed voting system reform, but these efforts were blocked by Radicals and more rurally based Conservatives in the Senate.[73]

The mobilization of the left and organized labour emerging from the war pushed voting system reform back onto the agenda. Efforts to change the system before had failed, but the spike in socialist support in 1914, combined with the social upheaval coming out of the war, made the issue more urgent. But the left was not strong enough to demand or inspire a switch to a fully proportional system.[74] The war had not overcome the historical divisions between the SFIO and the syndicalist labour movement that had made it one of the weakest left parties in Europe.[75] Nor could the French left draw on disgruntled agrarian labour as the German and Italian left did, because the peasantry in France was largely independent and conservative.[76] By contrast, the centre-right emerged from the war in better shape than its counterparts on the Continent. It had won the war and could focus public dissatisfaction on Germany and the promise of reparations.[77] Uncertainty about the strength of the left did fuel interest in voting system reform, but mostly because it might alter conventional deal-making at election time. French elites had considerable experience in managing competitive mass elections, unlike most of continental Europe. However, given that traditional methods of manipulating the results were slowly being eliminated (the 1914 election was arguably the first to make secret balloting effective), there was concern.[78] In light of this post-war shift, a key group of centre-right politicians was keen to form a Bloc National that could mobilize anti-socialist votes while marginalizing the clerical issue. Voting system reform would become a key part of its efforts.[79] When reform finally came late in 1919, France adopted a highly disproportional hybrid system that rewarded parties that could make effective alliances over those that did not.[80] Given that the SFIO, under pressure from their militants, had publicly eschewed electoral deal-making with the Radicals, the design was clearly aimed to work against them. Though described by some commentators as a compromise between the SFIO and Radicals, centre-right politicians had been the key players in its design and would become the main beneficiaries in its first trial.[81] In the 1919 election the SFIO increased its support from 1.4 million in the previous contest to 1.7 million but its seat total sank from 101 to 68.[82] Meanwhile the Bloc National won a majority of seats.

Anglo-American Countries

Just across the English Channel post-war politics shaped up very differently from the way it had on the Continent. The war did lead to a mobilization of labour and civil society, just as in Europe. The political arm of the left, the Labour party, did appear to be on the rise, set to benefit from wartime discontents and an extension of the suffrage to all working men. And the conventional party system was in disarray, with a rump of the once-governing Liberals in opposition, while a war-time coalition of Liberals, Labour party members, and Conservatives held power. The war had led to serious splits in all the parties, whether over war itself, the prosecution of the war, or how to respond to the increasing demands in Ireland for independence. When an all-party Speaker's Conference on electoral reform reported in favour of PR in 1918, the timing seemed right for reform. But British political elites had much experience with mass elections and managing splits in Parliament. The votes cast for reform were close, but in the end they failed. Instead of voting system reform, the political elites fashioned a different response to the threat of the left and the uncertainties of the party system with the one-time "coupon" electoral coalition of Lloyd George Liberals and the Conservatives.

Things might easily have gone the other way. In the votes in Parliament in 1917–18 Labour members supported PR (in three of the five divisions) and Asquithian Liberals supported AV, while Lloyd George Liberals and the Conservatives opposed both. In the House of

Lords, Conservatives supported PR both to limit the impact of the franchise extension and the power of the House of Commons.[83] The government's views were influenced no doubt by holding power but also the uncertainty about which direction the political system might be headed. Everyone expected a coming political realignment, either as a progressive alliance of Labour and the Liberals or an anti-socialist coalition of Liberals and Tories.[84] Changes to the franchise laws extending the vote to many more working men as well as all propertied women over 30 seemed to just about guarantee it. Lloyd George's top advisors spent much of 1918 working out different scenarios to remake the party system, by putting their leader at the head of a united Liberal party, or an all-party coalition, or a new party altogether.[85] No matter, it meant Lloyd George had little interest in seeing any of his potential vehicles limited by PR, whether by reducing the incentives for his opponents to work with him or limiting the mandate his party could receive.[86] Negotiations with other parties began in earnest when the war suddenly turned from stalemate to impending victory over Germany in the fall of 1918. But the prime minister soon found that others did not want to play along. The official Liberal party refused his terms for re-entering its ranks (essentially that he become leader of the Liberals and remain prime minister). It assumed that, despite Lloyd George's famous name and strong public identification with winning the war, he could not win anything without a proper electoral organization, which he lacked. Labour soon quit the government to run alone; it had no interest in all-party government under a wartime prime minister.[87] Previous efforts to hive off supporters from other parties to form a new Lloyd George venture had failed.[88] This left only the Conservatives, with whom Lloyd George's lieutenants quickly formed a pact for the coming election. The pact eliminated the pressure for voting system reform by essentially postponing the realignment of the party system.

It is hard to say what might have happened if the British election had not been held so quickly after the end of the war. With the flush of victory still present, the "coupon" election of 1918 delivered a convincing victory to the Lloyd George Liberals and their Conservative allies.[89] Still, the result was not merely reward for winning the war. Public expectations were high that the new ministry would embark on far-reaching social reform in the fields of housing and health.[90] But as labour strife engulfed Britain too in the spring and summer of 1919, and the Conservative-dominated coupon government did little to act on its promises, it became clear that the election had hardly represented much of a "consensus."[91] Yet the government now had a renewed mandate, as long as it could hold its coalition together, while the opposition Labour and independent Liberals were unsure whether this represented a new party or a stalling tactic by Lloyd George.[92] Hedging its bets, when PR came back to a vote in the House of Commons in 1920 Labour again overwhelming supported the change, and this time 80 per cent of independent Liberals did too, though this bid for reform was also unsuccessful.[93] While there had been much talk about electoral reform during the war, and PR had support from most of Labour, a good many Liberals, as well as Conservatives from the House of Lords, it never became a priority for a sitting government. Labour's full suffrage breakthrough in 1918 was modest, independent Liberals could not overcome the advantages of the "coupon" for coalition Liberals, and the Conservatives (in the House of Commons anyway) were satisfied with coalition rather than voting system reform to limit Labour, their Liberal opponents, and the democratic flood. Though Liberal and Conservative elites were concerned about the rise of Labour and the increase in direct action by organized labour in the years after the war, they pursued a number of potential responses to them.[94] It appeared that, despite their differences, the elites of the traditional ruling parties were not as easily panicked as their counterparts on the Continent.[95]

The social upheaval that flowed out of the war was not restricted to Europe and the British Isles. British dominions like Australia, New Zealand, and Canada also faced an upsurge in labour militancy and strikes, compounded by a poorly organized demobilization of soldiers. By the spring of 1919, all three countries were in the grip of an unprecedented labour revolt. In Australia the wartime National government had already reformed the voting system, introducing the majoritarian alternative vote late in 1918. Faced with an emerging farmers' party drawing from the same vote pool as National, and a resurgent Labor party easily gaining 40–45 per cent of the poll, AV promised to handle what the government thought might be a temporary foray of agricultural interests into politics. PR, on the other hand, might only entrench them. Labor, keen to return to power in a majority government, was not interested in PR either.[96] In New Zealand, Labour finally emerged as a political force in 1918, both in elections and direct action. Partly in response to Labour and the social instability, Parliament returned to the question of PR in 1919 but declined to adopt it (though only by a narrow margin).[97] Of the dominions, Canada led the way in its consideration of PR after the war, at least at the sub-national level, a surprising development given that both union density and labour party organization were much weaker than in New Zealand and Australia. At its peak in 1920, voting system reform was seriously considered in four Canadian provinces and promoted by three of the four active federal political parties.[98]

Efforts to reform Canadian voting systems picked up speed during the war as part of a larger political reform movement. A smattering of towns across Western Canada adopted PR by 1918, largely through the efforts of dogged local activists, and farmers and organized labour declared their support for its application to provincial and federal elections. But little had been accomplished before the outbreak of labour and soldier militancy in the spring of 1919.[99] As in Europe, the war fuelled a more considerable organization of civil society, strengthening farmers' movements and organized labour. Union membership increased dramatically with the demands of war production. And labour began moving left, first to embrace political action by a labour party, and then to support direct action to achieve labour's goals.[100] At the same time, Canada's farmers moved decisively to form their own political organization and run candidates in federal and provincial elections.[101] Yet it was only when the Winnipeg General Strike broke out in March 1919, sparking similar efforts across the west, that conventional political elites began to pay attention, calling for reforms that might help represent the "reasonable labour man." Suddenly, PR was embraced by worried business leaders and daily newspapers in several important locales. In Winnipeg, after an impressive showing by Labour in the civic election following the strike, the business-led Winnipeg Citizens League urged the province to introduce PR.[102] The government quickly adopted PR for both city council elections and urban constituencies in provincial elections, to minimize Labour's impact.

In other provinces, farmers were a much greater threat to the status quo, though labour was an important ally. In Ontario in 1919 and Alberta in 1920, farmer parties won power promising democratic reform, including PR. At the federal level, the party system was in disarray, with both major parties unsure of their status. The federal Liberals, split during the war over conscription and now facing challenges to their traditional voting base from farmers and labour, turned to PR as a means of hedging their bets, adopting it as policy at their first federal convention in 1919.[103] The Union government was not sure if it would carry on or split into its former parties. With farmers winning by-elections in 1919 and 1920, and labour militancy on the rise, Union

Liberals joined their former party members in supporting a committee vote endorsing the majoritarian alternative vote in 1921.[104] With an election due soon, reform appeared promising, as no fewer than three of the four political groups that would compete endorsed some form of voting system change.

The novel conditions of the new "total war" inaugurated by the First World War shifted the balance of power in western societies, discrediting traditional ruling elites, as they were held largely responsible for the carnage, while buttressing and expanding the organization of civil society, particularly organized labour. With peace, a new kind of war broke out, largely defined by class, as disgruntled civilians, disoriented soldiers, and more-confident labour movements and left parties began making demands. Though motivated by bread-and-butter issues like jobs and living standards, the post-war social upheaval was also infused by desires for democracy, socialism, and national self-determination. The Russian Revolution had multiple readings, heralding the end of the traditional conservative regimes of Europe, representing the possibility of change towards a more egalitarian society, and demonstrating the practicality of forcibly changing government. The Soviets inspired the left and labour movements in the west, motivated nationalist movements in the east and Ireland, and frightened conventional elites everywhere. The Soviet example of revolution, combined with the surge of left and labour militancy across western societies, shifted the overall public discourse solidly towards democracy and social change, forcing the right to make concessions to head off what appeared to be worse alternatives. But democratic concessions came at a price: voting system reform. The adoption of various forms of PR was understood by the right as essentially conservative insurance against democracy aimed at limiting the left. By 1921, every country in Europe had adopted some form of PR. Each country came to the reform by a slightly different route, reflecting differences in class and cleavage structures, political party development, and the specific historical interactions between the two.

Outside Europe, voting system reforms were also widely considered but ultimately less successful, reflecting different patterns of class compromise and greater elite experience with democratic or quasi-democratic forms of managing social disputes. In the United States very modest concessions made to organized labour near the war's end were accompanied by a state-sponsored "red scare" that effectively criminalized and crippled the left. American elites were unencumbered by the divisions that plagued their European counterparts, and American society was much less affected by the war and war-induced shortages than other warring nations. Though Americans workers did prove militant in the immediate post-war period, just as in Europe, the American state and its political class were less divided and more experienced in marginalizing class dissent.[105] Most importantly, neither labour nor the left managed to form a viable political party in the United States, one reason voting system reform never became an issue there. National elites amongst the rest of the victorious powers may have admired the American response to the challenge, but they were not in a position to reproduce it. Other English-speaking countries like Canada, Australia, and New Zealand struggled to find a response to labour and soldier discontent, while in Britain an expansion of the franchise made the Labour party more competitive and threatening.[106] In Europe, war victors France and Italy also witnessed a rise of labour militancy and uncertainty about political brokering. But for varying reasons, voting system reform in the victorious nations enjoyed less consensus than elsewhere, proving at best temporary in some locales or rejected without trial in others.

Conservative Resurgence and the Slow Decline of PR, 1922–1939

For most western countries, satisfying the minimum conditions for democratic rule (at least full male suffrage, parliamentary control of the executive, free and fair elections) coincided with the outbreak of the most serious social upheavals of the new century. Between 1917 and 1921 Germany, Finland, and Sweden would gain responsible government, Belgium, the Netherlands, Italy, and Britain would expand voting to full male suffrage, and France and Switzerland would address election improprieties. But these accomplishments were not merely responses to new public demands, as these specific changes had been long sought after. Instead, the shift to a minimal form of democracy was defensive, designed to head off and limit more thoroughgoing social, economic, and political demands. The war had altered the fundamental trajectory of the left and started to shift public thinking more generally, away from a bias for local provision of services to a more national orientation. Some thought this would require revolution to see through, but for many others democracy would suffice. Of the many voices clamouring to be heard above the tumult there were numerous, sometimes conflicting, proposals for social change, most of them reformist. But as Geoff Eley notes, it was the undercurrent of rebellion at home along with the spectre of revolution from abroad that ultimately forced democratic concessions from the political status quo in most countries at this particular historical juncture.[107]

However, it must be underlined that these concessions did not represent any serious recognition of public or labour demands coming out of the war by traditional elites, particularly as concerned substantive social policy, as much as a shift in the terrain upon which they would be fought against. As became clear in the 1920s, the powerful in all nations had no intention of surrendering their day-to-day control over most aspects of life to any publicly driven democratic process. Yet most discovered in the immediate post-war period that to maintain their control, and perhaps restore it to its former glory, would not be possible through some nineteenth century–style restoration. The new mass society could not be controlled in the same way as before. As Charles Mair notes, marginalizing the left, and the promise of substantive social policy it represented, would require a "significant institutional transformation" and "new institutional arrangements and distributions of power."[108] The adoption of PR can be seen as one of the first of these institutional changes, though it by no means exhausted the possibilities.[109]

In the years that followed, PR would be judged by how well it acted as a form of "conservative insurance" against democracy. Where PR succeeded it remained as a "condensation" of class forces embedding in the institutions of the state. Left support was rising in most Scandinavian countries in the 1920s, making them the most popular party and easily a majority-government winner in a first-past-the-post system. PR either kept them from power or severely limited what they could do as minority governments. Where PR was not required, it was eliminated. The French left remained organizationally weak throughout the 1920s, a condition exacerbated by the exit of a considerable number of members to form a Communist party in 1920. As such, it proved little threat to the centre-right parties. Though it re-established its election-only alliance with the Radicals in 1924 and defeated the right, its weakness meant it had little influence on the government. Faced with crippling competition from the Communists on the left, and an indifferent partner on the right, the SFIO finally agreed to Radical proposals for a return to France's status quo approach to voting, the second ballot.[110] As a result, France's semi-proportional voting system was repealed in 1927. And where PR failed, either in limiting the left or providing for a clear right-wing alternative, democracy itself was often sacrificed. Traditional elites in Germany and Italy had great difficulty adapting to a democratic brokering of convention and dissent, and PR, with its mathematically precise representation of political pluralism, only made things worse.[111] Though the left in both countries were severely limited in pressing their own agenda, the right felt unable to recapture control democratically. In the end, both PR and democracy were jettisoned.

The great era of voting system reform between 1915 and 1920 has tended to overshadow significant developments in the years following. These include repeals of PR in Italy, France, Australia, and Northern Ireland, failed efforts to adopt PR and AV in Britain and Canada, and a notable shift in left thinking on the desirability of PR as a democratic reform.

Anglo-American Countries

Despite considerable discussion, Anglo-American jurisdictions did not follow post-war Europe in shifting to new voting systems, at least at the national level. One key factor in the fate of voting system reform in the British dominions was the emergence of a critical reappraisal of PR by its long-time champions on the left, and here European experience was instructive. PR as conservative insurance appeared to deliver results in the Scandinavian countries in the interwar period, as the left quickly rose to become the dominant party in each by the late 1920s. Over time, the consensus for PR on the European left came under challenge, as working-class voting majorities failed to develop and bourgeois alliances kept social democrats from power. Scandinavian left parties, the largest in their parliaments by far by the mid-1920s, found themselves unable to act in government and began mooting a return to plurality voting.[112] Britain's Labour party also began moving away from its commitments on PR. As a minority government in 1923, Labour was permitted to do little with its first term in office.[113] When the Liberals – a party that had stalled or opposed most efforts for voting system reform when it was in office – sponsored a bill for PR in 1924, Labour members were outraged and for the first time an overwhelming majority voted against any change.[114] Left parties were learning that the intransigence to their policies from bourgeois forces was deep and would not be moved by rational arguments or appeals to noble sentiments. As their opponents were prepared to use everything in their power to limit working-class parties and the policies they sought, the left decided it could not afford to support democratic reforms on the basis of mathematical justice. In what would become an influential position paper on the left, Herman Finer argued that the U.K. Labour party should defend the plurality system and wait until the system's distortions started working in its favour. Finer and much of the Labour elite now believed that only with the clear majorities that plurality typically provided would the party be able to implement any of its program against the combined opposition of the bourgeois parties, the mainstream press, and their capitalist sponsors.[115] Certainly the difficulty left parties were having in Europe under PR only reinforced their thinking.

However, Labour did nearly introduce AV during its minority government from 1929 to 31. Another Speaker's Conference was struck, but no consensus on changing the voting system could be reached amongst the parties. For a time Lloyd George privately angled for Conservative support on a PR bill instead of AV, promising Liberal votes for a Tory ministry in return, but the Conservatives remained leery of deals with their former ally. Instead, Labour decided to offer the Liberals AV in 1931 if they would sustain Labour's minority government, a deal the Liberals heartily agreed to. However, though the bill was passed in both the House and the Lords, the Labour government fell before it was dispatched to the king. The new Tory-dominated National government never mentioned it again.[116]

Britain's dominions were much influenced by developments back in the "old county," though in some cases the influence was reciprocal. Certainly Australian experience both with voting system reform and Labor government influenced their British counterparts.[117] Though Australia's Labor party had initially supported PR at confederation, its subsequent success in gaining office at both state and federal levels decisively shifted its thinking. When added to the fact that all subsequent voting system reform initiatives were explicitly designed to keep Labor from government, the left's newfound respect for plurality was not difficult to understand. When Labor recaptured federal power in 1914, it brushed aside its opponent's royal commission recommendations in favour of AV. At the state level, Labor repealed PR in New South Wales after regaining office in 1925.[118]

The Canadian left took longer to rework its thinking on voting system reform. From 1919 to 1930, PR placed first on the annual list of demands made to Parliament from the national labour body. Fledgling left political groups like the Federated Labour Party, the Socialist Party of Canada, the Canadian Labour Party, and the "ginger group" of left / labour MPs in the federal Parliament, particularly J.S. Woodsworth, all vigorously called for PR to do justice to working people and their issues.[119] But this also reflected the weakness of Canadian left politics and the barrier that first-past-the-post seemed to represent. It was not until the 1930s that some debate about voting system reform emerged on the left, not coincidentally at the very moment that a national left party finally emerged on the federal scene.[120]

In the period between 1916 and 1923 voting systems enjoyed a fairly high level of public visibility in western Canada and Ontario. Reformers had secured a few municipal conversions to PR during the war, but the labour upheaval of 1919 boosted its consideration amongst the chattering classes and their powerful sponsors. By 1920, every major town in western Canada had adopted PR, and three provinces (Alberta, Manitoba, and Ontario) had undertaken to introduce it.[121] But in the economic downturn that marked the early 1920s, the inflated strength of post-war labour declined significantly.[122] Where labour remained strong and organized, as in Winnipeg and Calgary, PR was introduced and remained an institutional fixture into the 1950s. But where labour's organizational strength visibly declined, as in Vancouver, Victoria, and a host of smaller towns, PR was quickly repealed.[123] In Ontario, farmers and their urban labour allies shocked the country in the fall of 1919 by capturing provincial power in the nation's industrial heartland. Both groups were keen to introduce PR or some hybrid PR/AV system. A Special Legislative Committee on Proportional Representation reported in favour of PR for urban centres, and as the governing majority supported the initiative, it should have easily passed. But the mainstream parties, determined to prevent what they thought was an anomalous multi-party legislature from becoming permanent, began filibustering the bill. In a fit of pique the inexperienced farmer premier called a snap election, which the farmers and their labour supporters lost convincingly.[124] The only other provincial reforms occurred in 1924, when Alberta introduced PR for urban areas (as Manitoba had done in 1920), and both Manitoba and Alberta introduced AV in the rural constituencies of their provinces to ward off challengers to the farmer parties.[125]

At the federal level, the recently reunited Liberal party, the farmer-sponsored Progressive party, and various left and labour candidates campaigned with PR as part of their election platforms in the 1921 election. When the Liberals formed a minority government with tacit support from the Progressives, reform appeared imminent. But the new Liberal prime minister, Mackenzie King, proved to be a wily politician who would manage to elicit third-party support with (unfulfilled) promises of voting system reforms for the next decade and half. In some ways, King's hands were tied. His Quebec contingent, the bedrock of his support, were wholly opposed to PR lest it lessen their province's pivotal role in most governments.[126] On the other hand, the forces to his left, particularly labour, were too weak to make PR a serious demand. When a motion to endorse a trial run of PR in select urban locales came before the House of Commons in 1923, King declared it a free vote and it failed. Another attempt to bring in PR in 1924 failed even more spectacularly.[127] There was a disputed voice vote on AV in 1923 that supporters claimed committed the government to introduce it. Over the next seven years King would repeatedly tempt his sometime allies and taunt his opponents, claiming that the government was just about to introduce a bill to bring in majority voting, but his government never did.[128] King's promises were designed to string along his Progressive party supporters while he wooed their best MPs back into the Liberal party, or their electoral support shrank and their voters returned to the Liberal fold, a tactic that had essentially succeeded by 1930.[129]

Another round of voting system debate came out of the 1935 Canadian federal election. King, now leader of the opposition, campaigned on a promise to implement PR if elected instead of the ruling Tories.[130] As usual, King was hedging his bets in the face of considerable electoral uncertainty. A new national left party, the Co-operative Commonwealth Federation (CCF), had emerged from the depths of the depression and had made some impressive headway at the provincial level.[131] As working-class voters were normally a key Liberal constituency, this development worried King and his party elite. As it happened, the CCF did not make a significant breakthrough in the 1935 contest. Instead the Liberals returned with a majority government and King fulfilled his promise by shunting voting reform off into a parliamentary committee stacked with anti-reform members.[132] The committee did contain one labour member with some experience of PR in Manitoba. However, by the end of the process he too voted against change, declaring that the voting reforms in the west had not lived up to their expectations.[133] When the CCF finally won power at the provincial level in 1944, PR increasingly lost support in the party, leaving the Communists its only defenders on the left.[134]

Continental Europe

As an institutional reform, PR held its position not through abstract democratic reasoning but through its practical results. It helped keep the socialists at bay in Scandinavia, it isolated them effectively in the Benelux countries, and it proved useful in managing tense conflicts in Ireland.[135] But in other countries proportional voting did not effect a balance that traditionally powerful groups were prepared to settle for. In the three major continental countries of Europe – Germany, France, and Italy – PR did not survive the interwar period, though for very different reasons. In France, though the voting reforms of 1919 had been pushed along by labour unrest and the general air of revolution wafting throughout Europe, the actual system chosen also reflected the desires of the centre-right to marginalize both the left and religious issues. In its first trial in the fall of 1919, SFIO support increased but its legislative performance declined from pre-war levels while the new Bloc National won a majority of seats.[136] The coalition-hopping Radicals had thrown their lot in with the Bloc in 1919 but switched to the SFIO in 1924, leading a centre-left coalition to victory. However the left soon discovered that it had little influence over its government as the Radicals increasingly sought extra support from more centrist Bloc members. Though the SFIO was unhappy with these developments, its organizational weakness meant that the French party system as a whole was weak, and strong parties were key to exacting concessions that might last. Some blame the SFIO for the failure of the centre-left coalition to hold together because it joined the electoral Cartel des Gauches in 1924 but then refused to join the government that result from it.[137] But others argue that the SFIO was in a tight spot, caught between competition on its left from the Communists and demands from its own supporters to defend socialist policies.[138]

The SFIO had tried to get the Communists to agree to a broad centre-left alliance before the 1924 election, knowing that the hybrid voting system would punish any party without one, but without success.[139] The SFIO turned out to be right – as part of the Cartel it regained the seats it had lost in 1919. But the replacement of the Cartel-elected government just two years after the election pushed voting system reform back onto the agenda. The SFIO preferred a fully proportional system, as did many on the far right. But there was no majority for such an option. Meanwhile, various elements of the Radical centre promoted a return to the majoritarian double ballot, eventually convincing the SFIO to support a successful vote to reinstate it in 1927. Some have argued that the SFIO thought the reform would help it marginalize the Communists, but the logic of the double ballot would also help the SFIO force its far left competitors to cooperate at election time or risk total defeat, except where a Communist candidate could win a majority outright.[140] Yet all this did not settle the question: efforts to reform the voting system re-emerged in nearly every election cycle in the interwar period.[141]

Meanwhile in Germany and Italy no democratic compromise could be reached. After the Social Democrats squandered their advantage in the early days of the republic, a rejuvenated right pressed forcefully for a retreat from the social and economic promises made between 1918 and 1920.[142] Crippling reparations, runaway inflation, joblessness, and a resurgent nationalism conspired to make political negotiation next to impossible in a country with little experience of politically mediating struggles over state power. Reichstag elections were repeatedly stalemated, failing to produce an effective majority government. Though later scholars would heap blame on Weimar Germany's highly proportional voting system, contemporary participants and observers made little comment. For the most part the SPD stood behind PR as the one great reform of its republican "revolution," though as the twenties wore on some younger members began questioning its operation.[143] The Catholic Zentrum party did call for a review of PR, and two bills did come before the Reichstag, one in 1924 and another in 1930, proposing a shift to some hybrid majority/proportional system, but both failed.[144] When PR started registering a Nazi decline in 1933, Hitler solved the problem by seizing power and abolishing competitive elections altogether.

Italy dispensed with PR and elections much earlier than Germany. The first election under PR in Italy in 1919 brought to the surface all the contradictions then bubbling within the nation: urban versus rural, north versus south, liberationists versus imperialists, socialists versus everyone else, and so on. The ruling Liberals were shocked and unprepared for the results.[145] The Socialists gained 32 per cent of the vote, while the new Catholic party captured 20 per cent. But the national totals obscure the regional impact of the results. The left gained its 32 per cent of the total vote, mostly in the north, which meant that it had gained well over 50 per cent in most of the urban, industrialized parts of the country. Left support was strong even in the rural parts of the north.[146] Meanwhile, the south was dominated by the imperialist right, the most corrupt sections of the Liberal party, and Catholic supporters.

Italy was like two countries geographically and economically.[147] The left victories in the north fuelled its militancy and, amid the intransigence of parliament, furthered its commitment to direct actions like land seizures and cost-of-living protests. At the same time, centre-right dominance over the south fuelled its impatience with the left, inspiring direct actions of its own in the form of attacks on left politicians, labour leaders, and supporters. Each side built up its supporters' expectations, revolution on the left, imperial and territorial gain on the right, but neither could deliver on its promises.[148] Meanwhile the Liberals could not agree how to respond. With very little experience of brokering conflicts in a mass body politic, they blamed the voting system or secretly supported the right-wing militias to deal with the left.[149]

Another election in 1921 did not solve the crisis. Though Liberal fortunes improved and left support declined, the latter fell mostly because increasing right-wing vigilantism suppressed voter turnout and divided the left about how best to respond. By 1922 the country verged on civil war.[150] After the Fascist March on Rome, the Liberals invited Mussolini to form a government, though he had only a small parliamentary party, and agreed to grant him emergency measures to deal with the crisis. The Liberals were not prepared to make the leap from a party of notables to a genuine mass party and tried to use the Fascists as a temporary, proxy alternative.[151] One of Il Duce's initiatives was to change the voting system. The Liberals desperately wanted an end to PR, which they blamed for most of the post-war instability, in favour of a return to single-member ridings, a proposal Mussolini toyed with.[152] But in the end he proposed a skewed majority system that would award the leading party in the election two-thirds of the seats, providing it gained at least 25 per cent of the vote. The rest of the parties would share the last third proportionately. The Liberals supported the measure in 1924, assuming that they would be the prime beneficiaries and that they could introduce a single-member system later on.[153] However, even before the new system was passed, the Fascists had effectively terrorized democracy out of existence. Subsequent elections were mostly for show.[154]

After the initial burst of labour militancy in the two years following the First World War, the left ran into the entrenched wall of opposition from traditional elites and worsening economic conditions that only further weakened its impact and denuded its ranks. Efforts to further PR adoptions after the great wave of 1919–20 usually failed.[155] In countries using it, PR was judged not by the public promises made during its adoption, that it might further democracy and social inclusion, but by how effectively it marginalized the left. Where it succeeded, the partisan consensus for PR usually broke down, with the left complaining about its effects. Where the left proved weak, PR was often repealed as an unnecessary complication of democratic process. And where PR failed to stifle the left or offer a clear path to some kind of conservative control, democracy itself was often sacrificed.

However, while countries like Germany and Italy and regions like Central and Eastern Europe ultimately failed in establishing some kind of minimal democratic rule, most western countries muddled through the interwar period, maintaining mass suffrage, responsible government, and regular elections. The threat of democracy that elites feared proved manageable by a host of means: institutional reforms, the rise of mass parties of the centre and right, and the liberal application of money to the electoral process. The right was learning how to respond to the new era of mass politics and counter some of the organizational advantages of the left. In the end, the crisis passed and, much to the surprise of traditional and business elites, the sizeable working-class electorate in most countries did not translate into leftist majorities at the polls. Except where the left remained on the brink of power, the concessions of the immediate post-war period were either forgotten or whittled away. Where it was not already in place, elites lost interest in voting system reforms like PR, finding other less politically porous methods of protecting their interests.

Conclusion

The first two decades of the twentieth century bore witness to an increasingly pitched struggle for and against democracy in western countries. As the west became more urbanized and industrialized, a working class was made out of the struggles spawned by such enormous social and economic change. To represent this emergent working class, left political parties emerged out of numerous conflicting social movements distinguished by distinctive forms of organization and compelling explanations of working-class problems. These parties would eventually pose the most serious threat to the status quo that traditional elites had ever seen. The rise of working-class parties also increased interest in voting system reform, from the left to further electoral justice and better the representation of fledgling left and labour parties, and from the right to divide the proponents of accountable government and democracy and ultimately keep the left from power.

Before the First World War, PR was introduced primarily by conservative regimes to divide their opponents, thus defeating both liberal demands for responsible government and left demands for democracy. Elsewhere it made little progress despite considerable interest. But the onset of "total war" during the First World War shifted the balance of class forces, eventually strengthening the left by creating new networks of social organization and thereby the mobilization of a host of new social demands. Where the left could remain an explicit champion of democracy and oppositional force, as in continental Europe's neutral countries, its mobilizing efforts forced the pace of democratic reform and the adoption of PR. Elsewhere, the contradictory social alliances required for war-making put a lid on the democratizing efforts for most of the war that subsequently exploded in the immediate post-war period, fuelled by wartime privations and the example of revolution abroad. As the last barriers to at least minimal democratic rule fell, elites scrambled for ways to limit the working-class majority they assumed might come to power. PR became the key reform in a series of trade-offs for full suffrage or responsible government or free and fair elections, a way of managing the contradictions of a specifically capitalist-form democracy by embedding class compromises in the state institutions themselves as a kind of "condensation" of class forces.

But the elite responses coming out of the First World War were not uniform. While all western countries witnessed substantial social upheaval in the immediate post-war period and conceded various labour and social policy reforms, their varying responses were conditioned by the strength of their opponents, their own past experience with mass elections and labour politics, and the particular historical sequence of events. The conservative regimes dominating the European continent shifted decisively to PR as the key means of limiting the socialist left, a decision they hardly second-guessed, given the enduring strength of the electoral left and organized labour in most countries. Exceptions included Italy, where conservatives quickly acquiesced in the elimination of the democratic experiment, and France, where the weakness of the left fuelled the repeal of the semi-proportional voting system. In Anglo-American countries PR, though much discussed, was not introduced at the national level. Countries in the British orbit had much more experience in mass elections and more confidence in seeing their way through the upheavals of 1918–19. Where party competition put pressure on conventional elites, majority voting system reforms were much more readily introduced than PR. Of course, the fact that Britain had an election so close to the war victory may have insulated the polity from historically specific pressures that came later, the labour and social upheaval that could have motivated a move to PR.

In the end, voting system reforms could be found at the heart of most democratic transitions around the First World War as the left championed a substantive social and economic democracy and the right resorted to voting system reform in an attempt to hobble their efforts and reassert its own traditional control. But the move to adopt voting system reforms was not an automatic response. It represented a historically contingent strategy by both the left and right, one that could change as conditions changed, or as the combatants adapted to the new circumstances, or players learned new ways of achieving the same ends.

Chapter 6

The Cold War Democratic Compromise, 1940–1969

Introduction

Though not as broad or sweeping as the democratic reforms that emerged from the First World War, the fifteen-year period following the Second World War produced intense debate and pitched struggles over voting system reform in the United States and Europe, particularly as concerned proportional representation. Surprisingly, these post-war voting system reforms have been largely overlooked in most accounts of western democratic institutions and their development.[1] In Italy and France the question of the proper choice of voting system remained in flux into the 1950s, while in Germany the possibility of change remained on the agenda to the end of the 1960s. In the United States, voting system debate became intertwined with the Cold War both at home and abroad. The few municipal uses of PR in America came under fire as "un-American" forms of voting, especially where they allowed Communists or left-wing councillors to gain election. Most were repealed just after the war or at some point in the 1950s. Abroad, American commentators blamed PR for the rise of extremist or "anti-system" parties of both the left and right, while U.S. political science quickly weighed in on the topic with "proof" that PR led to a proliferation of parties, government instability, and weak accountability. Yet, by the 1960s, voting system reform as a topic of concern in western industrialized democracies had noticeably ebbed for both elites and academics. On the whole, Europe continued to use PR, despite lingering American opprobrium, while Anglo-American countries, for the most part, never seriously questioned their relative majority and majority systems. The French reform of 1958 proved to be the last successful voting system change until the resurgence of interest in the question in the 1980s and 1990s. The shift from widespread concern to indifference can be explained by changes in the nature of political competition facing western industrialized countries in the decades after the war.

Post-war voting system reform in Europe – and the American response to it – was given shape by the challenge of left politics that swept Europe following the Second World War. War had destroyed both the physical and ideological bases of pre-war Europe. Resistance to Nazi aggression and occupation helped forge a broad political consensus for far-reaching economic and democratic reforms, while utterly discrediting the traditional political class, many of which had collaborated with the invaders. With the decline of the traditional right went the last of the interwar ambivalence about democracy, at least at the level of public discourse. Everyone was a "democrat" now. Meanwhile the widespread recognition of the Soviet Union's key role in defeating fascism, and the leading role of Communists in the nationally based resistance movements, contributed to a decisive shift in public attitudes towards both. For their part, West European Communists eschewed their past dismissals of bourgeois democracy and became defenders of electoral and parliamentary power. Now they would seek socialism by the ballot box and enter coalitions with other parties. By 1946 the strategy appeared to be working: a broad coalition spanning the centre to the left had taken office throughout much of Europe, which included Communists as leading government parties in Italy and France. Initially, at these moments of democratic rebirth, a consensus for proportional voting stretched across the political spectrum – even the United States approved.

But the post-war resumption of democracy would prove to be decidedly more social than before. With the crippling deprivations of the Great Depression and the recent dynamic state mobilization for war still fresh in their minds, western publics became convinced that governments could be a lot more active in securing the economic and social well-being of their citizens. State economic planning, widespread nationalizations of industry, various plans for the extension of social entitlements in the form of welfare states – all these developments seemed to suggest that the left's historic dream of an economic democracy was at hand. Yet the challenge of the left, and the undeniably popular social agendas it sponsored, did not go unanswered. Even before the end of Second World War the United States, with some help from Britain, began making plans to challenge the strengthened political left they could see emerging. Buttressing and rebuilding a right-wing alternative, while attempting to divide the left or hive it off from centrist political forces, became the cornerstone of American foreign policy even before the launching of the Cold War. Over the next decade, while some modest concessions on social policy were granted, an American-fuelled counter-attack by the European right would destroy the post-war consensus.[2] The manipulation of voting systems became one weapon among many to limit and divide the left. Only with the effective marginalization of the left, either through electoral defeat or by narrowing the scope of its economic and democratic agenda, would voting system reform fade from the political radar.

The history of voting system reforms after the Second World War fall into four broad periods: the left and centre coalitions of 1945–7, the making of the Cold War from 1947–51, the marginalization of the left 1951–9, and the decline of voting system reform 1959–75. While significant battles over voting systems occurred in New York City, Australia, and Canada, and some minor tweaking of voting formulas took place in a number of Scandinavian countries, the most dynamic struggles played out in France, Italy, and Germany. In this chapter we'll sketch out the reform process in these countries to explain why they were so contested.

Italy

In Europe, voting system reform emerged out of a serious post-war confrontation between left and right as the Continent's three largest countries had to rebuild their economies and political institutions at the war's end. Arguably the first of Europe's three largest countries to begin democratic renewal was Italy. Many of the key elements that would form Italy's institutional terrain (voting rules, divisions of power, the role of parliament, etc.) and largely set the parameters for political and social struggle in the post-war period had their origin in the turbulent and uncertain years between 1944 and 1947. The period was marked by a pervasive uncertainty about what different social and political forces might do, and the relative balance of power among them. As old and new political forces emerged from the resistance to Fascist rule, all were careful to avoid actions or institutional arrangements that might allow their present or future marginalization.[3]

In 1943 the combined effect of an orchestrated strike wave in the north, the defeat of the Germans at Stalingrad, and the Allied landings

in Sicily moved Italy's ruling elites to abandon Mussolini and switch
sides to the Allies. The struggle to reshape the Italian regime began almost as soon as Mussolini was pushed out of the ruling Fascist council.
For a time the new government tried to reinvent itself as a Salazar-style
authoritarian regime, hoping to gain western support and German acquiescence by playing up the threat of left-wing insurgency. Instead,
the Germans invaded, the government fled to the south, and resistance
forces seriously considered forming a separate, explicitly anti-Fascist
government.[4] Throughout 1943–4 resistance forces in central and northern Italy grew exponentially, with membership estimated at between
two and five hundred thousand active partisans, largely under the direction of Communist and Socialist organizers. For many on the left,
conditions appeared ripe for a social revolution and the establishment
of something more than a bourgeois democracy. Indeed, by April 1945
the largely left-leaning partisans would control over half of Italy, with
Soviet troops just across the border in Austria, and a socialist Yugoslavia
established right next door.[5] Though urged to recognize and join the
provisional government in the south by the Allies in late 1943 and early
1944, resistance forces appeared to be at an impasse, unwilling to sanction the existing, Fascist-tainted government and seemingly unable to
form one of their own.[6]

The arrival back in Italy of Communist Party (PCI) leader Palmiro
Togliatti in March 1944, fresh from exile in the Soviet Union, broke the
stalemate. Whether acting under direction of the Soviets or his own
assessment of the situation, Togliatti shifted the PCI away from its
position in favour of a new government and towards joining the existing one in the south.[7] Togliatti argued that Communists must join a
"national solidarity" government to assure that genuinely "popular
democracy" would be attained with the end of war. PCI leadership
tipped resistance support in favour of joining the government, with
Togliatti himself appointed minister of justice.[8] Between 1944 and
1947 the PCI refrained from mobilizing its potentially considerable
popular support into public demands for immediate social reforms.
Instead, the Communists encouraged unions to focus on increasing
productivity rather than wages, resisted calls for increasing government control over the economy, and put their energy into constitutional design and negotiations with an eye to future left democratic
victories at the polls. Here Togliatti was pursuing a strategy of studied
moderation in an attempt to appeal to middle-class voters, just as
many other Socialist and Communist parties across Europe were

doing.[9] And for a time, it appeared to be working. As Sassoon notes, between 1945 and 1950 pro-capitalist parties took a beating electorally in Europe, with only the confessional variants succeeding. Though the centrist Christian Democrats (DC) made a respectable showing in the 1946 Constituent Assembly elections, the Italian Socialist Party (PSI) and the PCI collectively attained more votes. The idea that post-war elections would give rise to a broad left government spanning from the PCI to the left of the DC did not just seem plausible but likely.[10]

With that view in mind, the PCI bargained for a constitution sanctioning a strong parliament, with few impediments to majority rule. Given the conservative blocking role of upper houses across Europe in the interwar period, a coherent left alternative had emerged that hardly differed from the British notion of "parliamentary supremacy." In the end, the Communists compromised a great deal with their governing coalition partners, particularly the DC. Though they gained a high degree of parliamentary sovereignty, and thus few impediments to any future left majority government's policy objectives, they gave in to DC demands for regional government, an upper chamber, an independent judiciary, and the reaffirmation of the 1929 Concordat with the church recognizing Catholicism as the state religion.[11] Clearly elements within the DC and other political forces were worried about future left, and specifically Communist, voter appeal and were keen to include constitutional recourses to resist any potential parliamentary left majority, particularly one dominated by the Communists. The DC and right-wing parties also explored a host of non-constitutional reforms to achieve their ends, including PR and compulsory voting, the latter initiative described by one contemporary commentator as a measure to counter the "zeal of left wing voters."[12] In the end, left opposition essentially eliminated compulsory voting, but all parties agreed on the need for proportional representation. PR appeared to flow logically from the resistance-era period of cross-party cooperation, and the Communists, keen to remain within the rubric of a broad progressive alliance, readily agreed to it. But the potential strength of the left was never far from being a central factor in any consideration of voting rules.[13]

Many commentators have suggested that PR appeared a "natural" response to the instability of the times, given that no political group could be certain of its electoral strength.[14] But the response was less natural than a clear-headed appraisal of the political relationships that existed between the emerging mass parties. For the left, PR would assure that Socialists and Communists would not split its vote. Though there was serious talk of uniting the two large left parties, they could not complete the negotiations before the first electoral contest and as such competed for election to the Constituent Assembly separately. For the right, PR would limit the damage that a majority system might inflict on it as a result of a decisive left victory and could increase its influence in the event that the left failed to reach a majority. For socially progressive centrists in the DC, PR would increase its chances of playing a pivotal role in post-war government, limiting some of the left's centralizing proclivities, providing the left did not win an outright majority.[15] An all-party committee examining voting systems deliberated through the fall of 1945, submitting a report in November essentially calling for a return to the PR system introduced in 1919. The American-dominated Allied Control Council raised no objections to the return to PR, commenting that the draft electoral law was "in keeping with modern developments in democratic practice." The final law was put in place in March 1946 in time for the first post-war national elections set for June.[16]

In the 1946 Constituent Assembly elections a centre-left majority stretching from the Communists to the Christian Democrats emerged committed to sweeping social and economic changes. As in France, the United States poured money into Italy to shore up conservative political forces and fuel dissent in the ranks of the centre-left. Yet American efforts in Italy were in a class of their own, representing the first major covert operation for American intelligence in peacetime.[17] The breakthrough for the Americans came in May 1947 when they finalized a secret deal with De Gasperi, the leader of the DC, that would see him expel the Communists from his governing coalition in return for U.S. economic aid.[18] The subsequent announcement of the Marshall Plan only days later was clearly part of these negotiations, though the timing was meant to allow the DC to take credit for the better economic times that would follow. But the United States did not limit their efforts to this. After all, the various U.S. interventions had not managed to split the Italian left. In fact, the Communist and Socialist parties were closer than ever and had forged an agreement to run as a joint slate in the coming contest, a factor many commentators thought would improve their prospects. As President Truman feared the Communists might win the 1948 elections, the U.S. state intervened aggressively in the election campaign with both overt and covert operations.[19] Historian Paul Ginsborg suggests that "American intervention was breath-taking in its size, its ingenuity and its flagrant contempt for any principle of non-interference in the internal affairs of another country." The U.S. administration immediately designated $176 million of interim aid to Italy in the first three months of 1948, after which the Marshall Plan kicked in. Local U.S. representatives made sure that the arrival of American supplies received extensive coverage in the media, just to underscore the good intentions of the west.[20] But U.S. officials also repeatedly warned Italian voters that a Communist victory would spell doom for the country's economy and the future of American economic aid. At the covert level, the CIA and the American state department funnelled money to a host of parties and organizations opposed to the Communists.[21]

In the end, the DC won an impressive victory: 48 per cent of the popular vote and a majority of seats. The left, by contrast, stumbled badly. Running on a joint ticket, the PCI and PSI gained only 31 per cent, down 8 per cent from their combined support in 1946 when they ran separately. The left defeat reflected a number of developments they could not effectively anticipate or respond to: the rise of virulent western anti-communism, the DC's ability to cast itself as both reformist and traditional, and the high level of American aid, both overt and covert, to the centre-right parties. But it also reflected the economic and social organization of the country, one characterized by highly uneven development, low levels of urbanization, and lingering economic insecurity in rural areas. Left support remained high in urban areas, particularly in the north, but slipped in central Italy, and failed to take hold at all in the largely undeveloped south. That left Italy's still predominantly rural population under the influence of traditional community leaders like the church, landowners, and now, by extension, their chosen political party, the DC.[22] In fact, arguably key to the DC's success as a national party was its ability to mimic the mass party form of the left in the centre and north while absorbing the clientelist networks of the traditional right in the south.[23] This was possible, according to Percy Allum, because the DC was a special form of mass party, comprising a party elite and a mass base connected indirectly through Catholic mobilizing organizations, a much more flexible arrangement than the more centralized left parties.[24]

The depth of the left's poor showing surprised everyone, including the left. It spent most of the end of the 1940s and early 1950s trying to get back into government, convinced that a majority of the populace supported its agenda of social and political reforms.[25] Certainly the DC had sounded like it supported many of the broad social reform aims during the Constituent Assembly negotiations. Indeed, De Gasperi had described the DC at its 1946 party congress as "a party of the center that leans to the left."[26] Reformers on the left of the DC had been key in drafting the social commitments in the recently approved constitution, a document that received full public support from the DC leadership.[27] But its impressive single party majority victory, the only one in the history of Italian democracy (excluding the Fascist gerrymander) in the twentieth century, along with the local effects of the Cold War and the changing nature of its voting support, moved the DC to shift its electoral strategy.[28] The electoral weakness of the left certainly put few apparent restraints on the DC's actions. Under the influence of the United States, the Catholic hierarchy, and Italy's business lobby group Confindustria, the DC embarked on a majoritarian strategy that included abandoning its social commitments, committing Italy to a western defence alliance, and reversing its pre-constitution commitments to decentralization and proportionality.[29] Now that the extent of left support had been exposed and found wanting, the DC felt more confident about its chances under a form of majority voting rules. DC leaders also saw an opportunity to impose some discipline on the smaller parties that they had to rely on, as well as the fractious factions within the party.[30]

The cornerstone of the DC's new direction was the implementation of a new voting law, one that mirrored Mussolini's infamous majoritarian gerrymander in everything but scope. Under the new rules, any party or alliance of parties that received more than 50 per cent of the vote would receive a bonus, pushing it up to 65 per cent of the total representation, a comfortable working majority, while other parties would share what was left proportionately. Some voting system reform along these lines had already occurred at the local level, with the result that the DC could rule alone in some cases, and DC leaders could more effectively control their many factions.[31] While the DC already had a majority of seats at the national level, even it recognized that its record 48 per cent of the popular vote would probably decline in coming elections, so majorities in the future were far from assured. At the level of public discourse, the DC attempted to defend what amounted to a blatant gerrymander as a much-needed reform designed to help stabilize Italian democracy.[32] But given the scope of its recent impressive victory, one that nearly captured a majority of Italian voting support, its rationale appeared weak and self-serving.[33] In fact, as was clear to everyone, the majority law was designed primarily to ensure that the left remained marginal and unthreatening.[34]

For its part, the left throughout this period, particularly the PCI, stuck diligently to strictly democratic confrontation. The Communists quickly discovered the benefits of political decentralization and argued that the 1948 constitutional settlement implied a consociational, rather than majoritarian, democratic practice. All parties should actively participate in governing, they argued, and Communists took seriously the work of parliament, amending legislation and proffering contributions of their own. In truth, the left had little choice.[35] Though the lightning mobilization of approximately nine million former partisans after the attempt on PCI leader Togliatti's life in 1948 suggested the potential brute strength of the left forces, a force that might easily have taken over northern Italy in 1943–4, the situation was changed by the late forties and early fifties.[36] Not only was the state stronger militarily, but left support was hindered everywhere by the pervasive effects of unemployment and state repression. The Cold War and American funding for right-wing unionists had helped fracture the Italian labour movement into three separate confederations in 1948, and the economic conditions kept unions weak and dependent on their political party sponsors.[37]

However, the left did organize considerable legislative and extra-parliamentary opposition on two issues in this period: Italy's entrance into NATO, and the adoption of the new voting law. The DC, like all the other parties, had campaigned in 1948 to keep Italy neutral in the emerging superpower polarization.[38] But perhaps because they felt they had the upper hand after the election, and certainly in response to American pressure, the DC leadership decided to accelerate the country's integration into the U.S. orbit by accepting membership in NATO and the establishment of American military bases in Italy. Though the left ultimately failed to block either initiative, it did mobilize considerable public opposition to both, particularly the voting reform. Dubbed the "swindle law" by its critics, the left hammered home how similar the new law was to the previous fascist law, successfully tarring its sponsors as "authoritarian."[39] Polling from the period revealed that voter knowledge of the new system was low and that few supported the change, confirming the elite nature of the proposal. In fact, given the choice, most voters, regardless of party, preferred the 1946 PR system.[40] De Gasperi defended the reform as necessary to sustain Italian democracy against challenges from its internal enemies. In his view, Italy's special needs required a "protected democracy," including not just electoral engineering but exceptional laws limiting civil liberties and extending police powers. After a bitter struggle, the DC succeeded in adopting the new voting system but failed to reap the majoritarian bonus in the 1953 election, falling short by just 57,000 votes.[41]

DC elites were disturbed at how the new system appeared to become a key campaign issue and worried that the repeated charges of authoritarianism from the left might stick in the public mind, casting the party too far from the centre and risking their control of the political system. The reform was also unpopular with the smaller centrist parties that the DC needed if it was to avoid having to form coalitions with the far right (in fact, the defection of some of its centre allies was one reason the DC failed to make the threshold).[42] In retaliation, the centre refused to join a new De Gasperi administration, and the post-war hero of the right was forced to step down.[43] In addition, there was disagreement within the DC about the advisability of the law, with various factions fearing how the new rules would affect the party.[44] Meanwhile, the PSI had begun running local slates separately from the Communists in some locales, particularly those using PR. This moved the breakaway socialists in the small Social Democratic Party to pressure the DC to repeal the bonus system.[45] As such, under pressure from its centrist allies, and with an eye to perhaps splitting the PSI off from their Communist partners, the DC abandoned its majoritarian strategy both within and outside the party, agreeing to repeal the bonus majority system in 1954 and return to the post-war system of PR, a decision that would remain unchallenged for over two decades.[46]

France

French reforms of the immediate post-war period also reflected the legacy of resistance-era coalitions and the new popularity of the left and general public acceptance of its ideas, specifically as concerned nationalizations and social security.[47] Communists particularly were held in high esteem, both for their leadership in resisting the Nazis and the war-earned prestige of the Soviet Union. As Donald Sassoon notes, everywhere Communists were considered the "bravest of the brave" for their daring work and sacrifices in the underground resistance movement. In addition, their unwavering focus on defeating the Nazis, to the exclusion of economic or political questions, earned them the respect of non-leftists, clearly establishing their credentials as patriotic national defenders.[48] Even with the end of war, the Communists largely eschewed social and economic demands, urging workers to increase production and get the economy back on track before seeking wage gains and social improvements. As in Italy, the French Communist party (PCF) was keen to sustain a popular democratic alliance that would drive out fascism and eliminate the anti-democratic reactionary forces within France.[49] In this, unity was more easily achieved as the French collaborators with the Nazis at Vichy – forces that included most of the business community and the traditional right-wing parties – were stymied in their efforts to rehabilitate themselves.[50] Unlike the Italian Fascist remnants that propped themselves in power between the resistance and the invading Allies, Vichy could offer little to Allied forces and only posed a threat to de Gaulle's claim to leadership.[51] As the Allies advanced into France, de Gaulle approached cooperation with the left, even the Communists, pragmatically, recognizing he would have to work with them to establish a new civil administration and consolidate his influence.[52]

When finally ensconced back in France in 1944, de Gaulle faced the dilemma of attempting to forge ahead with his own personal brand of reformism, particularly his penchant for a strong presidency, or reckoning with the concerns, and potential power, of the resistance parties. When it came to voting systems, de Gaulle now preferred the single-member plurality approach, because it would award decisive victory to the leading candidate. His constitutional advisor Michel Debré called for a return to the Third Republic second ballot system, modified to allow the leading party to win all the seats in a multi-member constituency. But the biggest resistance parties, the Communists, Socialists, and recently formed Christian Democrats (known as the MRP in France), were united in demanding proportional representation.[53] To some extent the issues were the same as in Italy. The parties were unsure of their electoral strength, and none wanted to risk coming up on the wrong side of an all-or-nothing majority-style electoral contest.[54] Like its cousins in the Italian PCI, the PCF viewed PR both as an extension of the resistance coalition and a means of assuring it would not be marginalized. The French Socialists (SFIO) also heralded PR to further left unity, prevent vote-splitting, and allow some distance to remain between themselves and their resistance partner to the left, just as activists in the PSI were doing.[55] And the new Christian Democrat MRP, like the DC in Italy, also understood PR as means of assuring a key role for more centre-left reformers.[56]

But there were factors related specifically to the legacy of voting system manipulation in the Third Republic and electoral competition in

France that influenced the decision as well. A consensus had emerged across the political spectrum in favour of PR just before the war, with the lower house passing a bill in favour of adopting it in 1939 (though it was later defeated in the Senate).[57] The French left had long advocated the adoption of a real PR system, as opposed to the limited form used for two elections after the First World War. Neither the PCF nor the SFIO would countenance a return to the second ballot of the pre-war regime.[58] Not only would the second ballot make left unity more difficult, as it had before the war, but both parties blamed the system for weakening parties and maintaining the influence of local notables in national politics.[59] The MRP was also concerned about the power of local members in any new voting system arrangements. As a new party, the MRP would have few "notables" or well-known local candidates. But more to the point for the MRP as Christian Democrats, it thought the second ballot would encourage polarization around economic issues that would bury clerical concerns. By contrast, with PR religious issues would be represented and not so easily marginalized.[60] Thus all three of the major resistance-era parties valued PR over the second ballot, as the latter risked restoring some of the power of the now-discredited traditional players and polarizing politics in a way that could hurt each one of the partners.[61] In the end, de Gaulle went with PR, mostly for fear that the Communists might end up first-past-the-post under his preference. And given that the purpose of the first election was to establish a Constituent Assembly, PR made also sense from the point of view of representing the nation. Yet in a sop to its critics, the 1945 version of PR was still a more limited form than that of many of its European counterparts, with the allocation of seats occurring only at the departmental level instead of a national one.[62]

The outcome of France's first post-war national election delivered an outright majority of seats to the parties of the left: the PCF and SFIO. Technically, de Gaulle still headed the government and the Constituent Assembly was supposed to be focused on designing a new constitution rather than holding government actions to account. But de Gaulle had no party – deliberately so, as he called for a politics of government that was above parties – and he soon found that his cabinet, a mixture of resistance party representatives and others, was increasingly divided along party lines. Disgusted, de Gaulle surprised everyone by quitting politics in January 1946, opening the way for the first elected civilian administration to take power in a decade. At first PCF leader Maurice Thorez attempted to form a left government with the Socialists, but the latter, fearing absorption by the larger, better organized left party, insisted on a broader coalition that would include the MRP. Meanwhile, the MRP refused to serve under a Communist premier and suggested a Socialist head the government. Despite being the largest party, the PCF acquiesced, and a tripartite government of the centre-left came to power under a Socialist prime minister.[63]

The new administration acted quickly to introduce a host of progressive legislation and nationalize key industries, suggesting that the "moment of antifascist possibility" might be at hand.[64] However, the government soon split on its constitutional proposals. The PCF and SFIO proposed a unicameral parliament, much like the one they were presently governing, with elections conducted by PR but with a national allocation replacing the less proportional departmental formula used in 1945. Given the anti-democratic character of the Senate in the Third Republic, the left was keen to move to a British-style system of parliamentary supremacy that would see power exercised by strong, disciplined parties.[65] The national allocation of PR would more correctly represent the big parties, and the proposal also included a 5 per cent threshold to limit the rise of any Weimar-style small parties (one of de Gaulle's concerns with a national allocation). If left proposals for unicameralism and a party-centred democracy were consistent across Europe, so was the opposition to them coming from Christian Democratic parties. In Italy the DC complained that the left's proposals would risk turning parliament into a "committee for public safety," while in France the MRP worried about a dictatorship of parties controlling both the legislature and civil society.[66]

As the governmental allies could not agree, it appeared the public would be the final arbiter. In 1945 de Gaulle had insisted that the new constitution be submitted to a public vote, motivated in part by concern about the strength of the Communists and the role they might play in the process. The Socialists and MRP agreed for similar reasons.[67] With an outright majority of seats, the left could disregard its centrist coalition partner's concerns and put its unicameral option directly to the public in a referendum in May 1946. It failed, though narrowly, with voting patterns for the left constitution faithfully reproduced a month later in elections for a new constituent assembly: 47 per cent for the PCF and SFIO. Only a bare majority turned down the unicameral option. Six months later, a paltry 38 per cent would approve the new proposed constitution, but with 31 per cent opposed and 31 per cent abstaining, it passed on a split vote.[68] Though the key divisive issue in the left's failed constitutional proposal was unicameralism and not the proposed change to a national allocation of PR, the choice of voting system and its details were left out of the new constitution. Yet none of the major parties moved to make a change at this time. The 1945–6 constitutional negotiations had been characterized by mutual suspicion and strategic calculation of the tripartite partners, with each group attempting to concede as little as possible. Thus the 1945 departmental PR system remained in force.[69]

Yet the debate over the voting system in France was quickly taken up with the post-1947 developments in Europe. The Cold War altered politics across Europe by expanding the incentives to remake the liberation-era coalitions. Anti-communism helped the discredited forces of the right regain their political footing and credibility, increasing their influence in public debate and a variety of political parties. The recently formed Christian Democratic parties, clearly centre-left forces in the immediate post-war period, increasingly began to feel the pull of a right-wing electorate and American influence. By 1947, particularly in Germany and Italy, Christian Democrats shifted decisively to the right, breaking publicly with the centre-left post-war consensus and eschewing cooperation with the left.[70] Left unity was also under strain. Given that centre-left governments faced seemingly intractable problems in rebuilding their economies and providing for their citizens, American promises of aid proved attractive to political forces on both the left and right. Meanwhile American support for the anti-Communist left fuelled debates within the left about the future of unity between Communists and Socialists, contributing to splits in Italy and France.[71] By late spring 1947 the liberation-era coalitions had been sundered, with the left pushed out of government in Italy and the Communists forced out in France.[72]

The remaking of political coalitions across Europe also contributed to a revival of voting system reform, though the nature of the political split in various countries influenced the timing of the process. In Italy, as the left forged a stronger electoral pact and the centre-right could not be sure of its political strength, PR remained uncontested in the run-up to the 1948 election. Basically, the bipolar nature of political competition between left and right in Italy made moves away from PR risky.[73] But in France, where the split had divided the left and buttressed the political centre, discussion of constitutional and electoral reform quickly re-emerged. For some, PR no longer appeared necessary to sustain centre-left unity, while for others PR was no longer required to contain a potential left majority. The new governing bloc could see advantages in voting systems that would push voters towards the centre, while the traditional centre-right, galvanized by the break in left-wing unity, also pushed for electoral and parliamentary reforms.[74] However, unlike in Italy, the French centre could not subordinate the right. The return of de Gaulle to active political life at this time, and his sponsorship of a political movement keen to overhaul the existing constitution, meant that the government faced opposition on both the left and right. For their part, France's Christian Democrats in the MRP, a key force in the new centrist coalition, opposed any efforts to diminish PR for fear that clerical issues might be sidelined.[75] Yet despite an apparent lack of consensus about alternatives, the electoral predicament of the centre government in France would keep electoral reform on the agenda throughout the next decade.

In both the French and Italian cases the state of the left would prove crucial to the timing and success of voting system reform. The different outcomes to the end of liberation-era centre-left government in 1947 had roots in the pre-war experiences of the left in both countries. The French left had a long history of bitter electoral competition, with Communists and Socialists locked in suicidal, mutually destructive competition for most of the interwar period. Only when Communist voters deserted their party at the polls in 1932 did the relations between the two parties change.[76] And though their unity in the Popular Front led the left to victory in 1936, relations remained strained, particularly after a host of Socialists voted to make the Communist Party illegal in 1939 and then opted to join the reactionary Vichy regime in 1940. Even through the resistance, many Communists and Socialists remained wary of one another.[77] But in Italy both parties had suffered persecution and proscription under the Fascist regime and long worked together to overthrow it. Their organizations had strong links and throughout the late 1940s seriously considered a possible merger. American efforts to divide the Italian left accomplished little in 1947–8, eventually succeeding in hiving off only a small rump of the Socialist right wing into a separate Social Democratic party.[78] By contrast in France, Socialists were more evenly split on cooperation with the Communists and, as such, more susceptible to continued American pressure. Cold War rhetoric then only intensified fears that some French Socialists had long harboured about their Communist allies. When the split came, it was welcomed by many in the SFIO, though ultimately divisions on the French left destabilized the party system, creating space for new initiatives on the right and a shift away from the post-war centre-left policy consensus.[79]

Conventional accounts of French voting system reforms in the 1950s explain them both as a necessary response to the "wrecking tactics" of extreme parties and as the means of preventing the election of a Weimar-style anti-system majority. According to these commentators, the political centre found itself short of allies, as it could not embrace the Communists to the left or the various anti-Republican Gaullists to the right. Yet as municipal election results had demonstrated as early as 1947, the far left and right might plausibly attain a majority of seats in the National Assembly between them if voting patterns remained constant. Thus voting system reform emerged as the only obvious solution to these problems.[80] But this reading of the events dramatically underplays the choices available to the political players and the contexts influencing their decisions. For instance, both Communists and Gaullists repeatedly made overtures to the government to realign the coalition to include them, but without success.[81] Ultimately, the narrow options faced by the centre parties had less to do with the behaviour of the political "extremes" than the nature of the bargains they struck with each other and the American state. Voting system reform then proved a convenient way to maintain these arrangements rather than break or renegotiate them.

Arguably the key decision affecting the new centre government's political options involved its acceptance of the U.S.-sponsored Marshall Plan of economic reconstruction. Of course, the influence of American money was hardly new in France.[82] American money had poured into France in the immediate post-war period to bolster non-left organizing.[83] In 1946, U.S. policymakers had hinted to the respected SFIO leader Leon Blum when he visited Washington that more money would flow to France if the Communists were forced out of the government. And throughout the spring of 1947 the French Socialist premier struggled to find an excuse to dismiss the Communists from his government, primarily to placate the Americans, who he feared might cut off aid to France.[84] But when the Marshall Plan was launched in June of 1947, these subtle directives became more explicit as nearly everyone could see how the initiative was directed against the Soviet Union, despite initially including them. In many countries parliamentary Socialists struggled with the American offer, often agreeing to participate only after much internal debate and anguish over the decision.[85] French Socialists were also deeply divided about the Marshall Plan and how it might prevent them from working with the Communist Party in future. Just a few months before, the SFIO parliamentary leadership had just barely won a party vote to remain in government after expelling the Communists.[86] Of course it was possible in the fluid political conditions of 1947 for Socialists to believe that conditions imposed today might be changed tomorrow, that U.S. directives against the Communists might be weakened. But the Marshall Plan would prove a one-way street, fuelling international economic and political relationships in such a way that any reconsideration would be very costly.[87]

Of course, local conditions, not just American influence, mattered in the outcome. Between 1947 and 1950 Socialist ambivalence towards the PCF tended to dissipate as the latter organized large-scale strikes and public demonstrations against the centre government the SFIO initially led and then subsequently participated in. It and others would accuse the Communists of "wrecking tactics" as the PCF repeatedly stalled legislation in both houses of parliament. But the Communists, no doubt angry at being shut out of government, also gave voice to considerable public frustration with the stalling of the post-war consensus, particularly on economic issues. Thus the public mobilizations were designed to force the government to readmit them and move on the centre-left agenda that a majority of voters had endorsed in 1947.[88] Over the course of two years the anti-Communist forces within the SFIO eventually emerged victorious within the party through a combination of principled ("the Communists are not democratic") and pragmatic ("we cannot go back on Marshall Plan commitments") rhetoric, furthering their commitment to a centrist coalition strategy.[89] With the settlement of the German question by its division in 1949, East and Western Europe quickly fell into two wholly separate political territories under distinctly different imperial influence. The Marshall Plan had greased the political passage of the Cold War in Western Europe by assuring that the centre-left coalitions of the immediate post-war period could not be easily reassembled. The alleged "wrecking tactics" of the French Communists had little influence either way. On a more covert level, American subsidies to the French Socialist party and its newspaper via the American Federation of Labour no doubt only reinforced its resolve to resist Communist calls for unity.[90]

The forced exit of the Communists required the governing coalition to expand by drawing more support from the centre or right of the political spectrum. However, unlike the Italian Christian Democrats, the MRP could not take effective control of the new coalition or subordinate the other parties under its leadership because France's rural class structure had spawned a much more independent politics and the new party proved ill-equipped to adapt to changing circumstances.[91] Instead, the new coalition multiplied the potential for division in the new government by bringing in the traditionally anticlerical Radical party.[92] Nor would the coalition look much further to the right, as the shift in the governing coalition had coincided with the return to politics of de Gaulle and his anti-republican vehicle, the RPF. By August of 1947 de Gaulle's quasi-party had attracted immense public and media interest, as well as a sizeable caucus in the National Assembly, drawn mostly from the ranks of conservative and centre-right parties. Though de Gaulle would later attempt to negotiate with the centrist government, his initial re-emergence was marked by stinging criticism of the republican regime and demands for immediate constitutional and parliamentary reform. As with the Communists, RPF supporters were vociferously critical of the centre government, attempting to block its initiatives in both the lower house and the Senate.[93]

The hostility of the new right and the various proscriptions against seeking support from the Communist left pushed the new centre government towards considering reforms that would buttress it politically. Arguments against PR specifically had been made by the Radicals during the Constituent Assembly negotiations, and de Gaulle's new RPF had made a return to the second ballot one of its key demands after its municipal election successes in 1947.[94] But it was only with the end of tripartism and the marginalization of the Communists that voting system reform moved up the government's agenda. The first indication of a break with the post-war consensus on voting rules came when parliament voted to shift the method of indirect election for senators away from one that essentially mirrored results in the lower house to one resembling pre-war approaches, specifically to put the Communists at a disadvantage.[95] But reforming the lower house, where the balance of legislative and executive authority lay, would prove a more protracted and unpredictable struggle. Radicals and most conservatives hated the PR system and wanted a return to the second ballot system that had worked so well for them in the past. In fact, the reintroduction of the second ballot for Senate elections from non-urban areas very quickly led to Radical and conservative gains in the upper house.[96] But the MRP was adamantly opposed to moves away from PR. It feared that a return to the second ballot would marginalize clerical issues and only further polarize political competition.[97] Debate over voting system and

constitutional reform continued throughout 1948–9, with little movement between the Radical and MRP positions. However, by 1950, with
a national election within sight, and the new RPF gaining support from
both parties, they began to shift. MRP members, discouraged and de-
pleted by defections to the RPF, passed a resolution at their 1950 convention agreeing to some form of voting system reform. Meanwhile
Radical party leaders now recognized that MRP concerns had to be addressed for any reform proposal to move forward. Throughout these
debates the Socialists had continued to support PR but also made it
clear that they were open to alternatives, particularly the second ballot.[98] The centre coalition now agreed that some change was in order,
though it still struggled over just what to replace PR with.

Throughout 1950–1 various voting system reform proposals vied
for support in the National Assembly. The centre parties, now generally referred to as kind of "third force" between left and right, were
agreed that any reform would be aimed primarily at marginalizing the
Communists and hopefully opening up more potential support for the
government. The Socialists, Radicals, and conservatives thought that a
single-member second ballot system would accomplish this, but the
MRP disagreed, worrying that it might lose run-offs to the RPF.[99] By
contrast, the MRP called for various mixtures of PR and majority voting. But none of these efforts managed to gain enough support to pass
both houses.[100] In fact, on 21 February 1950 no fewer than eight different voting system reform proposals were considered and defeated by
either the Assembly or the Senate.[101] Negotiations for reform in this
period were hindered by the stark decline in party discipline since
the end of Communist participation in government. For a brief time the
Communist threat had forced parties away from the decentralizing
pressures long present in French politics. In fact, the liberation-era
centre-left consciously acted to buttress central government with its
electoral and constitutional designs of 1945–6. But the Senate reforms
of 1948 and return of the Radicals to pre-eminence weakened party
discipline, reviving the influence of local notables in national affairs.[102]
The national leaders of the MRP and Radical parties could not even
ensure that local branches would abide by election agreements to work
with the Socialists, their governing ally.[103]

By late spring 1951, with an election just one month away, the
National Assembly finally agreed on a new voting system for the lower
house.[104] The MRP proposed a system that retained multi-member ridings and PR in a single ballot format but added a majority element.

Basically, the new rules would see any party or coalition of parties that gained a majority of the votes in a multi-member riding get all the seats available. If no party or coalition gained a majority, then seats would be distributed, as before, by PR. This proposal was clearly biased against the Communists as they had little hope of forming any alliances. But it would also limit the Gaullist RPF if the "third force" parties could maintain their coalition for electoral purposes. As a safeguard against any local break in the ranks, the government added a further twist, barring party coalitions from the ballot in the Paris region, where the PCI and RPF were the strongest. There could be little doubt that the government's new voting system amounted to little more than a ger-rymander against its political opponents.[105] Voting results on the question confirmed its partisan character: the SFIO, MRP, and Radicals were firmly in favour, while the PCF and the RPF were solidly op-posed. Only the non-RPF right was split, with about half supporting each side, reflecting perhaps relative measures of conservative hatred for both the Communists and the centre-government.[106] The new sys-tem then promptly delivered on its partisan promise, skewing the re-sults of the 1951 election to the benefit of the third force parties. The French voting system reform of 1951 emerged from rather tortuous and uncertain negotiations amongst the governing parties, against a back-drop of historically specific international political developments and national party competition. These contexts did not determine the re-sults – indeed, voting system reform nearly did not happen before the 1951 elections – but they did give shape to the options as the different parties saw them.[107]

By 1951 the Cold War had thoroughly infused domestic politics across western countries, contributing to the rightward drift of social democratic and formerly centrist parties, while commitment to the Marshall Plan made a retreat to the left and Communist support very difficult. Voting system reform offered a way out of a potentially devas-tating bout of political competition for the third force parties, though the differing interests and competitive positions of the coalition parties nearly scuttled the deal. In the end, the voting system design adopted clearly acknowledged the fractious unity of the coalition by structuring rewards for centrist unity and disabling such rewards for their oppo-nents and coalition defectors.

Though the centrist "third force" parties had benefited, as predicted, from the rather convoluted new voting system they adopted just be-fore the 1951 election, the results were embarrassingly one-sided and crude. The new system had clearly discriminated against the far left and right with representation that appeared to flout the public's voting intentions. The Communists and the Gaullist RPF were outraged by the results, while few government members would publicly defend the system.[108] One contemporary observer described it as "the least honest system in French history," but others were more blunt, dubbing it "bastard PR."[109] Not surprisingly, a new round of debate over voting system reform emerged in the National Assembly, with just as little consensus about an appropriate alternative. Complicating these negotiations were divisions within the "third force" government over economic policy and constitutional issues. The marginalization of the Communists by the Socialists and MRP, subsequently reinforced by the government's commitment to the stipulations of the American Marshall Plan, took pressure off the centre-right to cooperate on economic policy. The Socialists had brought down successive administrations before the 1951 election precisely because Radicals and Conservatives were pushing policy towards the right. But after the 1951 contest the Socialists themselves were marginalized and failed to return to the government benches. As they refused to work with the Communists and could not seem to slow the drift of French government policy to the right, the Socialists ended up as isolated in policy as their former allies, despite the fact that a majority of voters in 1951 again supported the former progressive alliance of PCF, SFIO, and MRP.[110] At the same time, de Gaulle's decision to withdraw from politics again, this time in protest about the lack of movement on constitutional reform, scattered the members of his RPF amongst other parties on the right and a more flexible new grouping, the Social Republicans. This sudden decline in political competition from both the left and right contributed to an increasing fragmentation of the centre along class and foreign policy lines.[111]

By 1955 the centre coalition had split in two, unable to agree on economic policy or the correct response to social and political unrest in French possessions overseas. Meanwhile, evidence of a thaw in the relations between Socialists and Communists emerged as the two parties worked together at the local level in a few locales.[112] Amid much uncertainty, successive efforts were made to introduce a new voting system, including bids for PR, the second ballot, and other hybrid models, but all were defeated. Though no one really liked the status quo, no party or coalition seemed able to marshal the necessary support to change it. There were concerns within the centre-right government that the MRP,

Socialists, and Communists had the necessary votes to reintroduce the 1946 PR system if they worked together. As a result, the prime minister repeatedly used procedural methods to block all efforts at reform by the other parties. Meanwhile, his own government also wanted reform but could not agree internally what the best alternative might be. Finally a decision of sorts was made with the unexpected fall of the government in 1956. In a bid to block yet another effort at voting system reform, the prime minister declared the opposition motion a vote of confidence in the government. When the prime minister lost, he dissolved the Assembly, thus bringing back into play the very system that no one really wanted to use.[113]

The 1951 voting system reform was designed to benefit the centre at the expense of the far left and right, an objective it largely achieved in that instance. But by 1956 the centre had split into two loosely competing coalitions, and the voting arrangements were to have decidedly different effects. The key wrinkle in the 1951 model was the bonus it awarded parties that could make effective electoral alliances: where any alliance gained a majority of the vote, it would win all the seats in a district. But divisions within the centre meant that alliances did not win many majorities, and the overall effect of the system was similar to the 1946 PR model. The failure of the centre meant that Communists won their proportionate share of seats, making them once again the largest single party in the National Assembly. But the proportionality of the results also allowed a new right-wing populist party, representing the tax grievances of farmers and small business and a pro-empire position on Algeria, to break into the political system at the expense of the more traditional forces of the centre-right and the remnants of de Gaulle's old RPF.[114] The "anti-system party" majority that the reform was designed to limit appeared to be on the horizon anyway. Not surprisingly the new National Assembly quickly returned to the question of voting system reform, though the parties still could not agree on an alternative. The dwindling MRP sponsored a bill for PR that gained Communist support and passed in the lower house, only to be defeated in the Senate.[115] Despite many efforts, the normal pattern of party competition and coalition trade-offs did not seem able to produce any agreement on reform, despite near-unanimous opposition to the status quo. The rural factor in France, like Italy, played a key role politically, as both countries shared uneven capitalist development and lower levels of urbanization than western averages. However, unlike Italy, centrist political forces in France could not dominate rural politics or the small business sector.[116] This was in part an unanticipated product of the economic restructuring brought on by the Marshal Plan and American pressure to open up the French economy. As the centre government moved to modernize the French economy, many of the traditional protections for rural farmers and small business were reduced or eliminated. These economic grievances, abetted by nationalist indignation with the decline of empire, eventually fuelled a right-wing populist response that further limited the movement of the political centre.[117]

The break came with the constitutional crisis of 1958. Military leaders working with Gaullist politicians, frustrated with the waffling of the government in Paris over the future of Algeria, staged a rebellion and threatened to invade continental France unless their demands were met. To make clear their determination, they invaded and gained possession of the French island of Corsica. The military's efforts quickly polarized French society, pushing the country to the brink of civil war, with many on the right not-so-secretly welcoming a military intervention.[118] Meanwhile, the Communists appeared to be the only party clearly stating their willingness to resist the army and protect the present state.[119] Though de Gaulle's knowledge of or involvement in the military's plans remains hotly debated, there is no denying that he responded to the crisis strategically, refusing to denounce the insurrection while at the same time offering his services as caretaker prime minister with emergency powers. Meanwhile the insurgents appeared to be stalling on their deadlines to invade, based on how the government responded to calls to install de Gaulle. After a tense few weeks, de Gaulle negotiated a deal that would see himself installed as prime minister for a limited time with a mandate to prepare a new constitution that would be subject to a public vote. In what might be described as a voluntary coup d'état, the centre surrendered government to de Gaulle under threat from the right and the military, but also out of a sense of frustration with the blocked nature of the political system. With a resurgent Communist party vying for a new popular front, and a militant right teetering towards insurrection, the centre hoped a populist general and war hero like de Gaulle would hold the country together through the crisis until such time as the centre could resume governing.[120] But de Gaulle had his own ideas. The crisis of 1958 was an opportunity to take up his long-sought-after constitutional changes to strengthen executive power, weaken the legislative branch, and marginalize the Communists.[121] Though the Gaullists claimed they sought only parliamentary reforms, a course of action the centre supported, a more grand set of plans were actually initiated when de Gaulle took power that would eventually include changes to the head of state, the relationship of the executive and the legislature, and the choice of voting system.

When de Gaulle was invested as prime minister in the spring of 1958, he was given strict guidelines, one of which explicitly removed the question of voting system change from his jurisdiction. But de Gaulle and his advisors managed to circumvent the prohibition through a constitutional sleight of hand. A minor clause in his proposals gave the provisional leadership the power to determine the voting system before the first election under the new constitution. Though the Communists campaigned against it, de Gaulle's constitution passed easily, and he used his new powers to introduce a retooled version of France's traditional voting system, the second ballot.[122] He also had constituency boundaries redrawn to discriminate against the Communists (though not the Socialists, whom he wished to balance against some of his more rightwing support).[123] Both reforms accomplished their purpose: in the first elections under the new rules, the Communists gained 19 per cent of the vote but just 2 per cent of the seats, while de Gaulle's supporters were over-represented, transforming 20 per cent of the vote into 42 per cent of the total seats. The 1958 reforms proved to be just the first in a series of institutional changes de Gaulle would see implemented over the next decade, all with the purpose of strengthening executive control and breaking the practice of legislative deadlock endemic to French politics.[124] However, these subsequent changes depended on the effective marginalization of the Communist left, which his second ballot voting system reform would finally achieve.

In Europe, voting system reform eventually gave way to other methods of political control. As the Italian Socialists turned right after 1956, they repudiated electoral cooperation with the Communists and inched closer to the DC, eventually joining a coalition government in 1963. With the Italian Communists now as isolated as the French, the DC found considerable room to move between left and right.[125] In France, de Gaulle's shake-up of the political system in 1958 brought about a new constitution and voting system, which had the immediate effect of dramatically under-representing and effectively marginalizing the Communist party. But de Gaulle did not stop there. Over the next decade, now as president, he relentlessly pursued further structural and constitutional reforms to bring the republic closer to his long-term vision of politics, often through questionably democratic means.[126] By the mid-1960s he had largely succeeded in marginalizing the radical right and shifting the political institutions of the state from parliamentary to presidential forms. Though de Gaulle would eventually over-play his populist hand and have to resign after losing one of his "appeal to the people" referendums, the political stalemate he had inherited had been broken. The Communists were in decline, the French economy and class structure fell more in line with western industrial averages, and no one was talking about electoral or constitutional reform.[127] The shift to a presidential focus politically in the 1960s also contributed to Communist decline, as a PCF candidate for such an office could hardly expect to gain sufficient cross-party support, leaving the Socialists in a better position to mop up left and centre votes.[128]

Germany

German political renewal at the end of the war was more complicated than in Italy or France. The four occupying powers – Britain, France, the Soviet Union, and the United States – had different ideas about politics, political institutions, and the future of Germany. Divided amongst the four into different "temporary" zones of influence, German parties and political institutions developed along different lines, depending on their particular occupation authority's preferences. All were concerned to avoid the instability of the Weimar regime, which they blamed on excessive party fragmentation and PR.[129] Of course, German politicians had their own ideas about remaking post-war politics, including the selection of a new voting system, and they were not without influence.[130] The experience of PR under the Weimar, including the view that it had helped the Nazis to power, also fuelled serious debate about voting systems both within and across the emerging political forces.[131] SPD members who spent the war in Britain returned home with a new appreciation of majority government and first-past-the-post elections.[132] The newly formed Christian Democrats in the CDU also seemed impressed with the potential stability that might come with relative majority or majority voting. But there were deep divisions within both parties about the choice of voting system. Both CDU and SPD members in the Soviet zone insisted on PR, while CDU members in areas of SPD strength in the north also raised objections to majority proposals.[133] Yet the national focus of some of these early debates amounted to little, given the lack of any pressing need to make a decision on a Germany-wide voting system. As long as the occupying powers continued to negotiate over the future of Germany – including settlement of issues like reparations, economic trade, the withdrawal of occupation forces, and the territorial reunification of the country – no national elections could conceivably be held.

The unresolved issues that stalled political developments at the national level in Germany were less of a barrier to a revival of politics at the local level, if only because each occupation force could control the activities within its own zone. And each occupier each took up its mandate in a slightly different fashion. The Soviets were the first to introduce PR for their zone and the only occupying power to positively embrace it, both to protect the Communist KPD, which appeared to be in a junior position to the SPD locally, and to demonstrate a commitment to pluralism to their allies.[134] Over the next five years the Soviets would consistently call for PR to be applied to regional and national levels in Germany.[135] In the French zone, authorities operated with little input from local Germans, introducing PR for local elections largely because France had just embraced PR. The French addressed the stability question not through electoral engineering but by establishing a firm limit over the number of parties, allowing just four to register.[136] The British introduced relative majority voting for the first local elections in their zone in 1946, reflecting a bias towards their own way of doing things, though a measure of PR was introduced at German insistence via a compensatory list.[137] Only the Americans left the decision about the voting system to the local Germans, choosing to make their influence felt most directly through the licensing of parties and more informal channels. However, the U.S. military command made their preference for PR known. At this time, between 1945 and 1947, both the American military and the U.S. State Department favoured PR for European elections. The military favoured PR to further its goal of governing with local support and creating consensus, thus preventing the occupation from becoming the focus of any emerging opposition politics. The State Department favoured PR to bolster both the non-Communist left and non-left parties at a time when, in its view, elections were less about government than the creation of constituent assemblies. In Germany particularly, as long as the questions of reparations and reunification remained open, the United States also wanted to appear to remain friendly to Soviet interests and open to any number of outcomes. As it happened, the Germans in the U.S. zone decided in favour of PR for local and Land elections, in most cases simply re-establishing the system last used in 1933.[138]

Two years into the occupation, national politics in Germany remained in stasis, with local politics under the control of the Allies. The Soviets were the first to sanction a return to party politics and arguably allowed the greatest freedom for popular economic policy development, at least initially.[139] But Russian retribution for the German invasion, combined with the inability of Soviet occupiers to match western aid levels, led to a massive migration of Germans into the western zones, effectively undermining stabilization efforts. Not that economic conditions were much better in the British, French, and U.S. zones.[140] Yet the United States was not prepared to move on economic questions until they could be sure that increased aid would not end up in Soviet hands as German reparations. At the same time American occupiers intervened to forestall grassroots German responses to the crisis, dismantling the local Antifas committees (spontaneous anti-facsist local governments), installing conservative politicians as temporary administrators, and preventing elected regional Länder from moving on nationalizations and other popular economic initiatives, even going so far as to use their economic influence over fellow allies Britain and France to limit such efforts in their zones as well.[141] By 1947, with little agreement amongst the Allies about reparations, reunification, arrangements for the end of the occupation, etc., the United States moved to press ahead with its agenda, eventually bringing Britain, France, and West German politicians in line with its plan to establish, at least temporarily, a separate western German state that would be wholly within the orbit of the capitalist west.[142]

The Germans themselves were divided on the wisdom of establishing separate states out of the East–West division of occupation zones, with most accepting it only because it represented a step towards regaining some real sovereignty. As a result, the process of state formation in what would become West Germany was halting and uncertain and stressed the temporary nature of the arrangements.[143] The Germans were reluctant to call what they were preparing a constitution, lest it appear to forgo some future reunification of east and west; nor were they prepared to imbue their document with populist sentiment or approval. The American military governors quickly became exasperated with German reticence, though some recognized the contradictions inherent in an occupying power pressing for a constitution animated by the principle that "all power issues from the people." Yet American influence would ultimately give shape to some key aspects of the German document, particularly federalism and voting rules.[144] The design of West Germany's political system differed markedly from the Weimar approach in other ways as well. In establishing the new regime there was no constituent assembly, no public input, and no referendum on the results of the deliberations. Instead, delegates appointed by the regional Land governments formed a Parliamentary Council in late 1948 that drafted a Basic Law rather than a full-blown constitution, again underlining the temporary nature of the decisions, and the draft was ultimately subjected to veto and amendment by the Land governments and the occupying powers.[145] The voting system would prove to be a serious point of division amongst the emerging constellation of political forces in the new state, as well as a point of contention with the Allied powers.[146] Dividing Germany altered the strength of different parties, leading to changes of policy on the desirability of different voting systems amongst them and their friends and enemies in the military government.

At the end of the war, voting system debate varied within and across parties.[147] There were some in the new Christian Democratic Party, with their Bavarian partners, the Christian Socials, who were interested in the Anglo-American relative majority system. These proponents highlighted how a plurality system would create personal links between politicians and voters and would deliver more stable majority government, but their potential to dominate such a system also figured prominently in their thinking.[148] There was debate on the initiative, however, with CDU branches in SPD-dominant areas and the Soviet zone remaining strong defenders of a return to PR.[149] But overall, views were not rigid on the question anywhere. Nearly all parties initially called for a return to PR, just to be on the safe side, with the CDU-controlled American zones making no move away from Germany's traditional form of proportional voting.[150] The SPD had some new converts to relative majority voting, particularly those who had lived out the war in Anglo-American countries, but the party also had strong proponents of its historical attachment to proportional voting.[151] Most of the smaller parties were for PR, though a few of the regionally concentrated ones dissented in favour of plurality, recognizing how it might be of advantage to them.[152] The Americans and the British favoured their own relative majority system, but under the pressures of occupation politics, the military authorities and the U.S. State Department endorsed PR as a means of creating consensus and shunting criticism away from the Allied powers.[153] Besides, U.S. authorities saw the local and regional Land elections as less about producing government than a kind of weak constituent assembly, thus it was only proper that they should be focused on representativeness, as they would be temporary, by definition.[154]

However, with the move towards creating an independent West Germany, firm opinions about voting systems rapidly crystalized. The SPD shifted decisively back to a defence of PR, as the loss of the Soviet zone represented a considerable weakening of its electoral position.[155] Meanwhile, sensing an advantage coming out of the local and Länder elections, CDU opinion hardened in favour of plurality voting.[156] U.S. constitutional advisors came out strongly against PR, supporting the CDU proposal in favour of adopting Anglo-American methods. But American influence appeared to come too late. The decision-making process was influenced by the make-up of the regional Land administrations, nearly all of which had been elected by some form of PR. The Allies' expedient support of proportional voting had led to a Parliamentary Council deadlocked between the equal voting power of the CDU and the SPD, and thus between what were now two opposed visions of the proper voting system.[157] After five months of deliberations, an SPD-led majority in the Parliamentary Council, with crucial votes from the smaller parties, triumphed over the CDU with its compromise proposal for "personal" PR, a voting system that would combine an even amount of representation from single-member ridings and party lists.[158] In the debates, the CDU had made much of the need for a constituency-representative link along the lines of the American and British model to make politicians more responsible and accountable. The SPD model addressed that concern, though the PR aspect undermined the CDU desire for strong, single-party majority government.[159] In the end, the proposal reflected many influences – British, American, German – and the two years of practice with hybrid models at the local and Land level.[160] The parliamentary council then submitted the new electoral law to the military authorities in late February 1949 for approval.[161]

On 2 March the military government rejected the new voting system, declaring the Parliamentary Council "not competent" to make such a decision. Instead it insisted that voting rules be established by each Länder, though these regional governments could adopt the Parliamentary Council's model if they wished. The decision meant that West Germany could end up using a hodgepodge of voting methods for the same election. The military government's decision was a surprise to everyone. The minister-presidents of the various Länder were already on record calling for a uniform national voting system. Various experts had been consulted and concurred. The Parliamentary Council had publicly struck up a committee to make a decision on the question as far back as September 1948. Yet the rejection of the voting law was "the first official word from the military governors on the subject." John Golay, who provided one of the few detailed accounts of this controversy in English, suggested that this "tardy" decision originated in a French and American "penchant for federalist decentralization."[162] One high-ranking U.S. official justified the decision by pointing to American state-level control over the federal election law. But the Germans were unconvinced, countering that the U.S. constitution granted the federal government power to establish a federal electoral system, a power exercised federally in 1842 to force states to abandon multi-member plurality elections in favour of single-member plurality. A more compelling explanation of the authorities' decision was that they feared the hybrid PR system would aid the left. By pushing the decision over the voting system to the Länder level, the military governors were giving the CDU another chance to secure an Anglo-style first-past-the-post system. If the CDU Länder made the switch, it would put pressure on the SPD governments to do the same or allow their adversaries to reap the rewards of over-representation where they were strong, and maximal representation where they were weak.[163]

The Parliamentary Council protested at this turn of events. With a CDU representative speaking for the group, it argued that the federal lower house could not be chosen by different methods in different regions of the country as it "might result in a completely false representation of the opinions of the electorate." The minister-presidents agreed unanimously that a uniform voting system was needed and called on the military government to approve the hybrid-PR model. The occupation authorities relented but insisted on a number of minor changes to the original proposal. The Parliamentary Council complied, resubmitting the voting law on 10 May. On 23 May it met for the last time to essentially bring the Basic Law into effect. But the debate over the voting system did not end there. Though the military governors had confirmed the Parliamentary Council's right to establish the voting rules just two weeks before, they now invited the minister-presidents to propose further changes if they were not happy with the existing model. In fact, they suggested that if a "substantial majority" of the Länder did not favour the current system, they would consider changing it. As five of the eleven Länders were controlled by the CDU, a "substantial majority" for the Parliamentary Council model might not exist. Indeed, this time the minister-presidents did offer amendments, calling for a shift from a 50:50 breakdown between single-member ridings and party list–seats to a 60:40 split, as well as the introduction of a threshold that would limit small parties. They did not try to replace the Parliamentary Council's work entirely, such as by insisting on a uniform single-member plurality system, but the suggestions did reduce the overall proportionality of the system and disadvantage non-regional smaller parties.[164]

The parties that had formed the majority in the Parliamentary Council, the authors of the original hybrid system, objected when they heard about the proposed changes, arguing that the minister-presidents had no right to interfere with their decisions. The SPD leader complained that the western allies were "breaking with the Bonn Constitution within a few days of approving it" while accusing the CDU of conspiring with the occupiers for its own gain. The SPD declared it might boycott the elections if the changes went through. Meanwhile, the SPD/FDP minister-presidents who had gone along with the others in proposing amendments to the Parliamentary Council's voting system were inundated with negative responses from their party organizations about their actions. At the next minister-presidents' meeting on 10 June, the SPD/FDP leaders moved to reopen the question of their involvement in the process, resulting in a letter to the military government from the Länder heads questioning its right to intervene in such matters. They underlined that the beginning of constitutional life must not be marred by "shadows of doubt," and as such disavowed the power granted to them by the occupation authorities. But the military governors were not deterred by these protests and simply ordered the proposed changes to be implemented.[165] Besides watering down the Parliamentary Council's model voting system, the CDU won other victories in the battle over West German electoral law. It managed to have the new voting system, the 1949 electoral law, enacted only on a temporary basis for the life of the first parliament.[166] Thus the new legislators would possibly have the opportunity to revisit the debate after the elections, depending on the balance of the outcome. American influence had been a key factor in the decision to leave the voting system itself outside of the constitution-like Basic Law, thus facilitating its reform in the future by a simple majority vote.[167]

Not surprisingly, voting system reform remained a topic of debate in West Germany throughout the 1950s, as the right-wing CDU sought to entrench its position as the dominant party. The controversial division of the occupied Germany territory in 1949 put the new West Germany on the front lines of the Cold War and tipped its domestic politics to the right. As these political conditions began to change, the CDU attempted to secure a majoritarian voting system that would reward it with clear control of the legislative arena. However, the immediate post-war practice of proportionality in sub-national elections had led to a fairly even split between left and right in terms of representation, allowing the SPD and centre parties to block this move and introduce a new hybrid PR system, at least on a temporary basis. The question of voting system reform remained a priority for the CDU, and it argued for a change to some form of majority voting throughout the 1950s.

When the temporary voting law adopted in 1949 elapsed before the 1953 federal election, the issue came again before parliament. The CDU proposed a British-style single-member plurality system, dropping the current proportional element. The SPD countered by proposing essentially the same system used in 1949. In response, the CDU cabinet introduced a proposal for a two-vote system, with one to be cast in a single-member district and other for a supplementary list. The system would essentially reward parties that could make alliances, like the CDU and its partners, and punish those that could not, like the SPD. Commentators drew comparisons with the Italian bonus law of the same year, while much of the public perceived it as a "law" to preserve the current governing coalition. Poor responses from other parties and the public moved the CDU to back down and instead offer a run-off system, with some option for different parties to pool support. In the end, a CDU politician proposed a two-ballot version of the 1949 PR system, which passed, supported by everyone, though again the law would be in force for only one election.[168]

Throughout 1955 and 1956 the CDU floated a plan that would keep the mixed system but sever the relationship between the single-member ridings and the compensatory list, with the effect of greatly reducing the proportional outcome. But this plan also failed when its centrist allies split on the issue. Once again the CDU re-passed the hybrid-PR system in 1957, this time deleting the one-election expiry clause.[169] By the end of the decade the CDU would even appeal to the SPD to support a shift to majority voting as a way of pushing the smaller parties out of political competition, an argument some on the left found attractive. But the CDU's dominant position in the political system throughout the 1950s ultimately moved its competitors, both large and small, to oppose reform. Ironically, the party did not lack the votes to secure a new voting system, having won an outright majority of seats in the elections of 1953 and 1957. But its need to gain super-majorities to pass the western integration treaties meant it did not force through voting system reform for fear of alienating its centrist allies.[170] After the treaties were passed, the CDU shifted its appeals for reform from the centre to the left, a dialogue that continued well into the 1960s.

By the 1960s, Germany was only European country where the voting system remained an issue, driven primarily by the now long-governing CDU. For some time Germany's political right was becoming increasingly frustrated with the demands of its long-time centrist partners, the FDP. With the western integration treaties duly passed, and the German SPD fresh from a significant round of revisionism that moved the party closer to the centre, the CDU proposed that a historic "grand coalition" of the two major parties take government and, among other things, pass a new voting law that would weaken or eliminate the smaller parties. The SPD refused the offer in 1962 but in the face of yet another defeat at the polls finally agreed to the deal in 1966. A legislative committee of the two parties was struck to consider how to replace the mixed-plurality/PR system with some form of plurality voting, pure and simple. After considerable research by the committee and independent studies by both parties, and amid substantial public interest and debate over the "best electoral system," the SPD backed off its commitment to voting system reform, opting to form a coalition itself with the estranged FDP. The SPD feared it might end up a permanent loser in a single-member plurality system, and its opposition to change helped link the centre parties to the left rather than the right. The CDU was incensed but isolated. Attempts to woo back the FDP failed while appeals for public support fell flat. The public could see little reason for reform, and polls consistently registered high levels of support for PR. By the early 1970s the CDU reluctantly dropped the issue after a quarter century of effort.[171]

Conclusion

For most democratic countries coming out of the Second World War, voting system reform did not emerge as a key issue. But this should not be interpreted to mean that voting systems were not considered important. For countries already using PR, like most of the smaller democracies in Europe, the strength of the post-war left assured that other political forces had little interest in agitating for any change: PR remained the best method of limiting the left's electoral power. In Anglo-American countries PR had never really been necessary to contain the threat of democracy or the left. Either the left was too weak (Canada, New Zealand) or traditional elites were more confident (Britain, Australia) that they could manage the "leap in the dark" towards some form of limited democratic government. But simply counting the number of countries taking up voting system reforms after the war does not capture the scope and intensity of the debate on the question. At the war's end, the choice of voting rules in Europe's three largest countries – Italy, France, and Germany – became intensely political questions, ones that involved both national and international dimensions. Within each country an unstable but potentially governing majority of the centre and the left gave voice to broad and sweeping public demands for both social and economic change. Set against this were the disorganized and discredited forces of the right, desperate to limit this expansive democratic agenda. Nearly all forces initially approved of PR to either manage their unwieldy coalition (the centre and the left) or to place some limits on their adversaries (the right).

But beyond these national disputes was an emerging international struggle for dominance driven by American designs for a new world economic order. American influence would also be important in decisions over voting rules. As the key occupying power in post-war Europe, the United States made its initial preference for PR clear as a means of limiting the left and holding national disputes in check while it negotiated with the Soviet Union. American influence would ultimately help tip the political scales in Europe back to the right, and in doing so alter the debate over voting systems. As the Cold War took hold across Europe, and a coalition of the right and the centre replaced the centre and left in government across the Continent, the post-war consensus for PR gave way to a new majoritarian strategy designed to marginalize the large, powerful, and electorally popular Communist parties. Both the American state and American academe provided support for efforts to dislodge proportional voting in favour of a U.S.-style first-past-the-post system.

Yet U.S. influence, both financial and intellectual, could not assure the success of any desired changes. Instead, the struggle over voting system reforms in Italy, France, and Germany played out against distinctive backdrops involving the nature of political party resources and competition, nationally specific cleavage structures, and the unpredictable effects of previous political decisions. In the end, contingent factors in each country contributed to the success or failure of each reform, though the drive for reform was the same everywhere – to assure democracy remained safe for capitalism and free from left interference. The decisions were political, and political actors sometimes misjudged circumstances or their opponents. By the 1960s the political threat of the left and its agenda had diminished to the point where voting system reforms appeared no longer necessary to contain them. In the absence of such a challenge, the political coalition required to effect change – an unwieldy and unstable group even when threatened – could not be secured.

De Gaulle's voting system reform of 1958 proved the last to be successful for some time. Though discussion of voting systems continued into 1960s in Germany and Ireland and emerged as a political issue in the Netherlands, the political conditions were not conducive to successful reform. Political elites might have wanted reform desperately, but they could not convince their allies or the public that the need was either pressing or in the public interest. By the 1960s the political landscape had changed. The driving force behind post-war voting system reforms had been the strategic position of the left. In the immediate post-war period the strength of the left in Europe had made PR a consensus position across the political spectrum, just as the marginalization of Communist parties motivated attempts to repeal PR later. Anything less than this level of Cold War threat made attempts at voting system reform appear partisan and immediately suspect. For the better part of three decades after 1960, voting system reform was off the political agenda in western democracies.

Chapter 7

The Neoliberal Democratic Realignment, 1970–2000

Introduction

The 1990s witnessed an explosion of interest in electoral systems, mul-tipartism and political institutions generally. This was hardly surpris-ing, given the epoch-shifting events that marked the opening of the decade: the fall of the communist bloc in 1989–90, the reunification of Germany in 1990–1, the end of apartheid in South Africa in 1994, and the return to democratic rule in a host of Latin American countries. After all, new democracies would need to establish some means of electing their new representative chambers. But the focus on demo-cratic institutions held the spotlight throughout the 1990s as the result of an even more surprising development: the successful reform of long entrenched electoral systems in established democracies. Italy and New Zealand adopted new voting systems in 1993, Japan followed suit in 1994, and Britain introduced myriad new systems for local, regional, and European elections in 1997.[1] To many – academics, political com-mentators, politicians – these last developments were inexplicable. Calls for voting system reform had long been dismissed as simply grumbles from the politically marginalized, not to be taken seriously. However, when the issue seemed to take root firmly in the 1990s, over-coming entrenched party and political elite opposition in a host of countries, commentators were at a loss to explain its sudden viability.

Since then, a number of tenuous efforts at explanation have emerged, most focusing on the general trend towards de-alignment in western party systems, the breakdown of traditional cleavages, the changing values of modern citizenry, and the achievement of a new institutional equilibrium or "modernization." Thus the recent institutional fluidity within modern democracies is claimed to represent the influence of a changing electorate, one less focused on material, Cold War–era electoral competition, in favour of post-material issues and less party-directed political participation. Commentators suggest that in New Zealand, Italy, and Japan public frustration with politics led to a break with politics-as-usual and traditional parties loyalties, and that this eventually fuelled a shift from party competition as the key political focus to institutional reform. Or analysts focus on how various contingent factors (corruption, policy reversals, etc.) acted on longstanding structural problems (lack of alternation in government) to fuel reform in favour of a new institutional equilibrium, particularly with reference to Italy and Japan. In Britain, voting system change has also been credited to delayed institutional and political modernization.[2] One needn't look far into each context to spot these factors seemingly at work in the different reform efforts. And yet something seems missing from these accounts, something about how these reforms may be related to the larger political struggles going on in western industrialized countries.

The big picture of the most recent era of voting system reform is harder to see because it has emerged more slowly and produced much less decisive shifts in how democracy appears to operate. As the "golden age" of the post-war democratic era began to pass in the 1970s, a host of ideas emerged about what caused its demise and what should be done to revive it or replace it. Unlike the previous post-war eras of democratic struggle, this latest period was drawn out over a longer period of time and lacked the seemingly clear-cut options facing previous generations. For a time governments across the west seemed to move in different directions: some opted to deepen government involvement in the economy, others stuck to the Keynesian status quo, while still others experimented with then-radical "neoliberal" market reforms. In each country proponents of these different approaches struggled to gain the upper hand, though eventually variants of the neoliberal approach would become the new democratic consensus position. But how and when this occurred would depend on the balance of political forces in each country. In some cases neoliberal champions simply won power (the United States, the United Kingdom, Canada) and set about reshaping the democratic system along new lines. But in others they faced significant political opposition. In some cases, these struggles to reshape contemporary democracy spilled over into battles to change institutional rules like voting systems.

The most recent period of voting system reform then represents both departures and continuities with past reform efforts. The contemporary left, both as a party and extra-parliamentary force, is no longer a threat worthy of voting system reform. Thus, in a departure from the efforts that followed both world wars, changes in voting systems today are not being sought to limit the left electorally. Yet recent voting system reforms are still being sought to accomplish specific political and economic goals as a kind of "politics by other means," particularly where the balance of power in different political systems has proven difficult to shift. Thus contemporary struggles over voting systems, as with similar battles following the First and Second World Wars, are related to important struggles over national and international political economy and their relation to how contemporary democracies function. And here the role of left parties, the structure of nation-based party systems, and the continuing, if weakened, influence of traditional cleavage structures have been important factors. In France, New Zealand, Italy, and the United Kingdom, struggles over party systems, the strategic positioning of the left, and decisions about neoliberal economic restructuring have been important catalysts to voting system reform, despite the fact that similar battles in other countries have not produced the same institutional changes. In this chapter we'll examine these recent reforms and the factors outlined above to explain why this is so.

Ireland, the Netherlands, and Canada

The voting system came under scrutiny in a few other locales in the 1960s and 1970s but the forces driving the process failed in their efforts to change them. Ireland had used the STV form of PR from its inception, later entrenching it in a new constitution passed in 1937. Though it was initially introduced by the British to weaken the influence of republican agitators, and later to protect the Protestant minority in the south, it had served mostly to balance the bitter sectarian divisions of the republicans themselves and represent a small Labour party. Though he championed the system during the 1937 constitutional revisions, Eamon de Valera, the leader of the subsequently dominant Fianna Fail party, decided that British-style voting and the governing majorities it tended to produce might have a lot to recommend it. But the party's campaign to repeal the system in 1959 and again in 1968 appeared self-serving and partisan. After all, no other party or public body supported the change, and no public demand could be said to be motivating it. In the end a majority of voters defeated the repeal effort in both cases.[3]

Voting system reform also became an issue in the Netherlands in the 1960s, given prominence by the breakthrough of a new party into the political system. The Democrats 66 offered a populist and reform-oriented set of proposals to shake up the Dutch political system and break the stasis it claimed characterized policy development and political competition. It called for an elected head of state and a move away from the proportional voting that it blamed for the lack of legislative change from election to election. Instead, it called for the introduction of a British-style constituency system that would "polarise the political spectrum and thus provide a direct link between election results and the formation of a new government."[4] Though it gained a considerable following for a time, it failed to convince other parties or enough voters to embrace its approach. By the mid-1970s its electoral support had declined and the debate over voting system reform tapered off.[5] D66 carried on, however, using its electoral leverage to have committees examine the issue in 1989 and 1994, this time angling for a German-style MMP system. But neither initiative produced any changes. Attempts to reduce the proportionality of the Dutch PR system through more minor reforms were pursued repeatedly in the 1970s and 1980s but also failed.[6]

Canada can be seen as a striking example of how crisis – even one directly connected to representative institutions – does not automatically contribute to voting system change. For a time in the 1970s some change of voting system was touted in Canada, at least amongst elite opinion-makers. Scholars had long noted the regional biases in Canada's traditional first-past-the-post voting system, that it benefited parties with regionally concentrated support while punishing those without, but the major parties appeared to have little incentive to change it.[7] The 1976 Quebec provincial election victory for the separatist Parti Québécois broke through the complacency about institutional reform. Now a better reflection of the polity, both its regional differences and its shared national aspirations seemed imperative to stave off a nasty break-up of the country. In one response, Prime Minister Trudeau established the Pepin-Robarts Task Force on Canadian Unity to sound out a way forward. Reporting in 1979, the commissioners recommended a host of institutional reforms, including a slight element of proportionality for elections to the House of Commons.[8]

Over the next few years, Canadians produced report after report in favour of mildly proportional reforms, exhibiting a hitherto little-known passion for electoral engineering.[9] The key concern was to eliminate the sometimes wild distortions that appeared between what were real patterns of regional voting and the artificially inflated regional results that parties achieved in first-past-the-post elections. Yet, with hindsight, consideration of these reforms appeared to be highly influenced by the proximity of the crisis. After Quebec voted "no" to negotiations around sovereignty association in 1980, what little pressure existed to fix Canada's problems via representation visibly slackened. Shortly thereafter, Liberal Prime Minister Trudeau toyed with a proposal to add a mild element of PR to the House of Commons and gained the support of Ed Broadbent, leader of the New Democratic Party, to seriously consider it. But when NDP elites and activists voted against their leader's decision at the party's 1981 national convention, even this meagre initiative was shelved.[10] Ironically, the separatist Parti Québécois government was also embroiled in debate over voting system reform throughout this period, split between members committed to reform as a matter of principle, and more pragmatic activists and legislative members keen to hold onto government. Though the party and the government officially studied the question, its ultimate defeat as policy in the 1980s surprised few.[11] Proposals for a PR-elected Senate were floated a decade later during constitutional negotiations but again amounted to little.[12] It appeared that repeated crises involving regionalism, separatism, and the constitution were not enough to get voting system reform an effective public or party hearing in Canada.

Just as concerns over minority representation alone could not secure voting system reform in the nineteenth century, attempts to change modern voting systems to further majority government in Ireland, provide for government alternation in the Netherlands, or address regional disputes in Canada all failed.

France

Canadian failure in the 1970s and 1980s is striking when compared to the (temporary) French success in changing their voting system just a few years later. In 1985, France switched from its traditional second ballot voting system, used continuously since 1958, to a PR system much like the one it had adopted in 1945. The decision was immediately controversial, with little public or elite support. President Francois

Mitterrand defended the move in terms of electoral fairness (that PR would more accurately reflect party support), his Socialist[13] party's longstanding commitment to the change, and the fact that the government had already introduced PR for local and regional elections. He claimed the decision was above politics, as the previous right-wing administration had also introduced PR for elections to the European Union.[14] But his opponents and most academic commentators cried foul, accusing the Socialist party of electoral self-interest and institutional manipulation. Sub-national election results over the previous three years had suggested that the first left government in modern French history was heading for a crushing defeat.[15] Critics argued that Mitterrand was interested in PR only to help mitigate his party's expected losses in the coming election and as a means of splitting his right-wing opposition. There were forces even within the Socialist government against the change, as they felt it would limit the party's return to power.[16] Certainly France was not facing anything like the regional or separatist threats that Canada was dealing with. Yet voting system reform was moving forward, apparently just to prevent the reigning government from losing too badly in the coming elections.

As an explanation for the change, the Socialist party's immediate electoral self-interest goes only so far. In the French case, the larger social and economic context behind the Socialist party's strategy is crucial to making sense of their efforts. Mitterrand did not merely seek to shore up Socialist representation and encourage party fissures on the right with his adoption of PR; he hoped to shift his party's location in the party system towards the centre, thus marginalizing the Communists on the left and drawing centrists away from the political right. The Socialists' experience in government from 1981 to 1985 convinced party elites that something about their political coalition-making would have to give. Mitterrand had been elected president in 1981 by linking a Socialist-dominated united-left with centrist political support, which he quickly turned into a left parliamentary majority in early legislative elections shortly thereafter.[17] After two decades of effort, the left was finally in power nationally in France. But this governing coalition immediately faced seemingly insurmountable problems of national economic decline, international economic pressure, and conflicting policy objectives from its far left and centre. Not only did the government have to manage the inflated expectations of its followers, but its bold policy prescriptions to go beyond the post-war Keynesian consensus now faced dire economic conditions and powerful national and international opposition to even the maintenance of the status quo. Though the government initially attempted to introduce its program through 1981–2, it eventually lost its nerve, given the scope of the problems, lack of partners elsewhere in Europe, and its own internal divisions.[18] Resisting the pressures for neoliberal policies coming from both inside France and internationally would have required a social mobilization that neither of the decaying party organizations on the left felt confident it could muster. While there were forces within the Socialist party keen to defend national economic sovereignty in the face of emergent globalizing pressures, others were keen to "modernize" the party and its policy commitments. When Mitterrand failed to convince others in the European Union to join France in defending the post-war model of economic regulation, the balance of forces within the party shifted to the right. The Socialists embarked on a dramatic reversal of economic policy, the Communists left the government, and a host of neoliberal policies were introduced, despite the opposition of most of the government's supporters.[19]

Voting system reform emerged out of the Socialists' governing, coalition-making, and electoral difficulties, informed by their organizational decline and the sense that no alternatives to neoliberal economic policies were viable. The two left parties were now split on economic questions, with the Communists accusing the Socialist government of ruling in the interests of the rich and middle classes. This was a serious split, given that the two parties had spent most of the 1970s sealing a deal that was committed to a detailed democratic socialist program, one that sought to move on the longstanding left demands for some kind of economic democracy.[20] So Mitterrand's turn to the right economically in 1983–4 was not just any old policy change – it represented a dramatic shift in the western left's democracy imaginary. The break meant that relations between the Socialist and Communist parties from 1984 (when the four Communist ministers resigned) to the run-up to the next legislative elections in 1986 remained adversarial. Yet given the coalition-making pressures created by the second ballot, the Socialists would need to come to some understanding with Communists before the election in 1986 or risk splitting left support. And policy differences were not the only difficulty facing the left. The increasing weakness of the PCF (polls in 1985 suggested the party was down to just 10 per cent, half of its 1978 total) was a problem for the Socialists as well, as it represented a declining pool of second ballot support.[21] This was another reason that Socialists were keen to find some way to reach towards the political centre for governing allies. It was here that the Socialist leadership became serious about making some change to the electoral rules. The government's subsequent decision to adopt PR eliminated the need for the two left parties to cooperate electorally, thus weakening left electoral pressure for the Socialists to moderate their embrace of economic liberalism. Though they expected to lose the coming election, Socialist strategists felt PR would allow for a more "orderly retreat" from government.[22] In the long run, they believed that their tough economic decisions would redound to their favour, eventually contributing to a return to power, perhaps with more centrist allies, especially as they expected PR to help split the already fractious French right.[23]

Mitterrand's strategy was plausible, given the rancorous political infighting that had dogged the French right from the late 1970s into the 1980s. But in the end the president's right-wing opponents outmanoeuvred him by working out an effective electoral agreement to resist the fragmenting pressures of the new PR system.[24] And given that the PR model adopted was only regionally proportional, the right managed to turn a plurality of support into a majority of seats.[25] Still, the right majority was narrow, and the Socialist hope to draw centrist politicians away from the new government and into a coalition with them might still have come to pass but for a number of obscure Gaullist constitutional provisions that allowed the new right-wing prime minister to essentially rule by decree and repeal PR without parliamentary debate.[26] Though the right had just won a majority under PR, it still favoured the second ballot as the best way to manage its coalition and with public opinion in its favour it quickly restored it. The Socialists had hoped to use PR to rejig the party system and their place within it, but the immediate gambit failed. (As it turned out, the party system changed even without PR.)[27] The mainstream right did not need PR to pursue its agenda (especially after the Socialists themselves had opened the door to neoliberalism), and a move away from it would lessen the impact of far-right competitors like the National Front. Nor did a left divided on its basic economic vision for France pose a threat in need of containment. Indeed, when the Socialists returned to power in 1988 they too lost interest in PR, having succeeded in moving themselves more firmly into the centre, amid collapsing support for the PCF.[28]

Voting System Reform in the 1990s

At the start of 1990s a public discussion of voting system reforms seemed to bubble up in various established democracies, though few credited it as a serious threat to existing institutional arrangements. The temporary switch to PR in France was seen as an aberration, a peculiar but very French exception to an almost iron law of political science and pragmatic political analysis that insisted that institutions like voting rules simply could not be changed under normal (i.e., non-crisis) political circumstances. Yet by the end of the decade three established democracies had changed their voting systems, another had introduced changes at the sub-national level, and the discussion of voting system reform appeared to be spreading to even more countries. The reforming countries – New Zealand, Italy, Japan, the United Kingdom – appeared to have little in common at first glance. Nor were the different processes or results of change remotely similar, beyond a broad public revolt against existing political forces and a shift to some new form of voting. As a result, most explanations of the changes have focused on the de-alignment of party systems across western countries, combined with the changing values of citizens and decline of traditional cleavages, and a host of country-specific conjunctural factors. There is little doubt that party system change was key in spurring reform, but this had less to do with value change or an end of the salience of traditional (particularly class) cleavages. Instead, all countries, influenced by the changing international economy and pressures from within and outside their borders, witnessed left parties attempting to shift positions on the ideological spectrum. These efforts sparked a struggle over politicized cleavages and, as in France, created an opening for the consideration of institutional reforms like changes to the voting system. In some cases, the institutional reform terrain was taken up by popular forces to limit the movement of left parties, while in others left parties pushed the issue to marginalize former supporters or create space for their own political reinvention.

New Zealand

In 1993 a bare majority of New Zealand's voters opted for a new proportional voting system in a binding referendum. While scholars have argued over the fine points of the process leading to change, the broad contours of the story are fairly consistent across differing accounts and can be briefly sketched out. Historically, New Zealand developed a two-party system with highly majoritarian tendencies. From the 1930s on, the Labour and National parties campaigned on explicit programs and were seen to enjoy a "mandate" if they won a majority of seats, even if that rested on a minority of votes. High voter turnout and alternation in government were seen by many as confirmations of the legitimacy and effective functioning of the system. Then, from the 1970s on, the traditional system broke down amid the rise of third parties, highly disproportional or perverse election results, and the apparent end of the mandate approach to campaigning. Analysts explain these developments as resulting from the breakdown of traditional trading relationships, the de-alignment and diversification of the electorate, incomplete institutional reform, and a new policy independence of the major parties who appeared to be no longer bound to traditional cleavages like class. By the late 1980s, the rapidity of political and economic change, combined with the dramatic shift to the right of the traditionally collectivist Labour Party, fuelled complaints about New Zealand's highly majoritarian democratic system, focusing particular attention on the voting system. Labour empowered a royal commission to study voting system reform and promised a binding referendum on the issue while campaigning in 1987 but later shelved the report and declined to act. But public disgust with both major parties and politicians in general moved a National government to honour the referendum pledge in the early 1990s.[29]

Conventional explanations of New Zealand's reforms essentially rest on de-alignment, peppered with some recognition of institutional factors and political misjudgment. These behavioural explanations, buttressed with neoclassical assumptions about economic performance, suggest that voters started moving away from the major parties in the 1970s for social and economic reasons. This led to highly disproportional election results in 1972 and 1975, and perverse results in 1978 and 1981 (when the most popular party – Labour – lost both elections). Though they elected few members, new third parties opened new policy space, specifically bringing ideas of economic liberalization to mainstream political discussion. De-alignment is also credited with weakening the hold of traditional political cleavages over the two main parties, contributing to a decline in the mandate approach to campaigning. Both National in 1978 and Labour in 1984 took up radically new policy directions once in office that they did not mention at election time, much less campaign on. For most analysts, the close proximity of more than a decade of curious election results, combined with public frustration over the lack of barriers to Labour's radical new policy direction, conspired to bring a normally ignored institution like the voting system under public scrutiny and criticism. From there, repeated political misjudgments kept the issue in the public realm: striking a royal commission, promising a binding referendum, finally holding a vote on the question. In the end, all the political prevarication on the issue was blamed for aiding its success, with the result characterized as a kind of "voters' vengeance."[30]

The wheels for voting system reform were set in motion shortly after Labour gained election in 1984. The party's surprising losses in 1978 and 1981 had raised the profile of the issue for party activists in a way that could not simply be buried, now that the party was in power. Additionally, the new justice minister, Geoffrey Palmer, was a former law professor who had written a book calling for a more proportional voting system. With support from his caucus, Palmer established a royal commission on the electoral system in 1985, appointing a group of independent political and legal experts to carry out the work and providing them with fairly broad terms of reference to examine the voting system. Their report came in late 1986 and endorsed a change to a mixed-member proportional (MMP) voting system to better reflect party support and the gender and ethnic diversity of the country. Given their independence and the clarity with which they made their case and recommendations, the report was favourably received by civil society. Soon after a new advocacy Electoral Reform Coalition (ERC) emerged to champion the recommendations and assure the government would act on them. But most of Labour's parliamentary caucus wanted nothing to do with the new proposals, damning the process that produced them as a "runaway commission."

The issue might have died at that point but for a slip-up during a televised leaders' debate in the 1987 general election. Prime Minister David Lange, an avowed opponent of the MMP proposals, nonetheless promised to hold a referendum on the issue in response to a question from an ERC represenstative. He would later claim he had misread his notes about his government's policy. When a re-elected Labour government failed to move on the referendum pledge in their next term, disgruntled Labour backbenchers kept raising the issue in the legislature, and eventually the opposition National party promised to hold a vote if they won the next election. When National gained office in 1990, they did follow through with the referendum, but not without adding a few twists of their own. The royal commission had called for referendum choice between New Zealand's existing plurality system and their proposed MMP alternative. In what appeared to be a bid to confuse the issue, National struck upon a two-vote process. In the first referendum, voters would make two choices, one indicating a desire for change from the status quo or not, and another expressing a preference amongst four different voting system options. If a majority of voters wanted a change, and if there was a clear choice amongst the alternatives, then a second vote would be held a year later and voters would choose between the existing plurality system and the most popular alternative.

If National had been hoping to muddy the waters, the results were disappointing. With 54 per cent voter turnout in a stand-alone referendum, 85 per cent of those voting said they wanted to change the voting system and 70 per cent chose MMP as their preferred alternative. Little more than a year later, in a vote that coincided with the general election and much higher turnout (83 per cent), 54 per cent of voters chose MMP over New Zealand's traditional plurality system.[31]

While the broad outlines of the conventional explanations are un-controversial, the emphasis on de-alignment and an undifferentiated public disaffection obscures a great deal about why the reform was ultimately successful. In the end, de-alignment was much less important in furthering reform than the struggle to alter the cleavage structure of New Zealand politics. Conventional accounts gloss over the struggle within the Labour party over contentious issues like economic liberalization, tending to over-estimate the degree of cleavage decline. And in their focus on a "voters' vengeance" fuelling voting system reform, they also fail to note the important cleavage dimension here too: that "yes" and "no" in the referendum vote divided broadly along left and right cleavage dimensions.

As Peter Mair has noted, de-alignment is often wrongly explained by cleavage decline.[32] Though parties may change, the cleavages that sustained them may in fact remain. For instance, strong class cleavages in Scandinavia have witnessed the rise of new or renewed left parties recently as social democratic parties have moved closer to the political centre. In New Zealand, the rightward drift of Labour in the late 1980s was answered by strong showings for the more leftist New Labour and its progressive coalition partners in the Alliance in the 1990s. Of course, cleavage structures can and do change. In New Zealand new dimensions have opened up to include environmental concerns, gender issues, and visible minority and indigenous Maori representation. No doubt the class cleavage itself has changed considerably with the internationalization of the economy and downsizing of the government workforce. The point here is that parties and cleavages are related in a dynamic way, and changes in their relations require explanation, not simply assertions or correlations. In New Zealand, the historically dominant class cleavage did not simply decline under demographic pressures or changes in lifestyles of working people. There were explicit efforts to remake it, diminish it, or sustain it.

Historically, New Zealand's cleavage structure was premised on an urban working class, farmers, middle-class professionals and small entrepreneurs, and a nation-based business sector. In a country long dependent on Britain for trade, early political competition witnessed various coalitions of these groups battle each other while seeking economic guarantees from the state. Initially farmers dominated Parliament, sometimes working with organized labour, sometimes opposing it. A Labour party emerged during the First World War and became a contender for government only amid the economic crisis of the 1930s.[33] Unlike Europe, or even neighbouring Australia, the rise of a state-oriented Labour party in New Zealand did not spark a movement for electoral reform, for a number of reasons. First, as in most Anglo-American countries, the franchise and responsible government were extended in a gradual and rather ambiguous manner. For instance, though effective full male, and later female, suffrage came early in New Zealand, democratization remained arguably incomplete until 1947, when the country became officially independent from Britain.[34] Second, by that time, Labour's opponents had managed to unite behind a single party banner (National) and accepted some aspects of Labour's interventionist agenda. By contrast, in Australia, opponents of their Labor party could not merge, and voting system reforms were passed at both the state and federal level. Of course, timing is important. For instance, in Australia, the nature of farming and ranching led to early efforts to unionize and the rapid emergence of a competitive, potentially governing Labor party before the First World War. Many of the same fears motivating electoral reform in Europe at the time were also present in Australia. In New Zealand, however, farming was organized very differently, and the social basis for a politicized class cleavage came only later. By the time Labour took power in 1935, many of its statist proposals were being popularized across western industrialized countries and had gained broad popular support, especially given the economic conditions of the time.[35]

Though largely put in place by Labour in the 1930s and 1940s, the post-war welfare state was presided over by the National Party, which forestalled Labour's return by maintaining the redistributive welfare state while satisfying business and farmers with tariffs and subsidies.[36] But the breakdown of the U.S.-led system of managed world trade in the 1970s created real economic problems for New Zealand, compounded by the shift of British trade interests from its former colonies to Europe. Both Labour and National struggled to formulate and implement a viable alternative. In 1975, National moved decisively onto Labour territory, introducing an active Keynesian policy of public investment and demand management. By the early 1980s, amid a record recession, Keynesian approaches were under intense criticism everywhere.[37] In New Zealand, National's move left alienated many supporters and helped boost third-party voting to its highest levels ever: to approximately 20 per cent in 1978, 1981, and 1984.[38] Campaigning in the 1984 election, Labour gave little indication that it would move far from National's basic policy direction.[39]

Much has been written about Labour's neoliberal policy innovations after returning to government in 1984. Some suggest it "abandoned outright" its traditional social democratic commitments, effectively becoming a party of the "new right," while others characterize its actions as representing a "decisive break with the past."[40] Why an established party with a stable base of support would do such a thing generated a host of explanations. Some pointed out that the Labour party caucus was no longer recruited from the working class and that the professionals who had mostly replaced them understood the "left" more in lifestyle terms rather than class. Others suggested that the new Labour government had a core of neoliberal ideologues who worked effectively with neoliberal colleagues in the influential Treasury Department. Still others pointed to the necessity of the reforms or the influence on Labour party leaders of the success of the fledgling neoliberal New Zealand Party in the 1984 election.[41] However, all appeared to agree that the weakening of class cleavages facilitated the process. Certainly, at an organizational level, Labour's membership decline and move to advertising-based voter contact mirrored larger first-world trends away from direct links with supporters. Labour's re-election in 1987 amid declining support for third parties appeared to further buttress this view, suggesting that the party faced no real penalties for its actions.[42]

In toting up the many changes from 1984 to 1990, Labour's policy shift appears to most commentators as decisive, right-wing, and unimpeded by much effective opposition. But a closer look at the actual decision-making process suggests that Labour's efforts were neither brazenly right-wing nor free from consideration of its traditional supporters. Wendy Larner argues that while Labour recognized the need for market reforms, it initially tried to introduce "more market" as a "means of achieving social democracy."[43] The previous National government had left New Zealand with a huge public debt and floundering economy. Debates within the Labour party reflected a concern to stimulate growth as one means of maintaining and possibly furthering equity through the party's traditional focus on social spending. One way to accomplish this was by exacting greater efficiencies through the public sector portion of the economy. Buttressing this view is Labour's early rejection of privatization as a means of reforming the public sector. Instead, Labour established state-owned enterprises (SOE) that would remain publicly owned but operate more like businesses.[44] Labour's distinctive approach to "market reform" is also evinced by stipulations that SOEs were to be "good employers" and have a "sense of social responsibility."[45] It was only later in Labour's second term, amid a crushing economic downturn and a struggle within the party, that the onus shifted to privatization.[46]

There is also much evidence that Labour's traditional class cleavage exercised much pull, particularly in its first term. Early in the first term, the Labour government reinstated compulsory unionism, scrapped wage controls, and allowed hikes as high as 15 per cent in the traditional national awards system. In education, Labour reduced class sizes and hired more teachers, awarding them pay increases in the range of 25–36 per cent. Nurses also witnessed pay increases of 31–38 per cent. No social programs were cut in the first term, and a royal commission on social policy report in 1986 was supposed to form the basis of an expanded social safety net in Labour's second term.[47] In other words, though Labour presided over a liberalizing of trade and economic regulation, its approach to industrial relations and social programs remained consistent with the party's social democratic legacy. And the party's strong anti-nuclear stand furthered its appeal with post-material voters.

The more decisive shift to the right occurred in Labour's second term. Labour secured re-election in 1987, though it did not escape unharmed. Labour's vote fell in its traditional safe seats (though not to the point of losing them), precisely amongst the poor and working classes most vulnerable to an internationalized market economy. Meanwhile, the party did receive considerable financial support from the business community and voting support from fans of neoliberalism.[48] This new coalition of supporters behind Labour would prove highly unstable. When the economy dipped instead of recovering in the late 1980s, the party was literally wrenched apart trying to sort out its direction. Amid ferocious battles at all levels of the party, the Labour government turned towards more and more neoliberal "solutions."[49] By 1989 the parliamentary caucus was hopelessly divided, and a breakaway left party, New Labour, was launched. Divided, Labour lost the 1990 election badly and then witnessed a new, more decisively neoliberal National Party apply those policies to key Labour constituencies.[50]

The failure of Labour's economic policies has also produced much debate. For the left, Labour's actions betrayed an ideological zeal for essentially unworkable economic ideas. For the right, Labour's failure was chalked up to "sequencing" errors, particularly its failure to liberalize employment and social policy. But reliance on "ideology" or "error" as explanations again ignores important cleavage dimensions. Labour's "sequence" of economic reforms was not in error, but instead faithfully reflected its contradictory cleavage bases. Early liberalizations targeted farmers and business, traditionally National Party constituencies, not working people directly.[51] However, in liberalizing financial markets, trade, and investment, New Zealand's business sector was nearly completely remade in the period between 1985 and 1987, creating a new constituency of support for Labour. It helped that at this point National remained unclear about its approach to neoliberalism.[52] Thus Labour went into the 1987 election with support from opposing sides, and that tension carried through into a battle for control of the party and the legislative caucus over the next three years.

Dissent with the policy drift of Labour amongst supporters, activists, and members eventually spilled over into the emerging public campaign for voting system reform. Though the issue had supporters from across the spectrum, Labour would prove a key source of experienced leaders, organizers, and perhaps most importantly, organizational links and resources, particularly from organized labour.[53] Meanwhile Labour backbenchers in Parliament kept the issue on the agenda, either reminding the leadership of its promises or introducing their own private member's bills to force the issue to a public vote. In the end, against the wishes of most of its parliamentary party, Labour members and supporters decisively threw their support behind the proportional options in the two referendums.[54] In fact, public surveys suggested that voting system reform essentially divided along the left/right cleavage line, with Labour, New Labour, and a significant portion of the centrist New Zealand First electorate for change, while National voters stood opposed.[55] The business community, also sensing how voting system reform was connected to resistance to the neoliberal reforms it supported, came out decisively against PR, pouring money into an anti-reform campaign that outspent its rivals nearly five to one.[56] In the end, the business-sponsored opposition managed to push the status quo single-member plurality system to nearly the same levels of public support as the proportional reform proposal. The new mixed-member proportional (MMP) system barely passed with just 54 per cent of the referendum vote.[57]

Voting system reform in New Zealand emerged against a backdrop of economic crisis and the political responses to it. The crisis was real. New Zealand's post-war economic regime could no longer be sustained in the face of changing world patterns of trade, particularly the loss of its main trading partner, Britain. But the political responses to the economic crisis were not preordained by circumstances or economic theory.[58] Instead, the Labour party embarked on a series of reforms that reflected both the pull of existing cleavages and the new cleavages its actions produced. These reforms sparked considerable opposition within the party, leading to battles for control of the party structure, caucus revolts, breakaway parties, and a humiliating loss in the 1990 election.

Weaved throughout all this was discussion of New Zealand's voting system. Though initially investigated to satisfy Labour members' concerns about the perverse election results of 1978 and 1981, the voting system issue gained saliency amongst the party grassroots amid these struggles over policy and accountability, particularly between 1986 and 1990.[59] When National came to power in 1990 pursuing a more vigorous neoliberal approach, Labour activists and other progressives put even more energy into voting system reform. As survey work appears to confirm a strong left cleavage behind the pro-reform results, we may conclude that the victory was less an example of "voters' vengeance" than a specifically Labour voters' vengeance. Why National went ahead with the referendum remains unclear. The decision has been variously described as an attempt to wrong-foot Labour, cash in on public reform sentiment (while attempting to rig the process to fail), and the politicians' hubris that voting system reform would not catch on with the average voter.[60] The result demonstrates how actors can seriously misjudge reform processes they do not completely control.

Italy

While New Zealanders agitated for a referendum on the voting system in the early days of the new National government, Italians were also attending to the question of voting system reform, though they already had a citizen-driven initiative-referendum mechanism to draw on. On 9 June 1991 Italian voters gave decisive support to a referendum initiative to eliminate multiple-preference voting in elections.[61] Though preference voting – a feature of the country's party list PR system long blamed for aiding corruption and vote-peddling – was hardly considered Italy's most serious institutional deficiency, the campaign against it became a rallying point for public frustration with the political system generally.[62] The referendum proved to be the first step in a decade-long struggle for institutional and political reform, a struggle that would lay low the existing party system and challenge more central institutions like the country's controversial proportional voting arrangements. By 2000, the voting system alone had been subject to four separate reform initiatives. Why and how voting system reform became arguably the key strategy in a larger process of political and state reform is the subject of much debate and little consensus.

The 1991 referendum victory appeared to spark an unstoppable political and institutional unravelling. In the 1992 national elections the traditional ruling bloc of parties lost their majority for the first time since 1948. In the same year a judicial inquiry into political corruption in Milan uncovered a dense and far-reaching web of illegal political kickbacks. As the investigation (dubbed *Tangentopoli* – "kickback city") expanded, a considerable number of parliamentarians were eventually brought up on corruption charges. Facing political and legal challenges, and mindful of new referendum campaigns aimed at reforming local and national elections, politicians tried to reform themselves, with mixed results. Though a bicameral commission of parliament in 1992 managed to reform local election laws, no agreement could be reached on a new national voting system. Despite all the upheaval, it appeared that many politicians still believed the crisis would blow over.[63]

The results of the 1993 referendum to effectively replace the Senate's version of PR with a much less proportional mixed system clearly signalled that there would be no return to "normal." Turnout exceeded the 1991 preference referendum; 75 per cent of registered voters came to the polls, with 82.7 per cent in favour of reducing proportionality. Though parliament toyed with other less far-reaching voting reforms, in the end it altered the electoral laws in line with the referendum results.[64] The 1994 national election, the first conducted under the new mixed system of single-member plurality (75 per cent of the seats) and compensatory list (25 per cent of the seats), pleased no one. Under the new rules even more parties managed to gain entry to parliament, government was still the product of coalition wrangling, and the promise of more stable government remained unfulfilled: the new administration fell in less than a year. Attention now shifted to eliminating the last vestiges of proportionality altogether.

The renewal of the party system so clearly marked in the 1994 election appeared to change the dynamic and possibilities for more far-reaching electoral and constitutional reforms.[65] Where the old leading parties had been either committed to proportional voting (Communists) or unwilling to risk change (Christian Democrats, Socialists), the new leading parties (Forza Italia, Democratic Party of the Left) were committed to majoritarian over proportional voting rules, though agreement on a specific alternative eluded them. In fact, the 1996 national election was dominated by competing visions of a reformed Italian state and its institutions from both the right and left coalitions. However, when the new centre-left government began pursuing arguably neoliberal policies, the right-wing Forza Italia cooled its reform rhetoric for fear of being pushed too far from the centre.[66] The lack of consensus on an acceptable alternative ultimately hobbled the efforts of a new bicameral committee of parliament in 1997 and 1998.[67] The failure triggered yet another round of referendums in 1999 and 2000, both times with the express purpose of repealing the proportional element of the voting system. Surprisingly, the first initiative in 1999 narrowly failed for lack of quorum, while a second effort in 2000 witnessed voter turnout plunge to just 32.4 per cent, suggesting the limits of referendum-driven reform had been reached.[68] With the election of an apparently stable majority government in 2001, arguably the key objective of reform forces, it appeared possible that the era of voting system reform was now over.[69]

More startling than the scope and depth of the changes to the Italian political system in the 1990s for many observers was the fact that change occurred at all. Just one year prior to the preference referendum in 1991, veteran Italian political scientist Gianfranco Pasquino described voting system reform as an "obscure object of desire," noting that "there is nothing more political than reforming an electoral system" and "nothing more difficult ... than reforming a consolidated electoral system."[70] Given that nearly all political parties, large or small, had an interest in maintaining the existing system, it was not clear how any reform would be possible.

A host of explanations have surfaced that largely agree on the key events contributing to Italy's recent party system change and institutional reform – the fall of Communism, the rise of the Northern League, *Tangentopoli*, the judicial "clean hands" investigations, and the pressures of European economic integration – though each tends to assign greater weight and decisive influence to a different one. Beyond assessing the precise balance of factors propelling the changes was the question of timing: why did reform appear to become possible only in 1990s? Many of the complaints – corruption, clientelism, lack of alternation in government, etc. – were longstanding and publicly well known. What had prevented them from fuelling reform previously? Here a number of theories point to a combination of forces, specifically the impact of particular conjunctural factors (i.e., the specific events mentioned above) on lingering and widespread structural problems (e.g., the need for thoroughgoing state reform, the unsustainable costs of clientelism, the increasing economic and social integration with Europe).[71]

But here, as with our previous example, insufficient attention tends to be paid to the role of parties, and the cleavages sustaining them, in fuelling the reform. This is surprising, given that few doubt the importance of Italy's distinctive party system in giving shape to the post-war democratic system and its institutions. The strength of the left coming out of the Second World War had assured the adoption of a highly proportional voting system. However, when a united left comprising the Socialist (PSI) and Communist (PCI) parties did poorly in the initial legislative election of 1948, the centre-right Christian Democrats (DC) tried to reform the system towards a more majoritarian orientation. Yet this turned out to be risky strategy. Though the DC and its coalition partners nearly achieved a majority in 1953, the PCI moved ahead of the PSI and became the leading party on the left, a position it subsequently never relinquished. In fact, voting support for the PCI only increased over the next two decades. As a result, the DC backed away from majoritarianism for fear it might one day benefit the left and push the DC too far from the centre.[72] As long as the DC could straddle the centre-right and use the state to distribute largesse, an acceptable political stasis could be maintained.[73]

Aiding this was the state and organization of Italy's economy. Italy's post-war economic development has been described as an example of "bastard modernization."[74] Development has been highly uneven:

somewhat industrial in the north, still highly agricultural in the south. For most of the post-war period, the DC patched together a national coalition with business preferments in the north and subsidies for the south. An elaborate system of clientelism effectively traded votes for government largesse, aided by Cold War–inspired preferential treatment from the United States, fuelling widespread inefficiencies and corruption. The fact that the largest alternative party was the Communists served only to lodge the DC in place. However, rising labour militancy and the breakdown of the post-war regime of managed international trade in the 1970s created both economic and political problems for the maintenance of the status quo. For a time, the PCI sustained the DC in power as part of its "historic compromise" strategy of getting closer to national power.

Into the 1980s, though the country's economic problems hardly abated, the status quo was reasserted by the DC in coalition now with the rightward-moving PSI. Interest in institutions like voting systems also revived after an absence of more than two decades. As early as the late 1970s, various members of the DC and PSI had mooted calls for consideration of the German mixed system or the French double ballot. The Bozzi commission of the 1980s explored voting system reform but lacked sufficient political party support to do anything about it. Countless academics called for reform, particularly for a British-style single-member plurality system, but they too lacked any party elite backers or public influence.[75]

The key barrier to change was opposition from most members of the two key parties, the DC and the PCI. Both feared that any shift away from PR would benefit the other. Though many observers credit de-alignment with breaking the deadlock, pointing particularly to the rise of the Northern Leagues, it was arguably this and realignment on the left that opened the space for institutional reform.[76] Long before the fall of the eastern bloc, Italy's "frozen" party system was starting to melt. Under Bettino Craxi, the PSI moved to the right and manoeuvred itself to the front rank of the coalition government with the DC.[77] The PCI too was re-examining its position in the political system, given the meagre results obtained from its "historic compromise" strategy.[78] Throughout the late 1980s the PCI debated its future, embarking on thoroughgoing reform in March 1989, *before* the unanticipated fall of the eastern bloc.[79] With the PSI enacting arguably right-wing policies in coalition with the DC, the PCI attempted to reposition themselves as social democrats. But in doing so, the party fractured, with a significant group of members splitting off to form a new party, Communist Refoundation. Though the split initially weakened the PCI, now renamed the Democratic Party of the Left (PDS), it ultimately strengthened its focus and altered its strategy. Severed from the more orthodox elements of its old class cleavage, the PDS had more freedom to move towards the centre. As a result, the party, long the strongest defender of PR, now committed itself to voting system reform favouring a French-style majority system. The PDS believed that a majority system would help break the clientelist links that fuelled corruption and kept the DC in power.[80] As for the DC, the party's long-running internal warfare took on a new dimension as the "glue" that held the organization together, patronage and clientelism, increasingly came into conflict with the more global strategies of its business supporters, particularly in the north.[81] A key part of the success of new parties in the north resulted from the disaffection of key elements of the business class from the DC's traditional "political economy" of gaining votes in the south with patronage paid for by the north.[82]

In examining the upheaval in Italian politics in the 1990s, much attention has been paid to the independent-minded prosecutors, the non-party technocrats brought in to run the government at different times, and the renegade politicians like DC MP Mario Segni, who became publicly associated with leading the reform cause. But the role of the parties, particularly on the left, has tended to be overlooked. Though reformers in the 1990s struck upon the referendum as a means to electoral reform – successfully using it to end multiple preference voting in 1991 and effectively forcing a shift from the country's highly proportional party list form of PR to a less proportional mixed voting system in 1993 – it must be remembered that party organization played a strong role in facilitating this process. In fact, the signature campaigns to get the referendums before the public crucially benefited from the political parties, or the factions within them, who thought they could benefit from the changes.[83] Specifically, the remaking of the political left opened a space for a cross-cleavage campaign in favour of reform between various elements of the DC and the former Communists in the PDS. And the uneven party support for subsequent changes, specifically the indifference of Forza Italia and the opposition of Communist Refoundation, goes a long way towards explaining why efforts to eliminate proportionality altogether, either by members of parliament (1992, 1997–8) or by public referendum (1999, 2000), failed repeatedly.[84]

Thus the actions of the judiciary, technocrats, and renegade politicians make sense only when put into a larger context of the party system change being fuelled by shifting cleavage structures, the challenges facing political organizations, and the new neoliberal economic environment encroaching on Italy as it became further integrated into the European Union.[85] Italy's post-war party system had grown out of the dramatic mobilizations for and against fascism at the end of the war, giving rise to an evenly balanced mass party system tipped only slightly in favour of the centre-right and against a Communist-dominated centre-left. As Italy was drawn into America's Cold War, an economic and political framework emerged to help maintain the DC in power, involving U.S. subsidies for trade and development, and an internal system of economic payoffs that sustained the political control of the centre-right. By the 1980s the political organizations sustaining these arrangements, on both the left and right, were in decline. Meanwhile, the economic relationships cementing the traditional deal-making of the political elites could no longer be sustained in contexts of European and American free trade. Without their payoffs and political direction, justices and many politicians became more "independent." As elites on both the right and left struggled to forge a new political identity and winning electoral formula, they deliberately, sometimes inadvertently, helped expose the deep corruption of the Italian political system, unleashing a strong public reaction against the status quo. Out of such tumult, political elites fought over voting system reforms as a means of securing both specific policy objectives (i.e., neoliberal reforms) and a strengthened position strategically in coming electoral contests, with results that were uneven, unpredictable, and – for some – disastrous.

Japan

The voting system reform process in Japan differed markedly from that in New Zealand and Italy in at least one important way – the parties rather than a citizen-supported referendum process could be seen as driving the change. In 1994 the first non–Liberal Democratic Party (LDP) government in thirty-eight years replaced Japan's traditional semi-proportional voting system with a mixed-member system consisting of three hundred single-member plurality seats and another two hundred seats elected from party lists. Voting system reform had long been a back-burner issue in Japanese politics, trotted out every few years by the reigning LDP to either discipline its rivals or appear to respond to seemingly endless corruption charges, but it always faced strong opposition from other parties and a majority within the LDP itself. Why did the status quo give way in 1994? Some analysts credited heightened public concern over corruption for fuelling the reform, along with an emerging consensus amongst political commentators and elites that the country's persistent political problems (money politics, one-party dominance, factionalized parties) were the product of its traditional single nontransferable vote system (SNTV).[86] But others pointed to a new instability in the party system itself, noting divisive struggles within all parties around key issues like economic development, market liberalization, and foreign diplomacy.

Politicians and academic commentators have long focused on SNTV as a key determinant of Japan's party system, particularly in producing some its more negative traits, such as long periods of one-party rule, party factionalization, and the never-ending quest for campaign finances.[87] The first concerted push to change the system came shortly after the return of governing control to the Japanese in the early 1950s.[88] Initially, the opposition Socialist party (JSP) lobbied for an Anglo-American single-member plurality (SMP) system hoping to benefit from right-wing vote splits between the Liberal and Democratic parties. But when those right parties fused into a single governing party in 1955 and forged ahead with voting system reform, specifically an SMP system, the JSP balked and organized ferocious opposition, preferring instead a proportional system or the status quo. After heated wrangling, the LDP let the matter drop, but not for long.[89] Electoral reform issues generally returned to the legislature in response to allegations of corruption. Between 1960 and 1972 seven advisory councils on electoral reform were convened, six with an explicit focus on the voting system. But consensus was difficult to achieve: typically the LDP stuck by its proposals for SMP, while the opposition parties called for PR or adjustments to SNTV. In the end, most reports were simply filed away. Put simply, individual LDP legislators could see little point in changing a system that had worked so well for them.[90]

Interest in voting system reform re-emerged from all parties in the late 1980s and early 1990s as a series of high-profile scandals toppled two LDP prime ministers and a host of high-ranking legislators. Opposition parties, revelling in the LDP loss of control in the now-PR elected upper house, supported change as a possible way of forcing the LDP from government. Meanwhile various factions within the LDP considered a focus on voting system reform an effective pre-emptive move that might stall more thoroughgoing reforms and allow the party to stay in power.[91] But the mixed system proposal that emerged from the Eighth Electoral Reform Commission in 1990 earned only criticism from the opposition and indifference from the LDP.[92] Finally, a new scandal in 1992 resurrected the discussion and, amid calls from the opposition for thoroughgoing campaign finance reforms, the LDP introduced legislation for a full SMP system in 1993. At this point, the opposition broke with its traditional objections to mixed systems and proposed a fully proportional MMP system as an alternative. This shift in the opposition ranks would prove decisive. The subsequent debate on these proposals split the LDP, toppled the government, and led to the first non-LDP administration since 1955.

In the July 1993 lower house elections a historic non-LDP coalition government emerged, though it agreed on little but the need for voting system reform.[93] The key division concerned economic policy, with many of the former LDP members supporting economic liberalization, while JSP members defended Japan's highly state-regulated system. As a result, the new coalition government made political reform its top priority, but even here it had difficulty carrying out its objectives. JSP members were divided over the proposed electoral reforms, and seventeen eventually voted against the government bill when it reached the upper house, causing it to fail.[94] Now the coalition leaders turned to the LDP to work out a compromise. LDP influence reduced the new system's proportionality and gutted provisions to reduce the impact of money on campaigns. After the new voting system was finally adopted in January 1994 the non-LDP coalition government slowly imploded, incapable of managing its policy contradictions.[95] Just five months later, the LDP was back in power, first in coalition with its longtime rival, the JSP, and after its demise in the 1996 elections, with other parties. Though complaints about the new system abounded, no serious effort emerged to replace it.[96]

Analysis of Japan's 1994 voting system reform has focused heavily on the timely conjuncture of repeated scandal and corruption, with increasing public pressure for a political response, alongside an emerging consensus amongst the political class that the country's traditional single non-transferable voting system has been responsible for much of what ails the political system (e.g., excessive party factionalization, one-party rule, the corrupting influence of money on politicians and policy outcomes, etc.). While these factors were undoubtedly influential, they fail to explain why voting system reform succeeded in the

1990s when it had failed so many times before. Scandal, promises of reform, blaming the voting system – these decade-old factors had done little to challenge either the LDP or SNTV before.[97]

The key difference between the 1990s and previous eras of voting system reform was a markedly changed international environment, both politically and economically. As a front-line Cold War state, the bulwark of American foreign policy in the region, Japan found that its meteoric economic growth was greatly aided by technology transfers and privileged terms of trade with the United States.[98] But the end of the Cold War brought new pressure from U.S. politicians and business to "open Japan for business" and alter the lopsided trade relationship. The restructuring of international trade along free market lines put enormous pressure on Japan to open markets and internationalize corporate ownership, decision-making, and investment.[99] It also made Japan's clientelistic form of politics, where votes and campaign funds were essentially traded for extensive, often unnecessary, public works and government contracts, more politically risky. As Japan's competitive position in the world economy declined, and the economy stagnated at home, support for decentralization, deregulation, and neoliberal policies emerged within the LDP itself, despite the party's traditional reliance on a strong hand in economic affairs to pay back contributors and voters. At the same time, more and more voters and business leaders were questioning whether contemporary conditions required their traditional fidelity to the LDP.[100] Younger members of the LDP, less secure in their positions, were more aware of these rumblings and more willing to take them seriously.[101]

The end of the Cold War also showed up the irrelevance of an LDP dominance based on the need to protect Japan from "socialism," both externally and internally. In fact, by the late 1980s and 1990s, the JSP was one of the strongest defenders of Japan's distinctive brand of state-interventionist capitalism.[102] But the JSP was also facing internal pressures for change, fuelled in part by a reorganization and centralization of the labour movement that helped fund the party.[103] This also reflected ideological differences within the party and the union movement, with the left committed to some degree of anti-capitalism, while the right sought a Blairite "third way." As a result, the left in the JSP, fearing a new voting system might break up the party, opposed voting system reform, and many of its legislators broke ranks to vote against it. Meanwhile, the right in the JSP thought a new voting system would weaken its left, thus aiding the development of a new government-oriented, centre-left party. Both sides were proven correct when the JSP was practically wiped out in the 1996 lower house elections, the remnants joining the centrist Democratic party.[104] However, the increase in Communist party support that coincided with the fall of the JSP suggests that the class cleavage, though weak, remained relevant.

It would appear then that party elites and key actors in civil society were the catalyst for voting system reform, rather than any strong changes in public opinion about the parties or the ongoing corruption scandals. Actors within both major parties were looking for alternative arrangements to further their own goals and shift the basis of Japanese politics, while elements of both organized labour and business were keen on new options as well. In the case of labour, unions found themselves in a difficult spot. They were politically and financially committed to the various left-wing parties, particularly the front-running JSP. But since the late 1970s they had made some inroads with the LDP, as the party's electoral support kept declining and it sought out new allies to sustain its government. But here was the contradiction: links to the governing party gave the unions much more influence than they ever had by supporting the chronic opposition on the left, but that influence was checked by their low position in the hierarchy of LDP supporters. Basically, any labour demands that conflicted with business interests were rejected or ignored.[105] By the late 1980s, the failure of these multiple political strategies was evident to labour's leadership. As a result, under the banner of a new united trade union federation (Rengo), organized labour renewed its efforts to unite all the leftist parties to create a potentially alternative governing party, one that might increase its influence. By 1990, it had nearly succeeded, and unity talks between the various parties had advanced to a considerable degree. However, the Gulf War and possible Japanese participation in it drove a wedge between the different players, and negotiations collapsed. With this failure, key elements in organized labour announced they would shift funding towards any political forces that could help create this alternative party, a major blow to the JSP particularly.[106]

Thus the heightened impact of otherwise ostensibly normal political conditions in Japan – money politics, corruption, complaints about the negative effects of the voting system – gained their saliency amid a process of sometimes subtle, sometimes not-so-subtle, party realignment and pressure for neoliberal economic restructuring. The perceived end of the "1955 system" and the economic logic that had fuelled LDP politics was one reason that so many politicians were willing to take up voting system reform and pursue new political allegiances.[107] The challenge to the post-war economic system also encouraged a realignment of forces within the JSP, leading to a break in its historic approach to institutional reform, arguably the catalyst for the subsequent events. According such importance to the left here may seem surprising, given the lopsided nature of LDP dominance in Japanese politics, and the slow decline in JSP support from the 1960s. But as with Italy, the clientelistic nature of the political system was held in place by the character of the party system, specifically the existence of a main opposition party that appeared unelectable. The JSP had remained the key opposition party for a host of reasons, including its strong commitment to peace and anti-militarism.[108] Changing economic and international factors only further weakened the JSP's competitive position electorally into the 1990s, and its strategic responses and internal divisions helped break the dualism that had long characterized the Japanese political system, creating an opening for institutional reform. As the union leaders seeking reform recognized, the JSP was too weak to act as a pole for an alternate governing party but too strong to be ignored in any negotiations about what to do.[109]

Given the obvious decline of the traditional party system in the 1990s, based on a left-right dualism shaped in and designed to serve the Cold War, elements within both the LDP and the JSP saw voting system reform as a means to break out of political arrangements that appeared decreasingly viable. Scandal was less important in fomenting reform than the changing international terms of trade that were weakening the LDP's traditional clientelistic forms of political control and the fact that Japan's business class was no longer united behind the post-war "Japan Inc." strategy of strong national tariffs and high exports. Support for neoliberal restructuring of Japan's economy was increasingly dividing the traditional LDP ranks, leading to breakaway political formations that ultimately cost the centre-right its control of the government in the 1990s. Meanwhile, Japan's left was also divided about the way forward, with the dominant force within the JSP in favour of reform as a means of refashioning the party as the logical pole of attraction for all those wanting a change in government. The JSP interpreted the increasing fragmentation within the LDP ranks as opportunity to move towards this goal and accepted an LDP proposal for voting system reform, with disastrous results. Voting system reform did not end LDP control of Japanese politics, let alone aid the left, but it did give voice to neoliberal political forces and move its traditional governing party closer to neo-liberal positions on a host of issues.

United Kingdom

The last voting system reforms adopted in the 1990s occurred in Britain. But unlike that of its predecessors, the British reform process has been a more muted and limited affair, both in the political circumstances surrounding it and the impact of the changes on the national political scene. Since 1997 and the return of Labour to the government benches, Britain has moved from a longstanding defence of single-member plurality for every kind of election to a startling embrace of electoral system pluralism, adopting no fewer than five separate voting systems for different electoral purposes, all in less than five years. After gaining power, veteran political observers expected to see Labour give most of these proposals a "kick into the long grass": endless rounds of study, committee hearings, expert counsel, etc. Instead, Labour took up action very shortly after assuming government in May 1997. Elections for a Northern Irish constitutional assembly were held later in May, the government announced a switch to PR for European elections in July, and referendums on establishing local assemblies for Scotland and Wales were held in September. Plans for the return of London's local government were also quickly pulled together, complete with directly elected mayor and council. All these new representative structures involved countless decisions about design, composition, decision rules, and constitutional powers. Curiously, the voting systems for all contained some element of proportionality, a clear departure from British electoral traditions. Nationally, voting system reform was also under consideration. By December 1997 Labour struck an independent commission on the electoral system, dubbed the "Jenkins Commission" after its chair, Lord Jenkins. Labour, after less than a year in power, appeared firm in its resolve to hold a referendum on Britain's voting rules.

The rise of voting system reform in British circles was as surprising as it was meteoric. A decade earlier, the topic was the province of mostly ignored constitutional reform groups like Charter 88, and the third-place Alliance (an electoral alliance of the Liberal and Social Democratic parties).[110] This is not to say that Britain's traditional SMP voting system had not come under recent scrutiny and criticism. It had, but few expected decisive action from the parliamentary Labour party. After all, in a 1977 free vote on whether to adopt a party list PR system for

European elections, Labour leaders appeared indecisive, and half the caucus joined with the Tories to vote it down.[111] Two decades later, most spent mired in opposition after four successive defeats at the polls, Labour still seemed lukewarm about change. In fact, new leader Tony Blair declared he was unconvinced of the merits of PR shortly before the 1997 campaign.[112] These were all facts that made his party's speedy adoption of a flurry of proportional and semi-proportional voting systems shortly after taking office all the more curious.

Though never dominating public discussion, voting system debates had been percolating through British public consciousness for at least two decades. The governing Conservatives brought the topic back to life in 1973 when they mandated the use of PR for elections in Northern Ireland as one response to emerging social and political tensions there.[113] However, the representational quirks of Britain's traditional first-past-the-post system really made headlines when the party with the most votes lost the February 1974 election. In that instance Labour triumphed over the Conservatives, despite enjoying slightly less public support. In a way, this just reversed a previous injustice; in 1951 it was Labour who suffered, losing to the Tories despite getting more votes. But the situation in the 1970s was complicated by a further injustice to the third-place Liberals, a party whose negligible support in 1951 (3 per cent) had mushroomed to 20 per cent in the back-to-back elections of 1974. Yet the Liberals secured less than 2 per cent of the seats in the House of Commons, fewer seats in fact than much less popular regional parties. These disturbing trends motivated a number of ruminations about electoral reform, including the highly touted Hansard Commission Report of 1976 that called for a semi-proportional additional member system (AMS).[114]

The question of voting system reform remained within sight in the 1980s but well beyond political reach. When the new Social Democrat / Liberal Alliance gained 25 per cent of the popular vote in the 1983 election (just 3 per cent less than Labour) but only a handful of seats, another round of hand-wringing occurred, though little came of it.[115] The problem was simple: both Conservatives and Labour utterly opposed any change. Without support from either of the two major parties, the parties generally perceived to have a realistic chance of forming governments, the issue was a non-starter.[116]

The break came with the third straight defeat for Labour in 1987. At this point the "Labour Campaign for Electoral Reform" started to gain ground within the party as both members and a few MPs began to worry that the pendulum might not ever swing back.[117] Whether to let off steam or hedge its bets in the event of another loss, Labour established a working group on electoral reform under Raymond Plant in 1990. The Plant reports sketched out many of the innovative ideas Labour would later introduce in government, particularly on sub-national reform and European elections. But Plant's call for a new national voting system, the semi-proportional "supplementary vote," still proved too controversial for the party, despite Labour's fourth consecutive defeat in 1992. In the convention debate on the issue, Plant's proposal was voted down, but supporters did manage to commit the party to a national referendum on the question.[118]

The Labour party's shift on voting system reform has been explained in a number of ways. Some credit leader Tony Blair's stated desire to move Britain away from confrontation and towards a more consensual style of politics. Others point to it as a component of Labour's new commitment to broader constitutional reform, accountability, and consultation.[119] No doubt interest within the party and some of its supporters was motivated by a host of different concerns: bettering the representation of women and minorities, addressing public disengagement from politics, etc. Less idealistically, there have been suggestions that Labour may just have been trying to "wrong-foot" the Conservatives and keep them on the defensive, just as the Tories used to do to them.[120] With strategy in mind, Dunleavy and Margetts suggest the promise of voting system reform was extracted by the centre Liberal Democrats in return for Lib/lab cooperation with tactical voting in the constituencies to defeat the Tories in the general election.

Less attention has been paid to how Labour's position may reflect larger struggles and changes within the party itself. Today's Labour is hardly recognizable when compared to the party as it existed for most of the post-war period. Under Tony Blair the party jettisoned much of its traditional policy program, weakened the influence of activists in the party, and strengthened the hand of the leader to act unilaterally.[121] Some claim to see a similar pattern at work in the Labour government's democratic reforms.

A good deal of Labour's motives can be seen in its shifting positions on Scottish and Welsh devolution. Historically Labour opposed it for the same reasons that left parties everywhere opposed federalism, bicameralism, or a separation of powers – it might limit a central government's ability to act, particularly on the economy. As long as Labour was committed to its traditional interventionist approach to government and the economy, the party vigorously resisted devolution.[122] The rise of the Scottish Nationalist Party (SNP) in the 1970s cut into Labour's support in the region, traditionally a stronghold for the party, forcing it to concede a referendum on the issue in 1979. Though a majority endorsed the idea, it failed for lack of turnout. Tight competition with the SNP forced Labour to pay close attention to Scottish affairs in the 1980s and 1990s. In a series of constitutional conventions starting in 1989, Labour endorsed devolution and eventually a proportional scheme to elect a Scottish Parliament.[123] At the same time, Labour was in the process of backing off its traditional policy commitments to interventionism and an expanded welfare state, distancing itself from the "class politics" of "old Labour."[124] Thus Labour commitments to decentralization and "democracy," an apparent opening of the political system, must be balanced against its new commitments to neoliberalism, which have the effect of dramatically narrowing what this expanded democratic space can talk about.[125]

While reformers applauded what they saw as the good faith of the Labour government in keeping its promises about voting reform for European elections, the new London council, and devolution, critics charged that Blair's zeal for the job was all about settling scores within his own party. For instance, Labour members of the European Parliament (MEPs) complained that the leader deliberately introduced the party list form of PR for European elections to gain control over nominations and root out one of the final bastions of opposition to his remaking of the party.[126] Blair's later effort to rig Labour's nomination for the London mayoralty against his leftish MP Ken Livingstone appeared only to confirm this assessment. Even the government's much-vaunted power-sharing approach to devolution was decidedly asymmetrical and reflected Labour's biases about proportional voting. A dose of PR for the regions meant they would be much more representative, but it could also mean they would be less decisive, less likely to challenge the dominance of Westminster.[127]

Labour's institutional reforms around devolution and more proportional voting systems developed out of countless consultations – Scotland's constitutional conventions, contributors to the Plant reports, interaction and negotiation with community groups and even other political parties. In the run-up to the 1997 general election, Labour was keen to build the broadest coalition behind its program. The party went so far as to work publicly with the third-place Liberal Democrats in 1996, signing a number of pre-election agreements on democratic and constitutional reform.[128] But all this should not obscure where Labour's self-interest also dictated its commitment to reform. Labour's choices of voting system for Scotland and Wales were both designed to favour Labour, as subsequent election results have largely borne out.[129] It might be countered that Labour's keen action on devolution and voting system reform reflected its commitment to values supporting local governance and inclusion, or represent in part a principled response to public and stakeholder demands, but such views should not obscure how these decisions also reflected a pragmatic calculation of how much these policies would help the party without interfering with its own source of power at Westminster.[130] Thus Blair's efforts appear similar to Mitterrand's introduction of an element of PR to French municipalities and regions in the early 1980s – to more effectively "divide and rule" other political jurisdictions. The fact that Labour has repeatedly stalled on electoral reform at the national level only lends further credence to this interpretation.

Few leaders legislate away their own power base. But Labour's rapid work on devolution and the reform of European voting convinced many pundits that the party just might be serious about applying reform to itself as well: elections to the House of Commons. Of course, as a party Labour did not endorse any specific change to the country's voting system. Instead, it committed itself to a process where change could be considered, first through extensive research and consultation, and then via a national referendum on the question. For many in Labour, the promise was hardly threatening, as they felt confident that tradition would win out over "foreign" ways of doing things. Thus little opposition emerged when the Labour government appointed the Jenkins Commission in December 1997 to get the process started.

But before the commission could submit its report, a host of political developments began to subtly undermine Labour's continued commitment to the process. The initial results in Scotland under their additional member system of PR (essentially the MMP form of PR under a different name) witnessed a significant drop in Labour support from the national elections just one year earlier, forcing Labour there into a coalition government with the Liberal Democrats. This fuelled opposition within Labour's parliamentary caucus and furthered the organization of an explicitly anti-PR group of MPs. The report from Lord Jenkins did little to quell the growing opposition or inspire new support.[131]

Submitted in October 1998, the Jenkins report recommended the mildly proportional alternative vote plus, rejecting both the German-style MMP and Britain's traditional choice of proportional voting, STV. Many cried foul, claiming Jenkins's cosy relations with the new prime minister had influenced his deliberations. Dunleavy and Margetts report that Jenkins had an interim meeting with Blair where the prime minister nixed his plan to promote a more proportional additional member voting system.[132] Though Jenkins later denied improper influence, his conclusions bore a striking resemblance to Labour's own maximal position.[133] This perhaps pragmatic accommodation to power did little to speed the process. Interest in a report so timid in its recommendations for change evaporated quickly.[134] In the end, Labour broke its promise to hold a referendum on the question in its first term, though to keep Liberal Democrat support at election time it suggested it would be held in the future.[135] Yet afterward, a number of Labour MPs publicly spoke against the idea, government ministers floated non-proportional alternatives to Jenkins's proposals, and Blair continued to make vague promises to restart the process but refused to provide specific details.[136]

The remaking of Britain's Labour party in the 1980s and 1990s involved a calculated effort to resituate the party more closely to the perceived centre of British politics in the aftermath of the Thatcherite right-wing juggernaut. Tony Blair's New Labour gave up any pretence of class politics and instead embraced key elements of the new neoliberal economic model. Yet before his election victory in 1997 Blair could not be sure whether his lunge for the centre would work, and as a back-up he attempted to form a broad anti-Conservative coalition to secure victory, even countenancing electoral cooperation with the third-place Liberal Democrats.[137] In this context of uncertainty about reshaping Britain's party system, Labour leaders and activists made a weak commitment to consider slightly proportional voting system reforms. Labour's victories in 1997, 2001, and 2005 effectively shelved voting system reform initiatives at the national level, despite some positive noises on the issue early in Labour's first term.[138] However, for other electoral purposes – devolved regional government in Scotland, Wales, and Northern Ireland, local government in London, and for European elections – Labour's leadership turned to voting system reform as a means of dividing their political opponents in the party system and marginalizing opponents of New Labour's neoliberal project within the party as well.

Conclusion

Voting system reform burst onto the political agendas of a number of established democracies in the 1990s, fuelled by voter dissatisfaction with conventional politics and a larger process of party system change.

Yet in each case, the confluence of events had a slightly different trajectory. In New Zealand, citizens pushed voting system reform as a response to their frustration with the Labour party and its attempts to reposition the party on the political spectrum. In doing so, they faced opposition from both major parties. The public was also a force in Italy too, though here there were more traditional political forces also interested in change, particularly the former communists in the new social democratic party. In Japan voters were also fed up with politics as usual, though they expressed little interest in voting system reform. Here the parties championed a new voting system as a means of remaking their political coalitions and repositioning themselves in the party system – voter concerns simply formed a convenient backdrop. And in Britain, voting system reform emerged as part of Labour's campaign to return to government and shift the party towards the centre. As it turned out, Labour did not need a new voting system to reform itself, though the introduction of PR and semi-PR systems for European elections and at the sub-national level did serve the leadership's interest in dividing other levels of government and extending central party control over all aspects of the party. In all cases, the impinging changes in international political economy, with support both within and outside the nation-state, put pressure on traditional political coalitions and conventional approaches to economic regulation. In each country, the decisions of left parties and the nature of the support or opposition they faced, would prove a key factor in how voting system reform emerged, or whether it emerged at all.

In this examination of successful voting system reform in a number of countries, reform emerged as left parties tried to redefine themselves and their place in the party system. Earlier public discussions on the subject in Ireland, the Netherlands, and Canada – where the left was not factor – stalled. France was the turning point. Faced with declining party capacities, a weak partner on the left, and national and international pressures to abandon the post-war economic compromise, the Socialists moved to the right and turned to PR to shift the party system in their favour. Though PR did not last, the shift in the French party system did occur, setting an example for how institutions could serve as renewed sites of struggle in securing other political and economic ends.

French political struggles involving party and class in the late 1980s were not unique. By the 1990s all western countries witnessed an intensification of neoliberal pressure and a decline of left parties (if not support). In New Zealand, Italy, Japan, and the United Kingdom, this also manifested in institutional struggles and reform, though in different ways. In New Zealand support for voting system reform emerged primarily out of struggles within the Labour party over its government's neoliberal economic policies. As activists lost the battle within the party, reform became an attractive strategy to discipline the party and open up new avenues of resistance to neoliberalism (through the election of new parties). In Italy, increasing European economic integration highlighted the unsustainability of the country's clientelist politics and economy. Though sustained by the DC and an opportunistic PSI, business and regional unrest cut into their traditional voter base. When the PCI reinvented itself as the social democratic PDS, it precipitated a split with its more orthodox left wing and eased its move to the centre. Subsequently the party decided to reassess its strategies and reversed its longstanding support of PR, thus opening a space for electoral reform. But when it pursued neoliberal policies in government, both the right and far left fought to stem the process of electoral reform (the right because it wanted to occupy that policy space, and the far left because it opposed it). In Japan the influence of the left was arguably the weakest, given the strength of the LDP hold on power. Still, the pressures of a changing international economy altered the incentives for both LDP and opposition parties, leading to consensus on voting system reform after decades of intransigent debate. The decision of the left-led opposition to compromise arguably started the process. In Britain, voting system reform emerged as part of Labour's broad coalition strategy to get back into power after an eighteen-year absence and to aid Tony Blair in his struggle to remake the party and marginalize his left critics.

Across all three countries a number of factors coincided, contributing to voting system reform, including a changing international political economy that required some local response, a change in the relationship of left voters and their parties, changes to the national and international media systems accentuating election campaign style over substance, and changes within left parties strengthening leadership groups at the expense of members and activists. How those factors aided electoral reform depended on the particular development of the party system in each country and the nature of past institutional manifestations of party struggle. The role of left parties, more than others, has been highlighted because historically the left's statist aspirations fuelled previous democratization efforts. In the early twentieth century, and again after the Second World War, the left mobilized a sizeable working-class constituency and aroused powerful opposition, often leading to struggles for proportional voting where government was within its grasp. But the recent breakdown of the post-war regime of international trade, along with the increasing estrangement of left parties from their core support, has led to struggles to reorient the left away from its traditional state approach and policy goals. These struggles created an opening for the reconsideration of voting systems, either to fight the neoliberalization of the left, as in New Zealand, or help entrench it, as in France, Italy, Japan, and the United Kingdom.

Chapter 8

Conclusion

It had long been considered a truism of modern political science that voting systems in western industrialized countries were nearly impossible to change, barring severe political crisis. In fact, true to this conservative bias, a host of political scientists had predicted that the latest round of reforms in the 1990s would not succeed – just before they did.[1] Just as the changes in Eastern Europe, Germany, and South Africa had evaded the predictive capacities of contemporary political scientists, so too did the latest round of voting system reform catch the profession unaware and scrambling for some means to explain it. As Pippa Norris candidly admitted on behalf of the discipline shortly after the first wave of reform in the early 1990s, "We lack a theoretical framework to understand how political systems reform basic constitutional principles."[2] Needless to say, the work that has emerged since then has focused mostly on recent events, with little attempt to fashion a comparative explanation across space, let alone historical time.

This book set out to discover what commonalities existed, if any, across the range of cases of voting system reform in western industrialized countries over the last century. Previous scholarship and the striking cross-national trends in voting system reform in a number of different historical periods suggested that something common was at work. Quantitative studies matched the incidence of multiparty politics and the rise of left parties specifically with voting system reform but struggled to say just why or how they were related. Given their inattention to historical contexts, they could only speculate about the relationships. Other scholars who did attend more to the specific contexts of voting system reform did so in a way that ignored the sequence of historical events, either offering a summary of all the protagonists calling for reform (suggesting that reform came to satisfy their demands) or reading a causal account back from what appeared to be its later effects (the fact that PR better represented minority opinion meant that PR must have been introduced to accomplish this). Given the paucity of historical and comparative work on voting system reform specifically, most of these observations had remained untested.

By contrast, this study has focused on the importance of context in explaining change, working up an over-arching explanation through a close examination of all the cases of serious voting system reform efforts in western industrialized countries. This has involved taking insights from past work (the influence of multipartism, left parties, democratization) and connecting them to the larger historical contexts within which these actors and processes were embedded. By using a critical institutionalist approach, we have attempted to link some of the larger social dynamics animating western societies to these struggles over institutional rules. This was accomplished by paying closer attention to the historical fluidity of terms like *democracy*, recognizing that what democracy would be has never been fixed. Instead, the parameters of democracy in western societies have themselves been the subject of social and political struggle, initially to gain or resist something called "democratic government" and then to control or shape what states might do under such a label. As a result, the book has focused on struggles to politicize economic and social cleavages, how this informed and affected the party system and spawned responses from other political forces. Specifically it has attended to the emergence of a working-class cleavage, and its subsequent manifestation as a political cleavage in socialist and labour parties. Past work had suggested that left parties were key to reform. This study sought to explain why this was so, focusing particularly on the perceived threat left parties posed to the political system through their promotion of a distinct "democratic imaginary," and how this influenced institutional reforms like a change in voting system. It was suggested that voting system reforms have largely been a response to these challenges, though each particular context witnessed the manifestation of this threat in distinctive ways that involved different mixes of players and unique combinations of events.

The results of this study confirm that there is something common to all efforts at voting system reform in western countries. Reforms have emerged in the context of historical struggles to either limit or expand the popular democratic character of western governing systems. In each of the historical periods, from the late nineteenth century, to the

First World War, to the Cold War, to the 1990s, struggles to make and unmake political cleavages and alter the national/international regulation of capitalism have spurred voting system reform. But this is too broad a claim, almost as broad as previous explanations that attributed change in voting systems to multipartism or left parties. That is why attention has been paid here to the historical sequence of events, to allow an explanation of just *how* these factors have influenced this process. In different historical periods and in different places within any given period, struggles over voting system reform have been mediated by variations in class structure, political development, party system dynamics, and the impact of international events.

This attention to the specific contexts of reform initiatives and the sequence of historical events has challenged many conventional assertions of past work on the subject. Commentators on nineteenth-century voting system reforms focused on the importance of demands for minority representation and the key interventions of voting system reform associations and intellectuals. But attention to the historical details of the various efforts provides scant evidence for such views. Braunias and Rokkan's characterization of the nineteenth century as the "minority representation" phase of voting system reform cannot be sustained – nowhere in western countries did minority concerns fuel a change of voting system at the national level in the nineteenth century (or thereafter), and even changes at the cantonal level in Switzerland, allegedly to address minority concerns, are poorly documented. Instead, voting system reform emerges as a serious issue in this period only under the pressure of class factors, specifically the twin impact of the emergence of a new working-class cleavage and its manifestation politically in unions and left political parties. Though religious and ethnic minorities long called for voting system reforms to accommodate them in the nineteenth and early twentieth century, they got little response until left parties began organizing working people politically in the 1890s. This is clear from the only case of successful national voting system reform in the nineteenth century, Belgium in 1899, and with conservative responses to the left in Germany and Sweden in the same period.

Over the last century, then, voting system reform in western industrialized countries has borne the distinct imprint of class via these struggles over democracy. In nearly all our cases, stretching from the late nineteenth century to the late twentieth century, from New Zealand to the heart of Europe, behind the struggles to change the voting system were struggles to alter the balance of power affecting the state. In every period under study and in all the countries sponsoring a national change, the point was to shift whatever was the conventional understanding of what the state "should" do, to remake the boundaries of what was acceptable politically as democratic action. Left political parties, whether on the rise or in decline, were key actors fuelling considerations of change. On occasion other factors – like concern for the political inclusion of religious and ethnic minorities, or a desire for single-party governing majorities or alternation in government – have been raised, but they have never secured a voting system reform on their own. Close attention to the historical sequence of the events leading to successful voting system reforms clearly demonstrates that these concerns have required the added stimulus of class-based disputes to force through any change.

The findings of these historical explorations of different western countries in previous chapters suggest that class has defined the process of voting system reform over our different historical periods, primarily because of the tensions inherent in first establishing and then maintaining the specifically capitalist form of democracy that emerged in western countries. This tension was fuelled primarily by the rise of left political parties throughout western countries in the late nineteenth century. Left parties championed democracy as a means of turning the state towards the economic and social concerns of the working class, and their distinctive form of organization allowed them to mobilize mass levels of support. Throughout the twentieth century the left's expansive "democratic imaginary" inspired mass support and strong opposition from bourgeois forces and traditional political elites. Voting system reforms emerged again and again as one means of responding to the political machinations of the left.

Voting system reform *specifically* became central to the management of capitalist democracy in a host of cases because voting rules essentially establish the aperture of the political system (under conditions of full suffrage and responsible government), regulating how open or closed political competition will be. Where the left appeared strong and set to take power, PR was attractive to conventional political elites as a means of limiting the burgeoning left-wing levels of support and maximizing their own. Essentially the right sought assurances that if the left were to wield majority power, it would require a real majority of popular support, unlike the inflated majorities the right had long enjoyed under plurality and majority voting systems. But these responses to the left were not consistent across all jurisdictions. Though Anglo-American

countries seriously considered voting system reforms, particularly after the First World War, their political elites tended to be more experienced with mass political processes affecting government than their
counterparts in Europe, and more confident about being able to contain
them without changing voting procedures. At the same time, the Anglo-
American left was defined more in terms of "political labour" than
socialism and as such appeared to pose less of a threat than the more
explicitly socialist parties of Europe (and it also appeared electorally
weaker; where it was strong – Australia – it did inspire modest voting
system reforms). Even within Europe, the left's challenge was not consistent. Important differences in class structures, for instance, contributed to the institutional weakness of the French left and the limited and
temporary nature of its voting system reforms in a number of periods.

We can make similar observations in comparing the left's influence
across the four key periods of reform, highlighting the reciprocal influences between the left and its opponents, how changing material conditions have influenced the capacity of the left, and how international
events like war and revolution have had a great impact on reform results. In the late nineteenth century the left proved too weak in most
cases to secure full male suffrage, let alone anything that might prop-
erly be called democracy, though conservative regimes struck upon PR
as a means of dividing their opponents and avoiding both parliamentarization and democracy, and many did take up reform in the early years
of the twentieth century. In the period around the First World War concerns about the rising power of the left and the uncertain conditions of
war motivated a shift to PR in a few neutral countries in Europe. After
the war, faced with the influence of the Russian Revolution and domestic social upheaval, a form of minimally democratic rule was established almost everywhere in western countries, with PR as the price of
liberal and conservative acquiescence, at least in Europe. Similar conditions held PR in place in much of Europe following the Second World
War, though in the Continent's three biggest countries debate over voting systems would be influenced by the strength of public commitment
to a nebulous "social" democracy, the electoral strength of western
Communist parties, the proximity of the Soviet Union, and eventually
the pressures of the Cold War.

But by the 1990s the "threat" of the left to capitalist democracies had
largely evaporated. Now voting system reform emerged as a result of
the weakness of the left, as a response by left parties to help fix a new
centrist position for themselves in the political spectrum, or as a means

by which social forces could attempt to hold left parties to their historic cleavages, or push polities towards a more full embrace of neoliberalism. Over the course of the twentieth century the organizational methods of left mass parties were eventually mimicked by the right, while other capitalist activity eventually mobilized working people away from left networks of support, through consumerism, urban sprawl, or the state sponsorship of social services provided formerly by the left. Though the class cleavage has remained salient, class as a political cleavage had lost much of its power by the 1990s. This is one reason that the latest wave of reform is so different. Here the left itself has tried to manipulate the voting rules to sustain its competitive position, often by distancing itself from its own political coalition. Or left supporters have tried to use voting system reform as a means of anchoring left parties to their traditional constituencies. Or the right has attempted to change voting systems to break up the party system coalitions hindering its radical transformation of the mode of economic regulation, thus seeking by institutional change an opening to force through neoliberal reforms, an example of a reversal of the class "threat."

In all this, the historical dimension of the conclusions must be underlined. Attempts at "process tracing" miss the point. There are no singular or static processes that can be mapped. Historical struggles are too contingent; political actors and their choices are fundamentally too unpredictable. Instead, the best we can do is attempt to retrospectively explain why we think different struggles turned out the way they did or why certain actors made the decisions they did. In this study, voting system reform in the twentieth century west has been linked to ongoing struggles over the shape of democracy itself, struggles involving the management of the tension between their capitalist context and democratic pretensions. That has relied on a class threat from the left to hold any tension. But prior to the rise of an organized left, voting system reforms emerged as a means to political advantage by traditional competing elites (as in Denmark, Britain, the United States, and Canada in the mid- to late nineteenth century), or where the left remained weak, voting system reforms proved attractive to colonial powers as a method to divide and rule (as in the British and French Empires from the late nineteenth to mid-twentieth centuries). With the near collapse of the left as an electoral, mobilizing, or counter-hegemonic threat today, the conditions that fuelled consideration of new voting systems in the twentieth century in western industrialized countries may not hold. As voter turnouts plummet in western countries and election campaigns appear more and more defined by those who finance them, existing mostly in a virtual rather than physical space, the critical tension in capitalist democracies may be decisively shifting.[3] Voting system reform processes continue to unfold around the world in the twenty-first century, but whether the dynamic sketched out here will continue to fuel them can be ascertained only by bringing these historical and comparative insights into dialogue with a context-specific exploration of these new conditions and possibly new dynamics.

Notes

Chapter 1

1 Alan Renwick, *The Politics of Electoral Reform: Changing the Rules of Democracy* (Cambridge: Cambridge University Press, 2010), 1.
2 Ibid., 41.
3 For example, Renwick's *Politics of Electoral Reform*; André Blais, ed., *To Keep or to Change First Past the Post: The Politics of Electoral Reform* (Oxford: Oxford University Press, 2008); Michael Gallagher and Paul Mitchell, eds., *The Politics of Electoral Systems* (Oxford: Oxford University Press, 2005).
4 Nor is this new insight. Benjamin Barber quotes historian Alfred A. Cobban making a similar complaint in 1960: "The political scientist, in so far as he wishes to remain a scientist, is limited to the study of techniques. A good deal of what is called political science, I must confess, seems to me a device, invented by academic persons, [for] avoiding that dangerous subject politics, without achieving science." As cited in Benjamin Barber, "The Politics of Political Science: 'Value-Free' Theory and the Wolin-Strauss Dust-up of 1963," *American Political Science Review* 100, no. 4 (Nov. 2006): 539–45.
5 Amongst academics, there exist differences in typologizing the various voting systems (whether they should be considered majority or proportional or mixed, etc.), with some categorizing voting systems on the basis of their constituent components (decision rule, districting, ballot structure, etc.), while others focus more on the results various voting systems produce (plural, majority, or proportional). For the former view, see André Blais, "The Classification of Electoral Systems," *European Journal of Political Research* 16, no. 1 (1988): 99–110; and Louis Massicotte and André Blais, "Mixed Electoral Systems: A Conceptual and Empirical Survey," *Electoral Studies* 18, no. 3 (1999): 341–66. This study will follow the latter approach,

which aligns more closely with historical usage and follows the practices of political actors rather than academics.

6 For just a few representative works, see Maurice Duverger, *Political Parties* (1954; repr., London: Methuen, 1963); David P. Quintal, "The Theory of Electoral Systems," *Western Political Quarterly* 23, no. 4 (1970): 752–61; Douglas Rae, *The Political Consequences of Electoral Law* (New Haven: Yale University Press, 1971); Vernon Bogdanor and David Butler, eds., *Democracy and Elections: Electoral Systems and Their Political Consequences* (Cambridge: Cambridge University Press, 1983); Gary W. Cox, *Making Votes Count: Strategic Coordination in the World's Electoral Systems* (Cambridge: Cambridge University Press, 1997).

7 Pippa Norris, "Introduction: The Politics of Electoral Reform," *International Political Science Review* 16, no. 1 (1995): 4.

8 This process is neatly summed in David Brian Robertson, "The Return to History and the New Institutionalism in American Political Science," *Social Science History* 17, no. 1 (Spring 1993): 1–36.

9 Initially a critique from the left, interest in the state eventually spread across the spectrum in political science. From the left, see Ralph Miliband, *The State in Capitalist Society* (1969; London: Quartet Books, 1973); James O'Connor, *The Fiscal Crisis of the State* (New York: St Martin's, 1973); and Nicos Poulantzas, *Political Power and Social Classes* (1968; London: Verso, 1978). For its incorporation into the mainstream of political science, see Eric A. Nordlinger, *On the Autonomy of the Democratic State* (Cambridge: Harvard University Press, 1981); P. Evans, D. Rueschemeyer, and T. Skocpol, eds., *Bringing the State Back In* (Cambridge: Cambridge University Press, 1985); and Peter A. Hall and Rosemary C.R. Taylor, "Political Science and the Three New Institutionalisms," *Political Studies* 44, no. 5 (1996), 936–57.

10 Matthew Shugart, "Comparative Electoral Systems Research: The Maturation of a Field and New Challenges Ahead," in *The Politics of Electoral Systems*, ed. M. Gallagher and P. Mitchell (Oxford: Oxford University Press, 2005), 51; Kenneth Benoit, "Electoral Laws as Political Consequences: Explaining the Origins and Change of Electoral Institutions," *Annual Review of Political Science* 10, no. 1 (2007): 387.

11 For a laudable exception to this trend, see Michael Bernhard, *Institutions and the Fate of Democracy* (Pittsburgh: University of Pittsburgh Press, 2005). As Bernhard notes, the "failure of fully understand the motivations of actors can lead to mistaken conclusions about what the outcomes of processes of institutional choice meant or even the significance of the outcome in general," while a "failure to adequately understand the historical background of

a process of institutional choice can lead to mistaken interpretations of the significance of outcomes" (14).

12 The concept of "deep politics" is borrowed from Luckham, Goetz, and Kaldor and is meant to contrast the conventional political science characterizations of politics as merely political elite or voter behaviour and institutional processes with an approach that examines the intersections between society and institutions, recognizing that societies everywhere are unequal and that this affects the interactions. In other words, for them, the social relations that exist in democracies and the character of social and state conflict must be factored into any analysis of "actually existing democracy." See Robin Luckham, Anne Marie Goetz, and Mary Kaldor, "Democratic Institutions and Democratic Politics," in *Can Democracy Be Designed?*, ed. S. Bastian and R. Luckham, 14–59 (New York: Zed Books, 2003).

13 As quoted in Arend Lijphart, *Electoral Systems and Party Systems: A Study of Twenty-Seven Democracies, 1945–1990* (Oxford: Oxford University Press, 1994), 139.

14 R. Kenneth Carty, André Blais, and Patrick Fournier, "When Citizens Choose to Reform SMP: The British Columbia Citizens' Assembly on Electoral Reform," in Blais, *To Keep or to Change First Past the Post?*, 150, 158.

15 These problems are explored in Dennis Pilon, "Investigating Media as a Deliberative Space: Newspaper Opinions about Voting Systems in the 2007 Ontario Provincial Referendum," *Canadian Political Science Review* 3, no. 3 (Sept. 2009): 1–23.

16 For some insight into non-Western voting systems and patterns of reform, see Mark P. Jones, "A Guide to the Electoral Systems of the Americas," *Electoral Studies* 14, no. 1 (1995): 5–21; Andrew Reynolds, *Electoral Systems and Democratization in Southern Africa* (Oxford: Oxford University Press, 1999); Bernard Grofman, Sung-Chull Lee, Edwin A. Winckler, and Brian Woodall., eds., *Elections in Japan, Korea, and Taiwan under the Single Non-Transferable Vote* (Ann Arbor: University of Michigan Press, 1999); and Karen L. Remner, "The Politics of Institutional Change: Electoral Reform in Latin America, 1978–2002," *Party Politics* 14, no. 1 (2008): 5–30. For a discussion of how non-Western patterns of "modernization" differed from Western experience, see Paul Cammack, "Democratization and Citizenship in Latin America," in *Democracy and Democratization*, ed. Gerraint Parry and Michael Moran, 174–95 (London: Routledge, 1994).

17 For examples of this sort of indiscriminate comparison between Western and non-Western countries, see Mathew Soberg Shugart, "'Extreme' Electoral Systems and the Appeal of the Mixed-Member Alternative," in *Mixed*

Member Electoral Systems: The Best of Both Worlds?, ed. M. Shugart and Martin P. Wattenberg, 25–51 (Oxford: Oxford University Press, 2001); Josep Colomer, "The Strategy and History of Electoral System Choice," in *Handbook of Electoral System Choice*, ed. J. Colomer (New York: Palgrave-Macmillan, 2004), specifically section 3, "The Electoral System Evolution," 53–68; Benoit, "Electoral Laws as Political Consequences," 363–89; and Krister Lundell, *The Origins of Electoral Systems in the Postwar Era* (New York: Routledge, 2009). For a rare example of a study of electoral reform that does appreciate the specificity of non-Western development, see Sunil Bastian, "The Political Economy of Electoral Reform: Proportional Representation in Sri Lanka," in Bastian and Luckham, *Can Democracy be Designed?*, 196–219.

18 It should be underlined that European and Anglo-American countries can be considered "similar" only in the broadest terms, as remarkable differences in economic and political development exist among them. The most obvious examples include the stark differences in political development between Continental Europe and the Anglo-American countries, and the economic differences between northern and southern Europe. Yet these countries are more similar to each other in economic and political terms than they are to non-Western countries.

19 See John R. Commons, *Proportional Representation*, 2nd ed. (1907; reprint, New York: August M. Kelley Publishers, 1967); Clarence G. Hoag and George Hallett Jr, *Proportional Representation* (New York: Macmillan, 1926); Joseph P. Harris, "The Practical Workings of Proportional Representation in the United States and Canada," *National Municipal Review* 19, no. S5 (May 1930): S335–S83; and Ferdinand A. Hermans, *Democracy or Anarchy? A Study of Proportional Representation* (1941; New York: Johnson Reprint, 1972).

20 Richard Bendix, *Nation-Building and Citizenship: Studies of Our Changing Social Order* (New York: Wiley, 1964); Duverger, *Political Parties*; Stein Rokkan, *Citizens, Elections, Parties* (New York: David McKay, 1970).

21 Vernon Bogdanor, "Conclusion: Electoral Systems and Party Systems," in Bogdanor and Butler, *Democracy and Elections*, 252; Arend Lijphart, *Patterns of Democracy* (New Haven: Yale University Press, 1999), 306.

22 Andrew McLaren Carstairs, *A Short History of Electoral Systems in Western Europe* (London: George Allen and Unwin, 1980), 4; Bo Sarlvik, "Scandinavia," in Bogdanor and Butler, *Democracy and Elections*, 123.

23 Norris, "Introduction," 3–4.

24 Patrick Dunleavy and Helen Margetts, "Understanding the Dynamics of Electoral Reform," *International Political Science Review* 16, no. 1 (1995): 11;

David Farrell, *Electoral Systems: A Comparative Introduction* (New York: Palgrave, 2001), 179.

25 See Pippa Norris, *Electoral Engineering: Voting Rules and Political Behavior* (Cambridge: Cambridge University Press, 2004), specifically chapter 1.

26 See various contributors to R.J. Dalton, S.C. Flanagan, and P.A. Beck, eds., *Electoral Change in Advanced Industrial Democracies: Realignment or Dealignment?* (New Jersey: Princeton University Press, 1984).

27 See Dunleavy and Margetts, "Understanding the Dynamics of Electoral Reform," 24–5; David Denemark, "Choosing MMP in New Zealand: Explaining the 1993 Electoral Reform," in Shugart and Wattenberg, *Mixed Member Electoral Systems*, 71–5; Mark Donovan, "The Politics of Electoral Reform in Italy," *International Political Science Review* 16, no. 1 (1995): 51–2; Raymond Christensen, "Electoral Reform in Japan: How It Was Enacted and Changes It May Bring," *Asian Survey* 34, no. 7 (July 1994): 594–9; and Eugene L. Wolfe, "Japanese Electoral and Political Reform: Role of the Young Turks," *Asian Survey* 35, no. 12 (Dec. 1995): 1070–3.

28 For a discussion of these developments, see Mark Donovan and David Broughton, "Party System Change in Western Europe: Positively Political," in *Changing Party Systems in Western Europe*, ed. D. Broughton and M. Donovan, 255–74 (London: Pinter, 1999).

29 Norris, "Introduction," 7; Shugart, "'Extreme' Electoral Systems and the Appeal of the Mixed-Member Alternative," 26–8.

30 Dunleavy and Margetts, "Understanding the Dynamics of Electoral Reform," 25–7; Patrick Dunleavy and Helen Margetts, "The United Kingdom: Reforming the Westminster Model," in Colomer, *Handbook of Electoral System Choice*, 301; P. Dunleavy and H. Margetts, "From Majoritarian to Pluralist Democracy? Electoral Reform in Britain since 1997," *Journal of Theoretical Politics* 13, no. 3 (2001): 310–11.

31 Shugart, "'Extreme' Electoral Systems and the Appeal of the Mixed-Member Alternative," 25–7.

32 Ibid., 27–8.

33 Keith Jackson and Alan McRobie, *New Zealand Adopts Proportional Representation* (Aldershot: Ashgate, 1998), 19–20.

34 See Ronald Rogowski, "Trade and the Variety of Democratic Institutions," *International Organization* 41, no. 2 (Spring 1987): 203–23; Kathleen Bawm, "The Logic of Institutional Preferences: German Electoral Law as a Social Choice Outcome," *American Journal of Political Science* 37, no. 4 (1993): 965–89; and F.E. Lehoucq, "Institutional Change and Political Conflict: Evaluating Alternative Explanations of Electoral Reform in Costa Rica," *Electoral Studies* 14, no. 1 (1995): 23–45. Another version of this argument

focuses on how winners tend to like existing rules, and losers are more open to change. See Shaun Bowler, Todd Donovan, and Jeffrey A. Karp, "Why Politicians Like Electoral Institutions: Self Interest, Values, or Ideology," *Journal of Politics* 68, no. 2 (May 2006): 434–46.

35 See the debate in a special issue of the *Journal of Theoretical Politics*, particularly Gerard Alexander, "Institutions, Path Dependence, and Democratic Consolidation," *Journal of Theoretical Politics* 13, no. 3 (2001): 249–70; and Kenneth A. Shepsle, "A Comment on Institutional Change," *Journal of Theoretical Politics* 13, no. 3 (2001): 321–25.

36 Colomer, "Strategy and History of Electoral System Choice," 3–10.

37 Thomas Cusack, Torben Iversen, and David Soskice, "Economic Interests and the Origins of Electoral Systems," *American Political Science Review* 101, no. 3 (Aug. 2007): 373–91; Carles Boix, "Setting the Rules of the Game: The Choice of Electoral Systems in Advanced Democracies," *American Political Science Review* 93, no. 3 (Sept. 1999): 609–24; Barbara Sgouraki Kinsey and Olga Shvetsova, "Applying the Methodology of Mechanism Design to the Choice of Electoral Systems," *Journal of Theoretical Politics* 20, no. 3 (2008): 303–27; Josephine T. Andrews and Robert W. Jackman, "Strategic Fools: Electoral Rule Choice under Extreme Uncertainty," *Electoral Studies* 24, no. 1 (2005): 64–85. Some analysts working in this tradition do attempt to gauge uncertainty; see Jean-Benoit Pilet and Damien Bol, "Party Preferences and Electoral Reform: How Time in Government Affects the Likelihood of Supporting Electoral Change," *West European Politics* 34, no. 3 (2011): 568–86.

38 For a review of recent developments, see Ellen M. Immergut and Karen M. Anderson, "Historical Institutionalism and West European Politics," *West European Politics* 31, nos 1–2 (Jan.–Mar. 2008): 345–69.

39 Renwick, *Politics of Electoral Reform*, 24; Marcus Kreuzer, "Historical Knowledge and Quantitative Analysis: The Case of the Origins of Proportional Representation," *American Political Science Review* 104, no. 2 (May 2010): 369–92. Others are not so sure that the problem is merely one of mixing methods. For an excellent review of the methodological limits of quantitative as compared to historical work, see Giovanni Capoccia and Daniel Ziblatt, "The Historical Turn in Democratization Studies: A New Research Agenda for Europe and Beyond," *Comparative Political Studies* 43, nos 8–9 (2010): 945–7.

40 However, though not explicitly a historical institutionalist analysis, Lundell does discount rational choice arguments for most voting system adoptions in the postwar period, arguing that cultural and institutional legacies were more important. Following Massicotte et al., for instance, he suggests that

colonial inheritance explains most voting system origins in the former British and French colonies. See Krister Lundell, *The Origins of Electoral Systems in the Postwar Era* (New York: Routledge), esp. chaps 5 and 6; and Louis Massicotte, André Blais, and Antoine Yoshinaka, *Establishing the Rules of the Game: Election Laws in Democracies* (Toronto: University of Toronto Press, 2004).

41 For example, see Jenifer Hart, *Proportional Representation: Critics of the British Electoral System, 1820–1945* (Oxford: Clarendon, 1992); Jackson and McRobie, *New Zealand Adopts Proportional Representation*; Shaun Bowler and Bernard Grofman, eds., *Elections in Australia, Ireland, and Malta under the Single Transferable Vote* (Ann Arbor: University of Michigan Press, 2000).

42 Renwick, *Politics of Electoral Reform*, 2, 7. A notable exception is Bernhard, *Institutions and the Fate of Democracy*, which compares the development of democratic institutions, including the voting system, in Poland and Germany after both world wars.

43 Renwick sets out the details of his framework in chapters 2, 3, and 4.

44 Other examples include Gideon Rahat and Reuven Y. Hazan, "The Barriers to Electoral System Reform: A Synthesis of Alternative Approaches," *West European Politics* 34, no. 3 (2011): 478–94; Marc Hooghe and Kris Deschouwer, "Veto Players and Electoral Reform in Belgium," *West European Politics* 34, no. 3 (2011): 626–43; Gideon Rahat, "The Study of the Politics of Electoral Reform in the 1990s: Theoretical and Methodological Lessons," *Comparative Politics* 36, no. 4 (July 2004): 461–79.

45 Renwick, *Politics of Electoral Reform*, 101–2.

46 George Ross, "Destroyed by the Dialectic: Politics, the Decline of Marxism, and the New Middle Strata in France," *Theory and Society* 16 (1987): 27, 31. The government's efforts are given in more detail in George Ross and Jane Jenson, "Strategy and Contradiction in the Victory of French Socialism," in *Socialist Register 1981*, ed. R. Miliband and J. Saville, 98–103 (London: Merlin, 1981); Maurice Larkin, *France since the Popular Front, 1936–1996*, chap. 19, "Keynesianism in One Country: The Socialist Experiment," 356–81; and Donald Sassoon, *One Hundred Years of Socialism* (New York: New Press, 1996), chap. 19, "The French Experiment," 534–71.

47 These problems are summed in Ellen M. Immergut, "Historical-Institutionalism in Political Science and the Problem of Change," in *Understanding Change: Models, Methodologies, and Metaphors*, ed. Andreas Wimmer and Reinhart Kossler, 237–59 (Basingstoke: Palgrave, 2005).

48 For a discussion of the second wave and its proposed solutions, see B. Guy Peters, Jon Pierre, and Desmond S. King, "The Politics of Path Dependency: Political Conflict in Historical Institutionalism," *Journal of Politics*

67, no. 4 (Nov. 2005): 1275–1300; Sven Steinmo, "Historical Institutionalism," in *Approaches and Methodologies in the Social Sciences*, ed. Donatella
Della Porta and Michael Keating, 118–38 (Cambridge: Cambridge University Press, 2008); Peter A. Hall and Kathleen Thelen, "Institutional Change
in Varieties of Capitalism," *Socio-Economic Review* 7 (2009): 7–34.

49 See Jane Jenson and Frederic Merand, "Sociology, Institutionalism and the
European Union," *Comparative European Politics* 8, no. 1 (2010): 80, 82.

50 Ibid., 82.

51 An obvious example of this tradition would be Charles Mair, *Recasting
Bourgeois Europe* (1975; Princeton: Princeton University Press, 1988).

52 Amel Ahmed, "Reading History Forward: The Origins of Electoral Systems
in European Democracies," *Comparative Political Studies* 43, nos 8–9 (2010):
1059–88; Amel F. Ahmed, "Constituting the Electorate: Voting System
Reform and Working Class Incorporation in France, the United Kingdom
and the United States, 1867–1913" (PhD diss., University of Pennsylvania,
2006); Dennis Pilon, "Explaining Voting System Reform in Canada: 1874
to 1960," *Journal of Canadian Studies* 40, no. 3 (Autumn 2006): 135–61; Sanil
Bastian, "The Political Economy of Electoral Reform: Proportional Representation in Sri Lanka," in *Can Democracy Be Designed?*, ed. S. Bastian and
R. Luckham, 196–219 (London: Zed Books, 2003); and David Pottie and
Shireen Hassim, "The Politics of Institutional Design in the South African
Tradition," in Bastian and Luckham, *Can Democracy Be Designed?*, 60–92.

53 Monique Leyenaar and Reuven Y. Hazan, "Reconceptualising Electoral
Reform," *West European Politics* 34, no. 3 (2011): 437–55.

54 Colin Hay, *Political Analysis* (Houndmills: Palgrave Macmillan, 2002), 53.

55 Ibid., 54. These problems are neatly summed in Capoccia and Ziblatt,
"Historical Turn in Democratization Studies," 945–7.

56 Hay, *Political Analysis*, 53.

57 As cited in Dietrich Rueschemeyer, "Can One or a Few Cases Yield
Theoretical Gains?," in *Comparative Historical Analysis in the Social Sciences*,
ed. J. Mahoney and D. Rueschemeyer, 305–36 (Cambridge: Cambridge
University Press, 2003).

58 E.P. Thompson, *The Poverty of Theory* (Manchester: Merlin, 1978), 67.

59 P.A. Lewis, "Agency, Structure and Causality in Political Science: A
Comment on Sibeon," *Politics* 22, no. 1 (Feb. 2002): 17–23; Hay, *Political
Analysis*, chap. 3.

60 James Mahoney and Dietrich Rueschemeyer, "Comparative Historical
Analysis: Achievements and Agendas," in Mahoney and Rueschemeyer,
Comparative Historical Analysis in the Social Sciences, 4, 6.

61 Hay, *Political Analysis*, 47. This is succinctly captured by Bonnell as "history mediated by theory." See Victoria E. Bonnell, "The Uses of Theory, Concepts and Comparison in Historical Sociology," *Comparative Studies in Society and History* 22, no. 2 (Apr. 1980): 156–73.

62 Kathleen Thelen and Sven Steinmo, "Historical Institutionalism in Comparative Politics," in *Structuring Politics: Historical Institutionalism in Comparative Politics*, ed. S. Steinmo, K. Thelen, and F. Longstreth (Cambridge: Cambridge University Press, 1992), 9.

63 Capoccia and Ziblatt, "Historical Turn in Democratization Studies," 943.

64 However, it should be underlined that there is and has never been *one* comparative historical method – the term captures a multitude of different approaches that all loosely draw on history to make comparisons. For an early statement of this heterogeneity, see Theda Skocpol and Margaret Somers, "The Uses of Comparative History in Macrosocial Inquiry," *Comparative Studies in Society and History* 22, no. 2 (Apr. 1980), 174–97.

65 See Hugh Stretton, *The Political Sciences* (London: Routledge and Kegan Paul, 1969), 60–1; A. Hacker, "Inescapable Subjective Judgments," in *The Practice of Comparative Politics*, ed. P. Lewis, D. Potter, and F. Castles, 214–27 (London: Longman, 1978).

66 See Mahoney and Rueschemeyer, "Comparative Historical Analysis," 8; and G.K. Roberts, "The Explanation of Politics: Comparison, Strategy and Theory," in *The Practice of Comparative Politics*, 2nd ed., ed. P.G. Lewis, D.C. Potter, and F.G. Castles (London: Longman, 1978), 293.

67 Renwick, *Politics of Electoral Reform*, 3–4. Again, Bernhart and Renwick are exceptions.

68 This is not to disparage Carstairs's accomplishment, which covered a number of countries across a considerable amount of time in one short book. Indeed, this study will draw on insights from Carstairs when relevant. Rather, the point is to underline that while most of political science eschews historical analysis as insufficiently rigorous, they nonetheless rely on it when convenient or necessary, and that, when they do, they do not appear to apply much rigour in deciding what to use. For an illustrative example, see André Blais, Agnieszka Dobrzynska, and Indridi H. Indridason, "To Adopt or Not Adopt Proportional Representation: The Politics of Institutional Choice," *British Journal of Political Science* 35, no. 1 (2004): 182–5, 189. In this piece, Blais et al. rely primarily on quantitative techniques but bolster their claims by citing historical work, which basically amounts to Carstairs. Nor do political scientists, as a rule, tend to appreciate the complexity of historical analysis or the depth and range of

debates amongst historians. For an example of this superficial gloss on history from political science, see Thomas Cusack, Torben Iversen, and David Soskice, "Coevolution of Capitalism and Political Representation: The Choice of Electoral Systems," *American Political Science Review* 104, no. 2 (May 2010): 393–403, and particularly in their attached "Web Appendix." For an introduction to the debates amongst historians about studying politics, see David M. Craig, "High Politics and the New Political History," *Historical Journal* 53, no. 2 (2010): 453–75. On the increasing research importance of history to political science, see Julian E. Zelizer, "What Political Science Can Learn from the New Political History," *Annual Review of Political Science* 13, no. 1 (2010): 25–36.

69 Mair, *Recasting Bourgeois Europe*, 5.

70 Ibid.

71 Ibid., 6.

72 Blais, Dobrzynska, and Indridason, "To Adopt or Not Adopt," 182.

73 Capoccia and Ziblatt make this point effectively when they argue that only deep historical analysis of the contexts can discover what actors themselves thought they were doing in the episodes that scholars have identified as moments of "democratization." See Capoccia and Ziblatt, "Historical Turn in Democratization Studies," 937.

74 Critical theory obviously has many meanings and applications. For our purposes, it will be understood as a loose body of thinkers who challenge the pluralist understandings of social power and organizing dominant in political science and the atomistic social ontologies that often accompany them. For arguably the classic statement of the need for critical theory in social science, see C. Wright Mills, *The Sociological Imagination* (New York: Oxford University Press, 1959). For a more recent discussion, see Clyde W. Barrow, "The Intellectual Origins of New Political Science," *New Political Science* 30, no. 2 (2008): 215–44; and Harry F. Dahms, ed., *No Social Science without Critical Theory* (Bingley, UK: Emerald, 2008).

75 Jenson and Merand, "Sociology, Institutionalism and the European Union," 82.

76 Dan Krier, "Finance Capital, Neo-Liberalism, and Critical Institutionalism," *Critical Sociology* 35, no. 3 (2009): 404.

77 Sunil Bastian and Robin Luckham, "Introduction: Can Democracy be Designed?," in Bastian and Luckham, *Can Democracy Be Designed?*, 2.

78 Luckham, Goetz, and Kaldor, "Democratic Institutions and Democratic Politics," 21.

79 A good example of how to make these links and why they are important can be found in Doug McAdam and Sidney Tarrow, "Ballots and

Barricades: On the Reciprocal Relationship between Elections and Social Movements," *PS: Perspectives on Politics* 8, no. 2 (June 2010): 529–42.

80 Ran Hirschl, *Toward Juristocracy: The Origins and Consequences of the New Constitutionalism* (Cambridge, MA: Harvard University Press, 2004); Stephen Gill, *Power and Resistance in the New World Order*, 2nd ed. (Houndmills: Palgrave Macmillan, 2008).

81 Representative examples of this approach could include: Seymour Martin Lipset, *Political Man: The Sociological Bases of Politics* (1960; Garden City: Anchor Books, 1963), 27–63; Samuel Huntingdon, *The Third Wave: Democratization in the Late Twentieth Century* (Norman: University of Oklahoma Press, 1991); and the contributions to Larry Diamond and Marc F. Plattner, eds., *The Global Resurgence of Democracy*, 2nd ed. (Baltimore: Johns Hopkins University, 1996). While widely celebrated by many political scientists, these works have also been subject to extensive critiques. See Paul Cammack, "Political Development Theory and the Dissemination of Democracy," *Democratization* 1, no. 3 (1994): 353–74; Dietrich Rueschemeyer, Evelyne Huber Stephens, and John D. Stephens, *Capitalist Development and Democracy* (Chicago: Chicago University Press, 1992), esp. chap. 2; and Klaus von Beyme, *Parliamentary Democracy: Democratization, Destabilization, Reconsolidation, 1789–1999* (Houndmills: Macmillan, 2000), chap. 2. For a concise overview of these debates, see Jean Grugel, *Democratization: A Critical Introduction* (Houndmills: Palgrave Macmillan, 2002), chaps 2 and 3.

82 See Barrington Moore Jr, *Social Origins of Dictatorship and Democracy: Lord and Peasant in the Making of the Modern World* (Boston: Beacon, 1966); Goran Therborn, "The Rule of Capital and the Rise of Democracy," *New Left Review* 103 (May–June 1977): 3–41; Rueschemeyer, Huber Stephens, and Stephens, *Capitalist Development and Democracy*; and Geoff Eley, *Forging Democracy: The History of the Left in Europe, 1850–2000* (Oxford: Oxford University Press, 2002).

83 These contributions and the debates around them will be explored in more detail in chapter 3.

84 For instance, Pilon, "Explaining Voting System Reform in Canada," 135–61; Bastian, "Political Economy of Electoral Reform," 196–219; and Ahmed, "Reading History Forward," 1059–88.

85 For a concise review of the methodological challenges of historical-comparative research, particularly concerns about the use of secondary sources, see W.L. Newman, *Social Research Methods: Quantitative and Qualitative Methods*, 4th ed. (Boston: Allyn and Bacon, 2000), 395–412.

86 Theda Skocpol, ed., *Vision and Method in Historical Sociology* (Cambridge: Cambridge University Press, 1984), 382.

87 Skocpol, *Vision and Method in Historical Sociology*, 382–3; Ira Katznelson, "Reflections on History, Method, and Political Science," *Political Methodologist: Newsletter of the Political Methodology Section, American Political Science Association* 8, no. 1 (Fall 1997): 13.
88 Katznelson, "Reflections on History, Method, and Political Science," 12.

Chapter 2

1 For instance, see Phillip Green, "'Democracy' as a Contested Idea," in *Democracy*, ed. P. Green, 2–18 (New Jersey: Humanities, 1993); Charles Tilly, *Democracy* (Cambridge: Cambridge University Press, 2007); or Frank Cunningham, *Theories of Democracy: A Critical Introduction* (New York: Routledge, 2002).
2 For an illustration of such assumptions, see Thomas Carothers, "Democracy without Illusions," *Foreign Affairs* 76, no. 1 (Jan.–Feb. 1997): 85–99; or Larry Diamond, Juan J. Linz, and Seymour Martin Lipset, *Democracy in Developing Countries*. Vol. 4, *Latin America* (Boulder: Lynne Rienner, 1989). The operative word here is *tend*. Obviously there are political scientists who are aware of the disputes, both historical and contemporary, about the meaning of democracy, particularly within the subfields of political theory and critical democratization studies. My point here is simply that for many political scientists "democracy" is conventionally reduced to elections.
3 For instance, see Shugart and Wattenberg, *Mixed-Member Electoral Systems*; Colomer, *Handbook of Electoral System Choice*; Gallagher and Mitchell, *Politics of Electoral Systems*; and Blais, *To Keep or to Change First Past the Post?*, to name just a few. However, for an exception to this trend, see Richard Katz, *Democracy and Elections* (New York: Oxford University Press, 1997).
4 A.R. Myers, *Parliaments and Estates in Europe to 1789* (London: Thames and Hudson, 1975), 24–8.
5 Benjamin Ginsberg, *The Consequences of Consent: Elections, Citizen Control and Popular Acquiescence* (Reading: Addison-Wesley, 1982), 244.
6 C.B. Macpherson, *The Real World of Democracy* (1965; Concord: Anasi, 1992), 1.
7 For example, see David Collier and Steven Levitsky, "Democracy with Adjectives: Conceptual Innovation in Comparative Research," *World Politics* 49, no. 3 (Apr. 1997): 430–51; David Collier and Robert Adcock, "Democracy and Dichotomies: A Pragmatic Approach to Choices about Concepts," *Annual Review of Political Science* 2, no. 1 (1999): 537–65. Here a quote from Diamond, Linz, and Lipset from *Democracy in Developing Countries* is particularly telling: "We use the term 'democracy' in this study to signify a

political system, separate and apart from the economic and social system to which it is joined. Indeed, a distinctive aspect of our approach is to insist that issues of so-called economic and social democracy be separated from the question of governmental structure." As cited in John Markoff, "Where and When Was Democracy Invented?," *Comparative Studies in Society and History* 41, no. 4 (1999): 663.

8 For example, see Therborn, "The Rule of Capital and the Rise of Democracy"; Rueschemeyer, Huber Stephens, and Stephens, *Capitalist Development and Democracy*; Eley, *Forging Democracy*.

9 The goals of this chapter are modest – to highlight how political science has typically operationalized "democracy," compare this with some of the more critical work on struggles over the substantive meaning of democracy, and connect this with the voting system reform debates. The effort will be necessarily brief and somewhat impressionistic, as either of the first two topics could easily be the subject of its own book-length treatment. Here we should remember that the point of this chapter is to provide a context for the exploration of Western voting system reforms, the subject of the rest of the book, not provide a definitive account of political science as a discipline or debates over democracy.

10 See J. Roland Pennock, *Democratic Political Theory* (Princeton: Princeton University Press, 1979), for an example of the former, and the contributions by Arend Lijphart, Donald Horowitz, and Ian Shapiro in Robert A. Dahl, Ian Shapiro, and Jose Antonio Cheibub, eds., *The Democracy Sourcebook* (Cambridge, MA: MIT Press, 2003), for the latter.

11 A classic example of this approach, and its shortcomings, can be found in Gabriel Almond and Sidney Verba, *The Civic Culture* (Boston: Little, Brown, 1965).

12 For a brief treatment of the shifting social objectives of political scientists, see Kenneth Prewitt, "Political Ideas and a Political Science for Policy," *Annals of the American Academy of Political and Social Science* 600, no. 1 (2005): 14–29. For a somewhat sympathetic account of the history of American and British political science, see Robert Adcock, Robert Mark Bevir, and Shannon C. Stimson, eds., *Modern Political Science: Anglo-American Exchanges since 1880* (Princeton: Princeton University Press, 2007). For a more critical account, see the contributions by Phillip Mirowski, Margaret Somers, Sophia Mihic et al., and Emily Hauptmann in George Steinmetz, ed., *The Politics of Method in the Human Sciences* (Durham: Duke University Press, 2005).

13 See Fletcher M. Green, "Cycles of American Democracy," *Mississippi Valley Historical Review* 48, no. 1 (June 1961): 3. On European assumptions of U.S.

democracy, see William E. Lingelbach, "American Democracy and European Interpreters," *Pennsylvania Magazine of History and Biography* 61, no. 1 (Jan. 1937), 1–25.

14 As Bernard Crick described it, "The word [*democracy*], increasingly respectable though it was, was never used to characterize English life in general or English politics in particular. There were friends and foes of democracy, but no one in their right mind in 1913 would have called Britain, as it was, a democracy. It simply was not. It was a free society, it had a system of representative government in which some popular reforms were proving increasingly possible, but it was not democratic." See Bernard Crick, *In Defence of Politics*, 2nd ed. (Chicago: University of Chicago Press, 1972), 70.

15 See Commons, *Proportional Representation*.

16 For a sense of the vague and romantic nature of democracy for American social critics in the nineteenth century, see John M. Anderson, "Romantic Democracy," *American Quarterly* 2, no. 3 (Autumn 1950), 251–8. On the democratic aspirations of American populism, see Lawrence Goodwyn, *Democratic Promise: The Populist Moment in America* (Oxford: Oxford University Press, 1976).

17 Not that this was a new problem; see Pierre Rosanvallon, "The History of the Word Democracy in France," *Journal of Democracy* 6, no. 4 (1995): 140–54; Jon Roper, *Democracy and Its Critics: Anglo-American Democratic Thought in the Nineteenth Century* (London: Unwin Hyman, 1989).

18 Crick comments on this change in the discourse of "democracy": "Only with the First World War did it [i.e., the public] learn that it was fighting – being conscripted, indeed – *to preserve* democracy. The rhetoric of Lloyd George, the genial cynicism of Churchill and Max Aitken, the idealism of Woodrow Wilson, all contrived to rob the term of any precise meaning whatever. The word was established for the sovereign purposes of war at the cost of stripping it of any real political meaning. Sacrifices could be demanded in the name of democracy which could not be expected for mere patriotism for the social order as it was. Tories who should have known better, and radicals who did know better but who were hoping for better, conspired to make Britain (verbally) democratic. And it has remained (verbally) democratic ever since." Crick, *In Defence of Politics*, 70–1.

19 Walter J. Shepard, "Democracy in Transition," *American Political Science Review* 29, no. 1 (Feb. 1935): 4, 18–19. However, five years later, John Lewis, writing in the *American Political Science Review*, would rebut this dualism, claiming democratic control over the economy need not be a threat to liberty. No doubt influenced by the Depression-era conditions, Lewis noted that the "political liberty to starve or freeze when no job can be found is no

real liberty." See John D. Lewis, "The Elements of Democracy," *American Political Science Review* 34, no. 3 (June 1940): 467–80.

20 Clyde W. Barrow, "Charles A. Beard's Social Democracy: A Critique of the Populist-Progressive Style in American Political Thought," *Polity* 21, no. 2 (Winter 1988): 253–76; Peter Lamb, "Laski on Rights and the Problem of Liberal Democratic Theory," *Politics* 19, no. 1 (1999): 15–20. See also Harold Laski, *Democracy in Crisis* (London: George Allen and Unwin, 1933). Lippincott perceptively addressed this in 1940: "The question is, why have American political scientists given so little attention to the economic aspect of politics? The answer is to be found, I suggest, in our notion of the scope of political science, in our conception of scientific method, in certain American conditions, in our middle-class assumptions, and in certain conditions of academic life. Of all these factors, our conception of scientific method and our middle-class assumptions seem to be the most significant factors." See Benjamin E. Lippincott, "The Bias of American Political Science," *Journal of Politics* 2, no. 2 (May 1940): 125–39.

21 See Herbert McClosky, "The Fallacy of Absolute Majority Rule," *Journal of Politics* 11, no. 4 (Nov. 1949): 637–54; Kenneth J. Arrow, *Social Choice and Individual Values* (new York: Wiley, 1951); Robert Dahl, *A Preface to Democratic Theory* (Chicago: University of Chicago Press, 1956).

22 See Joseph P. Schumpeter, *Capitalism, Socialism and Democracy* (1943; New York: Harper Torchbooks, 1976), specifically, chaps 20–3; and Robert Dahl, *Who Governs?* (New Haven: Yale University Press, 1961). For less famous but illustrative contemporary examples, see Ralph Gilbert Ross, "Party and Politics," *Ethics* 64, no. 2 (Jan. 1954): 100–25; Hans Kelsen, "Foundations of Democracy," *Ethics* 66, no. 1 (Oct. 1955): 1–101; Richard Wollheim, "Democracy," *Journal of the History of Ideas*," 19, no. 2 (Apr. 1958): 225–42. For a discussion of these developments, see J.S. Maloy, "A Genealogy of Rational Choice: Rationalism, Elitism, and Democracy," *Canadian Journal of Political Science* 41, no. 3 (Sept. 2008): 756–7.

23 For contemporary examples of the critical challenge to the political science mainstream, see Philip Green and Sanford Levinson, eds., *Power and Community: Dissenting Essays in Political Science* (New York: Random House, 1970). For the participatory vision of democratic politics, see Carole Pateman, *Participation and Democratic Theory* (Cambridge: Cambridge University Press, 1970); C. George Benello and Dimitrios Roussopoulos, eds., *The Case for Participatory Democracy* (New York: Viking Compass, 1971); Terrence E. Cook and Patrick M. Morgan, eds., *Participatory Democracy* (New York: Harper and Row, 1971).

24 Their view was elaborated in a specially prepared report by academics Michel Crozier, Samuel Huntington, and Joji Watanuki, *The Crisis of Democracy: Report on the Governability of Democracies to the Trilateral Commission* (New York: New York University Press, 1975).

25 Maloy, "Genealogy of Rational Choice"; S.M. Amadae, *Rationalizing Capitalist Democracy: The Cold War Origins of Rational Choice Liberalism* (Chicago: University of Chicago Press, 2003); Gerry Mackie, *Democracy Defended* (Cambridge: Cambridge University Press, 2003).

26 For instance, see Joan Nelson, "The Politics of Economic Transformation: Is Third World Experience Relevant in Eastern Europe?," *World Politics* 45, no. 3 (1993): 433–63.

27 Daniele Archibugi, ed., *Debating Cosmopolitics* (London: Verso, 2003); Archon Fung and Erik Olin Wright, eds., *Deepening Democracy: Institutional Innovations in Empowered Participatory Governance* (London: Verso, 2003); Hilary Wainwright, *Reclaim the State: Experiments in Popular Democracy* (London:.Verso, 2003); Jeffrey D. Hilmer, "The State of Participatory Democratic Theory," *New Political Science* 32, no. 1 (2010): 43–63.

28 The narrowness of the debate amongst political scientists analysing democracy and development is neatly captured by Larry Diamond, who criticizes the "fallacy of electoralism" in some of his colleagues while offering a definition of "liberal democracy" that is hardly more expansive. See Larry Diamond, "Defining and Developing Democracy," in Dahl, Shapiro, and Cheibub, *Democracy Sourcebook*, 32–5.

29 Laurence Whitehead, "The Vexed Issue of the Meaning of Democracy," *Journal of Political Ideologies* 2, no. 2 (1997): 125.

30 Cammack, "Democratization and Citizenship in Latin America," 177.

31 Julia Paley, "Toward an Anthropology of Democracy," *Annual Review of Anthropology* 31, no. 1 (2002): 476.

32 Whitehead, "Vexed Issue of the Meaning of Democracy," 127.

33 Ibid., 129–30. Farr also makes the case that some concepts are necessarily historical – "revolution" in his example – and cannot be understood without historical anchoring. See James Farr, "Historical Concepts in Political Science: The Case of 'Revolution,'" *American Journal of Political Science* 26, no. 4 (Nov. 1982): 688–708.

34 Macpherson, *Real World of Democracy*, 1–2.

35 C.B. Macpherson, *The Life and Times of Liberal Democracy* (Oxford: Oxford University Press, 1977), 74–7.

36 Seymour Martin Lipset, "Some Social Requisites of Democracy: Economic Development and Political Legitimacy," *American Political Science Review* 53, no. 1 (Mar. 1959): 69–105.

37 These two traditions are concisely summed up in Grugel, *Democratization*, chaps 1–3.

38 Examples of this approach could include Bastian and Luckham, *Can Democracy Be Designed?*; Rueschemeyer, Huber Stephens, and Stephens, *Capitalist Development and Democracy*; and Eley, *Forging Democracy*. For a spirited defence of this approach and critique of the political science mainstream on democratization, see John Saul, "For Fear of Being Condemned as 'Old Fashioned': Liberal Democracy vs Popular Democracy in Sub-Saharan Africa," *Review of African Political Economy* 24, no. 73 (1997): 339–53.

39 Beyme challenges the "wave" theorists of democracy, who he claims mistake successful franchise extensions or the achievement of parliamentary control over the governing executive for democracy, with the result that they put the beginnings of the democratic era too early in historical time. Rather than an early- or mid-nineteenth-century beginning in Western countries, democracy comes mostly after the First World War. See Beyme, *Parliamentary Democracy*, 16–18.

40 See W.J. Hudson and M.P. Sharp, *Australian Independence: Colony to Reluctant Kingdom* (Melbourne: Melbourne University Press, 1988), 3–4, 51–8; Robert Craig Brown and Ramsay Cook, *Canada 1896–1921: A Nation Transformed* (Toronto: McClelland and Stewart, 1974), 280; and R. MacGregor Dawson, *The Development of Dominion Status* (Oxford: Oxford University Press, 1937).

41 For some insight into the this process in various locales across the West, see Ira Katznelson and Aristride R. Zolberg, eds., *Working-Class Formation: Nineteenth-Century Patterns in Western Europe and the United States* (Princeton: Princeton University Press, 1986); and Michael Mann, *The Sources of Social Power*. Vol. 2, *The Rise of Classes and Nation-states, 1760–1914* (Cambridge: Cambridge University Press, 1993).

42 Eley, *Forging Democracy*, 24–5, 62–84; E.J. Hobsbawm, "The Making of the Working Class," *Uncommon People: Resistance, Rebellion and Jazz* (1984; London: Weidenfeld, 1998), 60–1, 67, 69–70.

43 Sassoon, *One Hundred Years of Socialism*, xxi; Eley, *Forging Democracy*, 5–6, 21–2.

44 Robert J. Goldstein, *Political Repression in 19th-Century Europe* (London: Croom Helm, 1983), 238–9; G. Steinmetz, "Workers and the Welfare State in Imperial Germany," *International Labor and Working-Class History* 40 (Fall 1991): 29–30, 36.

45 The quote is from W.K. Hancock, an Australian economic writer in the 1930s, one of many opponents to economic initiatives of the Australian state before the Second World War. See Gregory Melleuish, "Bruce Smith, Edward Shann, W.K. Hancock: The Economic Critique of Democracy in Australia," *Australian Journal of Political Science* 44, no. 4 (2009): 579–95.

46 John Horne, "Remobilizing for 'Total War': France and Britain, 1917–1918," in *State, Society and Mobilization in Europe during the First World War*, ed. John Horne, 195–211 (Cambridge: Cambridge University Press, 1997); J. Cronin and P. Weller, "Working-Class Interests and the Politics of Social Democratic Reform in Britain, 1900–1940," *International Labor and Working-Class History* 40 (September 1991): 51; Eley, *Forging Democracy*, 134; Bernard Waites, *A Class Society at War: England 1914–1918* (New York: Berg, 1987), 30–1; Giovanna Procacci, "Popular Protest and Labour Conflict in Italy, 1915–18," *Social History* 14, no. 1 (Jan. 1989): 31–58; and Philippe Bernard and Henri Dubief, *The Decline of the Third Republic, 1914–1938* (Cambridge: Cambridge University Press, 1985), 48, 54, 71.

47 D.K. Buse, "Ebert and the German Crisis, 1917–1920," *Central European History* 5, no. 3 (Sept. 1972): 234–55; James Cronin, "Labor Insurgency and Class Formation: Comparative Perspectives on the Crisis of 1917–1920 in Europe," 125–52; Arnold J. Mayer, *Politics and Diplomacy of Peacemaking: Containment and Counter-revolution at Versailles* (New York: Alfred A. Knopf, 1967).

48 Eley, *Forging Democracy*, 156–7, 225.

49 See Mair, *Recasting Bourgeois Europe*, 153–93.

50 Gerd-Rainer Horn, "From 'Radical' to 'Realistic': Hendrik de Man and the International Plan Conferences at Pontigny and Geneva, 1934–1937," *Contemporary European History* 10, no. 2 (2001): 239–65; Joanne Pemberton, "The Middle Way: The Discourse of Planning in Britain, Australia and at the League in the Interwar Years," *Australian Journal of Politics and History* 52, no. 1 (2006): 48–63.

51 Bernard Rulof, "Selling Social Democracy in the Netherlands: Activism and Its Sources of Inspiration during the 1930s," *Contemporary European History* 18, no. 4 (2009): 475–97; Erik Hansen, "Depression Decade Crisis: Social Democracy and Planisme in Belgium and the Netherlands, 1929–1939," *Journal of Contemporary History* 16, no. 2 (1981): 293–322.

52 Edmond Taylor, "Democracy Demoralized: The French Collapse," *Public Opinion Quarterly* 4, no. 4 (Dec. 1940): 630–50; Sassoon, *One Hundred Years of Socialism*, 41–59.

53 Medearis traces the evolution of Schumpeter's elite democracy thinking in *Capitalism, Socialism and Democracy* as a reaction to the rise of organized labour and their success in affecting state policies under the American New Deal in the 1930s, actions "he deplored." See John Medearis, "Schumpeter, the New Deal, and Democracy," *American Political Science Review* 91, no. 4 (Dec. 1997): 819–32.

54 Antoine Joseph, "Pathways to Capitalist Democracy: What Prevents Social Democracy?," *British Journal of Sociology* 45, no. 2 (June 1994): 211–34.

55 Eley, *Forging Democracy*, 287–91; Geoff Eley, "Back to the Beginning: European Labor, U.S. Influence, and the Start of the Cold War," *International Labor and Working-Class History* 40 (Fall 1991): 93; Patrick T. Pasture, "The April 1944 'Social Pact' in Belgium and Its Significance for the Post-war Welfare State," *Journal of Contemporary History* 28 (1993): 695–714.

56 See T.H. Marshall, *Citizenship and Social Class and Other Essays* (Cambridge: Cambridge University Press, 1950); Grugel, *Democratization*, 16–17; David Held, *Models of Democracy*, 2nd ed. (Stanford: Stanford University Press, 1996), 234–5.

57 Bruce Kuklick, *American Policy and the Division of Germany* (Ithaca: Cornell University Press, 1972), 139.

58 Gabriel Kolko, *The Politics of War: The World and United States Foreign Policy, 1943–45* (New York: Vintage Books, 1968), 95, 34–6, 184, 345, 437, 443, 620.

59 The origins of the Cold War have remained in dispute for most of the post-war period, with successive waves of scholarship revisiting how both sides may have benefited from it. But lost in some of the debate is much of the incoherency surrounding the events and mixed motives of different players in the period. For instance, while there is no doubting the failure of "people's democracies" to live up to most basic definition of democratic freedom in the Cold War era, scholars have highlighted how things were not so clear or rigid in the years immediately following the war and before the Cold War began. Nor is there strong evidence that the Soviets from 1945 to 1947 were single-mindedly expansionist and keen to roll over Western Europe. By the same token, American motives are also subject to scrutiny in terms that country's shifting geopolitical and economic interests, rather than a simple-minded acceptance that it was performing a selfless defence of the "free world." See Melvyn P. Leffler, "From the Truman Doctrine to the Carter Doctrine: Lessons and Dilemmas of the Cold War," *Diplomatic History* 7, no. 4 (Fall 1983): 247–8; Leffler, "Inside Enemy Archives: The Cold War Reopened," *Foreign Affairs* 75, no. 4 (July–Aug. 1996): 120–35; Eley, "Back to the Beginning," 98; Michael F. Hopkins, "Continuing Debate and New Approaches in Cold War History," *Historical Journal* 50, no. 4 (2007): 913–34.

60 Jeffrey C. Isaac, *Democracy in Dark Times* (Ithaca: Cornell University Press, 1998), 32–3.

61 In American post-war discourse "democracy" retained strong influences from the various progressive movements that stretched back to the post–Civil

War period. "Progressivism" included many, sometimes conflicting, ideas about American society, history, and politics. However, American historian James Livingston suggests that three key themes animated progressive thinking: a belief in the fundamental division between agriculture and capitalism, the juxtaposition of business interests versus the forces of social and political reform; and a characterization of corporations as parasitic organizations. This progressive legacy now came under challenge in the 1950s from both the liberal centre and right of the American political spectrum, who vigorously denied any contradiction between business and democracy. On the progressive legacy, see James Livingston, "Social Theory and Historical Method in Williams's Work," *Diplomatic History* 25, no. 2 (Spring 2001): 251–74. For an exhaustive, if somewhat celebratory, examination of the post-war American remaking of democratic theory, see Amadae, *Rationalizing Capitalist Democracy*. For a more critical take on these developments, see Green, "'Democracy' as a Contested Concept," specifically 4–14.

62 See McClosky, "The Fallacy of Absolute Majority Rule"; Arrow, *Social Choice and Individual Values*; and Schumpeter, *Capitalism, Socialism and Democracy*, specifically, chaps 20–3.

63 For a summary of the relevant developments, see William Buxton, *Talcott Parsons and the Capitalist Nation-State: Political Sociology as a Strategic Vocation* (Toronto: University of Toronto, 1985), esp. chaps 9–11. For a contemporary review of issues related to this new "scientific" study of voting in the 1950s, see Walter Berns, "Voting Studies," in *Essays on the Scientific Study of Politics*, ed. Herbert J. Storing, 3–62 (New York: Holt, Rhinehart and Winston, 1962).

64 See April Carter, *Direct Action and Democracy Today* (Cambridge: Polity, 2005), chap. 3.

65 See Tim Parsons, "The Community Schools Movement," *Community Issues* 2, no. 6 (Dec. 1970): 1–77; Donald C. Rowat, *The Ombudsman Plan: Essays on the Worldwide Spread of an Idea* (Toronto: McClelland and Stewart, 1973).

66 See Jack L. Walker, "A Critique of the Elitist Theory of Democracy," *American Political Science Review* 60, no. 2 (June 1966): 285–95.

67 See Pateman, *Participation and Democratic Theory*; Benello and Roussopolous, *The Case for Participatory Democracy*; Cook and Morgan, *Participatory Democracy*.

68 Michael J. Crozier, Samuel P. Huntingdon, and Joji Watanuki, "From *The Crisis of Democracy*," in P. Green, *Democracy*, 102.

69 Peter Self, *Government by the Market?* (Boulder: Westview, 1993), 212; Eric Helleiner, *States and the Reemergence of Global Finance* (Ithaca: Cornell University Press, 1994), 115, 130.

70 Leo Panitch and Colin Leys, *The End of Parliamentary Socialism: From New Left to New Labour* (London: Verso 1997), 118–24; Sassoon, *One Hundred Years of Socialism*, 534–71, 706–13.

71 Self, *Government by the Market?*, 64–5; Noel Thompson, "Hollowing Out the State: Public Choice Theory and the Critique of Keynesian Social Democracy," *Contemporary British History* 22, no. 3 (2008): 355–82.

72 For details on this process, see various contributions to Herbert Kitschelt, Peter Lange, Gary Marks, and John D. Stephens, eds., *Continuity and Change in Contemporary Capitalism* (Cambridge: Cambridge University Press, 1999).

73 On the often unremarked political theory undergirding the analysis of various economists, see Conrad Waligorski, *The Political Theory of Conservative Economists* (Lawrence: University Press of Kansas, 1990). For a discussion of how economists may be used for political purposes, see Meghnad Desai, *Marx's Revenge* (London: Verso, 2002), particularly chaps 16, 17.

74 Ben Fine, "Economics Imperialism and the New Development Economics as Kuhnian Paradigm Shift?," *World Development* 30, no. 12 (2002): 2057–70; Gary J. Miller, "The Impact of Economics on Contemporary Political Science," *Journal of Economic Literature* 35, no. 3 (Sept. 1997): 1173–204.

75 See John Callahan, "Social Democracy and Globalization: The Limits of Social Democracy in Historical Perspective," *British Journal of Politics and International Relations* 4, no. 3 (Oct. 2002): 429–51; Mark E. Rupert, "(Re)Politicizing the Global Economy: Liberal Common Sense and Ideological Struggle in the US NAFTA Debate," *Review of International Political Economy* 2, no. 4 (Autumn 1995): 658–92; Helleiner, *States and the Emergence of Global Finance*.

76 For a good example of an analysis balancing the influence of political strategy with unpredictable events, see Colin Crouch, "Privatized Keynesianism: An Unacknowledged Policy Regime," *British Journal of Politics and International Relations* 11 (2009): 382–99.

77 Douglas Wass, *Decline to Fall: The Making of British Macro-Economic Policy and the 1976 IMF Crisis* (Oxford: Oxford University Press, 2008); Chris Rogers, "The Politics of Economic Policy Making in Britain: A Re-assessment of the 1976 IMF Crisis," *Politics and Policy* 37, no. 5 (Oct. 2009): 971–94.

78 Held, *Models of Democracy*, 262.

79 For an illustrative example of this process, see Stephen McBride, "Quiet Constitutionalism in Canada: The International Political Economy of Domestic Institutional Change," *Canadian Journal of Political Science* 36, no. 2 (June 2003): 251–73. For the impact of such politics on labour, see Gerald Friedman, "Is Labour Dead?," *International Labor and Working-Class History* 75 (Spring 2009): 126–44.

80 See P. Mair, "Party Organizations: From Civil Society to the State," in *How Parties Organize: Change and Adaptation in Party Organizations in Western Democracies*, ed. R. Katz and P. Mair (London: Sage, 1994), 4; Gerasimos Moschonas, *In the Name of Social Democracy* (London: Verso, 2002), specifically chap. 8, "Inside Social Democracy: Organization in Mutation," 120–53; D.L. Swanson and P. Mancini, eds., *Politics, Media and Modern Democracy: An International Study of Innovations in Electoral Campaigning and Their Political Consequences* (Westport: Praeger, 1996), "Introduction," as well as 11–14, 251; Elin H. Allern and Karina Pedersen, "The Impact of Party Organisational Changes on Democracy," *West European Politics* 30, no. 1 (Jan. 2007): 68–92.

81 See Benjamin Arditi, "From Globalism to Globalization: The Politics of Resistance," *New Political Science* 26, no. 1 (Mar. 2004): 5–22; Malcolm J. Todd and Gary Taylor, eds., *Democracy and Participation: Popular Protest and New Social Movements* (London: Merlin, 2004); and Boaventura De Sousa Santos, "The World Social Forum and the Global Left," *Politics & Society* 36, no. 2 (2008): 247–70.

82 Ernesto Calvo, "The Competitive Road to Proportional Representation," *World Politics* 6, no. 2 (Apr. 2009): 255.

Chapter 3

1 See Hoag and Hallett, *Proportional Representation*; Donald J. Ziegler, "Proportional Representation in the Social and Political Conflict in Germany, 1871–1920" (PhD diss., University of Nebraska, 1956); Robert L. Eckelberry, "The Swedish System of Proportional Representation" (PhD diss., University of Nebraska, 1964); Carstairs, *Short History of Electoral Systems in Europe*; Hart, *Proportional Representation*; Kathleen Barber, *A Right to Representation* (Columbus: Ohio State University Press, 2000); and Colomer, "Strategy and History of Electoral System Choice," 3–80.

2 Rokkan, *Citizens, Elections, Parties*, 157.

3 In fact, most of the sources themselves document just how marginal reformers were in this period, noting that Considerant's early proposals were considered "eccentric," or recounting J.S. Mill's rough treatment at the hands of his fellow MPs when he tried to broach the subject in 1867. See Ernest Naville, "PR in Switzerland," *PR Review* 1, no. 2 (Dec. 1893): 55; Carstairs, *Short History of Electoral Systems in Europe*, 138; E.J. Feuchtwanger, "Electoral Systems: An Anglo-German Comparison, 1867–1933," *Historical Research* 65, no. 157 (June 1992): 195–6.

4 See Ruth Berins Collier, *Paths towards Democracy: The Working Class and Elites in Western Europe and South America* (Cambridge: Cambridge University Press, 1999), 24–5; Rokkan, *Citizens, Elections, Parties*, 87; Beyme, *Parliamentary Democracy*, 27. Collier's work represents the most egregious example of this approach. She begins by defining democracy as a set of institutions (rule of law, franchise, elections, etc.) and democratization as the process by which these are sequentially introduced. But Collier is reading back from later events, assuming that because various countries do eventually become at least minimally democratic that these reforms are all steps toward that result – a dubious and historically false assumption. Another example of this reading back can be found in Markoff, who tends, with hindsight, to see liberal battles for constitutional or "responsible" government as a "democratic breakthrough." See Markoff, "Where and When Was Democracy Invented?"

5 As Therborn put it, "None of the great bourgeois revolutions actually established bourgeois democracy." See Therborn, "The Rule of Capital and the Rise of Democracy," 17.

6 There is much debate over just what constitutes the necessary conditions of democratic rule. Therborn defines bourgeois democracy as, at a minimum, requiring "1. a representative government elected by 2. an electorate consisting of the entire adult population, 3. whose votes carry equal weight, and 4. who are allowed to vote for any opinion without intimidation by the state apparatus." By Therborn's rather restrictive definition, few countries could claim to be democratic well into the twentieth century (for instance, because of restrictions against black voters he puts the United States' attainment of democracy at 1960). See Therborn, "The Rule of Capital and the Rise of Democracy," 4, 11, 16–17. While his conditions are certainly laudable in terms of what democratic process should attain at a minimum, they define away an important shift from the period of *regime censitaire* representative government to mass participation "accountable" government. Thus I would put the minimum conditions of arguably democratic government as requiring a significant degree of mass participation (i.e., at least male suffrage) and a government accountable to the electorate through regular elections. Of course, even when various countries appear to satisfy these two conditions, as France and Switzerland appear to by 1900, other factors must be included if they appear to negate or seriously impede either one. These qualifications involve the erratic administration of elections, including corruption, ballot stuffing, uneven enforcement of rules, and much else.

7 M. Levin, *The Spectre of Democracy: The Rise of Modern Democracy as Seen by Its Critics* (New York: New York University Press, 1992), 28. For an exploration of how similar anti-democratic sentiments fuelled later U.K. reform bill debates, see Robert Saunders, "The Politics of Reform and the Making of the Second Reform Act, 1848–1867," *Historical Journal* 50, no. 3 (2007): 571–91. Bernard Manin makes a similar point about American history, noting that U.S. founding father James Madison understood his proposal for "representative government" to be not merely a different kind of democracy, but a wholly different and altogether better alternative because it would allow society's natural elite – the wealthy – superior influence. See Bernard Manin, *The Principles of Representative Government* (Cambridge: Cambridge University Press, 1997), 2–4.

8 Beyme, *Parliamentary Democracy*, 16–17. However, Beyme makes the same mistakes as those he criticizes when he turns to electoral reforms, characterizing them as being motivated by aims to increase the "participation of new political forces in government." Here he appears to be echoing conventional political science generalizations rather than investigating them.

9 Rueschemeyer, Huber Stephens, and Stephens, *Capitalist Development and Democracy*, 6; Eley, *Forging Democracy*, 10.

10 Goldstein, *Political Repression in 19th Century Europe*, 333–4. This was also true in the United States where the expansion of the franchise to white males largely preceded the emergence of a significant working class. Alexander Keyssar agues that extensive manipulations of the franchise and other electoral laws occurred from the mid-eighteenth century on, spurred by increasing industrialization, the proletarianization of poor farmers, and the rapid, large-scale immigration of European workers into American cities. See A. Keyssar, *The Right to Vote: The Contested History of Democracy in the United States* (New York: Basic Books, 2000), 170. On the centrality of struggle in gaining concessions in the United States, see Frances Fox Piven, *Challenging Authority: How Ordinary People Change America* (Lanham: Rowman and Littlefield, 2006). More recently Adam Przeworski has argued that franchise reforms across the West were granted only when the lower classes were able to demand them, usually by organizing themselves in what appeared to be a politically threatening manner. See Adam Przeworski, "Conquered or Granted? A History of Suffrage Extensions," *British Journal of Political Science* 39 (2008): 291–321; and Przeworksi, "Constraints and Choices: Electoral Participation in Historical Perspective," *Comparative Political Studies* 42, no. 1 (Jan. 2009): 4–30.

11   The exception being Illinois, which used the cumulative vote for state leg-
     islative elections from 1870 to 1980. Denmark also used the single transfer-
     able vote beyond the 1850s but for a substantially reduced electorate.

12   Plurality voting, also known as "first-past-the-post" or "winner-take-all"
     or "x"-voting, requires only that a candidates gain more votes than any
     other single candidate. With two candidates running, the winner will most
     likely gain a majority of the votes. However, with more than two candi-
     dates running, a winner may succeed with less than a majority of the vote,
     and in evenly competitive cases even much less than 50 per cent. Majority
     voting systems seek to correct for this anomaly in plurality voting by as-
     suring that a winning candidate does gain a majority of the votes cast. This
     is most typically accomplished by conducting a second round of voting at
     a later date in those constituencies where no candidate gained a majority
     of the votes cast. In the nineteenth century a number locales even had pro-
     vision for a third round of voting (Switzerland, France). Plurality and ma-
     jority voting can be conducted in either single- or multi-member districts.

13   Though why estate voting tended toward plurality is less clear. See Rokkan,
     Citizens, Elections, Parties, 156; Peter Campbell, *French Electoral Systems and
     Elections since 1789*, 2nd ed. (Hamden: Archon Books, 1965), 21. There is some
     evidence that voting was the subject of much debate in the late Roman peri-
     od and again in the Middle Ages amongst religious scholars, though it is
     not clear if these discussions had much influence on later developments.
     In Britain, plurality was formally adopted in 1430 to select two knights from
     every shire to attend Parliament. See Hart, *Proportional Representation*, 5;
     Barber, *Right to Representation*, 161.

14   Hoag and Hallett, *Proportional Representation*, 162–3; Barber, *Right to Repre-
     sentation*, 3. For a summary of some of these pre-modern developments,
     see Colomer, "Strategy and History of Electoral System Choice," 13–42.

15   Hart, *Proportional Representation*, 5.

16   It is important to recall that neither parliaments nor representation were
     novelties of the nineteenth century. As A.R. Myers notes, both stretched
     back to the early days of feudalism. What was novel was the shift from
     representation based on social position – noble, landlord, clergy, sometimes
     peasant – to representation based solely on class, and from the overlapping
     and multiple sovereignties of the feudal system (in most cases with dimin-
     ishing effect in the face of royal absolutism anyway) to the idea of parlia-
     mentary supremacy. See Myers, *Parliaments and Estates in Europe*, 24–8.

17   Beyme, *Parliamentary Democracy*, 25–6.

18   Barber, *Right to Representation*, 3–4; Hart, *Proportional Representation*, 9, 12.

19 Swiss reformers first organized in 1865 and quickly articulated a now-familiar list of grievances against their majority voting system: distorted party results, poor representation of religious and ethnic minorities, etc. Belgian reformers established their association in 1881 and essentially did the same, highlighting problems of language and ethnic representation. But the Swiss waited until 1892 to see their first conversion to proportional voting, while Belgium adopted PR nationally late in 1899, literally in the very last days of the nineteenth century. See T. Clarke, "The Unfinished Paradigm: Political Economy of St Galen" (PhD diss., Cornell, 1981), 150, 184; Georg Lutz, "Switzerland: Introducing Proportional Representation from Below," in Colomer, *Handbook of Electoral System Design*, 283–4; E. Bonjour, H.S. Offler and G.R. Potter, *A Short History of Switzerland* (Oxford: Oxford University Press, 1952), 308–9.

20 Exceptions include Rueschemeyer, Huber Stephens, and Stephens, *Capitalist Development and Democracy*, 8, 59; and Eley, *Forging Democracy*, 10.

21 Rueschemeyer, Huber Stephens, and Stephens, *Capitalist Development and Democracy*, 95–7.

22 Goldstein, *Political Repression in 19th Century Europe*, 114–15.

23 Ibid., 105. David Bayley notes, "The first two decades of the nineteenth century were … a period of great unrest in England. A Prime Minister was killed in the lobby of the House of Commons in 1812; Luddite riots the same year brought more troops to the Midlands than Wellesley had taken to the Peninsula in 1808; and the Peterloo massacre of 1819 showed the bankruptcy of the existing police system." See D. Bayley, "The Police and Political Development in Europe," in *The Formation of National States in Western Europe*, ed. C. Tilly (Princeton: Princeton University Press, 1975), 357.

24 Levin, *Spectre of Democracy*, 27; Goldstein, *Political Repression in 19th Century Europe*, 157–8.

25 Philip Corrigan and Derek Sayer, *The Great Arch* (Oxford: Basil Blackwell, 1985), 147–8.

26 Kenneth Good, "The Drive for Participatory Democracy in Nineteenth Century Britain," *Commonwealth & Comparative Politics* 47, no. 3 (July 2009): 237–42; Goldstein, *Political Repression in 19th Century Europe*, 229, 258; E. Biagini, *Liberty, Retrenchment and Reform: Popular Liberalism in the Age of Gladstone, 1860–1880* (Cambridge: Cambridge University Press, 1992), 261–2.

27 Levin, *Spectre of Democracy*, 55.

28 Bayley, "Police and Political Development in Europe," 360.

29 Golstein, *Political Repression in 19th Century Europe*, 187–91.

30 E.P. Thompson, *Customs in Common* (New York: New Press, 1991), 224–7.

31 Eley, *Forging Democracy*, 18–19.

32 Goldstein, *Political Repression in 19th Century Europe*, 159–60.

33 Dorothy Thompson, *The Chartists* (London: Temple Smith, 1984), 20–1.

34 Though seldom referenced by democratization or electoral system scholars, there is a considerable literature on the electoral left and their democratic aspirations. In-depth overviews can be found in Adam Przeworski, "Social Democracy as a Historical Phenomenon," *New Left Review* 122 (1980): 27–58; Adam Przeworski, *Capitalism and Social Democracy* (Cambridge: Cambridge University Press, 1985); Sassoon, *One Hundred Years of Socialism*; Gerassimos Moschonas, *In the Name of Social Democracy* (London: Verso, 2002); and Eley, *Forging Democracy*. Of course, in highlighting the rise of distinctively organized working-class parties, it should be added that such innovation sprang from prior organizational forms like cooperatives, friendly societies, trade unions, etc.

35 Goldstein, *Political Repression in 19th Century Europe*, 238–9.

36 Eley, *Forging Democracy*, 62–3, 74–5; Rueschemeyer, Huber Stephens, and Stephens, *Capitalist Development and Democracy*, 79.

37 Eley, *Forging Democracy*, 62–3.

38 G. Steinmetz, "Workers and the Welfare State in Imperial Germany," *International Labor and Working-Class History* 40 (Fall 1991): 29–30, 36.

39 Robert Trelford McKenzie and Allan Silver, *Angels in Marble: Working Class Conservatives in Urban England* (London: Heinemann, 1968), 40, 43–56; Martin Pugh, *The Tories and the People 1880–1935* (Oxford: Basil Blackwell, 1985), 8, 140–1. See also John Vincent, "The Effect of Second Reform Act in Lancashire," *Historical Journal* 11, no. 1 (1968): 84–94.

40 Eley, *Forging Democracy*, 31–2, 58.

41 E.J. Hobsbawm, "The Making of the Working Class," *Uncommon People: Resistance, Rebellion and Jazz* (1984; London: Weidenfeld, 1998), 60–1, 67, 69–70.

42 Sassoon, *One Hundred Years of Socialism*, xxi.

43 Goldstein, *Political Repression in 19th Century Europe*, 253.

44 Mann, *Sources of Social Power*, 2:667.

45 The literature on class development highlights how Britain's slow economic development may have better facilitated incorporating the working class into the political system, whereas the rapid German industrialization contributed to more rapid social dislocation and class polarization. Meanwhile French capitalism remained less urban and proletarianized, partly because of the resilience of the small-holder peasantry and the success of artisans and rural powerbrokers in maintaining some of their regulatory privileges. In settler countries like the United States, Canada, Australia, and New

Zealand, capitalist development was more uneven, though state and class responses were muted by the absence of a traditional landed or aristocratic class and the need to attract and keep immigrants, factors contributing to somewhat malleable franchise laws and a partial integration of the emergent working classes. See Eley, *Forging Democracy*, 56–7; I. Katznelson, "Working-Class Formations: Constructing Cases and Comparisons," in *Working Class Formation: Nineteenth-Century Patterns in Western Europe and the United States*, ed. I. Katznelson and A.R. Zolberg (Princeton: Princeton University Press, 1986), 31; Rueschemeyer, Huber Stephens, and Stephens, *Capitalist Development and Democracy*, 139–40.

46 Rueschemeyer, Huber Stephens, and Stephens, *Capitalist Development and Democracy*, 84–5.

47 Maurice Cowling, *1867 Disraeli, Gladstone and Revolution: The Passing of the Second Reform Bill* (Cambridge: Cambridge University Press, 1967), 48–52, 58–60; J. Lawrence, "Popular Politics and the Limits of Party: Wolverhampton, 1867–1900," in *Currents of Radicalism: Popular Radicalism, Organized Labour and Party Politics in Britain, 1850–1914*, ed. E. Biagini and A. Reid (Cambridge: Cambridge University Press, 1991), 76. Before the adoption of the secret ballot, both parties were known to resort to coercive measures to gain working-class support, including having Liberal and Tory employers and landlords use threats over work and housing. However, Hanham also cites a number of examples where ignoring working-class voting strength cost Liberals and Tories seats as early as 1868. See H.J. Hanham, *Elections and Party Management* (London: Longmans, 1959), 95; and Patrick Joyce, "The Factory Politics of Lancashire in the Later Nineteenth Century," *Historical Journal* 18, no. 3 (Sept. 1975), 525–53.

48 Rueschemeyer, Huber Stephens, and Stephens, *Capitalist Development and Democracy*, 95–7. Hanham reviews the period from 1867 to 1900 in his chapter on "working-class radicalism," 323–43; as does J. Shepherd, "Labour and Parliament: The Lib-Labs as the First Working-Class MPs, 1885–1906," in Biagini and Reid, *Currents of Radicalism*, 187–213. However, Conservatives also made appeals to working-class voters; see McKenzie and Silver, *Angels in Marble: Working Class Conservatives*, 43–56. Though by the 1890s, considerable pressure for separate labour representation was building up in Britain as well, particularly after a series of anti-labour court decisions in 1895, and the explicitly socialist Social Democratic Federation began to make headway in some municipal elections. For national efforts, see James Hinton, *Labour and Socialism: A History of the British Labour Movement, 1867–1974* (Brighton: Wheatsheaf Books, 1983), 68, 70–2; for early municipal labour representation, see P. Thane, "Labour and Local Politics: Radicalism,

Democracy and Social Reform, 1880–1914," in Biagini and Reid, *Currents of Radicalism*, 244–70.

49 Opposition to working-class participation in politics emerged in all settler countries with the rise of working-class organization and strength, even the United States. In *Right to Vote*, A. Keyssar reviews how differently immigrants to the United States were treated, depending on whether they were destined for rural farming or urban labouring, and cites a number of influential periodicals and organizations calling for a restriction of working-class suffrage. In Canada, despite the explicitly undemocratic claims of the founding fathers, emergent Liberal and Conservative parties quickly began vying for working-class votes, though within limits. See Keyssar, *Right to Vote*, 170; G. Kealey, *Toronto Workers Respond to Industrial Capitalism, 1867–1892* (Toronto: University of Toronto, 1980). For New Zealand lib-labism, see B. Brown, *The Rise of New Zealand Labour* (Wellington: Price Milburn, 1962), 2–4; and B. Gustafson, *Labour's Path to Political Independence* (Auckland: Auckland University Press, 1980), 13–14.

50 Rueschemeyer, Huber Stephens, and Stephens, *Capitalist Development and Democracy*, 82, 107; Volker R. Berghahn, "On the Societal Functions of Wilhemine Armaments Policy," in *The Social History of Politics: Critical Perspectives in West German Historical Writing since 1945*, ed. Georg Iggers (New York: St Martin's, 1985), 159, 167, 171; Martin Kitchen, *The Political Economy of Germany 1815–1914* (London: Croom-Helm, 1978), 225–32.

51 Rueschemeyer, Huber Stephens, and Stephens, *Capitalist Development and Democracy*, 114–15.

52 Collier, *Paths towards Democracy*, 102–3. However, Bismarck kept control over the political system, despite enfranchising working men by maintaining control over the executive – the legislature could only advise, it could not control the government.

53 Katznelson, "Working-Class Formations," 39–40.

54 Ibid., 33–4; Rueschemeyer, Huber Stephens, and Stephens, *Capitalist Development and Democracy*, 87–8. Michael Mann notes the France's proletariat was also comparatively more decentralized and not exclusively reliant on wage-labour. See Mann, *Sources of Social Power*, 2:667.

55 Goldstein, *Political Repression in 19th Century Europe*, 270–1; Eley, *Forging Democracy*, 70; Rueschemeyer, Huber Stephens, and Stephens, *Capitalist Development and Democracy*, 90–1; Katznelson, "Working-Class Formations," 34–5.

56 Alistair Cole and Peter Campbell, *French Electoral Systems and Elections since 1789* (Aldershot: Gower, 1989), 71; Martin Pugh, *The Evolution of the British Electoral System, 1832–1987* (London: Historical Association, 1990),

16; Trevor Lloyd, "Uncontested Seats in British General Elections, 1852–1910," *Historical Journal* 8, no. 2 (1965): 260–5. In Britain up to 300 seats typically remained uncontested in the 1860s, slipping to just 43 in 1885. In France 80–90 per cent of seats failed to go to a second ballot in the 1870s–1880s, but that figure had dropped to 60–70 per cent by the 1890s.

57 Feuchtwanger, "Electoral Systems," 198. Nearly all contests were settled on the first ballot before the rise of the SDP as mass party; by 1912 fewer than 50 per cent were.

58 Eley, *Forging Democracy*, 79–80.

59 Fairbairn makes this case for the 1898 and 1903 German elections. See Brett Fairbairn, *Democracy in the Undemocratic State: The German Reichstag Elections of 1898 and 1903* (Toronto: University of Toronto Press, 1997), 252–3.

60 Duverger, *Political Parties*, xxxvi–xxxvii, 1–2. There were exceptions. In Britain, both the Liberals and Conservatives established nascent party organizations that sought to mobilize an increasingly mass electorate, particularly after the 1867 reforms, but these efforts paled in comparison to the more systematic approaches that would be inaugurated by left parties. For discussion of these early efforts, see M. Ostrogorski, *Democracy and the Organization of Political Parties. Vol. 1, England*, 1902; and J. Lawrence, "Popular Politics and the Limitations of Party: Wolverhampton, 1867–1900," in Biagini and Reid, *Currents of Radicalism*, 65–85.

61 Goldstein, *Political Repression in 19th Century Europe*, 322–3.

62 Though initially new members had to be sponsored by an existing member, these restrictions gave way early in the twentieth century. See Duverger, *Political Parties*, 72.

63 Ibid., 62–3.

64 Though much is often made of Roberto Michels's less than glowing account of left internal democracy in his 1915 account of the German Social Democratic party in his *Political Parties*, the great popularity of the book has arguably more to do with its conclusions than the depth of its analysis. Indeed, in one of the few critical investigations of Michels's work, Gordon Hands complains that *Political Parties* is "often cited but seldom read," that it "contains surprisingly little hard empirical evidence," and that "Michels' method can only be described as 'proof by anecdote.'" See Gordon Hands, "Roberto Michels and the Study of Political Parties," *British Journal of Political Science* 1, no. 2 (Apr. 1971): 155–72. More even-handed accounts manage to track the many tortuous debates on the left about how such democracy should be practised without losing sight of its real contribution in a historical period where democratic spaces were largely nonexistent.

For instance, see Logie Barrow and Ian Bullock, *Democratic Ideas and the British Labour Movement, 1880–1914* (Cambridge: Cambridge University Press, 1996).

65 Eley, *Forging Democracy*, 113.

66 Duverger, *Political Parties*, 169–71. Though the tenor of Duverger's comments tends to equate party discipline with authoritarianism, he does grant that socialist parties (as opposed to communist parties) have acted democratically, and that struggles for political influence on the part of the working classes has required disciplined organization. In a particularly insightful comment he notes, "For the masses the classic contrast between freedom and discipline which appeals to the middle classes has no meaning: they won freedom by discipline, not only technically, because of their size, but sociologically because of the mental attitude of their members; the parties of the masses had a natural tendency to be disciplined parties." The "mental attitude" Duverger refers to is the historical learning process of working people discovering over time that only by disciplined collective efforts could they achieve anything.

67 Sassoon, *One Hundred Years of Socialism*, 20–1.

68 Wolfgang Abendroth, *A Short History of the European Working Class* (New York: Monthly Review, 1972), 52–3.

69 Goldstein, *Political Repression in 19th Century Europe*, 262–3.

70 Ibid., 268; Douglas V. Verney, *Parliamentary Reform in Sweden, 1866–1921* (Oxford: Clarendon, 1957), 111.

71 Nor was the early Swedish left at this time the model of moderation it would later become. Goldstein quotes Swedish socialist leader and future PM Hjalmar Branting in 1886, declaring, "Universal suffrage is the price with which the bourgeoisie can buy a settlement through administration in place of liquidation ordered by the court of revolution." See Goldstein, *Political Repression in 19th Century Europe*, 268.

72 Verney, *Parliamentary Reform in Sweden*, 139.

73 Eckelberry, "Swedish System of Proportional Representation," 32–3.

74 Ibid., 36–8. The plan would effect a double blow to the left. As they were strong in urban areas, PR would in effect reduce their representation as the current system tended to over-represent them and better represent the right as a minority interest. Yet denying PR to the rural areas would mean that the left would not capture any support as a minority interest, while conservatives would continue to enjoying over-representation there as the dominant electoral force.

75 Ziegler, "Proportional Representation in the Social and Political Conflict in Germany," 32.

76 G. Eley, "The Social Construction of Democracy in Germany, 1871–1933," in *The Social Construction of Democracy, 1870–1990*, ed. G.R. Andrews and H. Chapman (New York: New York University Press, 1995), 106. Though conservatives too came up with novel institutional ways to frustrate the left, including using state patronage in rural areas to facilitate electoral fraud that favoured the right. See Daniel Ziblatt, "Shaping Democratic Practices and the Causes of Electoral Fraud: The Case of Nineteenth Century Germany," *American Political Science Review* 103, no. 1 (Feb. 2009): 1–21.

77 Ziegler, "Proportional Representation in the Social and Political Conflict in Germany," 64.

78 Ibid., 65–6.

79 Ibid., 70–90.

80 Janet L. Polosky, "A Revolution for Socialist Reforms: The Belgian General Strike for Universal Suffrage," *Journal of Contemporary History* 27, no. 3 (1992): 449–55. In contrast to Polosky, most conventional work on the adoption of PR in Belgium suggests it was produced by the emergence of multiple cleavage lines around religion, language, region, and class. The distinctive role of the Belgian left in accelerating the push for institutional reform has been largely overlooked, as has been the literature that makes this case. However, recently some scholars have questioned how distinctive Belgium's left politics in the 1890s really were. In *A House Divided*, C. Strikwerda argues that the unity of Belgium's working class has been generally overstated and that workers supported conservative and liberal political projects, as well as socialist efforts. While he is certainly correct to highlight the divisions amongst workers about political party commitments, the existence of such divisions does not really diminish the important historical role of the Belgian left in this period. The point is, Belgium's Socialist Party managed to organize successful demonstrations that achieved political results. Longstanding social divisions based on religion, language, and region had not managed to produce either franchise reforms or more proportional voting – only the rise of organized social divisions based on class managed to tip the reform scales. See C. Strikwerda, *A House Divided: Catholics, Socialists and Flemish Nationalists in Nineteenth-Century Belgium* (New York: Rowman and Littlefield, 1997).

81 Polosky, "Revolution for Socialist Reforms," 449, 452–4.

82 Carstairs, *Short History of Electoral Systems in Europe*, 52–3.

83 Strikwerda, *House Divided*, 120, 126.

84 E.H. Kossman, *The Low Countries 1780–1940* (Oxford: Clarendon, 1978), 476.

85 Ahmed, "Reading History Forward," 1077–80.

86 Kossman, *Low Countries*, 503; Strikwerda, *House Divided*, 261. Kossman
thought the moment particularly dangerous because "the Liberal party
also gave the impression of being ready to accept the risk of revolution"
to effect political change.

87 At the most basic level, party list forms of PR convert the popular vote attained by different parties into proportional levels of legislative representation. Thus, ideally, if a party were to receive 20 per cent of the popular
vote, it would receive 20 per cent of the seats in Parliament. Concretely,
however, party list systems might diverge quite substantially from pure
proportionality. A country could be divided into different multi-member
constituencies and the PR principle applied only within them (as opposed
to being pooled across the country as a whole). Such an approach would
discriminate against parties without a strong regional base. In the Belgian
example, urban districts were drawn to maximize anti-socialist representation, while the district magnitude (the number of candidates to be elected
in a particular district) of rural areas was kept low precisely to under-rep-
resent the left. Thus many have characterized these early Belgian reforms
as only a partial-PR system. For details, see Carstairs, *Short History of
Electoral Systems in Europe*, specifically the chapter on "Belgium."

88 Carstairs, *Short History of Electoral Systems in Europe*, 54.

89 Rueschemeyer, Huber Stephens, and Stephens, *Capitalist Development and
Democracy*, 62–3. However, while such "perceptions of threat" cannot be
strictly quantified, they are nonetheless real in their impacts. As the authors note, "These perceptions are not simply reflections of objective conditions but represent symbolic constructs that are subject to hegemonic
and counter-hegemonic contention. Once established, they often remain
a potent force for long periods of time."

90 Panebianco distinguishes left parties in terms of their "strong" or "weak"
institutionalization. Strong parties – like the German SPD, the French PCF,
and the Italian PCI – had strong, coherent, independent organizations and
could act "imperialistically" within their political environments to dominate their potential supporters. Weak parties by contrast – Britain's Labour
Party, and the French and Italian socialists – were historically more dependent on external organization and had to adapt themselves to their changing environment. See Angelo Panebianco, *Political Parties: Organization and
Power* (Cambridge: Cambridge University Press, 1988), 110.

91 Hart, *Proportional Representation*, 101. Jones suggests that a strong element
in the PR leadership group were driven by Liberal Unionist objectives and
sought the reform to limit Irish home rule over-representation. Meanwhile
other Liberal leaders, like Chamberlain, thought poorly of the limited vote

experiment with "minority representation." In the end, the shift to single member districts was seen as a better "minority representation" strategy to most Liberals and Conservatives. See Andrew Jones, *The Politics of Reform 1884* (Cambridge: Cambridge University Press, 1972), 102–3; J.P.D. Dunbabin, "Some Implications of the 1885 Shift towards Single-Member Constituencies: A Note," *English Historical Review* 109, no. 430 (Feb. 1994), 89–100; and Ted R. Bromund, "Uniting the Whole People: Proportional Representation in Great Britain, 1884–5, Reconsidered," *Historical Research* 74, no. 183 (Feb. 2001): 89–94.

92   Thus Carstairs characterized a number of European shifts to PR as uncontroversial because they enjoyed multi-party support. See Carstairs, *Short History of Electoral Systems in Europe*, particularly chapters on Scandinavia and Benelux countries.

93   Hart, *Proportional Representation*, 166.

94   There is some debate over which left parties supported PR and why. Penades argues that left parties divided on the question of voting reform, depending on their general "participation strategy," with some confident and others more "timid" about taking on the responsibility of governing. These strategies were, in turn, informed by left party links to unions, with strong links translating into support for majoritarian voting rules and weak ones leading to commitments to PR. But Penades's neat logic is too deterministic and ignores how left party positions could change or be influenced by historical events. For instance, he claims that Swedish, Australian, and U.K. left parties opposed PR but, as will be shown in later chapters, this is not entirely correct. All three parties would by the 1920s oppose PR but at earlier points had all expressed support. In fact, in the British House of Commons the U.K. Labour Party voted for PR in 1917 and again in 1920, only to turn decisively against it in 1924. See Alberto Penadés, "Choosing Rules for Government: The Institutional Preferences of Early Socialist Parties," in *Controlling Governments: Voters, Institutions, and Accountability*, ed. J. Maravall and I. Sanchez-Cuenca, 202–46 (Cambridge: Cambridge University Press, 2008).

Chapter 4

1   Pugh, *The Tories and the People*, 25–8; Walter Dean Burnham, "The United States: The Politics of Heterogeneity," in *Electoral Behaviour: A Comparative Handbook*, ed. Richard Rose (New York: Free Press, 1974), 662–4, 667–8; Leon D. Epstein, *Political Parties in Western Democracies* (New York: Praeger Publishers, 1967), 104–6, 110–12.

2 For example, extensive SPD social and cultural practices in Germany are re-
   counted in Vernon L. Lidtke, *The Alternative Culture: Socialist Labor in Imperial
   Germany* (New York: Oxford University Press, 1985); and Dick Geary, "Beer
   and Skittles? Workers and Culture in Early Twentieth-Century Germany,"
   Australian Journal of Politics and History 46, no. 3 (2000): 388–402; while more
   general trends toward working-class identity across Europe are explored in
   Dick Geary, "Working Class Identities in Europe, 1850s–1930s," *Australian
   Journal of Politics and History* 45, no. 1 (1999): 20–34.
3 Horne, "Remobilizing for 'Total War.'"
4 Sassoon, *One Hundred Years of Socialism*, 28–30.
5 Cronin and Weller, "Working-Class Interests," 51; Eley, *Forging Democracy*,
   134; Waites, *Class Society at War*, 30–1.
6 J. Hinton, "Voluntarism versus Jacobinism: Labor, Nation, and Citizenship
   in Britain, 1850–1950," *International Labor and Working-Class History* 48 (Fall
   1995): 74–5; Eley, *Forging Democracy*, 124, 131.
7 For Britain and Germany, see Eley, *Forging Democracy*, 131. For Italy and
   France, see Procacci, "Popular Protest and Labour Conflict in Italy"; and
   Bernard and Dubief, *Decline of the Third Republic*, 48, 54, 71.
8 The failure of parliamentarization in imperial Germany should not lead us
   to ignore some of the ways it could, nevertheless, influence government, or
   the pragmatic reasons that led different governments to seek its support.
   For a generous view of its power, see Marcus Kreuzer, "Parliamentarization
   and the Question of German Exceptionalism," *Central European History* 36,
   no. 3 (2003): 327–57; Margaret L. Anderson, *Practicing Democracy: Elections
   and Political Culture in Imperial Germany* (Princeton: Princeton University
   Press, 2000), 10. This tension between the king, his executive branch, and
   the various German parliaments is explored in Wolfgang J. Mommsen,
   "Kaiser Wilhelm II and German Politics," *Journal of Contemporary History*
   25 (1990): 289–316.
9 Collier, *Paths towards Democracy*, 101–3.
10 However, this point should not be overstressed. On the whole, Bismarck's
   federal design still privileged state power, particularly Prussia, by making
   the national Reichstag dependent on the states' house, the Bundesrat, both
   to introduce and enforce legislation and taxes. Prussia's national influence
   was assured because it held a majority of seats in the Bundesrat. See Gerald
   Feldman, *Army, Industry and Labor in Germany 1914–1918* (Princeton:
   Princeton University Press, 1966), 8–9. Bismarck was also motivated to
   limit the political influence of liberals and Austria-Hungary in the new
   German state. See Guenther Roth, *The Social Democrats in Imperial Germany*
   (Totowa: Bedminster, 1968), 34–6; and for a more extensive treatment,

Peter Steinbach, "Reichstag Elections in the Kaiserreich: The Prospects for Electoral Research in the Interdisciplinary Context," in *Elections, Mass Politics, and Social Change in Modern Germany: New Perspectives*, ed. Larry Eugene Jones and James Retallack, 131–8 (Cambridge: Cambridge University Press, 1992). For a brief summary of some of Bismarck's motives, see Gerhard A. Ritter, "The Electoral Systems of Imperial Germany and Their Consequences for Politics," in *Political Strategies and Electoral Reforms: Origins of Voting Systems in Europe in the 19th and 20th Centuries*, ed. S. Noiret (Baden-Baden: Nomos Verlagsgesellschaft, 1990), 53–4.

11 Kitchen, *Political Economy of Germany*, 122–6; W.L. Guttsman, *The German Social Democratic Party, 1875–1933: From Ghetto to Government* (London: George Allen and Unwin, 1981), 15, 22–4; Walter Kendall, *The Labour Movement in Europe* (London: Allen Lane, 1975), 89–90; Dick Geary, "Socialism and the German Labour before 1914," in *Labour and Socialist Movements in Europe before 1914*, ed. Dick Geary (New York: Berg, 1989), 102–5.

12 Guttsman, *German Social Democratic Party*, 27–40.

13 Germany's imperial parties were profoundly regional, having their roots in the quasi-independent states that preceded the formation of the Reich. For most of the imperial era (1871–1918) there were two main conservative parties (Deutsch-Konservative and Reichspartei), two main liberal parties (National Liberals and Progressives), a Catholic party (Centre party or Zentrum), the socialist SPD, and a smattering of regional or national minority parties (winning on average 10 per cent of the vote and seats). Only the SPD operated as a national party running candidates in all districts, while the other parties seldom fielded candidates in more than half the districts. References to "conservatives" or "liberals" in the literature then actually refer to a number of parties, though it is conventional to refer to them under these more general labels, except in cases where disagreements exists amongst them on a particular issue (e.g., between the more right-of-centre National Liberals and more left-of-centre Progressives). See Ritter, "Electoral Systems of Imperial Germany," 57–8.

14 Mary Nolan, "Economic Crisis, State Policy, and Working Class Formation in Germany, 1870–1900," in Katznelson and Zolberg, *Working-Class Formation*, 360.

15 Roth, *Social Democrats in Imperial Germany*, 6–9.

16 Ziegler, "Proportional Representation in the Social and Political Conflict in Germany," 75.

17 Fairbairn, *Democracy in the Undemocratic State*, 214.

18 Typical Continental majority voting in this period involved a two-round or three-round "run-off" ballot (in the two-round version, the system was

also known as the second ballot). If no candidates gained an outright majority in the first round of voting, then another round would be held at a later date. In some cases, the second ballot would be restricted to the two top vote-getters, but in other cases all candidates could stand again.

19 Merith Niehuss, "Historiography, Sources and Methods of Electoral and Electoral Law Analysis in Germany: 1871–1987," in Noiret, *Political Strategies and Electoral Reforms*, 145.

20 Stanley Suval, *Electoral Politics in Wilhelmine Germany* (Chapel Hill: University of North Carolina Press, 1985), 230–1.

21 Steinmetz, "Workers and the Welfare State in Imperial Germany," 27.

22 Ziegler, "Proportional Representation in the Social and Political Conflict in Germany," 65–6.

23 Ibid., 73.

24 Ibid., 77–9.

25 Ibid., 81–7.

26 Steinmetz, "Workers and the Welfare State in Imperial Germany," 24–5, 29.

27 Ziegler, "Proportional Representation in the Social and Political Conflict in Germany," 73–6.

28 James Retallack, "'What Is to Be Done?' The Red Specter, Franchise Questions, and the Crisis of Conservative Hegemony in Saxony, 1896–1909," *Central European History* 23, no. 4 (Dec. 1990): 303–6; Ziegler, "Proportional Representation in the Social and Political Conflict in Germany," 86–8. Some, like Cusack et al. and Retallack, argue that the anti-socialist unity of the centre and right in imperial Germany has been overdrawn and that, particularly at the state level, different alliances can be found. But Retallack's Saxony examples demonstrate only that liberals and conservatives had difficulty working together at times, not that liberals were prepared to work with socialists. In fact, much evidence of anti-socialist cooperation on other kinds of electoral reform aimed to limit the SDP can be found, including the plural voting law of 1909 (though it did not achieve its goals of limiting the left electorally). See Donald Warren, *The Red Kingdom of Saxony* (The Hague: Martinus Nijhoff, 1964), 78–9. Meanwhile, the claims of Cusack et al. that economic interests were bringing workers and employers together politically in certain locales in Germany relies, in part, on Wurttemberg's adoption of PR for evidence, but the specifics of the reform suggest otherwise. As detailed in Ziegler, only twenty-three of the ninety-one members to be elected to the upper chamber were chosen by PR. SPD calls to elect the entire chamber were rejected by the other parties as too "dangerous." See Cusack, Iversen, and Soskice, "Coevolution of Capitalism and Political Representation,"

399; and Zeigler, "Proportional Representation in the Social and Political Conflict in Germany," 81–2.

29 Ziegler, "Proportional Representation in the Social and Political Conflict in Germany," 70–1.

30 Abraham Joseph Berlau, *The German Social Democratic Party 1914–1921* (New York: Octagon Books, 1970), 44; Ziegler, "Proportional Representation in the Social and Political Conflict in Germany," 56–61. There were a few dissenters, including Eduard Bernstein, who felt PR would inhibit party solidarity, but they had little influence in the party on this issue. See Preston Hastings, "Proportional Representation and the Weimar Constitution" (PhD diss., University of North Texas, 1992), 33.

31 Though most left parties across Europe remained committed to PR as an issue through most of the pre-war period, the increasing success of left parties under plurality and majority rules did lead to debate within their ranks about the advisability of change. After the First World War, a number of left parties broke with the PR consensus, most famously Sweden's SDP and Britain's Labour Party.

32 Carl Cavanagh Hodge, "Three Ways to Lose a Republic: The Electoral Politics of the Weimar SPD," *European History Quarterly* 17, no. 2 (1987): 166–7.

33 P. Pulzer, "Germany," in Bogdanor and Butler, *Democracy and Elections*, 85.

34 Ziegler, "Proportional Representation in the Social and Political Conflict in Germany," 57–8. Party support for PR went so far as to eschew justifications for adopting it, even in party newspapers, by reference to how it would simply benefit their party.

35 Niehuss, "Historiography, Sources and Methods," 143–4. The inequalities were quite striking. Constituency sizes in 1912 ranged from 10,700 voters in Schaumburg-Lippe to 338,900 in a suburb of Berlin. See Ritter, "Electoral Systems of Imperial Germany," 60.

36 Nor did it stop them from responding in more creative ways. Anderson refers to "gerrymandering from below," the practice of changing SPD voters' addresses before an election for the purpose of getting more votes for the party in constituencies where they needed them. See Anderson, *Practicing Democracy*, 335–44.

37 S. Tegel, "Reformist Social Democrats, the Mass Strike and the Prussian Suffrage 1913," *European History Quarterly* 17 (1987): 307–8.

38 Comparing results from the 1907 and 1912 Reichstag elections, SPD support on the first round of majority voting increased from 73 to 144. Though the party lost a similar number of seats on the second round (30 to 34), their increase in outright victories on the first round in 1912 left the party with 110 seats, the most of any party. Meanwhile, first-ballot support for

the two liberal parties in terms of seats dropped by half between 1907 and 1912. Though both recovered to near their 1907 levels of representation by the second round, the trend was clear – declining first-ballot support would eventually deliver more first-ballot majorities to the SPD. Thus liberals began looking at PR to shore up their support. See Pulzer, "Germany," 87.

39 Willem Verkade, *Democratic Parties in the Low Countries and Germany* (Leiden: Universitaire Pers, 1965), 66–8. The 1912 election involved the most cooperation between socialist and liberal elites in terms of second-ballot non-competition, though liberal voters proved more reticent than SPD supporters to follow the plan. See Carl E. Schorske, *German Social Democracy 1905–1917: The Development of the Great Schism* (New York: Russell and Russell, 1955), 226–33; Gary P. Steenson, *"Not One Man! Not One Penny!" German Social Democracy, 1863–1914* (Pittsburgh: University of Pittsburgh Press, 1981), 53. On changing liberal views about the SPD and democracy, see Bruce B. Frye, *Liberal Democracy in the Weimar Republic* (Carbondale: Southern Illinois University Press, 1985), 31.

40 Pulzer, "Germany," 88.

41 The bias in the Prussian system was the most extreme. In 1913 the SPD attained 30 per cent of the popular vote in the state election, the most of any single party, but secured just 2.3 per cent of the seats. See Ritter, "Electoral Systems of Imperial Germany," 64.

42 Susanne Miller and Heinrich Potthoff, *A History of Germany Social Democracy from 1848 to the Present* (New York: St Martin's, 1986), 55–8; Richard Bessel, *Germany after the First World War* (Oxford: Clarendon, 1993), 3–4. Bessel presents a nuanced treatment of both working-class and SPD support for the war beyond merely nationalist enthusiasm, arguing that their support was both more measured and limited in scope.

43 Schorske, *German Social Democracy*, 307–12.

44 Hastings, "Proportional Representation and the Weimar Constitution," 37–40.

45 Wilhelm Deist, "The German Army, the Authoritarian Nation-State and Total War," in Horne, *State, Society and Mobilization in Europe*, 166–8; Robert B. Armeson, *Total Warfare and Compulsory Labor: A Study of the Military-Industrial-Complex in Germany during World War I* (The Hague: Martinus Nijhoff, 1964), 121–5.

46 Hastings, "Proportional Representation and the Weimar Constitution," 45–53.

47 Ziegler, "Proportional Representation in the Social and Political Conflict in Germany," 89–90.

48 Hastings, "Proportional Representation and the Weimar Constitution," 54–5.

49 Ziegler, "Proportional Representation in the Social and Political Conflict in Germany," 101–17.

50 John W. Mishark, *The Road to Revolution: German Marxism and World War I: 1914–1919* (Detroit: Moria Books, 1967), 163–71; Feldman, *Army, Industry and Labor in Germany*, 514; Bernhard, *Institutions and the Fate of Democracy*, 28–9.

51 Ebert admitted later that the short-lived parliamentary regime of Prince Max had agreed to demands for PR before turning over power to the left, an indication of the rapidly shifting conservative views on the reform. See Berlau, *German Social Democratic Party*, 209; Hastings, "Proportional Representation and the Weimar Constitution," 66–8.

52 R. Alapuro, *State and Revolution in Finland* (Berkeley: University of California Press, 1988), 90.

53 Carstairs, *Short History of Electoral Systems in Western Europe*, 111.

54 Alapuro, *State and Revolution in Finland*, 48.

55 David Kirby, "The Workers' Cause: Rank-and-File Attitudes and Opinions in the Finnish Social Democratic Party 1905–1918," *Past and Present* 111 (May 1986): 135–7.

56 Alapuro, *State and Revolution in Finland*, 109–10. However, the working class did not get the vote until after the revolution of 1905.

57 Osmo Jussila, "Nationalism and Revolution: Political Dividing Lines in the Grand Duchy of Finland during the Last Years of Russian Rule," *Scandinavian Journal of History* 2 (1977): 291.

58 On the role of language politics, see Jan Sundberg, "The Electoral System of Finland: Old, and Working Well," in *The Evolution of Electoral and Party Systems in Nordic Countries*, ed. B. Grofman and A. Lijphjart (New York: Agathon, 2002): 68–9, 74.

59 Osmo Jussila, Seppo Hentila and Jukka Nevakivi, *From Grand Duchy to Modern State: A Political History of Finland since 1809* (London: Hurst, 1995), 63, 69–70; Tuomo Polvinen, *Imperial Borderland: Bobrikov and the Attempted Russification of Finland, 1898–1904* (Durham: Duke University Press, 1995) 67, 275; Alapuro, *State and Revolution in Finland*, 112–13.

60 P. Haapala, "How Was the Working Class Formed? The Case of Finland, 1850–1920," *Scandinavian Journal of History* 12, no. 3 (1987): 193.

61 Alapuro, *State and Revolution in Finland*, 115, 121.

62 Both Jussila and Sundberg downplay the socialist influence. Jussila suggests that conventional elites were really just concerned about chaos and "anarchy" and that even the left eschewed revolution at this time in favour of nationalism. However, he then proceeds to recount in detail elite concerns about left organizing in the period after the general strike and how this influenced elite decisions about political reform. See Jussila,

"Nationalism and Revolution," 296, 307. Meanwhile, Sundberg claims that language politics were most important. He claims that the 1906 reforms were "not primarily the result of a strong Social Democratic mobilization" but instead the "weakness of the Russian government after the revolutionary action around the large empire." Yet the two factors are not mutually exclusive. Then later Sundberg admits that class consciousness did emerge before the first election in 1907 and the domestic social issues (read "class" issues) – not language issues – dominated the campaign, with the result that all other parties eventually "stood against the offensive from the left." These claims by Sundberg, which are not supported by any footnotes, are strongly challenged by the other Finnish sources cited here, which suggest left political organizing was established well before the 1905 revolts. See Sundberg, "Electoral Systems of Finland," 72, 74–5.

63 Haapala, "How Was the Working Class Formed?," 194.
64 Demands typically included specific calls for universal suffrage and a single house legislature but made no mention of PR. See D.G. Kirby, *Finland and Russia 1808–1920, From Autonomy to Independence: A Selection of Documents* (London: Macmillan, 1975), 104–17.
65 Klaus Tornudd, *The Electoral System of Finland* (London: Hugh Evelyn, 1968), 29–34; Carstairs, *Short History of Electoral Systems in Western Europe*, 113. Other guarantees against "excessive democracy" included qualified majority rules that required two-thirds votes in the legislature and the double passage of a bill through successive legislatures. See Jussila, Hentila, and Nevakivi, *From Grand Duchy to Modern State*, 81.
66 Alapuro, *State and Revolution in Finland*, 113, 127; Jussila, "Nationalism and Revolution," 292. Local Finish elites were also surprised at the strength of the left, both in terms of mounting the general strike and their competitive position in the first electoral contest following the revolt.
67 Tornudd, *Electoral System of Finland*, 27, 29; Carstairs, *Short History of Electoral Systems in Western Europe*, 113.
68 Eckelberry, "Swedish System of Proportional Representation," 19–21. Between 1872 and 1896 the percentage of the total rural population that could vote in lower house elections shifted from 5.7 to 6.2 (or between 22.0 and 23.4 per cent of men over the age of twenty-one).
69 In Sweden in this period, what would conventionally be understood as the upper house was referred to as the First Chamber, while the lower house was called the Second Chamber. For the purposes of this discussion, the terms *upper* and *lower house* will be used to avoid confusion.
70 Verney, *Parliamentary Reform in Sweden*, 88–90; Dankwart A. Rustow, *The Politics of Compromise: A Study of Parties and Cabinet Government in Sweden* (Princeton: Princeton University Press, 1955), 23–4, 40.

71 For a general overview of economic changes in this period, see Ulf Olsson, "Sweden and Europe in the Twentieth Century: Economics and Politics," *Scandinavian Journal of History* 18, no. 1 (1993): 7–11. For their connection to political mobilization, see N. Elder, A. Thomas, and D. Arter, *The Consensual Democracies: The Government and Politics of Scandinavian States* (Oxford: Martin Robertson, 1982), 29–42.

72 Rustow, *Politics of Compromise*, 54–6, 59–60; Verney, *Parliamentary Reform in Sweden*, 110–11.

73 Franklin D. Scott, *Sweden: The Nation's History* (Carbondale: Southern Illinois University Press, 1988), 404; Eckelberry, "Swedish System of Proportional Representation," 37–8. Before the 1890s, parliament was divided more along government/opposition lines than party lines, with shifting coalitions of conservatives usually controlling the government. Without formal parties, discipline was weak. With the entry of reformist liberal forces, and eventually socialists, into the lower house in the 1890s the "conservative" government absorbed most of its former opposition, whether they were farmers or more independent conservatives. Thus governments of conservatives and farmers after the electoral breakthrough for reformers in the 1890s can be identified somewhat accurately as Conservative, though a formal Conservative party and party organization would not emerge for another decade. For discussions of the fluid nature of Sweden's party system ca. 1860–90 and the emergence of more formal parties thereafter, see Stig Hadenius, *Swedish Politics in the Twentieth Century* (Boras: Swedish Institute, 1985), 12–21; and Bo Sarlvik, "Sweden: The Social Bases of the Parties in a Developmental Perspective," in *Electoral Behaviour: A Comparative Handbook*, ed. R. Rose, 372–81 (New York: Free Press, 1974).

74 Herbert Tingsten, *The Swedish Social Democrats: Their Ideological Development* (1941; Totowa: Bedminster, 1975), 374–7; Scott, *Sweden: The Nation's History*, 405; Verney, *Parliamentary Reform in Sweden*, 111–12; Rustow, *The Politics of Compromise*, 57.

75 Gullan Gidlund, "From Popular Movement to Political Party: Development of the Social Democratic Labor Party Organization," in *Creating Social Democracy: A Century of the Social Democratic Labor Party in Sweden*, ed. Klaus Misgeld, Karl Molin, and Klas Amak, 101–8 (University Park: Pennsylvania State University Press, 1992); Scott, *Sweden: The Nation's History*, 429–30, 434–5.

76 Scott, *Sweden: The Nation's History*, 424; Eckelberry, "Swedish System of Proportional Representation," 39.

77 Sheri Berman, *The Social Democratic Moment: Ideas and Politics in the Making of Interwar Europe* (Cambridge, MA: Harvard University Press, 1998), 99–101.

78 Leif Lewin, *Ideology and Strategy: A Century of Swedish Politics* (Cambridge: Cambridge University Press, 1988), 85; Eckelberry, "Swedish System of Proportional Representation," 41.

79 Lewin, *Ideology and Strategy*, 60.

80 Verney, *Parliamentary Reform in Sweden*, 134.

81 Rustow, *Politics of Compromise*, 62; Eckelberry, "Swedish System of Proportional Representation," 43–4. More rurally based Conservatives and farmers supported the change, while urban Conservatives opposed it. Liberals also opposed it, as urban areas were their key source of support.

82 Eckelberry, "Swedish System of Proportional Representation," 44.

83 Lewin, *Ideology and Strategy*, 69–70. With the expansion of the urban economy, more and more workers were surpassing the franchise property and income limits. See also Eckelberry, "Swedish System of Proportional Representation," 20.

84 Eckelberry, "Swedish System of Proportional Representation," 42.

85 Rustow, *Politics of Compromise*, 61–2.

86 Eckelberry, "Swedish System of Proportional Representation," 45–6.

87 Verney, *Parliamentary Reform in Sweden*, 140–1, 145; Rustow, *Politics of Compromise*, 63.

88 Eckelberry, "Swedish System of Proportional Representation," 52, 57–8, 63.

89 Ibid., 47, 59, 90, 104.

90 Ibid., 57–62, 70.

91 Rustow, *Politics of Compromise*, 65–6.

92 Eckelberry, "Swedish System of Proportional Representation," 60–1, 74. Just twelve independents were elected.

93 Verney, *Parliamentary Reform in Sweden*, 145. The Liberals now clearly saw the Social Democrats as their main competitive threat and shift from PR to majority voting as a means of limiting their impact and representation.

94 Rustow, *Politics of Compromise*, 68–70.

95 Eckelberry, "Swedish System of Proportional Representation," 115.

96 Scott, *Sweden: The Nation's History*, 416; Ingvar Ansersson, *A History of Sweden* (Stockholm: Natur Och Kultur, 1955), 407; Andrew A. Stromberg, *A History of Sweden* (New York: Macmillan, 1931), 758–9.

97 From the late 1890s Liberals relied on support from the urban middle classes, dissenting religions, and some small farmers in the north and west. The shift in Sweden's class structure, then, undermined their support in urban areas as the working class voted more heavily for SDP candidates. Later the Liberals would be further weakened by middle-class defections to the right in the face of labour militancy at the war's end. See Rueschemeyer, Huber Stephens, and Stephens, *Capitalist Development and Democracy*, 92–3.

98 One measure of the SDP's success in mobilizing workers was the dramatic increase in party members: from about 6–7000 in the early 1890s to over 100,000 between 1906 to 1908. See Tingsten, *Swedish Social Democrats*, 373.

99 Eckelberry, "Swedish System of Proportional Representation," 77.

100 Thomas T. Mackie and Richard Rose, *The International Almanac of Electoral History*. 2nd ed. (New York: Facts on File, 1982), 336, 340.

101 Scott, *Sweden: The Nation's History*, 428. In fact there were many in Conservative and royal circles who defended a more active intervention by the Crown in political affairs. See Lewin, *Ideology and Strategy*, 93–6.

102 Carstairs, *Short History of Electoral Systems in Western Europe*, 139–41. Though the 1910 referendum was close, with a majority of cantons and 48 per cent of voters in favour (twelve to ten). For a general overview of these efforts, see Lutz, "Switzerland: Introducing Proportional Representation from Below," 284–7.

103 Lutz, "Switzerland: Introducing Proportional Representation from Below," 286.

104 Between 1829 and 1882 the proportion of population eligible to vote expanded little, from 5.6 to 7.6 per cent. However, a Liberal administration won an outright majority of both seats and votes in every election but one between 1882 and 1903. Keen to further its nationalist cause against Swedish imperial power, and confident in its majority support, the Liberals slowly expanded the franchise, to 9.4 per cent of the population by 1885 and 19.7 per cent by 1900. Yet they retained indirect forms of election where the "primary" or eligible voters would elect "secondary" voters who would choose the actual representatives. Indirect voting was another institutional mechanism to control the electoral process and assure only "respectable" members of society would gain election. See Carstairs, *Short History of Electoral Systems in Europe*, 90.

105 A. Seip, "Nation-Building within the Union: Politics, Class and Culture in the Norwegian Nation-state in the Nineteenth Century," *Scandinavian Journal of History* 20, no. 1 (1994): 48.

106 Carstairs, *Short History of Electoral Systems in Europe*, 88.

107 Seip, "Nation-Building within the Union," 49.

108 Bernt Aardal, "Electoral Systems in Norway," in Grofman and Lijphart, *Evolution of Electoral Systems in Nordic Countries*, 179–80.

109 Ibid., 181–2.

110 Jostein Ryssevik, "Parties vs Parliament: Contrasting Configurations of Electoral and Ministerial Socialism in Scandinavia," in *Social Democracy in Transition: Northern, Southern and Eastern Europe*, ed. Lauri Karvonen and Jan Sundberg (Aldershot: Dartmouth, 1991), 32; Donald R. Matthews

and Henry Valen, *Parliamentary Representation: The Case of the Norwegian Storting* (Columbus: Ohio State University Press, 1999), 34, 37.

111 These calculations are drawn from Campbell, *French Electoral Systems and Elections*, and Cole and Campbell, *French Electoral Systems and Elections since 1789*, and include only attempts to change between majority and proportional voting systems. If efforts to shift from single-member to multi-member constituency systems are included, the figure rises to twenty-two.

112 D. Hanley, "France: Living with Instability," in Broughton and Donovan, *Changing Party Systems in Western Europe*, 48–9; Campbell, *French Electoral Systems and Election*, 23.

113 John Horne, "The State and the Challenge of Labour in France 1917–20," in *Challenges of Labour: Central and Western Europe 1917–20*, ed. Chris Wrigley (London: Routledge, 1993), 239–40; Roger Magraw, "Socialism, Syndicalism and French Labour before 1914," in Geary, *Labour and Socialist Movements in Europe before 1914*, 50–1.

114 The change can be seen with the steep increase in the number of constituency contests going on to a second ballot, beginning in the 1890s. See Cole and Campbell, *French Electoral Systems*, 71.

115 The character of the pre–First World War party system in France is complex and confusing, hindered by a lack of consensus amongst experts about how terms like *left* and *right* should be used and whom they should apply to. Scholars consistently apply *left* to republican forces and *right* to monarchist forces when dealing with the latter third of the nineteenth century but differ widely in incorporating the socialists after 1900. There is also confusion about the proper names for some parties – the Radicals are sometimes referred to as Radical Socialists, even though everyone seems to agree that the party was not socialistic in outlook. This is further confused by the shifting allegiances of many high-profile politicians of the period – Clemenceau, Briand, Millerand – who had roots on the left but ended up on the right. For some of the different treatments, see Gordon Wright, *Raymond Poincaré and the French Presidency* (New York: Octagon Books, 1967), 21; René Rémond, *The Right Wing in France: From 1815 to de Gaulle* (Philadelphia: University of Pennsylvania Press, 1966); Francis De Tarr, *The French Radical Party: From Herriot to Mendes-France* (London: Oxford, 1961), xviii–xix; J.F.V. Keiger, *Raymond Poincaré* (Cambridge: Cambridge University Press, 1997). The problem is discussed in Roy Pierce, "French Legislative Elections: The Historical Background," in *The French National Assembly Elections of 1978*, ed. Howard R. Penniman, 2–6 (Washington: American Enterprise Institute, 1980).

116 J. Salwyn Schapiro, "The Drift in French Politics," *American Political Science Review* 7, no. 3 (Aug. 1913): 384–94.

117 Ibid., 385.

118 Malcolm Anderson, *Conservative Politics in France* (London: George Allen and Unwin, 1974), 38.

119 For convenience, the different groups will be referred to from here on as Radicals, SFIO, Moderates, and Conservatives. While the members referred to under these labels operated within these loose parties throughout this period, the actual party names and their memberships did change from time to time.

120 David Goldey and Philip Williams, "France," in Bogdanor and Butler, *Democracy and Elections*, 65; Hanley, "France: Living with Instability," 54. However, given the fluidity of the party system, there were a few Radicals in favour of reform as well.

121 For instance, several Radical ministries before the war introduced some progressive legislation in terms of unions and social program but they were also extremely heavy-handed in their response to strikes and demonstrations, regularly using troops and firing on strikers. See James F. McMillan, *Twentieth Century France: Politics and Society 1898–1991* (London: Edward Arnold, 1992), 18–19; Robert J. Young, *Power and Pleasure: Louis Barthou and the Third French Republic* (Montreal and Kingston: McGill-Queen's University Press, 1991), 93. For a survey of republican and Radical progressive legislation and some of its shortcomings, see Roger Magraw, "Socialism, Syndicalism and French Labour before 1914," 48–100.

122 Goldey and Williams, "France," 68–9.

123 This demonstrates the overlap with and remaking of the old nineteenth-century republican/monarchist split, as electoral reform was long a republican issue (though focused on districting more than voting formula) to force politics away from local concerns and toward more disciplined parties. However, in this case the Moderates could be considered both republican and right-wing. See David Robin Watson, *Georges Clemenceau: A Political Biography* (Plymouth: Eyre Methuen, 1974), 78; and Pierce, "French Legislative Elections," 9–10.

124 Ahmed, "Constituting the Electorate," 116–18.

125 Ibid., 118–23.

126 McMillan, *Twentieth Century France*, 37–8; Keiger, *Raymond Poincairé*, 119.

127 "PR Review," *Equity Series* 12, no. 2 (Apr. 1910): 73–4; Benjamin F. Martin, *France and the Après Guerre 1918–1924* (Baton Rouge: Louisiana State University Press, 1999), 61. Apparently, Briand first supported the change and a positive vote endorsing PR was cast: 281 to 235. However, under

pressure from his Radical supporters he backtracked, calling for another vote, which reversed the decision, 291 to 235. See Ahmed's discussion of the legislative debates in "Constituting the Electorate," 123.

128 Keiger, *Raymond Poincaré*, 121, 127–8, 131; Wright, *Raymond Poincaré and the French Presidency*, 26, 73–4; Watson, *Georges Clemenceau*, 243–6; Young, *Power and Pleasure*, 113.

129 Campbell, "French Electoral Systems and Elections," 86, 89–91; Wright, *Raymond Poincaré and the French Presidency*, 112.

130 For a contemporary account of the issues fuelling interest in PR, see James W. Garner, "Electoral Reform in France," *American Political Science Review* 7, no. 4 (Nov. 1913): 610–38.

131 Schapiro, "Drift in French Politics," 393–4; Sassoon, *One Hundred Years of Socialism*, 12; Michelle Perrot, "On the Formation of the French Working Class," in Katznelson and Zolberg, *Working Class Formation*, 106–10.

132 Hanley, "France," 49–50. Magraw reports that over 60 per cent of the population could be considered "rural" in 1914, though some of these were workers in rural industry. Susan Milner notes that even when workers had urban jobs they still had strong roots in rural areas and shifted between the two, a trend that tapered off only after the Second World War. She suggests this may have had important implications for working-class collective action. See Magraw, "Socialism, Syndicalism and French Labour before 1914," 49; and Susan Milner, "France," in *The Force of Labour: The Western European Labour Movement and the Working Class in the Twentieth Century*, ed. Stefan Berger and David Broughton (Oxford: Berg, 1995), 215–16. However, having said all this, the SFIO did have some support with the French peasantry. See McMillan, *Twentieth Century France*, 26–7.

133 Abendroth, *Short History of the European Working Class*, 64.

134 The experiences of Denmark and the Netherlands can be fruitfully compared to the remaining neutral country on the European continent: Switzerland. Though the war undermined social and political stability there too, and the Swiss left undeniably benefited from the situation, the conditions did not result in voting system reform during wartime. A crucial difference, aside from the weakness of the Swiss left as compared to other major European countries, was the weakness of the federal government. The rise of the left in unitary states like Denmark and the Netherlands was more threatening than in decentralized federations like Switzerland. See Epstein, *Political Parties in Western Europe*, 32.

135 Carsten Due-Nielsen, "Denmark and the First World War," *Scandinavian Journal of History* 10, no. 1 (1985): 10; Erik Hansen, "Between Reform and Revolution: Social Democracy and Dutch Society, 1917–21," in *Neutral*

Europe between War and Revolution 1917–23, ed. Hans A. Schmitt (Charlottesville: University Press of Virginia, 1988), 183–4. Economic conditions remained fairly normal in neutral countries for the first two years of the war but deteriorated rapidly from 1916 on, as British naval blockades and German submarine warfare disrupted trade and shipping.

136 Kenneth Miller, *Government and Politics in Denmark* (Boston: Houghton Mifflin, 1968), 34; O. Borre, "The Social Bases of Danish Electoral Behaviour," in *Electoral Participation: A Comparative Analysis*, ed. R. Rose (London: Sage, 1980), 242; L. Johansen, "Denmark," in *European Electoral Systems Handbook*, ed. G. Hand, J. Georgel, and C. Sasse (London: Butterworths, 1979), 30. In qualifying Denmark's full male suffrage, Johansen notes that reforms in 1915 had the effect of trebling the vote for the lower house, an increase that cannot be explained solely by the extension of the vote to women.

137 Carstairs, *Short History of Electoral Systems in Western Europe*, 77–8; Miller, *Government and Politics in Denmark*, 35. However, though the SDP emerged in 1871 and elected two members to the lower house in 1884, their representation remained limited until the next century. The Danish party system, as elsewhere, remained fluid until the twentieth century. The Venstre, or "left party," emerged to represent farmers in the late nineteenth century, and are often referred to in English as "Liberals." Borre points out that initially the rise of left moved the Liberals to seek an accommodation with Conservatives. Only when they were rebuffed did they work more closely with the early socialists. See Borre, "Social Bases of Danish Electoral Behaviour," 243.

138 Peter J. Katzenstein, *Small States in World Markets* (Ithaca: Cornell University Press, 1985), 152; Borre, "The Social Bases of Danish Electoral Behaviour," 243; G. De Faramond, "The Nordic Countries: A Type of Democratic Spirit," in *A History of Democracy in Europe*, ed. A. de Baecque (Boulder: Social Science Monographs, 1995), 198. De Faramond suggests an agricultural crisis and serious labour agitation contributed to the dramatic Liberal-left victory at the polls in 1901.

139 Elder, Thomas, and Arter, *The Consensual Democracies?*, 37.

140 Ibid., 42.

141 Carstairs, *Short History of Electoral Systems of Western Europe*, 78.

142 Miller, *Government and Politics in Denmark*, 36.

143 Elder, Thomas, and Arter, *The Consensual Democracies?*, 50; Ben A. Arneson, *The Democratic Monarchies of Scandinavia* (New York: D. Van Nostrand, 1949), 54–5; Gosta Esping-Andersen, *Politics against Markets:*

The Social Democratic Road to Power (Princeton: Princeton University Press, 1985), 74.

144 Kenneth E. Miller, *Friends and Rivals: Coalition Politics in Denmark, 1901–1995* (New York: University Press of America, 1996), 4.

145 Jørgen Elklit, "The Best of Both Worlds? The Danish Electoral System 1915–20 in a Comparative Perspective," *Electoral Studies* 11, no. 3 (1992): 190–1; John Fitzmaurice, *Politics in Denmark* (London: C. Hurst, 1981), 17.

146 Johansen, "Denmark," 31.

147 Niels Finn Christiansen, "Reformism within Danish Social Democracy until the Nineteen-Thirties," *Scandinavian Journal of History* 3 (1978): 298; Carstairs, *Short History of Electoral Systems in Western Europe*, 79; Collier, *Paths towards Democracy*, 82; Miller, *Government and Politics in Denmark*, 60.

148 Elklit, "Best of Both Worlds?," 190.

149 Miller, *Friends and Rivals*, 9. For a review of these political machinations, see Jørgen Elklit, "The Politics of Electoral System Development and Change: The Danish Case," in Grofman and Lijphart, *Evolution of Electoral and Party Systems in the Nordic Countries*, 32–6.

150 Elder, Thomas, and Arter, *The Consensual Democracies?*, 36. The party was also strong at the municipal level, enjoying an outright majority on the Copenhagen city council by 1917 and strong showings in other cities. See Esping-Andersen, *Politics against Markets*, 74–5.

151 Miller, *Friends and Rivals*, 9–10.

152 Katzenstein, *Small States in World Markets*, 152; Carstairs, *Short History of Electoral Systems in Western Europe*, 79.

153 Sally Marks, *Innocent Abroad: Belgium at the Paris Peace Conference of 1919* (Chapel Hill: University of North Carolina Press, 1981), 40.

154 Hansen, "Between Reform and Revolution," 177.

155 Arend Lijphart, *The Politics of Accommodation: Pluralism and Democracy in the Netherlands* (Berkeley: University of California Press, 1968), 109–11; Rudy B. Andeweg, "Institutional Conservatism in the Netherlands: Proposals for and Resistance to Change," *West European Politics* 12, no. 1 (Jan. 1989): 45.

156 I. Scholten, "Does Consociationalism Exist? A Critique of the Dutch Experience," in *Electoral Participation: A Comparative Analysis*, ed. R. Rose (London: Sage, 1980), 340–1.

157 E. Hansen, "Workers and Socialists: Relations between the Dutch Trade-Union Movement and Social Democracy, 1894–1914," *European Studies Review* 7 (1977): 200–3, 209–10; E. Hansen and P. Prosper, "Transformation and Accommodation in Dutch Socialism: P.J. Troelstra and Social

Democratic Political Theory, 1894–1914," *European History Quarterly* 27, no. 4 (1997): 476.

158 Verkade, *Democratic Parties in the Low Countries and Germany*, 44–5.
159 Scholten, "Does Consociationalism Exist?," 340–1; Hansen, "Workers and Socialists," 201.
160 Scholten, "Does Consociationalism Exist?," 343–4.
161 Hansen and Prosper, "Transformation and Accommodation in Dutch Socialism," 482–3.
162 Verkade, *Democratic Parties in the Low Countries and Germany*, 45–9; Scholten, "Does Consociationalism Exist?," 344.
163 Hansen and Prosper, "Transformation and Accommodation in Dutch Socialism," 488–9; 493. Though the policy of tactical support for other parties was extremely divisive within the party, leading to an ongoing battle between the leadership and different left groupings at party conventions.
164 Carstairs, *Short History of Electoral Systems in Western Europe*, 62; Hansen and Prosper, "Transformation and Accommodation in Dutch Socialism," 481.
165 Verkade, *Democratic Parties in the Low Countries and Germany*, 50; Hansen, "Workers and Socialists," 218, 221–2; Hansen and Prosper, "Transformation and Accommodation in Dutch Socialism," 493. Though, ironically, shortly thereafter the SDP failed to consult the labour movement on its decision not to join in a coalition with the Liberals after their 1913 electoral breakthrough, a slight that created considerable tension between the two groups.
166 Hansen and Prosper, "Transformation and Accommodation in Dutch Socialism," 496.
167 Carstairs, *Short History of Electoral Systems in Western Europe*, 63.
168 E. Van Raalte, *The Parliament of the Kingdom of the Netherlands* (London: Hansard Society for Parliamentary Government, 1959), 21–2.
169 Hansen, "Between Reform and Revolution," 184–5; John P. Windmuller, *Labor Relations in the Netherlands* (Ithaca: Cornell University Press, 1969), 45, 50.
170 Scholten, "Does Consociationalism Exist?," 345.
171 Dick Seip, "The Netherlands," in *European Electoral Systems Handbook*, ed. Geoffrey Hand, Jacques Georgel, and Christoph Sasse (London: Butterworths, 1979), 195.
172 Hansen and Prosper, "Transformation and Accommodation in Dutch Socialism," 499.
173 Andeweg, "Institutional Conservatism in the Netherlands," 45; Hans Daalder, "The Netherlands: Opposition in a Segmented Society," in *Political*

Oppositions in Western Democracies, ed. R. Dahl (New Haven, CT: Yale University Press, 1966), 207; Lijphart, *Politics of Accommodation*, 109–11.

174 Hermann von der Dunk, "Conservatism in the Netherlands," *Journal of Contemporary History* 13 (1978): 753–4; Scholten, "Does Consociationalism Exist?," 346, 351. In fact, Scholten argues that the confessional parties, particularly the Catholics, did not want to normalize socialist political participation, let alone sanction their participation in government.

175 Ken Gladdish, *Governing from the Center: Politics and Policy-Making in the Netherlands* (Dekalb: Northern Illinois University Press, 1991), 26–8.

176 In the late nineteenth century, mainstream political forces in Britain, New Zealand, Australia, and Canada all offered "labour" candidates in elections who ran under the party banner but were clearly identified to voters as a kind of labour representative, either because they were working class or associated with a particular union. For examples, see John Shepherd, "Labour and Parliament: The Lib-Labs as the First Working-Class MPs, 1885–1906," in Biagini and Reid, *Currents of Radicalism*; Kealey, *Toronto Workers Respond to Industrial Capitalism*; Gustafson, *Labour's Path to Political Independence*; and R.A. Markey, "The 1890s as the Turning Point in Australian Labor History," *International Labor and Working-Class History* 31 (Spring 1987): 77–88.

177 For instance, see Fabian arguments against the establishment of an independent labour party, in M. Cole, *The Story of Fabian Socialism* (New York: John Wiley and Sons, 1961), 86–7.

178 Despite Eugene Debs's impressive run for president in 1912 when he gained 6 per cent of the national vote for the Socialist Party, and evidence that socialist success at the municipal and state legislative level had some influence on the pro-labour and pro-reform aspects of the Democratic Party program in 1914, the American left never made serious inroads into the national Congress, and thus never threatened the electoral viability of the existing centrist forces. See James Weinstein, *The Decline of Socialism in America 1912–1925* (New York: Monthly Review, 1967), 93–118.

179 "PR Review," *Equity Series*, Jan. 1911, 42; Hoag and Hallett, *Proportional Representation*, 188–9.

180 Harry Charles John Phillips, "Challenges to the Voting System in Canada, 1874–1974" (PhD diss., University of Western Ontario, 1976), 116; Canada, *House of Commons Debates* (30 Apr. 1917), p. 915.

181 Ralph Miliband characterized the British Labour Party's approach to power as "parliamentary socialism," while John Saville dubbed it "labourism." Both capture a great deal about the nature of "political labour"

in Anglo-American polities, particularly an abiding faith in constitution-alism and a belief in the neutrality of the state. Saville underlines the in-fluence of a deterministic gradualism from Fabian thinking in favouring such views. A number of historians have sketched out other influential currents informing labourist politicians, including British liberal radical-ism, American democratic radicalism, the Christian social gospel, as well as Fabian socialism, and, to a lesser extent, European Marxism. Unlike European socialist parties, then, political labour was a coalition with sub-stantial, sometimes dominant, non-socialist participation and leadership. Though often characterized as wild-eyed radicals by their political oppo-nents, political labour in most countries had set out from within existing political formations, usually Liberal parties, and as such tended to be more integrated into their political systems. For Miliband and Saville, see the relevant selections in David Coates, ed., *Paving the Third Way: The Critique of Parliamentary Socialism* (London: Merlin Press, 2003), specifi-cally 85–7. For the intellectual influences on political labour, see Craig Heron, "Labourism and the Canadian Working Class," in *Canadian Working Class History: Selected Readings*, ed. L. Sefton MacDowell and I. Radforth, 355–81 (Toronto: Canadian Scholars' Press, 1992); and Peter Campbell, *Canadian Marxists and the Search for a Third Way* (Montreal and Kingston: McGill-Queen's University Press, 1999).

182 Hoag and Hallett, *Proportional Representation*, 180–1, 190. A national reform association was not established in Canada until 1915, and it remained weak and largely ineffective. The American PR League did re-establish itself just before the war, becoming quite active between 1914 and 1932, but it never gained much influence beyond municipal applications.

183 Melvyn Dubofsky, "Abortive Reform: The Wilson Administration and Organized Labour, 1913–1920," in *Work, Community, and Power: The Experience of Labor in Europe and America, 1900–1925*, ed. James E. Cronin and Carmen Sirianni, 197–220 (Philadelphia: Temple University Press, 1983); Eley, *Forging Democracy*, 134.

184 The emergence of all-party coalition governments in wartime was widely interpreted in many countries as the arrival of non-partisanship and non-party rule. Many reformers hailed these developments as a step forward in democratic evolution. In the Canadian context, see Brown and Cook, *Canada 1896–1921*, 294–5.

185 As Lloyd George found out in his attack on landed property in the "People's Budget," the divide between landed and industrial wealth in Britain was not so easy to demarcate. In fact, there were close links between landed and urban wealth, and thus between the aristocracy and the industrial

and commercial business elites. See G. Searle, "The Edwardian Liberal
Party and Business," *English Historical Review* (Jan. 1983): 47–8. For a
more general discussion of the nature of British upper-class unity, see
Colin Leys, *Politics in Britain*, 2nd ed. (Toronto: University of Toronto
Press, 1989), 46–7.

186 Some MPs, particularly in the House of Lords, were worried about ex-
tending the franchise in 1867, and an amendment to add an element of
the limited vote to a few urban constituencies was animated, in part, by
fear of how a mass electorate might oppress "property and intelligence."
But its inclusion seemed haphazard and its survival more dependent on
Prime Minster Disraeli's "weariness rather than conviction." See Vernon
Bogdanor, *The People and the Party System* (Cambridge: Cambridge
University Press, 1981), 101–3.

187 Martin Pugh, "Political Parties and the Campaign for Proportional Representation 1905–1914," *Parliamentary Affairs* 33, no. 3 (Summer 1980): 295–6.

188 See Hanham, *Elections and Party Management*; Charles Seymour, *Electoral
Reform in England and Wales: The Development and Operation of the Parlia-
mentary Franchise, 1832–1885* (New Haven: Yale University Press, 1915);
Ostrogorski, *Democracy and the Organization of Political Parties*. Vol. 1, England.

189 H. Pelling, *The Origins of the Labour Party*, as cited in Feuchtwanger,
"Electoral Systems," 196.

190 Hinton, "Voluntarism versus Jacobinism," 72; Hinton, *Labour and
Socialism*, 61; Paul Thompson, "Liberals, Radicals and Labour in London
1880–1900," *Past and Present* 27 (Apr. 1964): 73–101.

191 P. Adelman, *The Rise of the Labour Party*, 2nd ed. (Harlow: Longmans,
1986), 26; H. Pelling, *A Short History of the Labour Party*, 3rd ed. (London:
Macmillan, 1968), 6.

192 Adelman, *Rise of the Labour Party*, 334. A few "labour" representatives had
been elected to Parliament since the 1880s, either as Liberals or by arrangement with the Liberal Party not to contest their constituency. By
1905 there were fifteen such Lib-Lab MPs in the House. Efforts to hive
these members away from the Liberals to stand as independent labour
MPs had largely failed, partly because few could see many differences between Liberal and labour positions on policy, but also because MPs were
not paid at this time, thus making "independent" politics more costly and
risky. But in 1903 the LRC succeeded in securing union funding to pay labour MPs elected under their banner. This allowed to the LRC to enforce
a degree of party discipline on its candidates and keep them from sliding
toward the Liberals. Liberal Party elites recognized that these developments would make labour candidates more competitive adversaries,

contributing to the interest in pact negotiations. See also Pelling, *Short History of the Labour Party*, 12–13.

193 M. Pugh, *State and Society: British Political and Social History 1870–1992* (London: Arnold, 1994), 130–1.

194 The alternative vote, or AV, is a majoritarian voting system and is intended to assure that the winning candidate gains a majority of the votes cast. However, unlike the second or multiple ballot approach where multiple rounds of voting occur, AV accomplishes this on one ballot by having voters mark a preference amongst candidates numerically. Thus voters would mark a 1 by their first choice, a 2 by their second, and so on. At the end of balloting, the first choices are added up, and any candidate who has gained a majority wins, and nothing further occurs. However, if no candidate gains a majority, then the lowest vote-getter is eliminated and that candidate's ballots are redistributed on the basis of the second preferences marked. This process of eliminating the least popular candidate and redistributing their ballots on the basis of preferences continues until a candidate secures a majority or all preferences have been exhausted. AV can also be used for multi-member constituencies. While AV will assure that district winners gain a majority of voting support, it does not address the other typical concern raised about plurality voting, namely the distortion between the proportion of the votes cast for parties and the proportion of seats won.

195 PR had long been a labour and left issue in Britain, with support from the early socialist Social Democratic Federation (SDF) in the 1880s and trade union support by the turn of the century. A number of unions even elected their own executives using PR. See Barrow and Bullock, *Democratic Ideas and the British Labour Movement*, 9, 17; Hart, *Proportional Representation*, 168; Pugh, "Political Parties and the Campaign for Proportional Representation," 303.

196 Macdonald's reasoning resembled the Fabian opposition to PR in that it might dilute leadership and make decisive government more difficult. The Fabians called for the elimination of the semi-proportional cumulative vote in 1901, then in use for school board elections, because it allegedly led to poor turnout and theological voting. See Barrow and Bullock, *Democratic Ideas and the British Labour Movement*, 147–8.

197 Pugh, "Political Parties and the Campaign for Proportional Representation," 299–303.

198 Keith Laybourn, "The Rise of Labour and the Decline of Liberalism: The State of the Debate," *History* 80, no. 259 (June 1995): 207–26.

199 P. Clarke, "The Electoral Position of the Liberal and Labour Parties 1910–1914," *English Historical Review* (Oct. 1975): 828–9.

200 N. Blewett, *The Peers, the Parties and the People*, as cited in H. Matthew, R. McKibbin, and J. Kay, "The Franchise Factor in the Rise of the Labour Party," *English Historical Review* (July 1976): 740.

201 P. Clarke, "Liberals, Labour and the Franchise," *English Historical Review* (Apr. 1977): 584.

202 Martin Pugh, *Electoral Reform in War and Peace 1906–18* (London: Routledge and Kegan Paul, 1978), 13–15; Pugh, "Political Parties and the Campaign for Proportional Representation," 299. Pugh suggests that the Liberal Cabinet almost included AV in the 1912 Franchise Bill but feared a delay in passing the bill.

203 Pugh, "Political Parties and the Campaign for Proportional Representation," 304.

204 The Liberals had long worried over the contradictions inherent in pursuing working-class votes. Since the early competition from municipal socialist and labour candidates in the 1880s and 1890s, Liberals found that to keep potential Labour voters they had to champion more radical policies. However, when they did take up more radical positions, they risked losing more middle-class voters to the Conservatives. Given that even the reformed franchise of 1885 was still heavily biased toward the middle class, the cost of competing with labour candidates on their own terms remained high, right up to 1918. See P. Thompson, "Liberals, Radicals and Labour in London," 78–80.

205 Searle, "Edwardian Liberal Party and Business," 40; Laybourn, "Rise of Labour and the Decline of Liberalism," 217.

206 Searle, "Edwardian Liberal Party and Business," 46. Searle notes that the Liberal defence of free trade kept many business supporters with the party, despite its social program.

207 G. Dangerfield, *The Strange Death of Liberal England 1910–1914* (1935; New York: Capricorn Books, 1961), 72–3. Others have characterized the basis of unity between the Liberals and Labour as less focused on social policy than a radical anti-Lords constitutionalism, particularly around the People's Budget of 1909 and the subsequent election. See Andrew Chadwick, "Aristocracy or the People? Radical Constitutionalism and the Progressive Alliance in Edwardian Britain," *Journal of Political Ideologies* 4, no. 3 (1999): 365–90.

208 V. Bogdanor, "Literature, Sources and Methodology for the Study of Electoral Reform in the United Kingdom," in Noiret, *Political Strategies*

and Electoral Reforms, 347. See also Dangerfield, *Strange Death of Liberal England*, 38.

209 Neal Blewett, "The Franchise in the United Kingdom 1885–1918," *Past and Present* 32, no. 1 (Dec. 1965): 31.

210 Matthew, McKibbin, and Kay, "Franchise Factor in the Rise of the Labour Party," 727–8.

211 Blewett, "Franchise in the United Kingdom," 34–5.

212 Ibid., 44. Registration was also a cost that fell unevenly on the parties, with Conservatives in a particularly good position to pay solicitors to make sure the rolls were full of Tory voters. While mostly adding to Blewett's analysis, Grace Jones argues that the registration and plural voting rules benefited the Tories primarily. See Grace A. Jones, "Further Thoughts on the Franchise 1885–1918," *Past and Present* 34 (July 1966): 134–8.

213 P. Clarke, "Electoral Position of the Liberal and Labour Parties 1910–1914," 830; P. Clarke, *Lancashire and the New Liberalism* (Cambridge: Cambridge University Press, 1971), 328. Labour also made dramatic gains at the local level between 1910 and 1914. See Laybourn, "Rise of Labour and the Decline of Liberalism," 214. One indication of Liberal interest in voting system reform was the private member's bill for AV in 1914 from Liberal C.H. Lyell, though he failed to convince the Liberal majority to support him. See Hart, *Proportional Representation*, 169–70.

214 Bogdanor, *People and the Party System*, 122.

215 P. Adelman, *The Decline of the Liberal Party 1910–1931* (Harlow: Longman, 1981), 5–6; Hinton, *Labour and Socialism*, 93–4.

216 Pugh, "Political Parties and the Campaign for PR 1905–1914," 301–2. Considerable debate had broken out in the Labour press about PR between 1912 and 1914, with Macdonald almost single-handedly squaring off against activists and other MPs in criticizing PR. For the 1914 convention vote on PR, Barrow and Bullock suggest Macdonald used his influence with the miners' unions to have the issue voted down. See Barrow and Bullock, *Democratic Ideas and the British Labour Movement, 1880–1914*, 274–83.

217 For an exploration of these debates within the Labour Party leadership, see R.I. McKibbin, "James Ramsay MacDonald and the Problem of the Independence of the Labour Party, 1910–1914," *Journal of Modern History* 42, no. 2 (June 1970): 216–35.

218 Pugh, "Political Parties and the Campaign for PR 1905–1914," 300–4.

219 Bogdanor, "Literature, Sources and Methodology for the Study of Electoral Reform in the United Kingdom," 350.

220 Hart notes that class factors emerged explicitly in the debate over PR for Ireland, with its supporters worrying that, if given the vote, the country's poor rural majority would deny the well-to-do adequate representation and thus influence. See Hart, *Proportional Representation*, 170–6. The 1914 bill would have applied PR to all of the Irish Senate and a proportion of the seats for the Irish House of Commons.

221 Pugh, *Electoral Reform in War and Peace 1906–18*, 70–2.

222 Pugh, "Political Parties and the Campaign for PR 1905–1914," 304–5.

223 Adelman, *Decline of the Liberal Party*, 18, 31.

224 Over his long political career Lloyd George shifted regularly between anti-business populism and an anti-left hysteria, considering a "government of businessmen" to answer the deadlock of 1910, a return to the progressive alliance whenever the war was over, the creation of a new centre party in 1919, and a formal left-liberal coalition to answer the Depression. See Searle, "The Edwardian Liberal Party and Business," 39–40; Clarke, *Lancashire and the New Liberalism*, 394; and Adelman, *Decline of the Liberal Party*, 29, 55.

225 Pugh, *Electoral Reform in War and Peace 1906–18*, 128–31, 163.

226 Hinton, *Labour and Socialism*, 102, 105–6; Hart, *Proportional Representation*, 182–3.

227 Pugh, *Electoral Reform in War and Peace, 1906–18*, 82–3.

228 Ibid., 6, 83, 115, 122.

229 Ibid., 109, 123–4, 158.

230 Ibid., 156, 163–4.

231 Homer Lawrence Morris, *Parliamentary Franchise Reform in England from 1885–1918* (New York: 1921), 188–9; Pugh, *Electoral Reform in War and Peace 1906–18*, 162.

232 Hart, *Proportional Representation*, 186; Pugh, *Electoral Reform in War and Peace 1906–18*, 165–6.

233 Carstairs, *A Short History of Electoral Systems in Western Europe*, 195–6.

234 Divisions existed within all parties of the period about PR (except the Irish nationalists), with the Conservatives most opposed, then the Liberals, and Labour most evenly divided. Labour's divisions shifted from slight favour to strong opposition in the five House of Commons votes on the issue that occurred between June 1917 and May 1918. Curiously, the negative votes in 1918 coincided with the party's reversal on the issue as policy when the party's conference voted in favour of supporting PR. For a breakdown of the votes, see Bogdanor, *People and the Party System*, 130–1.

235 There is some debate over the character of political labour in Australia. Nairn contends that Australia's Labor Party was essentially labourist and little interested in socialism, but Markey, in a literature review of the party's history, suggests that socialism and labourism were two important influences among many that contributed to ongoing party debate and organizational struggles, depending on the historical moment, at least until the party became a contender for government. Meanwhile Lovell claims that Australian socialism was unique, compared to European approaches, as a result of its strong working-class base rather than any theoretical innovations. Moore and Walter take up this debate in examining the shifting historical usages and meanings of "state socialism" as used by political actors. See B. Nairn, *Civilizing Capitalism: The Beginnings of the Australian Labor Party* (1973; Melbourne: Melbourne University Press, 1989); Markey, "The 1890s as the Turning Point in Australian Labor History," 79; and David W. Lovell, "Australian Socialism to 1917: A Study of the Relations between Socialism and Nationalism," *Australian Journal of Politics and History* 40, no. 4 (1994): 151; Tod Moore and James Walter, "State Socialism in Australian Political Thought: A Reconsideration," *Australian Journal of Politics and History* 52, no. 1 (2006): 13–29. There was also a pronounced American influence, particularly the ideas of Edward Bellamy and Henry George. See L.G. Churchward, "The American Influence on the Australian Labour Movement," *Historical Studies: Australia and New Zealand* 5, no. 19 (Nov. 1952): 258–77.

236 Louise Overacker, "The Australian Labor Party," *American Political Science Review* 43, no. 3 (Aug. 1949): 678–9; Markey, "The 1890s as the Turning Point in Australian Labor History," 79; P. Loveday, "New South Wales," in D.J. Murphy (ed.), *Labor in Politics: The State Labor Parties in Australia 1880–1920*, (St Lucia: University of Queensland Press, 1975), 25.

237 Farrell and McAllister argue that explanations of voting system reform that focus solely on party self-interest cannot explain why preferential ballots specifically became so popular in Australia and demonstrate the key role of various voting system reformers. While an important nuance about why Australia has used the specific systems it has, the point is less salient on the question being pursued here, namely why such systems were chosen when they were and what political purposes their designers thought they would serve. See David Farrell and Ian McAllister, "1902 and the Origins of the Preferential Systems in Australia," *Australian Journal of Politics and History* 51, no. 2 (2005): 155–67.

238 B.D. Graham, "The Choice of Voting Methods in Federal Politics, 1902–1918," *Australian Journal of Politics and History* 8, no. 2 (Nov. 1962): 167–9.

239 Alexander Brady, *Democracy in the Dominions: A Comparative Study in Institutions*, 3rd ed. (Toronto: University of Toronto Press, 1958), 204–5, 207; G.S. Reid and Martyn Forrest, *Australia's Commonwealth Parliament: Ten Perspectives* (Melbourne: Melbourne University Press, 1989), 14–15.

240 Graham, "Choice of Voting Methods in Federal Politics," 167–8.

241 Joan Rydon, "Electoral Methods and the Australian Party System," *Australian Journal of Politics and History* 2, no. 1 (Nov. 1956): 76.

242 David Farrell and Ian McAllister, *The Australian Electoral System* (Sydney: University of New South Wales Press, 2006), 32–4; Graham, "Choice of Voting Methods in Federal Politics," 168–9. From then on, Labor remained largely hostile to all voting system reforms. For a review of Labor Party debates on the issue up to 1950, see L.F. Crisp, *The Australian Federal Labour Party, 1901–1951* (London: Longmans, Green, 1955), 217–20.

243 Graham, "Choice of Voting Methods in Federal Politics," 169–70.

244 Ben Reilly and Michael Maley, "The Single Transferable Vote and the Alternative Vote Compared," in *Elections in Australia, Ireland, and Malta under the Single Transferable Vote*, ed. S. Bowler and B. Grofman (Ann Arbor: University of Michigan Press, 2000), 41.

245 John Rickard, *Class and Politics: New South Wales, Victoria and the Early Commonwealth, 1890–1910* (Canberra: Australian National University Press, 1976), 242–54.

246 Scott Bennett, "Political Corruption, the Fall of the Braddon Government and Hare-Clark Voting: E.T. Miles, 1899–1900," *Tasmanian Historical Research Association: Papers and Proceedings* 39, no. 4 (Dec. 1992): 156.

247 Patrick Weller, "Groups, Parliament and Elections: Tasmanian Politics in the 1890s," *Tasmanian Historical Research Association: Papers and Proceedings* 21, no. 2 (June 1974): 89–103.

248 C. Hughes, "STV in Australia," in *Elections in Australia, Ireland, and Malta under the Single Transferable Vote*, ed. S. Bowler and B. Grofman (Ann Arbor: University of Michigan Press, 2000), 158–9. However, despite what reformers had intended, STV did not ultimately eliminate the need to form a formal centre-right party in Tasmania. Eventually the anti-Labor forces did meld into the Liberal party, with links to the same national political party. Nor did STV slow the advance of Labor or block their entry to government. Labor's support rose to 39 per cent in 1909, allowing them to form a short minority government (one week). In 1914 Labor returned to power for two years with Liberal support. Finally, in 1934 Labor won their first majority government and held power in Tasmania uninterrupted until 1969. See Hughes, "STV in Australia," as well as Michael Denholm, "Playing the Game: Some Notes on the Second Earle

Government, 1914–1916," *Tasmanian Historical Research Association: Papers and Proceedings* 23, no. 4 (Dec. 1976): 149–52.

249 Anti-party sentiments were rife amongst voting system reformers in the late nineteenth and early twentieth centuries, though the American political scientist John Commons was an exception. See R.B. Walker, "Catherine Helen Spence and South Australian Politics," *Australian Journal of Politics and History* 15, no. 1 (Apr. 1969): 35–46; Commons, *Proportional Representation*. This anti-party theme only intensified in the reform periods around the First World War. In wartime Britain, H.G. Wells, declaring the British masses "utterly disgusted with parties," summed up some of the key anti-party arguments of reformers, suggesting that PR was "organizer-proof," and that it would allow independents to get elected. See Hart, *Proportional Representation*, 192. For a representative sample of farmer and populist anti-party sentiments, see David Laycock, *Populism and Democratic Thought in the Canadian Prairies, 1910–1945* (Toronto: University of Toronto Press, 1990), 46–51, 80–5. Ireland actually incorporated anti-party and direct representation ideas into its Senate. Through an elaborate nomination process, different social groups (farmers, workers, religious elites, etc.) were supposed to gain representation, though the system never really operated in this manner, as party affiliation quickly became more important. See J.H. Whyte, "Ireland: Politics without Social Bases," in *Electoral Behavior: A Comparative Handbook*, ed. Richard Rose (New York: Free Press, 1974), 625.

250 Rickard, *Class and Politics*, 242–54; Graham, "Choice of Voting Methods in Federal Politics," 170.

251 Rydon, "Electoral Methods and the Australian Party System," 76; Farrell and McAllister, *Australian Electoral System*, 69.

252 Graham, "Choice of Voting Methods in Federal Politics," 170–1.

253 The degree of the devastation can be seen in comparing the number of Labor governments at the state and federal level between 1915 and 1916. In just one year the party slipped from holding power in seven governments to just one (Queensland). See D. Murphy, "Queensland," in Murphy, *Labor in Politics*, 194.

254 Ken Turner, "From Liberal to National in New South Wales," *Australian Journal of Politics and History* 10, no. 2 (Aug. 1964): 205–20.

255 Graham, "Choice of Voting Methods in Federal Politics," 170–1.

256 However, Stock suggests that perhaps a majority of farmers did not support conscription for fear of rural labour shortages, a factor that distanced them from the Liberals and National coalition, perhaps fuelling their independent political efforts. See Jenny Tilby Stock, "Farmers and the Rural

Vote in South Australia in World War I: The 1916 Conscription Referendum," *Historical Studies* 21, no. 84 (Apr. 1985): 391–408.

257 Indeed, by 1919 National legislators recognized that the popularity of former Labor and now Nationalist wartime prime minister W.M. Hughes was probably their key asset. See Conrad Joyner, "W.M. Hughes and the 'Powers' Referendum of 1919: A Master Politician at Work," *Australian Journal of Politics and History* 5, no. 1 (May 1959): 20. This insecurity also manifested at the state level, particularly New South Wales, where another Labor government had split and a National coalition had emerged. See Loveday, "New South Wales," 98–9.

258 Graham, "Choice of Voting Methods in Federal Politics," 172.

259 By this time farmers had already taken up direct political action successfully at the state level, making threats at the national level more serious. See J.R. Robertson, "The First Years of the Western Australian County Party, 1912–1916," *Historical Studies: Australia and New Zealand* 11, no. 43 (Oct. 1964): 343–60.

260 Graham, "Choice of Voting Methods in Federal Politics," 171.

261 Ibid., 172.

262 Reid and Forrest, *Australia's Commonwealth Parliament*, 116–18.

263 Graham, "Choice of Voting Methods in Federal Politics," 173–4. Farmer grievances over issues like price-fixing also played into broader concerns over the government's conduct of the war, with returning soldiers organizations also calling for reform. See Marian Sawer, "Australia: Replacing Plurality Rule with Majority-Preferential Voting," in Colomer, *Handbook of Electoral System Choice*, 478–9.

264 It also reflected the organizational weakness of the National party in 1918–19. See B.D. Graham, "The Place of Finance Committees in Non-Labor Politics, 1910–1930," *Australian Journal of Politics and History* 6, no. 1 (May 1960): 47.

265 Hughes, "STV in Australia," 160–1. Labor had formed a minority government in New South Wales in 1910 despite 49 per cent of the popular vote, a result that would have translated into a majority under normal circumstances. The key to the result was unity of the anti-Labor forces in not splitting their vote, aided by the just-introduced second ballot. However, in 1913 Labor's vote declined marginally, though this time the party did gain a majority of seats. Faced with the unpredictability of the voting system, and similar dynamics in the state to the national level in terms of a Lib-Lab National government, a shift toward a more proportional voting system reform must have appeared the best way to limit Labor. For vote totals, see Loveday, "New South Wales," 42.

266 Farrell and McAllister, *Australian Electoral System*, 40–1.
267 John E. Martin, "Unemployment, Government and the Labour Market in New Zealand 1860–1890," *New Zealand Journal of History* 29, no. 2 (Oct. 1995), 193–5; Erik Olssen, "The Working Class in New Zealand," *New Zealand Journal of History* 8, no. 1 (Apr. 1974): 44–60; James Holt, "The Political Origins of Compulsory Arbitration in New Zealand: A Comparison with Great Britain," *New Zealand Journal of History* 10, no. 2 (Apr. 1976): 106. As Holt makes clear, where unions were strong they did not typically support compulsory arbitration. However, where they were weak, governments had little incentive to introduce it. The novelty in New Zealand was the combination of a sizeable working-class electorate and the colony's need to hold onto immigrants.
268 Brown, *Rise of New Zealand Labour*, 2–4. Though Hamer notes that, despite the name, labour supporters were effectively marginalized in the organization, and Lib-Lab candidates tended to do poorly until 1908 (when independent labour politics emerged seriously). See David Hamer, *The New Zealand Liberals* (Auckland: Auckland University Press, 1988), 185–6.
269 Hamer, *New Zealand Liberals*, 110–12, 232, 234–5.
270 Ibid., 230.
271 Jackson and McRobie, *New Zealand Adopts Proportional Representation*, 25.
272 Hamer, *New Zealand Liberals*, 185. New Zealand Liberals faced pressures similar to those facing liberals everywhere, basically a tension between economic liberals pursuing business and middle-class support on the right ,and social liberals attempting to woo working-class support on the left.
273 Erik Olssen, "The Origins of the Labour Party: A Reconsideration," *New Zealand Journal of History* 21, no. 1 (Apr. 1987): 82; Olssen, "The Seaman's Union and Industrial Militancy, 1908–13," *New Zealand Journal of History* 19, no. 1 (Apr. 1985), 14–37.
274 Jim McAloon, "A Political Struggle: Christchurch Labour Politics 1905–1913," *New Zealand Journal of History* 28, no. 1 (Apr. 1994): 22–40; Libby Plumridge, "The Necessary but Not Sufficient Condition: Christchurch Labour and Working Class Culture," *New Zealand Journal of History* 19, no. 2 (Oct. 1985): 130–50; Hamer, *New Zealand Liberals*, 189–90.
275 B.D. Graham, "The County Party Idea in New Zealand Politics, 1901–1935," in *Studies of a Small Democracy*, ed. Robert Chapman and Keith Sinclair (Auckland: Blackwood and Janet Paul, 1963), 177–8.
276 Hamer, *New Zealand Liberals*, 185, 269. Hamer notes that elements within the governing Liberals, the opposition, and the business community were pressing for the creation of an anti-socialist party by 1908 and suggests that the second ballot emerged as an alternative.

277 David Hamer, "The Second Ballot: A New Zealand Electoral Experiment," *New Zealand Journal of History* 21, no. 1 (Apr. 1987): 102–5; Hamer, *New Zealand Liberals*, 266; Jackson and McRobie, *New Zealand Adopts Proportional Representation*, 25–6.

278 Hamer, *New Zealand Liberals*, 309–12, 321–2.

279 Ibid., 336.

280 Ibid., 344.

281 Hamer, "Second Ballot," 108–11; Jackson and McRobie, *New Zealand Adopts Proportional Representation*, 26.

282 Jackson and McRobie, *New Zealand Adopts Proportional Representation*, 28–9.

283 Hoag and Hallett, *Proportional Representation*, 197; *PR Review*, Oct. 1915, 12–13; *PR Review*, Jan. 1916, 24.

284 Leon Weaver, "The Rise, Decline, and Resurrection of Proportional Representation in Local Governments in the United States," in *Electoral Laws and Their Political Consequences*, ed. B. Grofman and A. Lijphart (New York: Agathon, 1986), 140–1.

285 Pilon, "Explaining Voting System Reform in Canada," 140–8.

286 Dennis Pilon, "Democracy, BC-Style," in *British Columbia Politics and Government*, ed. Michael Howlett, Dennis Pilon, and Tracy Summerville (Toronto: Emond Montgomery, 2010), 89.

287 Weaver, "The Rise, Decline, and Resurrection of Proportional Representation," 143–4; Joseph P. Harris, "The Practical Workings of Proportional Representation in the United States and Canada," *National Municipal Review* 19, no. S5 (May 1930): S339–S67.

288 Brown and Cook, *Canada 1896–1921*, 250–74; Murphy, "Queensland," 194; Pelling, *Short History of the Labour Party*, 38–9; Hinton, *Labour and Socialism*, 101; Adelman, *Decline of the Liberal Party*, 17–18.

289 R. Douglas, "The Background to the 'Coupon' Elections Arrangements," *English Historical Review* (Apr. 1971): 318–22.

290 Unlike in its dominions, the British realignment did not centre on conscription but more general questions about the conduct of the war. To avoid an election that he thought his party might lose, Liberal PM Asquith had managed to form an all-party coalition government in the spring of 1915. Conscription emerged as a potentially divisive issue in December, but Asquith stalled with half measures for a few months until he could no longer avoid it. The real split came when cross-party intrigue put his Liberal rival Lloyd George in the premiership in December 1916, and Asquith's supporters left the government for the opposition benches. See Adelman, *Decline of the Liberal Party*, 17–20.

291 Brown and Cook, *Canada 1896–1921*, 270–3.

292 *PR Review* 40 (Oct. 1916): 8; Phillips, "Challenges to the Voting System in Canada, 135.

293 The Union government's deputy PM and Finance Minister Thomas White ably defended the British anti-PR view in a pre-Union debate on the question in April 1917; see Canada, House of Commons *Hansard*, 30 Apr. 1917, 908–11.

Chapter 5

1 Carstairs, *Short History of Electoral Systems in Western Europe*, 91; Daalder, "The Netherlands" (1966), as cited in Scholten, "Does Consociationalism Exist?," 345.

2 Buse, "Ebert and the German Crisis," 234–55.

3 M. Macmillan, *Paris 1919* (New York: Random House, 2002), 248–9, 277.

4 Eley, *Forging Democracy*, 128–37. For a more in-depth treatment of Britain and Germany, see F.L. Carsten, *War against War: British and German Radical Movements in the First World War* (Berkeley: University of California Press, 1982).

5 Cronin, "Labor Insurgency and Class Formation," 125–52.

6 Eley, *Forging Democracy*, 152.

7 Ibid., 153–4. Another way to understand the dramatic increase in strikes is to examine the sharp incline in union densities across Western industrialized countries between 1914 and 1920. For example, in Britain, male union density rose from an already high 29.5 per cent in 1914 to 54.5 per cent in 1920. See George Sayers Bain and Robert Price, *Profiles of Union Growth: A Comparative Statistical Portrait of Eight Countries* (Oxford: Basil Blackwell, 1980), 37.

8 Anthony F. Upton, *The Finnish Revolution 1917–1918* (Minneapolis: University of Minnesota Press, 1980), 338–9; Haapala, "How Was the Working Class Formed?," 195; Collier, *Paths towards Democracy*, 88–9; Alapuro, *State and Revolution in Finland*, 176. In the spring of 1918 the Finnish "whites" considered repealing the universal franchise in favour of a more restricted version based on wealth and status. See Jussila, Hentila, and Nevakivi, *From Grand Duchy to a Modern State*, 123.

9 Eley, *Forging Democracy*, 153–63. For a more in-depth treatment, see F.L. Carsten, *Revolution in Central Europe 1918–1919* (Berkeley: University of California Press, 1972).

10 Gerhard Ritter, "The Second International, 1918–1920: Attempts to Recreate the Socialist International and to Influence the Peace Treaties," *Europa: A Journal of Interdisciplinary Studies* 2, no. 1 (Fall 1978): 11–32.

11 Macmillan, *Paris 1919*, 95. However, on the whole Macmillan downplays the impact of the revolutionary events across Europe, preferring to focus on the ideas and personalities of the great leaders as key factors in the post-war settlement. But this represents a backward step from previous generations of scholarship that managed to combine a sense of the revolutionary threat and its impact on society and elites. See John M. Thompson, *Russia, Bolshevism, and the Versailles Peace* (Princeton: Princeton University Press, 1966); and Mayer, *Politics and Diplomacy of Peacemaking*.

12 Hastings, "Proportional Representation and the Weimar Constitution," 68–9; Bernhard, *Institutions and the Fate of Democracy*, 32.

13 Hodge, "Three Ways to Lose a Republic," 175.

14 Hastings, "Proportional Representation and the Weimar Constitution," 73.

15 Mair, *Recasting Bourgeois Europe*, 56, 63. Contemporary discussants of the events could readily see these mixed motives of the various participants, particularly the far left's aim for revolution and the former Conservatives' desire for a return to monarchy and an end to democracy. See Walter James Shepard, "The New Government in Germany," *American Political Science Review* 13, no. 3 (Aug. 1919): 361–78; and Shepard, "The New German Constitution," *American Political Science Review* 14, no. 1 (Feb. 1920): 34–52.

16 Berman, *Social Democratic Moment*, 142; Bernhard, *Institutions and the Fate of Democracy*, 33–4. Gerwarth reviews how serious these concerns were, tracking ex-military involvement in the wave of "white terror" that swept the defeated central European countries in the years after the war's end. See Robert Gerwarth, "The Central European Counter Revolution: Paramilitary Violence in Germany, Austria, and Hungary after the Great War," *Past and Present* 200 (Aug. 2008): 175–209.

17 Mair, *Recasting Bourgeois Europe*, 65.

18 Ibid., 140.

19 Ibid., 54–6, 59–60.

20 Niehuss, "Historiography, Sources and Methods of Electoral and Electoral Law Analysis in Germany," 151; Bernhard, *Institutions and the Fate of Democracy*, 61.

21 Hastings, "Proportional Representation and the Weimar Constitution," 89, 118. While some, like the distinguished social scientist Max Weber, still had concerns about PR, they did not raise them publicly. See Wolfgang Mommsen, *Max Weber and German Politics* (Chicago: University of Chicago Press, 1984), 372, 388, 398.

22 Ziegler, "Proportional Representation in the Social and Political Conflict in Germany," 146.

23 In fact, as their vote went up, their number of seats in the Storting declined, from twenty-three in 1912 to nineteen in 1915 and eighteen in 1918.
See Ryssevik, "Parties vs Parliament," 31.

24 Matthews and Valen, *Parliamentary Representation*, 37.

25 Esping-Andersen, *Politics against Markets*, 79–80; Eley, *Forging Democracy*,
177; Sassoon, *One Hundred Years of Socialism*, 33; Sten Sparre Nilson, "A
Labor Movement in the Communist International: Norway, 1918–23," in
Schmitt, ed., *Neutral Europe between War and Revolution*, 135. Some argue
that Norway's left was markedly more radical than other comparable
Scandinavian countries and that this can be attributed to the country's
more rapid process of industrialization, but these conclusions are disputed. By contrast, Nilson suggests that the Norwegian radicalism was not
out of line with the more general levels of social upheaval emerging across
Western Europe between 1917 and 1921. See Trond Gilberg, *The Soviet
Communist Party and Scandinavian Communism: The Norwegian Case* (Oslo:
Universitetsforlaget, 1973), 17–22; Sten Sparre Nilson, "Labor Insurgency
in Norway: The Crisis of 1917–1920," *Social Science History* 5, no. 4 (Fall
1981): 393–416; and Nilson, "Factional Strife in the Norwegian Labour
Party 1918–1924," *Journal of Contemporary History* 16 (1981): 691–704.

26 Henry Valen and Daniel Katz, *Political Parties in Norway* (London:
Tavistock, 1964), 26; Carstairs, *Short History of Electoral Systems in Western
Europe*, 91–2; Aardal, "Electoral Systems in Norway," 186–7.

27 Carstairs, *Short History of Electoral Systems in Western Europe*, 141. In 1908
the Social Democrats gained 18 per cent of the popular vote but just 4 per
cent of the parliamentary seats, while in 1911 they secured 20 per cent of
the vote but only 9 per cent of the seats. Only in 1914 did their popular
vote and seat total resemble each other.

28 Lutz, "Switzerland: Introducing Proportional Representation from Below,"
286.

29 Heinz K. Meier, "The Swiss National General Strike of November 1918," in
Schmitt, *Neutral Europe between War and Revolution*, 78, 81. Though the general strike was rooted primarily in domestic political concerns, conservative elites were convinced it was revolutionary in character and responded
with a mixture of repression and reform, sending strike leaders to jail but
then agreeing to send strike demands for PR to a referendum.

30 Carstairs, *Short History of Electoral Systems in Western Europe*, 141; Katzenstein,
Small States in World Markets, 155. Steinberg notes that the federal government had promised a referendum on PR before the 1914 election, but as
the election results effectively marginalized the left, they felt free to stall.
One effect of this decision was to move even party-oriented members of

the left, including Socialist party and trade union elites, to support direct action approaches like the political strike, a shift that helped give rise to the general strike in the fall of 1918. See Jonathan Steinberg, *Why Switzerland?* 2nd ed. (Cambridge, UK: Cambridge University Press, 1996), 55–9. However, not everyone agrees that left activism moved the reform process decisively. Lutz claims that no single factor can be credited with moving the adoption of PR in Switzerland, yet in his own account he carefully outlines how it was only when the left appeared threatening that the entrenched opposition to reform gave way. See Lutz, "Switzerland: Introducing Proportional Representation from Below," 286–7, 290, 292.

31 Johansen, "Denmark," 56; Elklit, "Best of Both Worlds?," 195.

32 Carol Gold, "Denmark, 1918," in Schmitt, ed., *Neutral Europe between War and Revolution*, 89–95.

33 Due-Nielsen, "Denmark and the First World War," 16–17.

34 Christiansen, "Reformism within Danish Social Democracy," 307–9; Miller, *Government and Politics in Denmark*, 37; Gold, "Denmark, 1918," 105–8.

35 Miller, *Friends and Rivals*, 13–15.

36 Johansen, "Denmark," 33; De Faramond, "Nordic Countries," 198.

37 Berman, *Social Democratic Moment*, 118–20; Carl-Goran Andrae, "The Swedish Labor Movement and the 1917–1918 Revolution," in *Sweden's Development from Poverty to Affluence 1750–1970*, ed. Steven Koblik, 232–53 (Minneapolis: University of Minnesota Press, 1975); Verney, *Parliamentary Reform in Sweden*, 209; Bo Sarlvik, "Party and Electoral System in Sweden," in Grofman and Lijphjart, *Evolution of Electoral and Party Systems in Nordic Countries*, 241.

38 Ernest Mahaim, "Proportional Representation and the Debates upon the Electoral Question in Belgium," *Annals of the American Academy of Political and Social Science* 15, no. 3 (May 1900): 396; Polosky, "A Revolution for Socialist Reforms," 452–4.

39 John Fitzmaurice, *The Politics of Belgium* (London: C. Hurst, 1983), 33; Verkade, *Democratic Parties in the Low Countries and Germany*, 31.

40 Verkade, *Democratic Parties in the Low Countries and Germany*, 33; Carstairs, *Short History of Electoral Systems in Western Europe*, 55.

41 Fitzmaurice, *Politics of Belgium*, 35–6; Marks, *Innocent Abroad*, 86–7, 171–83. Concern for social peace moved the monarch to force the pace of reform and depart from strict constitutionalism in expanding the franchise. Though some Conservatives complained, others approved of the breach to help stem the influence of revolution from abroad. See Val Lorwin, "Belgium: Religion, Class and Language in National Politics," in *Political Oppositions in Western Democracies*, ed. Robert Dahl (New Haven: Yale, 1966),

158; Hans A. Schmitt, "Violated Neutrals: Belgium, the Dwarf States, and Luxemburg," in Schmitt, *Neutral Europe between War and Revolution*, 207.

42 André Mommen, *The Belgian Economy in the Twentieth Century* (New York: Routledge, 1994), 3–8.

43 Marks, *Innocent Abroad*, 135–6, 204–5, 338.

44 Carstairs, *Short History of Electoral Systems in Western Europe*, 56.

45 Collier, *Paths toward Democracy*, 90. As in other countries on the Continent, important elements of the traditional Belgian elites, particularly Catholics, remained unconvinced of the merits of democratic government in the interwar period, a sentiment that only increased with crises of the 1930s. Thus the democratic bargain extracted during the upheaval immediately following the war could hardly been seen as fixed or beyond reversal. See Martin Conway, "Building the Christian City: Catholics and Politics in Inter-war Francophone Belgium," *Past and Present* 128 (Aug. 1990): 117–51. For post-war election results, see Verkade, *Democratic Parties in the Low Countries and Germany*, 91.

46 Paul Corner and Giovanna Procacci, "The Italian Experience of 'Total' Mobilization 1915–1920," in Horne, *State, Society and Mobilization in Europe*, 229–34.

47 Though Miller notes that the left did face some repression from the state, it hardly compares with the actions of other belligerent states. See James Miller, *From Elite to Mass Politics: Italian Socialism in the Giolittian Era, 1900–1914* (Kent, Ohio: Kent State University Press, 1990), 205–6. By contrast, Procacci argues that the Italian government entered the war without an electoral mandate, internally divided about the proper course of action, and that this created space for opposition to it from Socialists and others. See Procacci, "Popular Protest and Labour Conflict in Italy, 1915–18," 34.

48 Eley, *Forging Democracy*, 170.

49 Macmillan, *Paris 1919*, 285, 289–91, 293–5.

50 Mair, *Recasting Bourgeois Europe*, 110–11, 117; Carstairs, *Short History of Electoral Systems in Western Europe*, 154–5.

51 Miller, *From Elite to Mass Politics*, 3–5; Mair, *Recasting Bourgeois Europe*, 24–5; Ruescheneyer, Huber Stephens and Stephens, *Capitalist Development and Democracy*, 103–4.

52 Mair, *Recasting Bourgeois Europe*, 25–7.

53 Hartmut Ullrich, "Historiography, Sources and Methods for the Study of Electoral Laws in Italy," in Noiret, *Political Strategies and Electoral Reforms*, 314, 321–2.

54 Miller, *From Elite to Mass Politics*, 26, 126–7.

55 Gaetano Salvemini, *The Origins of Fascism in Italy* (New York: Harper and Row, 1973), 224–5.

56 Mair, *Recasting Bourgeois Europe*, 49. Davis points out that farm-workers had been amongst the first to organize a union federation (in 1901) and comprised 48 per cent of the total CGIL membership in 1914. See John A. Davis, "Socialism and the Working Class in Italy before 1914," in Geary, *Labour and Socialist Movements in Europe before 1914*, 213.

57 Eley, *Forging Democracy*, 170–1.

58 Ullrich, "Historiography, Sources and Methods," 325–6.

59 Alexander De Grand, *The Italian Left in the Twentieth Century* (Bloomington: Indiana University Press, 1989), 34–6; Eley, *Forging Democracy*, 171.

60 H. James Burgwynm, *The Legend of the Mutilated Victory: Italy, the Great War, and the Paris Peace Conference, 1915–1919* (Westport: Greenwood, 1993), 313–18.

61 Christopher Seton-Watson, *Italy from Liberalism to Fascism 1870–1925* (London: Methuen, 1967), 536, 547; Mair, *Recasting Bourgeois Europe*, 114–17. Though as Ulrich points out, he too had a volte face on the issue. See Ullrich, "Historiography, Sources and Methods," 326.

62 Ullrich, "Historiography, Sources and Methods," 328.

63 Herbert Tint, *France since 1918* (London: B.T. Basford, 1970), 10–12; Anthony Adamthwaite, *Grandeur and Misery: France's Bid for Power in Europe 1914–1940* (London: Arnold, 1995), 68–9; Mair, *Recasting Bourgeois Europe*, 77–8.

64 Anderson, *Conservative Politics in France*, 194–5; Martin, *France and the Après Guerre*, 51; McMillan, *Twentieth Century France*, 81–2, 86.

65 Roger Magraw, "Paris 1917–20: Labour Protest and Popular Politics," in Wrigley, *Challenges of Labour*, 136–8; Horne, "State and the Challenge of Labour in France," 247–51; Mair, *Recasting Bourgeois Europe*, 77–8.

66 Campbell, *French Electoral Systems and Elections*, 85, 89; Carstairs, *Short History of Electoral Systems in Western Europe*, 178.

67 Mair, *Recasting Bourgeois Europe*, 30–1.

68 Goldey and Williams, "France," 65.

69 Ibid., 68–9.

70 Ibid., 69.

71 Mair, *Recasting Bourgeois Europe*, 97.

72 Eley, *Forging Democracy*, 117–18.

73 Campbell, *French Electoral Systems and Elections*, 86, 90–1.

74 Kathryn E. Amdur, *Syndicalist Legacy: Trade Unions and Politics in Two French Cities in the Era of World War I* (Urbana: University of Illinois Press, 1986), 263–4; Sassoon, *One Hundred Years of Socialism*, 52.

75 Kendall, *Labour Movement in Europe*, 37; McMillan, *Twentieth Century France*, 28–9; Eley, *Forging Democracy*, 64, 85; Sassoon, *One Hundred Years of Socialism*, 14.

76 Mair, *Recasting Bourgeois Europe*, 47. Though the left had important pockets of support in rural and semi-rural areas. See Magraw, "Socialism, Syndicalism and French Labour before 1914," 82–3.

77 Mair, *Recasting Bourgeois Europe*, 134.

78 Pierce, "French Legislative Elections," 2; Goldey and Williams, "France," 63.

79 Martin, *France and the Après Guerre*, 49–52; Bernard and Dubief, *Decline of the Third Republic*, 86; Mair, *Recasting Bourgeois Europe*, 92–3, 97–8.

80 Pierce, "French Legislative Elections," 8. Evidence of the bias can be seen in the result for the SFIO in the 1919 contest. Running without a deal with the Radicals, the socialists gained 23 per cent of the popular vote but only 11 per cent of the parliamentary seats. See Geary, "Paris 1917–20," 135.

81 Bernard and Dubief, *Decline of the Third Republic*, 87. On the "no alliances" policy, see Jean Lacouture, *Leon Blum* (New York: Holmes and Meier, 1982), 168–9.

82 Raymond Leslie Buell, "Political and Social Reconstruction in France," *American Political Science Review* 15, no. 1 (Feb. 1921): 5.

83 Pugh, *Electoral Reform in War and Peace*, 156; Bogdanor, *People and the Party System*, 130–1.

84 V. Bogdanor, "Electoral Reform and British Politics," *Electoral Studies* 6, no. 2 (1987): 116.

85 Douglas, "Background to the 'Coupon' Elections Arrangements," 328–9.

86 Hart, *Proportional Representation*, 183–4. Lloyd George's Cabinet initially tried to get the Speaker's Conference to reconsider its proposal for PR. When they refused, the government submitted the bill to the house, declaring the portions it did not like – specifically PR and the women's franchise – open to free votes.

87 Douglas, "Background to the 'Coupon' Elections Arrangements," 330.

88 Ibid., 325.

89 Adelman, *Decline of the Liberal Party*, 26–7.

90 Philip Abrams, "The Failure of Social Reform," *Past and Present* 24 (Apr. 1963): 43–4, 49. Mayer notes that Lloyd George campaigned on vague promises of "housing, better wages and better working conditions" to attract working-class votes but offered more concrete promises to the Conservatives in private. See Mayer, *Politics and Diplomacy of Peacemaking*, 138.

91 Ibid., 603. The character of the labour revolt in Britain in 1919 and the "coupon" government's mostly conservative response to it is explored in Chris Wrigley, *Lloyd George and the Challenge of Labour* (New York: St Martin's, 1990).

92 However, the official Liberal party's hostility to Lloyd George and his co-
    alition Liberals did much to fuel to uncertainty by effectively cutting off
    the latter's retreat back into the party. Throughout most of 1919 Lloyd
    George tried to establish the basis for a new "centre" party that would
    combine his Liberals with the Conservatives into a powerful anti-socialist
    bloc, but that plan was rejected by his own followers, as it would have
    been by most Conservatives party members as well. See Adelman, *Decline
    of the Liberal Party*, 28–9; Maurice Cowling, *The Impact of Labour 1920–1924*
    (Cambridge: Cambridge University Press, 1971), 94–6, 113–14.

93 Hart, *Proportional Representation*, 213–14; Carstairs, *Short History of Electoral
    Systems in Western Europe*, 196. The bill was sponsored by an Independent
    Liberal MP. Perhaps as an indication of the precariousness of their posi-
    tion, over half of the Coalition Liberals also supported the initiative.

94 Cowling notes that many at the time could see that Labour's modest re-
    sult in 1918 had more to do with the low turnout and bad timing of the
    election (bad for Labour, good for the Coalition) than their potential levels
    of support. See Cowling, *Impact of Labour*, 25. For the various strategies of
    anti-labour politics in the inter-war period, see Patrick Renshaw, "Anti-
    Labour Politics in Britain, 1918–27," *Journal of Contemporary History* 12
    (1977): 693–705.

95 Here discourse mattered. Though Britain and other Anglo-American locales
    witnessed a high degree of social upheaval following the war, the political
    manifestation of the "labour revolt" in labourism meant that it did not draw
    as readily on the threatening overtones as socialism did in Europe, no mat-
    ter how pragmatic and constitutional the latter actually were in practice
    (particularly in post-war Germany). This would become only too clear in
    British Labour's timid responses to the 1926 general strike, where the par-
    ty was concerned to underline its commitment to the constitution. See
    John Saville, "Labourism and the Labour Government," in Coates, *Paving
    the Third Way*, 87; Laura Beers, "'Is This Man an Anarchist?' Industrial
    Action and the Battle for Public Opinion in Interwar Britain," *Journal of
    Modern History* 82 (Mar. 2010): 30–60. Having said this, anti-labour elites
    were alarmed by the rise of labour militancy and were very active in com-
    bating it. See Arthur McIvor, "A 'Crusade for Capitalism': The Economic
    League, 1919–39," *Journal of Contemporary History* 23 (1988): 631–55.

96 Graham, "Choice of Voting Methods in Federal Politics," 274–5.

97 Jackson and McRobie, *New Zealand Adopts Proportional Representation*, 28–9.
    On the formation of the second Labour party, see Jack Vowles, "Ideology
    and the Formation of the New Zealand Labour Party: Some New
    Evidence," *New Zealand Journal of History* 16, no. 1 (Apr. 1982), 39–55.

98 Pilon, "Explaining Voting System Reform in Canada, 1874–1960," 146–7. For party platforms, see C. Stacey, *Historical Documents of Canada* (Toronto: Macmillan, 1972), 36, 40.

99 Pilon, "Explaining Voting System Reform in Canada, 1874–1960," 142–5.

100 G. Kealey and D. Cruikshank, "Strikes in Canada, 1891–1950," in *Workers and Canadian History*, ed. G. Kealey,(Montreal and Kingston: McGill-Queen's University Press, 1995), 368–71; Heron, "Labourism and the Canadian Working Class," 369. For more general background, see C. Heron, *The Canadian Labour Movements: A Short History* (Toronto: James Lorimer, 1989); M. Robin, *Radical Politics and Canadian Labour* (Kingston: Industrial Relations Centre – Queen's University, 1968); and James Naylor, *The New Democracy* (Toronto: University of Toronto Press, 1991).

101 J. Hopkins, *Canadian Annual Review 1919* (Toronto: Canadian Annual Review, 1920): 382–9.

102 J. Paul Johnston and Miriam Koene, "Learning History's Lessons Anew: The Use of STV in Canadian Municipal Elections," in Bowler and Grofman, *Elections in Australia, Ireland, and Malta under the Single Transferable Vote*, 213.

103 Phillips, "Challenges to the Voting System in Canada," 135–6.

104 Ibid., 165–6.

105 American labour experience in this period is ably summarized in D. Montgomery, *The Fall of the House of Labor* (Cambridge: Cambridge University Press, 1987), chap. 8. On the "exceptionalism" of the American ruling class, see Kim Voss, *The Making of American Exceptionalism: The Knights of Labor and Class Formation in the Nineteenth Century* (Ithaca: Cornell University Press, 1993); and Sanford Jacoby, *Masters to Managers: Historical and Comparative Perspectives on American Employers* (New York: Columbia University Press, 1991).

106 Though social upheaval was a concern in Britain too; see Hinton, *Labour and Socialism*, 109–16; and Cowling, *Impact of Labour*, 21, 25–6, 43–4.

107 Eley, *Forging Democracy*, 156–7, 225.

108 Mair, *Recasting Bourgeois Europe*, 8–9.

109 Other responses included the rise of business-funded anti-socialist leagues that produced millions of leaflets and broadsheets for public consumption, a dramatic increase in national business organizations like employers and trade associations with a social or public focus, and more direct links between business funding for anti-socialist politicians, as well as pressure for centre-right parties to mimic the organization of left mass parties. See Chris Wrigley, "The State and the Challenge of Labour in Britain 1917–20," in Wrigley, *Challenges of Labour*, 280–4; Kitchen, *Political*

Economy of Germany, 256; A.J. Heidenheimer and F.C. Langdon, *Business Associations and the Financing of Political Parties: A Comparative Study of the Evolution Practices in Germany, Norway and Japan* (The Hague: Martinus Jijhoff, 1968), 23–7; Verkade, *Democratic Parties in the Low Countries and Germany*, 31–3; McIvor, "'Crusade for Capitalism,'" 631–55.

110 Tint, *France since 1918*, 21–8; Keiger, *Raymond Poincairé*, 306. The right toyed with changing the voting system in 1923 when they realized that the SFIO and Radicals were patching up their alliance, and again in 1931. See Martin, *France and the Après Guerre*, 227–8; and Bernard and Dubief, *Decline of the Third Republic*, 177. On Communist competition for the SFIO and the nature of their relationship, see Bernard and Dubief, *Decline of the Third Republic*, 154–5; Louise Elliot Dalby, *Leon Blum: Evolution of a Socialist* (New York: Thomas Yoseloff, 1963), 213, 265–6; Lacouture, *Leon Blum*, 178–80, 184–8.

111 David Abraham, "Conflicts within German Industry and the Collapse of the Weimar Republic," *Past and Present* 88 (Autumn 1980): 88–128.

112 Verney, *Parliamentary Reform in Sweden*, 215–16; Florence E. Janson, "Minority Governments in Sweden," *American Political Science Review* 22, no, 2 (May 1928): 407–13.

113 Elmer D. Graper, "The British Election," *American Political Science Review* 19, no. 1 (Feb. 1925): 84–96.

114 Hart, *Proportional Representation*, 221–3; Carstairs, *Short History of Electoral Systems in Western Europe*, 196; Bogdanor, *People and the Party System*, 134.

115 Herman Finer, *The Case against PR* (London: Fabian Society, 1924).

116 Hart, *Proportional Representation*, 234–44. The fall of the minority Labour government and defection of Labour leader Ramsey Macdonald to the Conservative-dominated National government underlined the continuing instability and weakness of the centre-left in Britain in the inter-war period. Labour members were still fighting over whether to make stand-down agreements with Liberals to avoid vote-splitting into the late 1930s. See Martin Pugh, "The Liberal Party and the Popular Front," *English Historical Review* 121, no. 494 (Dec. 2006), 1327–50. As for the Conservatives, despite their victory, they too continued to worry about the implications of a future Labour majority in the House of Commons. While uninterested in PR, they did continue to pursue discussions about reforms to the House of Lords that would allow them to stymie any future Labour majority in the lower house. See W.A. Rudlin, "Report on House of Lords Reform in Great Britain," *American Political Science Review* 27, no. 2 (Apr. 1933): 243–9.

117 The commonwealth Labour parties were well aware of the developments concerning their counterparts in other jurisdictions. For instance, British

Labour had followed labour's efforts in New Zealand and was critical of that country's compulsory arbitration act. See Ralph H.C. Hayburn, "William Pember Reeves, the Times, and New Zealand's Industrial Conciliation and Arbitration Act, 1906–1908," *New Zealand Journal of History* 21, no. 2 (Oct. 1987): 251–69.

118 Hughes, "STV in Australia," 160–1.
119 Pilon, "Explaining Voting System Reform in Canada," 147.
120 H. Orliffe, "Proportional Representation," *Canadian Forum* 22, no. 205 (Feb. 1938): 388–90. Phillips sketches out the debate over PR amongst the members of the League for Social Reconstruction, a group of left-wing intellectuals who influenced the formation of Canada's left party, the Cooperative Commonwealth Federation (CCF) in the 1930s. See Phillips, "Challenges to the Voting System in Canada," 216.
121 Pilon, "Explaining Voting System Reform in Canada," 145.
122 Bryan Palmer, *Working Class Experience*, 2nd ed. (Toronto: McClelland and Stewart, 1992), 219–21.
123 Pilon, "Explaining Voting System Reform in Canada," 146–8.
124 Naylor, *New Democracy*, 224, 243; Phillips, "Challenges to the Voting System in Canada," 163.
125 Harold Jansen, "The Single Transferable Vote in Alberta and Manitoba" (PhD diss., University of Alberta, 1998), 47–8, 57.
126 Phillips, "Challenges to the Voting System in Canada," 174–5, 179–80.
127 Ibid., 176, 184–5.
128 Ibid., 191–8.
129 Kings's success in gathering third-party adherents back into the fold is recounted in John Herd Thompson and Allen Seager, *Canada 1922–39: Decades of Discord* (Toronto: McClelland and Stewart, 1985), chap. 6.
130 Phillips, "Challenges to the Voting System in Canada," 198–9.
131 Elections British Columbia, *Electoral History of British Columbia, 1871–1986* (Victoria: Queen's Printer, 1988), 173; Grace MacInnis, *J.S. Woodsworth: A Man to Remember* (Toronto: Macmillan, 1953), 286.
132 Phillips, "Challenges to the Voting System in Canada," 229.
133 Ibid., 238. The use of PR in Winnipeg long divided the left, with criticisms emerging shortly after its introduction and various challenges to its use mounted by Labour members of council from the late 1920s on. CCF members did not agree amongst themselves on its repeal at the provincial level in 1955. See Pilon, "Explaining Voting System Reform in Canada," 153–4; Jansen, "Single Transferable Vote," 219–23.
134 Pilon, "Explaining Voting System Reform in Canada," 150, 153. The Communists had gained representation in both the provincial house and city council under PR but failed to return any members after its repeal.

135 For a contemporary discussion of how non-socialist forces limited Sweden's Social Democrats, for instance, see Janson, "Minority Governments in Sweden," 407–13.

136 Mair, *Recasting Bourgeois Europe*, 104.

137 Donald G. Wileman, "What the Market Will Bear: The French Cartel Elections of 1924," *Journal of Contemporary History* 29 (1994): 483–500.

138 Tony Judt, "The French Socialist and the Cartel des Gauches of 1924," *Journal of Contemporary History* 11, nos 2–3 (July 1976): 199–215.

139 Ibid., 206–8.

140 Kreuzer, "Historical Knowledge and Quantitative Analysis," 377. Of course, incentives do not necessarily get results. In 1928 the Communists again refused to cooperate with the SFIO, with disastrous results for both parties. Only when the scale of the problem became apparent after the first ballot did the Communists scramble to make a few deals with the SFIO to stand down candidates. For a discussion of the Communists and their 1924 and 1928 alliance strategies, see Maxwell Adereth, *The French Communist Party: A Critical History (1920–84)* (Manchester: Manchester University Press, 1984), 46–8.

141 See Cole and Campbell, *French Electoral Systems and Elections*, 63–9.

142 Mair, *Recasting Bourgeois Europe*, 192.

143 Hodge, "Three Ways to Lose a Republic," 176.

144 Pulzer, "Germany," 90.

145 Seton-Watson, *Italy from Liberalism to Fascism*, 549.

146 Mair, *Recasting Bourgeois Europe*, 129–30.

147 Numerous authors attest to the bifurcated state of Italy's economic and political development, noting that, unlike most of western Europe, Italy did not become a predominantly urban, industrialized society until after the Second World War. See Tobias Abse, "Italy," in Berger and Broughton, *Force of Labour*, 138–9; John A. Davis, "Socialism and the Working Classes in Italy before 1914," in Geary, *Labour and Socialist Movements in Europe before 1914*, 210–11.

148 Eley, *Forging Democracy*, 171–4.

149 Mair, *Recasting Bourgeois Europe*, 315; Rueschemeyer, Huber Stephens, and Stephens, *Capitalist Development and Democracy*, 104–5.

150 Seton-Watson, *Italy from Liberalism to Fascism*, 587–90; Mair, *Recasting Bourgeois Europe*, 336.

151 Adrian Lyttleton, *The Seizure of Power* (Princeton: Princeton University Press, 1987), 11–12; Mair, *Recasting Bourgeois Europe*, 339, 350.

152 Salvemini, *Origins of Fascism in Italy*, 316. At one point, to distract Liberals from one of his many indiscretions, Mussolini did introduce a bill to return to single-member districts. See Lyttleton, *Seizure of Power*, 263.

153 Ullrich, "Historiography, Sources and Methods," 327–8; Mair, *Recasting Bourgeois Europe*, 346–7; Salvemini, *Origins of Fascism in Italy*, 392–6. Mussolini wanted to marginalize his political competitors both within and outside of his Fascist movement and considered a plurality and regionally based majority system before settling on his super-majority option. The negotiations are recounted in detail in Lyttleton, *Seizure of Power*, 121–35.

154 Mair, *Recasting Bourgeois Europe*, 344–6. Lyttleton notes that the election following the passage of the new voting system was characterized by fairly free and democratic administration in the northern cities, helping explain how the opposition gained 33 per cent of the total vote, but blatant intimidation and corruption everywhere else. See Lyttleton, *Seizure of Power*, 146–8.

155 Examples include efforts to change the voting system in Britain in 1924 and 1931, and in Canada in 1923 and 1934–6.

Chapter 6

1 For exceptions, see Renwick, *Politics of Voting System Reform*; Alan Renwick, "Electoral Reform in Europe since 1945," *West European Politics* 34, no. 3 (2011): 456–77; and Bernhard, *Institutions and the Fate of Democracy*.

2 Here Renwick and Bernhard both ignore the "politics" of the Cold War and the many ways in which American politicians and policymakers attempted to intervene in the internal politics of European countries to limit left projects for state-led economic and social programs, characterizing their efforts instead as simply supporting the establishment of sustainable democratic structures.

3 Paul Furlong, *Modern Italy: Representation and Reform* (London: Routledge, 1994), 54. For an interesting and detailed contemporary account of some of the elite machinations accompanying the transfer of governing responsibility from fascist to anti-fascist forces, see Howard McGaw Smyth, "Italy: From Fascism to the Republic (1943–1946)," *Political Research Quarterly* 1, no. 3 (Sept. 1948): 205–22.

4 Fernando Claudin, *The Communist Movement: From Comintern to Cominform* (Harmondsworth: Penguin, 1975), 345–7; Kolko, *Politics of War*, 45; Furlong, *Modern Italy*, 56.

5 David W. Ellwood, *Italy 1943–45* (Bath: Leicester University Press, 1985), 152, 155; Claudin, *Communist Movement*, 361; Kolko, *Politics of War*, 48.

6 Joan Barth Urban, *Moscow and the Italian Communist Party: From Togliatitti to Berlinger* (Ithaca: Cornell University Press, 1986), 148, 168.

7 Kolko, *Politics of War*, 52–4; Stephen Hellman, "Italian Communism in the First Republic," in *The New Italian Republic: From the Fall of the Berlin Wall to Berlusconi*, ed. Stephen Gundle and Simon Parker (London: Routledge, 1996), 72.

8 Ginsborg, *History of Contemporary Italy*, 43–4; Claudin, *Communist Movement*, 348–51; Urban, *Moscow and the Italian Communist Party*, 185.

9 Sassoon, *One Hundred Years of Socialism*, 103–4, 129.

10 Ibid., 140.

11 Ibid., 129.

12 Clifford A.L. Rich, "The Permanent Crisis of Italian Democracy," *Journal of Politics* 14, no. 4 (Nov. 1952): 665.

13 Mario Einaudi, "Political Change in France and Italy," *American Political Science Review* 40, no. 5 (Oct. 1946), 904, 908; Rich, "Permanent Crisis of Italian Democracy," 665.

14 Mario Amoroso, "Italy," in *European Electoral Systems Handbook*, ed. Geoffrey Hand, Jacques Georgel, and Christoph Sasse (London: Butterworths, 1979), 141; Christopher Seton-Watson, "Italy," in *Democracy and Elections: Electoral Systems and Their Political Consequences*, ed. Vernon Bogdanor and David Butler (New York: Cambridge University Press, 1983), 110; Ullrich, "Historiography, Sources and Methods," 330.

15 As Di Palma makes clear, these calculations informed all of the constitutional debates of the period and the struggles over the interpretations of the constitution that followed. See Guiseppe Di Palma, "The Available State: Problems of Reform," in *Italy in Transition: Consensus and Conflict*, ed. Peter Lange and Sidney Tarrow (London: Frank Cass, 1980),150–2.

16 Einaudi, "Political Change in France and Italy," 903–4.

17 Ronald L. Filippelli, *American Labor and Postwar Italy, 1943–1953* (Stanford: Stanford University Press, 1989), 131; Douglas J. Forsyth, "The Peculiarities of Italo-American Relations in Historical Perspective," *Journal of Modern Italian Studies* 3, no. 1 (1998): 2.

18 Eley, "Back to the Beginning," 102; Donald Sassoon, *The Strategy of the Italian Communist Party* (London: Frances Pinter, 1981), 60. The DC's tight relationship with Washington would keep both overt and covert aid money flowing into the country well into the 1970s. See E. Timothy Smith, *The United States, Italy and Nato, 1947–52* (New York: St Martin's, 1991), 35, 41.

19 Forsyth, "Peculiarities of Italo-American Relations," 14–15. Specific details of the many American plans are sketched out in James E. Miller, "Taking Off the Gloves: The United States and the Italian Elections of 1948," *Diplomatic History* 7, no. 1 (Winter 1983), particularly 42–3, 45–52.

20 Ginsborg, *History of Contemporary Italy*, 115. American attempts to influence Italian attitudes took many turns. Wagstaff reports how thousands
of Hollywood films were distributed in Italy throughout 1945–6 by the
Psychological Warfare Branch of the U.S. Army, dumping them at prices
that local film-makers and distributors could not match. See Christoper
Wagstaff, "Italy in the Post-war International Cinema Market," in *Italy in
the Cold War: Politics, Culture and Society 1948–58*, ed. C. Duggan and C.
Wagstagg, *Italy in the Cold War: Politics, Culture and Society 1948–58*
(Oxford: Berg, 1995), 93.

21 Filippelli reports that $US10 million were secretly diverted from the eco-
nomic stabilization fund to aid American interventions in the 1948 election, involving "pay for local election campaigns, anti-Communist
propaganda, and bribes." The United States also prepared contingency
plans involving the use of military force in the event of a Communist victory. See Filippelli, *American Labor in Postwar Italy*, 131; as well as James E.
Miller, *The United States and Italy, 1940–1950: The Politics and Diplomacy of
Stabilization* (Chapel Hill: University of North Carolina Press, 1986), 248;
Forsyth, "Peculiarities of Italo-American Relations," 2, 14; Smith, *United
States, Italy and Nato*, 35; and Ginsborg, *History of Contemporary Italy*, 116.

22 Alberto Martinelli, "Organized Business and Italian Politics: Confindustria
and the Christian Democrats in the Postwar Period," in *Italy in Transition:
Conflict and Consensus*, ed. Peter Lange and Sidney Tarrow (London: Frank
Cass, 1980), 72; Sidney Tarrow, "Italy: Crisis, Crises or Transition?," in
Lange and Tarrow, *Italy in Transition*, 174.

23 While mass parties on the left tried to make inroads into southern Italy
in the 1940s and did in fact make some progress, the poll for working-
class parties in the 1946 constituent assembly elections in the south was
less than half of their total in the north (21 per cent versus 52 per cent).
Meanwhile the DC's organization allowed it to move into previous Liberal
party territory in the south without really challenging the traditional clientelistic system of power. See P.A. Allum, "The South and National Politics,
1945–50," in *The Rebirth of Italy 1943–50*, ed. S.J. Woolf (Aylesbury:
Longmans, 1972), 106–7.

24 However, this initial organizational advantage would prove troublesome
for DC elites when those same Catholic organizations attempted to direct
party – and by extension government – policy. This contributed to the
DC's increasing use of state power for political purposes from the mid-
1950s on, precisely to limit Catholic influence over the political class. See
Percy Allum, "The Challenging Face of Christian Democracy," in Duggan
and Wagstaff, *Italy in the Cold War*, 121–2, 124–5.

25   Rich, "Permanent Crisis of Italian Democracy," 676.

26   Frederic Spotts and Theodor Wieser, *Italy: A Difficult Democracy* (Cambridge: Cambridge University Press, 1986), 21.

27   Sassoon, *One Hundred Years of Socialism*, 144–5.

28   Rich, "Permanent Crisis of Italian Democracy," 665–6.

29   There was debate within the DC about this shift to the right and away from a neutral foreign policy, but in the aftermath of the 1948 election victory this faction lost much of its influence (regaining it only with the shift to the left in the 1960s). See Robert Leonardi and Douglas E. Wertman, *Italian Christian Democracy: The Politics of Dominance* (New York: St Martin's, 1989), 54–5; Ginsborg, *History of Contemporary Italy*, 158.

30   Sassoon, *Strategy of the Italian Communist Party*, 87–9. At the same time, De Gasperi moved to weaken the influence of factions within his party with the introduction of a four-fifths majority rule at party conventions. See Leonardi and Wertman, *Italian Christian Democracy*, 59.

31   Norman Kogan, *A Political History of Italy: The Postwar Years* (New York: Praeger, 1983), 62.

32   Barbara Taverni, "For Italy in a Changing World: The Political Apogee of Alcide De Gasperi, 1948–1954," *Modern Italy* 14, no. 4 (Nov. 2009): 467; James R. Thayer, "The Contribution of Public Opinion Polls to the Understanding of the 1953 Election to Italy, West Germany and Japan," *Public Opinion Quarterly* 19, no. 3 (Autumn 1955): 260. Unlike Thayer, subsequent scholarly commentators have largely accepted the DC's stated rationale at face value, including Seton-Watson, "Italy," 116; and Ullrich, "Historiography, Sources and Methods," 332–4.

33   Indeed, contemporary academic commentary, itself hardly sympathetic to the electoral challenges of the Italian left, found the DC reasoning unconvincing and noted the proposed law's threat to small centrist parties. See Roy Pryce, "The New Italian Electoral Law," *Parliamentary Affairs* 6, no. 3 (1952): 269–76.

34   However, DC leaders were concerned about their ability to maintain their leading position in the political system, especially in light of local election results in 1951 and 1952 that suggested the party was losing ground to both the left and right, and Di Scala argues that this fuelled De Gasperi's interest in the voting system reform. See Spencer Di Scala, *Renewing Italian Socialism: Nenni to Craxi* (New York: Oxford University Press, 1988), 86; and Joseph G. La Palombara, "The Italian Elections and the Problem of Representation," *American Political Science Review* 47, no. 3 (Sept. 1953): 682–3, 685–6. Here De Gasperi and other secular Catholics worried about church influence on the party, particularly their pressure to resort to

alliances with the fascist right to defeat the left, if need be. Thus the bonus law would lessen the need for these sorts of distasteful arrangements as well. See Spotts and Wieser, *Italy: A Difficult Democracy*, 22–3.

35 Hellman, "Italian Communism in the First Republic," 74–5; Di Palma, "Available State," 151, 154; Spotts and Wieser, *Italy: Difficult Democracy*, 43.

36 Tom Behan, "'Going Further': The Aborted Italian Insurrection of July 1948," *Left History* 3, nos 2–4, no. 1 (Fall 1995/Spring 1996): 168–204; Claudin, *Communist Movement*, 477–8. Behan is not so sure that the "aborted" insurrection would have failed.

37 Miller, *United States and Italy*, 256–63; Marino Regini, "Labour Unions, Industrial Action and Politics," in Lange and Tarrow, *Italy in Transition*, 50; Frederico Romero, *The United States and the European Trade Union Movement, 1944–1951* (Chapel Hill: University of North Carolina Press, 1992), chap. 5, "Divisions and Realignments: The Italian Case," 138–74.

38 Smith, *United States, Italy and Nato*, 57.

39 Hellman, "Italian Communism in the First Republic," 74; Seton-Watson, "Italy," 116; Muriel Grindrod, *The Rebuilding of Italy* (London: Royale Institute of International Affairs, 1955), 83–4; Smith, *United States, Italy and Nato*, 94–5. Of course, the new law was not nearly as draconian as the Fascist version of 1923. As La Palombara notes, "While the latter granted two thirds of the seats to the party receiving a plurality of the vote, the former demanded that a group of joined parties get at least 50% plus one of the valid votes cast before it could benefit by the premium." But this misses the political overtones of the initiative. It didn't help that De Gasperi had forcefully opposed Mussolini's law in 1923 and at that time defended PR. See La Palombara, "Italian Elections and the Problem of Representation," 679.

40 Thayer, "Contribution of Public Opinion Polls," 262.

41 Ginsborg, *History of Contemporary Italy*, 142–3. The DC and its allies gained 49.85 per cent of the popular vote.

42 Grindrod, *Rebuilding of Italy*, 83, 90; Kogan, *Political History of Italy*, 64–5.

43 Smith, *United States, Italy and Nato*, 172.

44 Palombara, "Italian Elections and the Problem of Representation," 685.

45 Di Scala, *Renewing Italian Socialism*, 87, 99. Of course, the PSI did break with their Communist allies in 1956, leading to the decisive realignment of Italian politics in the 1960s that witnessed the party join the DC in government. For this shift, see Ilaria Favretto, "1956 and the PSI: The End of 'Ten Winters,'" *Modern Italy* 5, no. 1 (2000): 25–45; and for the shift cast into a longer time frame, see De Grand, *The Italian Left in the Twentieth Century*, esp. chap. 8, "The Left in the Years of Centrism, 1948–1960," 117–30.

46 Gianfranco Pasquino, "That Obscure Object of Desire: A New Electoral Law for Italy," in Noiret, *Political Strategies and Electoral Reforms*, 465; Di Palma, "Available State," 152. Besides, the manipulation of the voting system was not the only option open to the DC in maintaining their dominance. A number of scholars highlight how the Italian courts played a key role in negating some of the more radical elements of the post-war constitutional settlement, and through a series of decisions in the 1940s worked against the left more generally. Meanwhile, with control over the state, the DC stalled throughout the 1950s and 1960s in bringing into force various aspects of the constitution that might have offered some space to challenge their control. All this lends credence to Poulantzas's insight that the state offers many arenas for the powerful to pursue their interests, even if one locale (i.e., parliament) falls under more popular control. See Christopher Duggan, "Italy in the Cold War Years and the Legacy of Fascism," in Duggan and Walstaff, *Italy in the Cold War*, 4–5; Kogan, *Political History of Italy*, 105; Ginsborg, *History of Contemporary Italy*, 100; and Nicos Poulantzas, *State, Power, Socialism* (London: Verso, 1978), 138–9.

47 Richard F. Kuisel, *Capitalism and the State in Modern France* (Cambridge: Cambridge University Press, 1981), 202, 205.

48 Sassoon, *One Hundred Years of Socialism*, 91, 93; Andrew Shennan, *Rethinking France: Plans for Renewal 1940–1946* (Oxford: Clarendon, 1989), 93.

49 Claudin, *Communist Movement*, 330–2. The reputation of the Communist role in the resistance and the initial public goodwill toward the Soviet Union at the war's end also contributed to a strong movement within the Socialist Party in favour of close links with the PCF, either as part of a new political party drawn from the resistance forces or through a fusion of the two traditional parties of the left. See B.D. Graham, *The French Socialists and Tripartism 1944–1947* (Toronto: University of Toronto, 1965), 99; and Graham, *Choice and Democratic Order: The French Socialist Party, 1937–1950* (Cambridge: Cambridge University Press, 1994), 265. On economic issues, numerous authors have pointed out that Socialists in many countries were forwarding more radical demands than Communists in this period. For East Germany, see Phillips, *Soviet Policy towards East Germany*, 35; for Italy and France, see Donald Sassoon, "The Rise and Fall of West European Communism, 1938–1948," *Contemporary European History* 1, no. 2 (1992): 145, 147; and more generally, see Kolko, *Politics of War*, 5–6, 33; and Sassoon, *One Hundred Years of Socialism*, 89–91.

50 Anderson, *Conservative Politics in France*, 75; Shennan, *Rethinking Franc*, 79; René Rémond, *The Right Wing in France* (Philadelphia: University of Pennsylvania Press, 1966), 318.

51 Larkin, *France since the Popular Front*, 114–15.

52 Kolko, *Politics of War*, 76; Claudin, *Communist Movement*, 326. In fact, de Gaulle even welcomed the re-establishment of political parties, despite his distaste for them, to counter the organizational strength of the Communists in the resistance movement. See Robert Gildea, *France since 1945* (Oxford: Oxford University Press, 1996), 33.

53 Einaudi, "Political Change in France and Italy," 900.

54 Francois Goguel, *France under the Fourth Republic* (New York: Russell and Russell, 1952), 61.

55 Graham, *French Socialists and Tripartism*, 65.

56 Campbell, *French Electoral Systems and Elections since 1789*, 103; Larkin, *France since the Popular Front*, 138.

57 Goguel, *France under the Fourth Republic*, 60.

58 Besides pre-war complaints, the post-war consensus for PR was also influenced by the extensive committee work and reports prepared by Free France expatriates in London and Northern Africa during the war, particularly the contributions of Socialist members. See Shennan, *Rethinking France*, 112–15, 125; Goguel, *France under the Fourth Republic*, 59–60.

59 Goldey and Williams, "France," 71; Larkin, *France since the Popular Front*, 144. Concerns about the party system appear prominently in the Free France documents. See Shennan, *Rethinking France*, 112–15, 125; Goguel, *France under the Fourth Republic*, 59–60.

60 Robert G. Neumann, "The Struggle for Electoral Reform in France," *American Political Science Review* 45, no. 3 (Sept. 1951): 741; Roy Pierce, "The French Election of January 1956," *Journal of Politics* 19, no. 3 (Aug. 1957), 396–7. The MRP also had a historic interest in PR, as in its previous, more conservative incarnations, Catholic parties in the 1930s also supported the reform. See Goguel, *France under the Fourth Republic*, 59–60.

61 The PCI worried about being cut off from the Socialists, the SFIO were concerned about being stuck with the Communists and cut off from the MRP, and Christian Democrats feared that a Communist/anti-Communist polarization would force them to the right, thus limiting their ability to work with the left on their social objectives. See Goguel, *France and the Fourth Republic*, 61–2.

62 Larkin, *France since the Popular Front*, 138; Goguel, *France and the Fourth Republic*, 61. De Gaulle's modifications sparked complaints from the parties participating in his advisory body, the Consultative Assembly, who complained that such an "unfair, bastard system of representation" would primarily benefit the more conservative, rural areas. Angry that the Consultative Assembly's more proportional model had been rejected

by the provisional Cabinet in favour a more conservative proposal "prepared on de Gaulle's instructions," rank-and-file members of the SFIO voiced support for the Communists' challenge of the provisional government itself. The SFIO leadership, worried about the influence of their pro-Communist left, tried to respond by urging de Gaulle to reconsider, but to no avail. See Graham, *French Socialists and Tripartism*, 95; and Graham, *Choice and Democratic Order*, 278–9. The references to allocation at the "departmental level" refers to the administrative division of the country into smaller regional units.

63 Jean-Pierre Rioux, *The Fourth Republic 1944–1958* (Cambridge: Cambridge University Press, 1987), 97–8; Larkin, *France since the Popular Front*, 139–40; Graham, *French Socialists and Tripartism*, 138. On the Communists' superior electoral organization, see Graham, *Choice and Democratic Order*, 329.

64 Kuisel, *Capitalism and the State in Modern France*, 201; Irwin M. Wall, "The French Social Contract: Conflict amid Cooperation," *International Journal of Labor and Working Class History* 50 (Fall 1996): 117–18.

65 Einaudi, "Political Change in France and Italy," 904–5; Goldey and Williams, "France," 70. While a number of writers see in these left proposals some ominous Jacobin or totalitarian design, others note the influence of British institutions (where a number of expatriate French politicians spent the war) on their thinking. For this insight, see Shennan, *Rethinking France*, 139. For contemporary views of unicameralism as undemocratic and open to communist abuse, see Robert K. Gooch, "Recent Constitution-Making in France," *American Political Science Review* 41, no. 3 (June 1947): 429–46.

66 Einaudi, "Political Change in France and Italy," 905, 908.

67 Larkin, *France since the Popular Front*, 137–7.

68 Ibid., 142.

69 O.R. Taylor, *The French Fourth Republic* (London: Royal Institute of International Affairs, 1951), 16.

70 Leonardi and Wertman, *Italian Christian Democracy*, 45–6, 54–7; Sassoon, *One Hundred Years of Socialism*, 144–5, 159.

71 Eley, *Forging Democracy*, 302–3; Filippelli, *American Labor and Postwar Italy*, 95–6, 131–2.

72 In some cases the promised economic aid came with astonishing rapidity, as when the World Bank paid out $250 million in loans to France just four days after the PCF were pushed out of the French government. See John L. Harper, *America and the Reconstruction of Italy, 1945–1948* (Cambridge: Cambridge University Press, 1986), 127.

73 Di Palma, "Available State," 149–50.

74 Neuman, "The Struggle for Electoral Reform in France," 742.
75 Goguel, *France under the Fourth Republic*, 67–70; Neuman, "Struggle for Electoral Reform in France," 744–5.
76 Goldey and Williams, "France," 69.
77 D.S. Bell and Byron Criddle, *The French Socialist Party: Resurgence and Victory* (Oxford: Clarendon, 1984), 127.
78 Sassoon, *One Hundred Years of Socialism*, 109; Urban, *Moscow and the Italian Communist Party*, 16–17. Miller claims that serious divisions did emerge in the Italian left during this period, noting that a host of different Socialist groups competed locally in October 1947 in Rome. However, in the next sentence he notes that the key breakaway Social Democratic party did poorly in this contest, effectively undercutting his main point (though Miller blames their poor performance on PCI/PSI orchestrated "violence"). See Miller, *United States and Italy*, 236.
79 Younger militants in the Socialist party were particularly keen on close links with Communists and an orientation to political activism that highlighted working-class struggle (as opposed to making an outreach to the middle classes). Their strength in the party led to the formation a joint SFIO/PCF committee to examine the possible fusion of the two parties in 1944. As the war drew to a close in France, the PCF stepped up their campaign to merge the two left parties. Unity discussions dominated SFIO congresses in the summer of 1945 and 1946. For their part, Blum and the traditional SFIO leadership were wholly opposed to a merger with the Communists, though they were willing to work with them politically in the immediate post-war period. Yet Blum and his associates were not above playing up the Communist "threat" to Americans to increase aid to France. See Graham, *Choice and Democratic Order*, 265, 268, 336; and Graham, *French Socialists and Tripartism*, 65, 73, 99.
80 Larkin, *France since the Popular Front*, 165; Neuman, "Struggle for Electoral Reform in France," 742; Goldey and Williams, "France," 71.
81 Hanley, "France: Living with Instability," 56; Roy Pierce, "France Reopens the Constitutional Debate," *American Political Science Review* 46, no. 2 (June 1952): 435–6; David S. Bell, "The French Communist Party: From Revolution to Reform," in *The French Party System*, ed. Jocelyn A.J. Evans (Manchester: Manchester University Press, 2003), 32–3.
82 For a comprehensive overview of these many strategies by the American government, see Edward Rice-Maximin, "The United States and the French Left, 1945–1949: The View from the State Department," *Journal of Contemporary History* 19 (1984): 729–47.
83 Eley, *Forging Democracy*, 300.

84 Kuisel, *Capitalism and the State in Modern France*, 232; Larkin, *France since the Popular Front*, 154.

85 Geir Lundestad, *America, Scandinavia and the Cold War 1945–1949* (New York: Columbia University Press, 1980), 92: Jussi M. Hanhimaki, *Scandinavia and the United States: An Insecure Friendship* (New York: Twayne Publishing, 1997), 24–5, 34; Helge Pharo, "The Cold War in Norwegian and International Historical Research," *Scandinavian Journal of History* 10, no. 3 (1985): 166, 172.

86 Rioux, *Fourth Republic 1944–1958*, 126.

87 As Federico Romero notes, "With Marshall aid European integration in fact became the 'interlocking concept in the American plan for Western Europe': it was seen as the key to the growth of western economic and political strength and thus to a favourable balance of power on the continent." See Frederico Romero, "Interdependence and Integration in American Eyes: From the Marshall Plan to Currency Convertability," in *The Frontier of National Sovereignty: History and Theory 1945–1992*, ed. Alan S. Milward, Ruggero Ranieri, Frances M.B. Lynch, Frederico Romero, and Vibeke Sorensen (New York: Routledge, 1993), 156. For a "generous" view of the intentions behind the Marshall Plan, see Michael J. Hogan, *The Marshall Plan* (New York: Cambridge University Press, 1987). For a critique of this view, see Eley, "Back to the Beginning," 96–7.

88 D.S. Bell and Eric Shaw, *The Left in France: Towards a Socialist Republic* (Nottingham: Spokesman, 1983), 133. A considerable body of scholarship appears to dismiss genuine popular support for democratic socialism and the kind of economic democracy it promised by viewing the PCF as simply a conduit for Soviet ambitions. While few would dispute that the French Communists were very pro-Moscow, the story of PCF actions is much more complicated than simply acting for the Soviet Union. Indeed, when the party responded to the unhappiness of its own voters in 1947 over continuing wage austerity by supporting the Renault strike, it is still dismissed by these scholars as acting nefariously. This projection of motives prevents these analysts from exploring some of the other motives and legitimate concerns that may have been influencing decisions in this period. For a particularly Cold War version of these events, see the contributions to Andrew Knapp, ed., *The Uncertain Foundation: France at the Liberation, 1944–47* (Houndmills: Palgrave-Macmillan, 2007). For more balanced accounts of the many pressures influencing the post-war PCF, see Gino G. Raymond, *The French Communist Party during the Fifth Republic* (Houndmills: Palgrave-Macmillan, 2005); Adereth, *French Communist Party*, 145–7.

89 See Frederick F. Ritsch, *The French Left and the European Idea, 1947–1949* (New York: Pageant, 1966), 83–5, 108–11.

90 Larkin, *France since the Popular Front*, 159.

91 The striking emergence of Christian Democracy as a powerful electoral force across Europe's three largest countries after the Second World War tends to obscure some important differences in their social bases and competitive contexts. The DC managed to broker an effective urban/rural coalition in part because it absorbed the clientelistic networks that dominated the poor, particularly rural, Italian south. Italian Christian Democracy also benefited from the undisputed Catholicism of the country and its privileged position in the constitution and in civil society. French rural areas, by contrast, were not so uniformly poor, and the small-holding peasantry wielded their political power more independently. In addition, the MRP were less pragmatic in their approach to Christian politics, refusing to truck with rural "notables" or alter their Christian "zeal" in the face of a much more secular electorate. On the DC, see Allum, "The South and National Politics," 106–7; on the MRP, see Richard Vinen, *Bourgeois Politics in France, 1945–51* (Cambridge: Cambridge University Press, 1995), 166–7.

92 Neuman, "Struggle for Electoral Reform in France," 742.

93 Larkin, *France since the Popular Front*, 156–7; Pierce, "France Reopens the Constitutional Debate," 435–6.

94 De Tarr, *French Radical Party*, 49–50; Goguel, *France under the Fourth Republic*, 51, 62–3. France also continued to use its traditional second ballot voting system throughout this period under certain circumstances, for local elections up to 1947 (and thereafter locally in towns with under 9000 citizens; towns with larger populations then used PR), and for elections to the Council of the Republic where only a single member was returned (i.e., from some of the smaller French colonies). Thus past electoral practices never totally faded from the public's or the parties' collective memories. See Goguel, *France under the Fourth Republic*, 32, 64; Taylor, *French Fourth Republic*, 24.

95 The reformed Senate voting system combined PR in urban areas with majority voting in rural departments. For details, see Goguel, *France under the Fourth Republic*, 45–6; and Larkin, *France since the Popular Front*, 148. Not surprisingly, the PCF objected strenuously to a change that kept PR where the Communists were strong but eliminated it where they were weaker. For Communist objections, see Dorothy Pickles, *French Politics: The First Years of the Fourth Republic* (London: Royal Institute of International Affairs, 1953), 101.

96 Pierce, "France Reopens the Constitutional Debate," 423; Goguel, *France under the Fourth Republic*, 45–6.

97 Goguel, *France under the Fourth Republic*, 69.

98 Neuman, "Struggle for Electoral Reform in France," 749; Goguel, *France under the Fourth Republic*, 67–70.

99 For the most part, the MRP opposed two ballot approaches, though they did propose one of their own, a multi-member second ballot system where the centre parties would appear together on the ballot, thus forcing supporters of one of the centre parties to support them all. The Socialist position on voting systems started to shift in the late 1940s from a firm commitment to proportional representation, to mixed PR/majority approaches aimed at disadvantaging the Communists, to support for a return to the second ballot system by 1949, led by Blum. See Neuman, "Struggle for Electoral Reform in France," 743–4, 746–7; Goguel, *France under the Fourth Republic*, 72; Pickles, *French Politics*, 114.

100 Goguel, *France under the Fourth Republic*, 70–1.

101 Rioux, *Fourth Republic*, 164; Pickles, *French Politics*, 130–1.

102 Goldey and Williams, "France," 65.

103 Neuman, "Struggle for Electoral Reform in France," 746.

104 Though this too was controversial, with some claiming that the original motion had been defeated and then reintroduced by questionably constitutional means. See Neuman, "Struggle for Electoral Reform in France," 749.

105 Larkin, *France since the Popular Front*, 166–7.

106 Neuman, "Struggle for Electoral Reform in France," 750.

107 For a review of the negotiations, see Larkin, *France since the Popular Front*, 165–7; and Neuman, "Struggle for Electoral Reform in France," 742–50.

108 Campbell, *French Electoral Systems and Elections*, 123–4; Roy Pierce, "French Election of January 1956," 397.

109 Pickles, *French Politics*, 142; Goguel, *France under the Fourth Republic*, 77.

110 Goguel, *France under the Fourth Republic*, 44; Pickles, *French Politics*, 144.

111 Pierce, "French Election of January 1956," 392.

112 Ibid., 395.

113 Ibid., 397–8.

114 Pierce, "French Election of January 1956," 411.

115 Campbell, *French Electoral Systems and Elections*, 127.

116 However, this was in flux during the 1950s, as rural populations and their political power were in decline. France ended the Second World War with nearly half its population residing in rural areas and

a third involved in agriculture, high figures compared to other Western industrialized countries. Yet by the 1960s industrial development and migration to urban areas would bring it in line with Western averages. For these trends, see J.-J. Carré, P. Dubois, and E. Malinvaud, *French Economic Growth* (Stanford: Stanford University Press, 1975), 91, 94; and William G. Andrews, *Presidential Government in Gaullist France* (Albany: State University of New York, 1982), 204–5.

117 Kuisel, *Capitalism and the State in Modern France*, 249, 259, 269–70.

118 Larkin, *France since the Popular Front*, 265–7. For a more extensive but still succinct review of these events, see Phillip M. Williams, *Wars, Plots and Scandals in Postwar France* (Cambridge: Cambridge University Press, 1970), esp. chap. 7, "The Fourth Republic: Murder or Suicide?," 129–66.

119 Roy Pierce, *French Politics and Political Institutions* (New York: Harper and Row, 1973), 45.

120 Larkin, *France since the Popular Front*, 268; Gildea, *France since 1945*, 43.

121 Nicholas Wahl, "The French Constitution of 1958: II. The Initial Draft and Its Origins," *American Political Science Review* 53, no. 2 (June 1959): 358.

122 Pierce, *French Politics and Political Institutions*, 144; Wahl, "French Constitution of 1958," 367.

123 Campbell, *French Electoral Systems and Elections*, 129. Nor were these the only institutional reforms the Gaullists considered to target the Communists specifically. See Wahl, "French Constitution of 1958," 367.

124 John T.S. Keeler and Martin A. Schain, "Institutions, Political Poker, and Regime Evolution in France," in *Presidential Institutions and Democratic Politics*, ed. Kurt von Mettenheim (Baltimore: Johns Hopkins University Press, 1997), 91–3. For the election results, see Larkin, *France since the Popular Front*, 270.

125 Sassoon, *One Hundred Years of Socialism*, 228, 235.

126 Keeler and Schain, "Institutions, Political Poker, and Regime Evolution in France," 90–3.

127 Larkin, *France since the Popular Front*, 284–9, 327, 330. For structural changes, see Carré, Dubois, and Malinvaud, *French Economic Growth*, 90–1; Chris Howell, *Regulating Labour: The State and Industrial Relations Reform in Postwar France* (Princeton: Princeton University Press, 1992), 46; Andrews, *Presidential Government in Gaullist France*, 204–5.

128 David S. Bell, "The French Communist Party: From Revolution to Reform," in *The French Party System*, ed. Jocelyn Evans (Manchester: Manchester University Press, 2003), 33.

129 Daniel E. Rogers, *Politics after Hitler: The Western Allies and the Germany Party System* (Houndmills: Macmillan, 1995), 120–1.

130 However, this should not be overstressed. In more recent accounts German agency is inflated to the point where the influence of occupying powers and the shifting context of U.S.–USSR relations appear to disappear entirely. See Marcus Kreuzer, "Germany: Partisan Engineering of Personalized Proportional Representation," in Colomer, *Handbook of Electoral System Choice*, 222–36.

131 Niehuss, "Historiography, Sources and Methods," 156.

132 Anthony Glees, *Exile Politics during the Second World War: The German Social Democrats in Britain* (Oxford: Clarendon, 1982), 179, 183; Pulzer, "Germany," 93. Glees points out that SPD expatriates in Britain had prepared a number of documents concerning post-war constitutional and democratic renewal, including a provision for "one man constituencies with 'special measures' for dealing with small parties." See Glees, *Exile Politics during the Second World War*, 182–3.

133 Niehuss, "Historiography, Sources and Methods," 157; Pulzer, "Germany," 96. For the reasons for these internal party preferences, see below.

134 Pulzer, "Germany," 93; Peter Pulzer, *German Politics 1945–1995* (Oxford: Oxford University Press, 1995), 37–8. Most Cold War–era scholarship assumes that the Soviets only introduced PR in their zone to further their manipulation of the political system. For instance, Ebsworth complains that the Soviets introduced party list PR because it would privilege parties and party control, thus facilitating their long-term plan to absorb all of politics into a totalitarian system. However, this tendency to "read back" from the later events of the Cold War has come under challenge. More recent research suggests that Soviet intentions are not so easily discerned, particularly for the period between 1945 and 1947. Caroline Kennedy-Pipe argues that the Soviets were keen at this time to keep up good relations with the West to further their economic and security goals, and thus faithfully observed Western democratic norms. In some ways Soviet motives in introducing PR hardly differed from anywhere else – to help stabilize the local situation by assuring all significant groups were represented (except fascists). But, as Anne Phillips suggests, the Soviets had other reasons to prefer such arrangements; they were much poorer than their U.S. counterparts and needed the local population's help just to administer their territory. Nor do accusations of Sovietization ring true at this point (1945–6), as early efforts by the SPD to merge with the KPD in the East were rebuffed by local Communists and the Soviets who feared a negative U.S. reaction. See Raymond Ebsworth, *Restoring Democracy in Germany: The British Contribution* (New York: Praeger, 1960), 73; Caroline Kennedy-Pipe, *Stalin's Cold War: Soviet Strategies in Europe, 1943–1956*

(Manchester: Manchester University Press, 1995), 5; William David Graf, *The German Left since 1945* (Cambridge: Oleander, 1976), 25; and Anne L. Phillips, *Soviet Policy toward East Germany Reconsidered* (New York: Greenwood, 1986), 35–6, 44.

135 Though the Soviets abandoned PR and competitive elections with the entrenchment of the Cold War from 1948 on, they had consistently supported political pluralism and PR as long as some hope existed for negotiations with their former allies before then. To that end they endorsed PR for local elections in their zone in 1946, as part of the five lander constitutions in the East in 1947, and in various proposals for a reunited Germany between 1947 and 1954. See J.P. Nettle, *The Eastern Zone and Soviet Policy in Germany, 1945–50* (London: Oxford University Press, 1951), 96; V.M. Molotov, "Provisional Political Organization of Germany," in *Documents on International Affairs 1947–1948*, ed. M. Carlyle (London: Oxford University Press, 1952), 449.

136 Rogers, *Politics after Hitler*, 137–8.

137 Ebsworth, *Restoring Democracy in Germany*, 53. Though British authorities were tempted to simply impose a single member plurality voting system on their occupied territory, they opted to negotiate with the Germans instead. To their surprise, none of the German representatives to their advisory council expressed a desire to return to the Weimar form of PR, but neither did they accept the British system without reservations either, particularly as concerned its potential to "waste" votes for parties. From these discussions British officials and the German advisory council eventually "hammer[ed] out a compromise system" combining single member districts with a compensatory list. For more detail, see the chapter in Ebsworth, "Elections and Electoral Systems," 50–77.

138 Daniel E. Rogers, "Transforming the German Party System: The United States and the Origins of Political Moderation, 1945–1949," *Journal of Modern History* 65, no. 3 (Sept. 1993), 512–14; Pulzer, "Germany," 93–4; Rogers, *Politics after Hitler*, 135–6. Officially U.S. politicians, the State Department, and Occupation authorities were on record as opposing PR. When two visiting senators complained that U.S. military leaders in Germany were supporting PR for the proposed West German constitution, both the State Department and military leaders denied it, adding they had always been "skeptical of the democratic merits of PR." Yet from 1945 to 1947 they did nothing to impede its reintroduction into German politics and much to encourage it. Anti-PR German scholar F.A. Hermans, in a special 1970s addendum to his 1941 book, claims that U.S. military forces did influence the eventual restoration of PR in Germany by speeding entry to the county of pro-PR political scientists like James Pollack as

advisors, while delaying the return to Germany by those more critical, like himself. See Hermans, *Democracy or Anarchy: A Study of Proportional Representation*, 460.

139 Kolko, *The Politics of War*, 509; Phillips, *Soviet Policy towards East Germany*, 35.

140 A.J. Nichols, *The Bonn Republic: West German Democracy 1950–1990* (New York: Longman, 1997), 53–9.

141 Anthony Glees, *Reinventing Germany: German Political Development since 1945* (Oxford: Berg, 1996), 42–5; Mark Roseman, "Restoration and Stability: The Creation of a Stable Democracy in the Federal Republic of Germany," in *European Democratization Since 1800*, ed. John Garrard, Vera Tolz, and Ralph White (Houndmills: Macmillan, 2000), 153–4. A number of authors have underlined the subtle and not-so-subtle ways in which the U.S. occupying powers attempted to influence the re-emergence of politics in Germany, from privileging old-line parties and elites over the grass-roots Antifas organizations, to challenging the left wherever they appeared strong by insisting on the inclusion of more right-wing representatives. See Rebecca Boehling, "U.S. Military Occupation, Grassroots Democracy, and Local German Government," in *American Policy and the Reconstruction of West Germany, 1945–1955*, ed. Jeffrey M. Diefendorf, Axel Frohn, and Hermann-Josef Rupieper, 281–306 (Cambridge: Cambridge University Press, 1993); Diethelm Prowe, "Democratization as Conservative Stabilization: The Impact of American Policy," in Diefendorf, Frohn, and Rupieper, *American Policy and the Reconstruction of West Germany*, 325; Edward N. Peterson, *The American Occupation of Germany: Retreat to Victory* (Detroit: Wayne State University Press, 1977), 54; Gareth Pritchard, "Schwarzenberg 1945: Antifascists and the 'Third Way' in German Politics," *European History Quarterly* 35, no. 4 (2005): 499–522.

142 Roseman, "Restoration and Stability," 151–2; Kuklick, *American Policy and the Division of Germany*, 136–7, 230–1. On the halting nature of the decision to divide Germany, from the British perspective, see Josef Foschepoth, "British Interest in the Division of Germany after the Second World War," *Journal of Contemporary History* 21 (1986): 391–411.

143 Peterson, *American Occupation of Germany*, 193–5; Roseman, "Restoration and Stability," 152–4

144 Erich J. Hahn, "U.S. Policy on a West German Constitution, 1947–1949," in Diefendorf, Frohn, and Rupieper, *American Policy and the Reconstruction of West Germany*, 21.

145 Roseman, "Restoration and Stability," 153–4; Susan E. Scarrow, "Germany: The Mixed-Member System as a Political Compromise," in Shugart and Wattenberg, *Mixed-Member Electoral Systems*, 58.

146 Scarrow, "Germany: The Mixed-Member System," 63–6.

147 Niehuss, "Historiography, Sources and Methods," 157.

148 Scarrow, "Germany: The Mixed-Member System," 63; Pulzer, "Germany," 95.

149 Niehuss, "Historiography, Sources and Methods," 157; Pulzer, "Germany," 96. Kreuzer notes that divisions within the parties also influenced deliberations, with southern members of the SPD concerned to weaken the power of its traditionally more dominant northern section. See Kreuzer, "Germany: Partisan Engineering" 227.

150 Peter H. Merkl, *The Origin of the West German Republic* (New York: Oxford University Press, 1963), 86–7.

151 Pulzer, "Germany," 93, 96.

152 Scarrow, "Germany: The Mixed-Member System," 63.

153 Ibid., 59–60; Pulzer, "Germany," 93–4.

154 Pulzer, "Germany," 94.

155 Niehuss, "Historiography, Sources and Methods," 157.

156 John Ford Golay, *The Founding of the Federal Republic of Germany* (Chicago: University of Chicago Press, 1958), 139; Scarrow, "Germany: The Mixed-Member System," 63; Pulzer, *German Politics 1945–1995*, 50.

157 Pulzer, "Germany," 94–5.

158 Golay, *Founding of the Federal Germany Republic*, 141–2; Scarrow, "Germany: The Mixed-Member System," 63–4; Pulzer, "Germany," 97.

159 There were other, more subtle influences on the choices as well, with support for single-member districts in the CDU from those favouring greater party decentralization, while SPD elites noted how such arrangements would impair the competitive position of their rivals on the left, the KPD. See Merkl, *Origin of the West German Republic*, 88; Richard Scammon, "Postwar Elections and Electoral Processes," in *Governing Postwar Germany*, ed. Edward H. Litchfield (New York: Kennikat, 1953), 507.

160 Though recent authors like Shugart and Wattenberg characterize the West German mixed-member form of PR as the "best of both worlds," contemporary American scholarship of the period was less impressed. Commenting early on, Robert Neuman complained that the hybrid models, with their explicit exclusion thresholds, would be neither very representative nor stable: "Having thus violated one of the fundamental tenets of PR – the doctrine that all groups of voters must be represented, without achieving the stability, directness, and clear cut alternatives of the Anglo-American system, this modified PR version merely succeeds in combining the disadvantages of both electoral systems." A year later, Carl Friedrich similarly commented, "At present, it is anybody's guess how

this mongrel system will work; it is to be feared, however, that it will nei-
ther give a clear-cut majority, which is the virtue of the majority system,
nor 'reflect justly' the distribution of political sentiment among the elec-
torate, which is the virtue of P.R." See Shugart and Wattenberg, "Mixed-
Member Electoral Systems: A Definition and Typology," *Mixed-Member
Electoral Systems*, 9–24; Robert G. Neumann, "New Constitution in
Germany," *American Political Science Review* 42, no. 3 (June 1948): 458; Carl
J. Friedrich, "Rebuilding the German Constitution, II," *American Political
Science Review* 43, no. 4 (Aug. 1949): 712.

161 Golay, *Founding of the Federal Germany Republic*, 142.

162 Ibid., 142–3. Golay's work has more recently been supplemented by
Bernhard's *Institutions and the Fate of Democracy*.

163 Golay, *Founding of the Federal Germany Republic*, 143; Bernhard, *Institutions
and the Fate of Democracy*, 173.

164 Golay, *Founding of the Federal Germany Republic*, 144–5.

165 Ibid., 145–6.

166 Eckhart Jesse, "Electoral Reform in West Germany: Historical, Political and
Judicial Aspects," in Noiret, *Political Strategies and Electoral Reforms*, 375.

167 Pulzer, "Germany," 94–5.

168 James K. Pollock, "The West German Electoral Law of 1953," *American
Political Science Review* 49, no. 1 (Mar. 1955): 107; Bernhard, *Institutions and
the Fate of Democracy*, 175, 276n35. Pollock reported that the innovation
came from an FDP member and that it was opposed by the CDU, a view
later echoed by Kathleen Bawn. But Bernhard provides evidence of CDU
sponsorship and support of the bill embodying the changes.

169 Eckhard Jesse, "The Electoral System: More Continuity Than Change,"
in *Institutions and Institutional Change in the Federal Republic of Germany*,
ed. Ludger Helms (New York: St Martin's, 2000), 128–9.

170 Pulzer, "Germany," 98.

171 Eckhard Jesse, "The West German Electoral System: The Case for Reform,
1949–87," *West European Politics* 10, no. 3 (July 1987): 435–6; Jesse, "The
Electoral System: More Continuity Than Change," 129; Jesse, "Electoral
Reform in West Germany: Historical, Political and Judicial Aspects," 375–
6; Pulzer, "Germany," 98–102.

Chapter 7

1 By the 1970s Japan was increasingly being considered another "Western"
industrialized democracy. This was not the case in the immediate post-
war period, as the country had no democratic experience and operated

under American tutelage well into the 1950s. As such, Japan's voting system reforms in 1990s are included here while previous reforms in the 1920s and 1940s were not considered in relevant previous chapters.

2 For a sample of such approaches, see Norris, "Introduction," 3–8; Shugart, "'Extreme' Electoral Systems," 25–54; Scott Flanagan and Aie-Rei Lee, "Value Change and Democratic Reform in Japan and Korea," *Comparative Political Studies* 33, no. 6 (June 2000): 626–59; and Patrick Dunleavy and Helen Margetts, "From Majoritarian to Pluralist Democracy? Electoral Reform in Britain since 1997," *Journal of Theoretical Politics* 13, no. 3 (2001): 295–319.

3 Carstairs, *Short History of Electoral Systems in Europe*, 210–12; Paul McKee, "The Republic of Ireland," in Bogdanor and Butler, *Democracy and Elections*, 167, 183; M.A. Busteed, *Voting Behaviour in the Republic of Ireland* (Oxford: Clarendon, 1990), 47–53; Jane O'Mahony, "The Irish Referendum Experience," *Representation* 35, no. 4 (1998): 229; 2007; 42; Bill Kissane, "Éamon de Valéra and the Survival of Democracy in Inter-War Ireland," *Journal of Contemporary History* 42, no. 2 (2007): 222.

4 Monique Leyenaar and Jantine Oldersma, "The (In)Compatibility of Institutional Reform and Inclusiveness: The Case of the Netherlands," *Representation* 43, no. 2 (2007): 98.

5 Arend Lijphart, "The Dutch Electoral System in Comparative Perspective: Extreme Proportional Representation, Multipartism, and the Failure of Electoral Reform," *Netherlands Journal of Sociology* 14 (1978): 128–31; Rudy B. Andeweg, "Institutional Reform in Dutch Politics: Elected Prime Ministers, Personalized PR, and Popular Veto in Comparative Perspective," *Acta Politica* 32, no. 3 (Autumn 1997): 235, 238–9; Gladdish, *Governing from the Centre*, 102–5.

6 Leyenaar and Oldersma, "(In)Compatibility of Institutional Reform," 97–100; Henk van der Kolk, "Electoral System Change in the Netherlands: The Road from PR to PR (1917–2006), *Representation* 43, no. 4 (2007): 271–87.

7 Alan Cairns, "The Electoral System and the Party System in Canada, 1921–1965," *Canadian Journal of Political Science* 1 (Mar. 1968): 55–80.

8 F. Leslie Seidle, "The Canadian Electoral System and Proposals for Reform," in *Canadian Parties in Transition*, 2nd ed., ed. A. Brian Tanguay and Alain-G. Gagnon (Toronto: Nelson, 1996), 292.

9 Examples included proposals from the Pepin-Robarts Task Force on Canadian Unity, federal NDP leader Ed Broadbent, and William Irvine, *Does Canada Need a New Electoral System?* (Montreal and Kingston: McGill-Queen's University Press, 1979). For a comprehensive review up to 1985, see William Irvine, "A Review and Evaluation of Electoral System Reform

Proposals," in *Institutional Reforms for Representative Government, Royal Commission on Economic Union Research*, ed. Peter Aucoin (Toronto: University of Toronto Press, 1985), 38:71–98.

10 Donley Studlar, "Will Canada Seriously Consider Electoral System Reform? Women and Aboriginals Should," in H. Milner, ed., *Making Every Vote Count* (Peterborough: Broadview, 1999), 125.

11 Henry Milner, "Obstacles to Electoral Reform in Canada," *American Review of Canadian Studies* 24, no. 1 (1994): 39–55.

12 Richard Johnston, André Blais, Elisabeth Gidengil, and Neil Nevitte, *The Challenge of Direct Democracy: The 1992 Canadian Referendum* (Montreal and Kingston: McGill-Queen's University Press, 1996), 55–6.

13 France's socialists reorganized themselves in the late 1960s and changed their name from the SFIO to simply the Socialist party.

14 John Frears, "The French Electoral System in 1986: PR by Lists and Highest Average," *Parliamentary Affairs* 39, no. 4 (Oct. 1986): 489–90; Byron Criddle, "Electoral Systems in France," *Parliamentary Affairs* 45, no. 1 (Jan. 1992): 113–15. Though as Criddle points out, the small element of proportionality added to the municipal voting systems in 1982 appeared more like electoral engineering than the highly proportional party list system adopted for European elections in 1979.

15 D.S. Bell and Byron Criddle, "Presidential Dominance Denied: The French Parliamentary Election of 1986," *Parliamentary Affairs* 39, no. 4 (Oct. 1986): 477.

16 Andrew Knapp, "Proportional but Bipolar: France's Electoral System in 1986," *West European Politics* 10, no. 1 (Jan. 1987): 91–2. Criddle suggests that the Socialists' penchant for PR at sub-national levels had less to do with democratic idealism than Mitterrand's desire to "divide and rule" all competing political arenas. See Criddle, "Electoral Systems in France," 115.

17 The Socialists proved more effective at drawing second ballot support from centrist parties than the Communist party, particularly after they surpassed the Communists as the front-running party on the left in 1978. For a detailed breakdown of these trends, see Joseph A. Schlesinger and Mildred Schlesinger, "The Reaffirmation of a Multiparty System in France," *American Political Science Review* 84, no. 4 (Dec. 1990), 1077–1101.

18 Ross, "Destroyed by the Dialectic," 27, 31. The government's efforts are given in more detail in Ross and Jenson, "Strategy and Contradiction in the Victory of French Socialism"; Larkin, *France since the Popular Front*, 356–81; and Sassoon, *One Hundred Years of Socialism*, 534–71. For a review of the divisions within the Socialist party and their larger left coalition with the PCF in the 1970s, see Ross and Jenson, "Strategy and Contradiction" 72–103; Bell and Criddle, *French Socialist Party*, 61–148.

19 Debates within the government over the policy shift are recounted in Leo
    Panitch, "Socialist Renewal and the Labour Party," in Miliband and Saville,
    Socialist Register, 323–4; and Helleiner, *States and the Re-emergence of Global
    Finance*, 140–3. Yet it would be wrong to characterize the shift in govern-
    ment policy as a complete turnaround. As would be the case later in New
    Zealand, the left government did recognize the need to forward some of
    its traditional policy goals, even as it moved right on others. Thus the ex-
    pansion of certain social entitlements (higher minimum wage, shorter
    work week, improved social security) was accompanied by wage controls
    and higher unemployment. See Bell and Criddle, "Presidential Dominance
    Denied," 478–9.
20 Political scientists tend to give this debate on the left short shrift, ignoring
    the depth of the thinking on these alternatives and the degree of public
    support for their broad aims. For instance, Bell and Criddle complain that
    "the 1981 victory was neither the victory of a radical form of socialism,
    nor, arguably, was it a victory for a radical policy." In line with most other
    political scientists, they tend to dismiss socialist support amongst voters as
    easily as they accept the necessity and inevitability of neoliberal policies.
    See Bell and Criddle, *French Socialist Party*, 151. For exceptions to this
    trend, see Nancy I. Lieber, "Politics of the French Left: A Review Essay,"
    American Political Science Review 69, no. 4 (Dec. 1975): 1406–19; Joseph P.
    Moray, *Grand Disillusion: Francois Mitterrand and the French Left* (Westport:
    Praeger, 1997). For a brief description of 1981–3 government policies, see
    Elie Cohen, "A Dirigiste End to Dirigisme?," in *The Mitterrand Years: Legacy
    and Evaluation*, ed. Mairi Maclean (Houndsmills: Macmillan, 1998), 37–8.
21 Bell and Criddle, "Presidential Dominance Denied," 477–8.
22 Andrew Knapp, "Orderly Retreat: Mitterrand Chooses PR," *Electoral
    Studies* 4, no. 3 (1985): 255–60.
23 Knapp, "Proportional but Bipolar," 100–1; Larkin, *France since the Popular
    Front*, 378–80.
24 Ella Searls, "The French Right in Opposition 1981–1986," *Parliamentary
    Affairs* 39, no. 4 (Oct. 1986): 474–6; Knapp, "Proportional but Bipolar," 97–
    100; David Hanley, "Compromise, Party Management and Fair Shares:
    The Case of the French UDF," *Party Politics* 5, no. 2 (1999): 171–89.
25 For a concise overview of the workings of the system, see Knapp, "Pro-
    portional but Bipolar," 93–5.
26 Bell and Criddle, "Presidential Dominance Denied," 483; Knapp, "'Propor-
    tional but Bipolar,'" 104–6, 108. Specifically, Knapp notes how Chirac used
    articles 49.3 (non-confidence) and 38 (decree powers) to force the change
    back to the second ballot without parliamentary debate. Article 49.3 was

important because it forced deputies voting against a measure to effectively vote non-confidence in the government, a condition that ultimately forced most centre-right politicians into line to sustain the new right-wing government.

27 For a good discussion of how the Socialists managed the electoral dimensions of this realignment from the early 1980s to mid-1990s, see Vivian A. Schmidt, "Engineering a Critical Realignment of the Electorate: The Case of Socialists in France," *West European Politics* 13, no. 2 (2007): 192–215. Schmidt provides an illuminating account of how the Socialists made specific policy appeals to France's changing electorate, particularly different segments of the workforce, but, as with Bell and Criddle above, tends to be guided by deterministic assumptions about how economies work.

28 For instance, the Socialists returned to power in 1988 with centrist allies instead of the PCF. See Larkin, *France since the Popular Front*, 398–9. However, there is some evidence that Mitterrand did consider PR again when Socialist fortunes plummeted in 1991, but this time opposition within the party effectively opposed it. See Renwick, *Politics of Electoral Reform*, 104–6.

29 The basics of the story can be found in David Denemark, "Choosing MMP in New Zealand: Explaining the 1993 Electoral Reform," in Shugart and Wattenberg, *Mixed Member Electoral Systems*, 70–95; and Jackson and McRobie, *New Zealand Adopts Proportional Representation*.

30 See Denemark, "Choosing MMP in New Zealand," 70–95; Jack Nagel, "Social Choice in a Pluralitarian Democracy: The Politics of Market Liberalization in New Zealand," *British Journal of Political Science* 28, no. 2 (1998): 223–67; and Jack Vowles, "The Politics of Electoral Reform in New Zealand," *International Political Science Review* 16, no. 1 (1995): 95–115. While these authors have different perspectives on certain aspects of the reform process, their approach to the broad outlines of what occurred are roughly similar.

31 Succinct but detailed overviews of this reform process can be found in Denemark, "Choosing MMP in New Zealand," 84–6, 88–92; and Jack Nagel, "New Zealand: Reform by (Nearly) Immaculate Design," in Colomer, *Handbook of Electoral System Choice*, 530–6.

32 Peter Mair, "Parameters of Change," in *The West European Party System* (Oxford: Oxford University Press, 1990).

33 Christoper Wilkes, "The State as an Historical Subject: A Periodization of State Formation in New Zealand," in *State and Economy in New Zealand*, ed. Brian Roper and Chris Rudd (Auckland: Oxford University Press, 1993), 226–8; Robert Bremer with Tom Brooking, "Federated Farmers and the State," in Roper and Rudd, *State and Economy in New Zealand*, 108–12.

34 Brady, *Democracy in the Dominions*, 289.

35 Some claim that Labour's victory was less controversial because New Zealand had always had a relatively "egalitarian" approach to politics, pointing to the early emergence of welfare state there at the turn of the century. But others argue that New Zealand's welfare measures were meagre before Labour's win in 1935. See Chris Rudd, "The New Zealand Welfare State: Origin, Development, and Crisis," in Roper and Rudd, *State and Economy in New Zealand*, 227.

36 Wilkes, "State as an Historical Subject," 203–4.

37 For a critical discussion of this period, see Brian Roper, "The End of the Golden Weather: New Zealand's Economic Crisis," in Roper and Rudd, *State and Economy in New Zealand*, 1–25.

38 Nigel Roberts, "Nats, Fat Cats and Democrats: The Opposition Parties," in *The Fourth Labour Government*, ed. J. Boston and M. Holland (Auckland: Oxford University Press, 1987), 39.

39 Nagel, "Social Choice in a Pluralitarian Democracy," 251.

40 Denemark, "Choosing MMP in New Zealand," 81; Bruce Jesson, "The Disintegration of a Labour Tradition: New Zealand Politics in the 1980s," *New Left Review* 192 (Mar./Apr. 1992): 37; and J. Boston and M. Holland, "The Fourth Labour Government: Transforming the Political Agenda," in Boston and Holland, *Fourth Labour Government*, 2.

41 Jack Nagel reviews much of this debate in "Social Choice in a Pluralitarian Democracy."

42 For membership decline, see Barry Gustafson, *Social Change and Party Organization: The New Zealand Labour Party since 1945* (London: Sage, 1976). However, as Vowles notes, even then Gustafson had underlined that this could not be attributed to decline in Labour's support base amongst the working class, as little decline could be discovered. Since then, Vowles traces a continuing link between Labour and its traditional cleavages, with some expansion into white collar and professional ranks. See Jack Vowles, "The Fourth Labour Government: Ends, Means, and for Whom?" in Boston and Holland, *Fourth Labour Government*, 23–4.

43 Wendy Larner, "Governing Neoliberal New Zealand," *Studies in Political Economy* 52 (Spring 1997): 9. Whether Labour's leadership were being honest in this view is less relevant than the fact that they had to make a case within the familiar normative terms of their class cleavage. In other words, their appeals are evidence they recognized some limits to how they could act, what they could act upon, etc.

44 Larner, "Governing Neoliberal New Zealand," 17. The limits of Labour's "solution" to the problems that would increasingly face left parties

everywhere has received considerable critical attention: see Greg Albo, "'Competitive Austerity' and the Impasse of Capitalist Employment Policy," in *Between Globalism and Nationalism: Socialist Register 1994* (London: Fernwood, 1984), 144–70; and Alan Zuege, "The Chimera of the Third Way," *Necessary and Unnecessary Utopias: Socialist Register 2000* (Toronto: Fernwood, 1999), 87–114.

45 Larner, "Governing Neoliberal New Zealand," 22.

46 Thus Boston and Holland could write in 1987 that Labour's approach was not comparable to Thatcher's and still reflected "social democratic" values. See Boston and Holland, "Fourth Labour Government," 7.

47 Nagel, "Social Choice in a Pluralitarian Democracy," 254–5.

48 Ibid., 253–4. In fact, money from business, along with Labour's liberalization of media rules, aided the trend toward strengthening the leadership against activists in the party and moving campaigns decisively into paid media.

49 Opponents of Labour's right turn formed a "Broad Left" group that won control of the party machinery at the party conference in 1987, but it had marginal influence on what Mair described as the "party in government." Still deep divisions broke out in caucus, with Prime Minister Lange repeatedly breaking publicly with his finance minister, Roger Douglas, and his supporters, a situation that eventually led to Douglas's resignation in late 1988 and Lange's loss of the prime-ministership in 1989. See Jane Kelsey, *Economic Fundamentalism* (London: Pluto, 1995), 36–7.

50 Here we can see how the social impacts of neoliberal policies were percolating back up through the politics system, leading to party splits in an otherwise stable system – first in Labour in 1989 and then National in 1992–3. See G.A. Wood, "Globalization and Parliament," in *Sovereignty under Siege? Globalization and New Zealand*, ed. Robert Patman and Chris Rudd (Aldershot: Ashgate, 2005), 79–80.

51 Bremer, "Federated Farmers and the State," 125; Nagel, "Social Choice in a Pluralitarian Democracy," 259–60.

52 Jesson, "Disintegration of a Labour Tradition," 44–5, 51–2; Roberts, "Nats, Fat Cats and Democrats," 45–6.

53 Labour's neoliberal policies weakened the labour movement through both regulatory reform and public sector restructuring. For instance, changes to the Labour Relations Act of 1987 required unions to have at least a thousand members before they would be recognized by law to bargain with employers – this alone reduced the number of unions from 223 in 1986 to 112 in 1989. Meanwhile, public sector restructuring reduced the unionized civil service from 192,800 in 1985 to 162,342 in 1989. As a result, nine

unions decided to disaffiliate from the Labour Party between 1988 and 1990. The post-1990s National government targeted unions with even more draconian legislation, reinforcing union support for an end to single-party majority governments. See Cybele Locke, "'Blame the System, Not the Victim!' Organizing the Unemployed in New Zealand, 1983–1992," *International Labor and Working-Class History* 71 (Spring 2007): 179.

54 Jackson and McRobie, *New Zealand Adopts Proportional Representation*, 51, 125, 164, 170–1, 251–7. Undoubtedly, Labour supporters had numerous issue concerns driving their interest in voting system reform, including bettering gender and minority representation and re-engaging the broader public in the democratic process. But the argument here is that the neoliberal economic policy shifts were key in getting the issue on the table and moving a considerable number of people to examine it.

55 Peter Aimer, "From Westminster Plurality to Continental Proportionality: Electoral System Change in New Zealand," in Milner, *Making Every Vote Count*, 155. Aimer credits Labour and Alliance supporters with casting 70 per cent of the votes for MMP, while National supporters accounted for only 8 per cent. Aimer and Miller take this analysis further, breaking down both elite and mass support for change by party, demonstrating a surprisingly amount of support from Labour elites as well. They also highlight support from traditional Labour backers for the campaign, like the trade unions and women's groups. See Peter Aimer and Raymond Miller, "Partisanship and Principle: Voters and the New Zealand Electoral Referendum of 1993," *European Journal of Political Research* 41 (2002): 796–7, 799–800. These results closely mirror an earlier study by James W. Lamare and Jack Vowles, "Party Interests, Public Opinion, and Institutional Preferences: Electoral System Change in New Zealand," *Australian Journal of Political Science* 31, no. 3 (1996): 330–1.

56 Denemark, "Choosing MMP in New Zealand," 91.

57 For shifting poll numbers of the different systems, see Vowles, "Politics of Electoral Reform in New Zealand," 103–4, 109–10.

58 As Geoff Bertram makes clear in "Keynesianism, Neoclassicism, and the State," in Roper and Rudd, *State and Economy in New Zealand*, 26–49. Goldfinch and Malpass also underline the political nature of the "economic crisis" language by exploring how many of the claims about the New Zealand economy at the time were dramatically overstated and could not be squared with available evidence. See Shaun Goldfinch and Daniel Malpass, "The Polish Shipyard: Myth, Economic History and Economic Policy Reform in New Zealand," *Australian Journal of Politics and History* 53, no. 1 (2007): 118–37.

59 Alan Renwick, "Do 'Wrong Winner' Elections Trigger Electoral Reform? Lessons from New Zealand," *Representation* 45, no. 4 (2009): 362–3.

60 For a concise review and analysis of National's mixed motives on the voting system referendum, see Alan Renwick, "Why Did National Promise a Referendum on Electoral Reform in 1990?," *Political Science* 59, no. 1 (2007): 7–22.

61 Patrick McCarthy, "The Referendum of 9 June," in *Italian Politics: A Review*, vol. 7, ed. S. Hellman and G. Pasquino (New York: Pinter Publishers, 1992), 11.

62 P. Corbetta, and A. Parisi, "The Referendum on the Electoral Law for the Senate: Another Momentous April," in *Italian Politics: A Review*. Vol. 9, *Ending the First Republic*, ed. C. Mershon and G. Pasquino (Boulder: Westview, 1995), 76.

63 P. Furlong, "Political Catholicism and the Strange Death of the Christian Democrats," in Gundle and Parker, *New Italian Republic*, 65.

64 Simon Parker, "Electoral Reform and Political Change in Italy, 1991–1994," in Gundle and Parker, *New Italian Republic*, 45–6.

65 Though "renewal" is a rather misleading description of what has come to pass. The new major right-wing party is largely a media creation, with little internal democracy or membership base. It benefited from the commercialization and subsequent near monopolization of Italy's media system by its founder Berlusconi when he had strong links with the corrupt PSI-led government. See Stephen Gundle and Noelleanne O'Sullivan, "The Crisis of 1992–1994 and the Reform of Italian Public Broadcasting," *Modern Italy* 1, no. 1 (1995): 70–81; Joseph Farrell, "Berlusconi and the Forza Italia: New Forces or Old?," *Modern Italy* 1, no. 1 (1995): 40–52; and Gianpietro Mazzoleni, "The RAI: Restructuring and Reform," in Mershon and Pasquino, *Italian Politics: Ending the First Republic*.

66 S. Fabbrini, "Has Italy Rejected the Referendum Path to Change? The Failed Referenda of May 2000," *Journal of Modern Italian Studies* 6, no. 1 (Spring 2001): 48–50. Della Sala argues that the centre-left adopted neoliberal, market reforms as part of a larger strategy to break up the material basis of the centre-right's long dominance: clientelism. See Vincent Della Sala, "Politics through Markets: The Italian Left between the First Republic and EMU." Paper presented to the Annual General Meeting of the Canadian Political Science Association, Sherbrooke, 6–8 June 1999, 25–6.

67 Gianfranco Pasquino, "A Postmortem of the Bicamerale," in *Italian Politics: A Review*. Vol. 14, *The Return of Politics*, ed. D. Hine and S. Vassallo (New York: Berghahn Books, 2000), 102.

68 Fabbrini, "Has Italy Rejected the Referendum Path to Change?" 40, 52.

69 Though this proved incorrect as well when the ruling party changed the system back to full PR in 2005. For the political machinations behind this change, see Gianfranco Pasquino, "Tricks and Treats: The 2005 Italian Electoral Law and Its Consequences," *South European Society and Politics* 12, no. 1 (2007): 79–93.

70 Pasquino, "That Obscure Object of Desire," 479.

71 Stefano Guzzini, "The 'Long Night of the First Republic': Years of Clientelistic Implosion in Italy," *Review of International Political Economy* 2, no. 1 (Winter 1995): 27–61; M. Bull and M. Rhodes, "Between Crisis and Transition: Italian Politics in the 1990s," *West European Politics* 20, no. 1 (Jan. 1997), 1–13; Phillip Daniels, "Italy: Rupture and Regeneration?," in Broughton and Donovan, *Changing Party Systems in Western Europe*, 72–95.

72 Pietro Scoppola, "The Christian Democrats and the Political Crisis," *Modern Italy* 1, no. 1 (1995): 19.

73 Di Palma, "Available State," 152–3.

74 Guilio Sapelli, "The Italian Crisis and Capitalism," *Modern Italy* 1, no. 1 (1995): 91; Sidney Tarrow, "Italy: Crisis, Crises, or Transition?" in Lange and Tarrow, *Italy in Transition,* 174.

75 Review of the debate can be found in Paul Furlong, "Government Stability and Electoral Systems: The Italian Example," *Parliamentary Affairs* 44, no. 1 (Jan. 1991), 58–9; Pasquino, "That Obscure Object of Desire"; and G. Pasquino, "Reforming the Italian Constitution," *Journal of Italian Studies* 3, no. 1 (1998): 42–54.

76 Besides, as regional parties, the Northern Leagues would only benefit from any shift toward majoritarian voting, a fact DC elites were well aware of.

77 Stephen Gundle, "The Rise and Fall of Craxi's Socialist Party," in Gundle and Parker, *New Italian Republic*, 90.

78 Stephen Hellman, "Italian Communism in Crisis," in Miliband and Saville, *Socialist Register 1988*, 244–88.

79 Stephen Hellman, "Italian Communism in the First Republic," in Gundle and Parker, *New Italian Republic*, 82–3; Tobias Abse, "Italy: A New Agenda," in *Mapping the West European Left*, ed. Perry Anderson and Patrick Camiller (London: Verso, 1994), 217. For a detailed description of the reform process, from the 1987 election results on, see Leonard Weinberg, *The Transformation of Italian Communism* (London: Transaction Publishers, 1995), 51–63.

80 For background on the shifting strategies of the PDS and its key role in the new left bloc, see Martin Rhodes, "Re-inventing the Left: The Origins of Italy's Progressive Alliance," in Mershon and Pasquino, *Italian Politics: Ending the First Republic*, 113–34.

81 Guzzini, "'Long Night of the First Republic,'" 51–2; Patrick McCarthy, *The Crisis of the Italian State: From the Origins of the Cold War to the Fall of Berlusconi* (New York: St Martin's, 1995), 4. For business pressure for state-wide economic reforms, see Richard Deeg, "Remaking Italian Capitalism: The Politics of Corporate Governance Reform," *West European Politics* 28, no. 3 (2005): 521–48. For a brief account of the shifting basis of DC factionalist strife, see Kim Eric Bettcher, "Factions of Interest in Japan and Italy: The Organizational and Motivational Dimensions of Factionalism," *Party Politics* 11, no. 3 (2005): 349–54.

82 See Martin J. Bull and James L. Newell, "Italian Politics and the 1992 Elections: From 'Stable Instability' to Instability and Change," *Parliamentary Affairs* 46, no. 2 (Apr. 1993): 213; Sergio Fabbrini and Mark Gilbert, "When Cartels Fail: The Role of the Political Class in the Italian Democratic Transition," *Government and Opposition* 35, no. 1 (2000): 36–7; Michael E. Shin and John Agnew, "The Geographical Dynamics of Italian Electoral Change," *Electoral Studies* 26, no. 2 (2007): 300. For an effective account of how shifting political economy and globalization influenced the cultural aspects of the Lega Nord as a political phenomenon, see Anna Bull and Mark Gilbert, *The Lega Nord and the Northern Question in Italian Politics* (Houndmills: Palgrave, 2001).

83 Mark Donovan, "The Referendum and the Transformation of the Party System," *Modern Italy* 1, no. 1 (1995): 58–9. Gambetta and Warner go so far as to say that reform process was "under the control of the establishment," ironically the very group "against whom it was directed." While they correctly note that public participation in the details of the reform process was limited, they overstate the degree to which traditional elites "controlled" it. This has the effect of ignoring how much of the traditional elite coalitions had already broken down or were declining before the reform process emerged. See Diego Gambetta and Steve Warner, "Italy: Lofty Ambitions and Unintended Consequences," in Colomer, *Handbook of Electoral System Choice*, 239–40.

84 Pasquino, "Reforming the Italian Constitution," 42–4; Fabbrini, "Has Italy Rejected the Referendum Path to Change?," 48–50, 54.

85 Newell and Bull make this point, arguing that increasing integration into Europe raised anxieties amongst entrepreneurs about how the costs of corruption might limit their competitiveness economically on the Continent. See James L. Newell and Martin J. Bull, "Political Corruption in Italy," in *Corruption in Contemporary Politics*, ed. M. Bull and J. Newell (Houndmills: Palgrave Macmillan, 2003), 45. Meanwhile, other work has focused on how the breakdown of the traditional links between political and judicial

elites, and their informal mechanisms for dealing (or not) with corruption, were decisively weakened by the end of the Communist threat in 1989 and these changing economic circumstances. See Martin J. Bull, "Parliamentary Democracy in Italy," *Parliamentary Affairs* 57, no. 3 (2004): 563–4. Others highlight how post-war Italy had long been characterized by "politicized justice"; see Spotts and Wieser, *Italy: A Difficult Democracy*, 158–62; McCarthy, *Crisis of the Italian State*, 5. Another line of research notes how quickly the crusading justices were again marginalized by the political class after the crisis passed. See Donatella Della Porta and Alberto Vannucci, "Corruption and Anti-Corruption: The Political Defeat of 'Clean Hands' in Italy," *West European Politics* 30, no. 4 (2007): 830–53.

86 Rei Shiratori, "The Politics of Electoral Reform in Japan," *International Political Science Review* 16, no. 1 (1995): 92. SNTV is often referred to as a semi-proportional voting system because it is more open to multi-party competition than plurality or majority systems but much less accurate than PR systems. SNTV operates with multi-member districts where voters are limited to a single non-transferable vote. The system rewards parties that can organize their voters effectively. If a party puts up too many candidates, they may see their votes spread too thinly across their candidates and not elect anyone. If they run too few, they may not capture all the support they have in the constituency. In a sense, SNTV operates on the same principles as the limited vote, though in a more exaggerated way.

87 J.A.A. Stockwin, "Japan," in Bogdanor and Butler, *Democracy and Elections*, 210.

88 The debates amongst Japan's political class over the effects of SNTV stretch back to the early days of American occupation following the Second World War. However, except for some minor tinkering with the size the districts between 1946 and 1947, the system survived countless efforts to change it over the following decades. See Masaru Kohno, *Japan's Postwar Party Politics* (Princeton: Princeton University Press, 1997), 39–47.

89 S.R. Reed and M.F. Thies, "The Causes of Electoral Reform in Japan," in Shugart and Wattenberg, *Mixed-Member Electoral Systems*, 158–9.

90 Gerald D. Curtis, *The Logic of Japanese Politics: Leaders, Institutions, and the Limits of Change* (New York: Columbia University Press, 1999), 147–8.

91 Ibid., 21, 139.

92 Reed and Thies, "Causes of Electoral Reform in Japan," 163–5.

93 Steven R. Reed and Kay Shimizu, "An Overview of Postwar Japanese Politics," in *Political Change in Japan: Electoral Behavior, Party Realignment, and the Koizumi Reforms*, ed. S.R. Reed, K.M. McElwain, and K. Shimizu (Stanford: Walter H. Shorenstein Research Center Books, 2009), 13–14.

94 In an analysis of the reasons offered by the seventeen JSP members for voting against the reform, Kawato demonstrates that most highlighted democratic problems with the proposed SMP districts, along with their party's longstanding opposition to them, as well as their belief that the real issue that needed to be addressed was corruption, not the voting system. See Sadafumi Kawato, "Strategic Contexts of the Vote on Political Reform Bills," *Japanese Journal of Political Science* 1, no. 1 (2000): 46–7. See also Curtis, *Logic of Japanese Politics*, 159–60.

95 Curtis, *Logic of Japanese Politics*, 116.

96 Ibid., 168.

97 Kubota reports forty-two political scandals between 1955 and 1993, at a rate of at least one major scandal per year; Akira Kubota, "A Genuine Reform? The June-August 1993 Upheaval in Japanese Politics," *Asian Thought and Society* 17, nos 53–4 (May–Dec. 1993): 112. For evidence of the longstanding concerns about both factions and electoral reform, see Lee W. Farnsworth, "Challenges to Factionalism on Japan's Liberal Democratic Party," *Asian Survey*, 6, no. 9 (Sept. 1966): 501–9; Ronald J. Hrebenar, "The Politics of Electoral Reform in Japan," *Asian Survey* 17, no. 10 (Oct. 1977): 978–96.

98 William K. Tabb, *The Postwar Japanese System* (New York: Oxford, 1995), 92.

99 Particularly from the United States; Curtis, *Logic of Japanese Politics*, 199; see also Gregory W. Noble, "Japan in 1993: Humpty Dumpty Had a Great Fall," *Asian Survey* 34, no. 1 (Jan. 1994): 19–29; Masako Suginohara, "The Politics of Economic Nationalism in Japan: Backlash against Inward Foreign Direct Investment?" *Asian Survey* 48, no. 5 (2008): 845; Gavan McCormack, "Koizumi's Coup," *New Left Review* 35 (Sept.–Oct. 2005): 6; Hyeong-Ki Kwon, "National Model under Globalization: The Japanese Model and Its Internationalization," *Politics & Society* 33, no. 2 (June 2005): 232–7.

100 Choel Hee Park, "A Comparative Institutional Analysis of Korean and Japanese Clientelism," *Asian Journal of Political Science* 16, no. 2 (2008): 122–3; Shigeko N. Fukai and Haruhiro Fukui, "Elite Recruitment and Political Leadership," *PS: Political Science and Politics* 25, no. 1 (Mar. 1992): 33–4; Curtis, *Logic of Japanese Politics*, 21, 43, 52, 88; Ethan Sheiner, "Clientelism in Japan: The Importance and Limits of Institutional Explanations," in *Patrons, Clients, and Policies*, ed. Herbert Kitschelt and Steven I. Wilkinson, 288–94 (Cambridge: Cambridge University Press, 2007).

101 Otake Hideo, "Forces for Political Reform: The Liberal Democratic Party's Young Reformers and Ozawa Ichiro," *Journal of Japanese Studies* 22, no. 2 (Summer 1996): 273–82.

102 Curtis, *Logic of Japanese Politics*, 198.

103 Raymond V. Christensen, "Electoral Reform in Japan: How It Was
     Enacted and Changes It May Bring," *Asian Survey* 34, no. 7 (July 1994):
     596; Eugene L. Wolfe, "Japanese Electoral and Political Reform: Role of
     the Young Turks," *Asian Survey* 35, no. 12 (Dec. 1995): 1070–3.
104 Reed and Thies, "Causes of Electoral Reform in Japan," 171.
105 Lonny E. Carlile, "Party Politics and the Japanese Labor Movement:
     Rengo's 'New Political Force,'" *Asian Survey* 34, no. 7 (July 1994): 611–12.
106 Ibid., 613–18; Ray Christensen, *Ending the LDP Hegemony: Party Cooperation
     in Japan* (Honolulu: University of Hawaii Press, 2000), 28–30, 150–2.
107 Yet it is important to underline that these new ideas faced intransigent
     opposition from those still committed to the old ones. Thus business re-
     mained divided throughout this period between those still committed to
     "Japan Inc." and those seeking to join the U.S.-defined neoliberal global
     approach. For examples of these divisions on various issues, see Saori N.
     Katada, "From a Supporter to a Challenger? Japan's Currency Leadership
     in Dollar-Dominated East Asia," *Review of International Political Economy*
     15, no. 3 (2008): 399–417; Atsushi Kusano, "Deregulation in Japan and the
     Role of Naiatsu (Domestic Pressure)," *Social Science Japan Journal* 2, no. 1
     (1999): 65–84; Steven K. Vogel, "Can Japan Disengage? Winners and
     Losers in Japan's Political Economy, and the Ties That Bind Them," *Social
     Science Japan Journal* 2, no. 1 (1999): 3–21; Yuko Suda, "Japan's Telecom-
     munications Policy: Issues in Regulatory Reform for Interconnection,"
     Asian Survey 45, no. 2 (2005): 241–57. In this, the status quo was strength-
     ened by public ambivalence about reform, particularly as it applied to the
     economic social pact that defined the post-war Japanese economy, namely
     lifelong employment, on-the-job training, and seniority based–pay. See
     EeHwan Jung and Byung-you Cheon, "Economic Crisis and Changes in
     Employment Relations in Japan and Korea," *Asian Survey* 46, no. 3 (2006):
     458–9; McCormack, "Koizumi's Coup," 7; Yong Wook Lee, "The Japanese
     Challenge to Neoliberalism: Who and What Is 'Normal' in the History of
     the World Economy?," *Review of International Political Economy* 15, no. 4
     (2008): 506–34.
108 Ian Neary, "Parliamentary Democracy in Japan," *Parliamentary Affairs* 57,
     no. 3 (2004): 668; Mayumi Itoh, "Japanese Constitutional Revision: A
     Neoliberal Proposal for Article 9 in Comparative Perspective," *Asian
     Survey* 41, no. 2 (2001): 313–14; Steven R. Reed, "The 1993 Election and the
     End of LDP One-Party Dominance," in *Japanese Electoral Politics: Creating
     a New Party System*, ed. S.R. Reed (London: Routledge Curzon, 2003), 8.
109 Carlile, "Party Politics and the Japanese Labor Movement," 614.
110 Some argue that groups like Charter 88 became influential with political
     elites in the late 1980s and early 1990s, particularly the Labour Party after

1992. However with Blair's majority government win in 1997, such influence notably waned. See Michael Rustin, "Revisiting Charter 88," *Parliamentary Affairs* 62, no. 4 (2009): 568–79.

111 David Farrell, "The United Kingdom Comes of Age: The British Electoral Reform 'Revolution' of the 1990s," in Shugart and Wattenberg, *Mixed Member Electoral Systems*, 525.

112 Ibid., 521.

113 David Butler, "Electoral Reform and Political Strategy in Britain," in Noiret, *Political Strategies and Electoral Reforms*, 457.

114 Pippa Norris, "The Politics of Electoral Reform in Britain," *International Political Science Review* 16, no. 1 (1995): 72–3. For a detailed discussion of this period, see Bogdanor, *People and the Party System*, chap. 2, "1974–79," 144–74.

115 Hart, *Proportional Representation*, 284. For instance, the 1983 Campaign for Fair Votes, an eclectic group of Liberal and Conservative politicians, gathered over one million signatures calling for a referendum on PR, to no avail.

116 Even hoping for a "hung" Parliament was far from a sure thing. The third-place Liberals had supported a minority Labour administration twice in the past (1929–31, 1976–9) but failed to extract any concessions on voting system reform. See Hart, *Proportional Representation*, 244–5.

117 Though LCER was formed in 1976. See Hart, *Proportional Representation*, 285–6.

118 Norris, "Politics of Electoral Reform in Britain," 74–5; Mark D. Stuart, "Managing the Poor Bloody Infantry: The Parliamentary Labour Party under John Smith, 1992–94," *Parliamentary Affairs* 59, no. 3 (2006): 411.

119 For an illuminating discussion about Labour's motives in touting larger political and party reforms, see the debate amongst Mair, Marquand, McKibbin, and Barnett in the 2000 issues of *New Left Review*. McKibbin's intervention is the strongest, highlighting some of the social and historical pressures forcing Labour to move on decentralization (i.e., Scotland, London) despite their discomfort with it, which is one reason the Labour leadership fought so hard to limit what these new bodies could do (i.e., campaigning to limit Scottish taxing powers). McKibbin rightly connects all this with Labour's embrace of neoliberalism and the decline of the party organization as a means of reaching voters (thus strengthening attempts by the leadership to control the party's image through the media). See Ross McKibbin, "New Labour: Treading Water?," *New Left Review* 4 (July–Aug. 2000): 69–74.

120 Farrell, "United Kingdom Comes of Age," 528.

121 Paul Webb and Justin Fisher, "The Changing British Party System: Two-Party Equilibrium or the Emergence of Moderate Pluralism?," in

Broughton and Donovan, *Changing Party Systems in Western Europe*, 24–5; Panitch and Leys, *End of Parliamentary Socialism*, esp. chap. 10.

122 A number of authors have attempted to flatten the distinctions between the recent Blairite revisionism and previous rounds of Labour's ideological self-reflection, casting it as change in scale but not type. Thus New Labour is found to be lurking in the Crosslandite revisionism of the 1950s or the pragmatic governing decisions of Wilson/Callaghan in the 1970s. The problem with these attempts is that they ignore what was a loose post-war consensus about the role of an active state in ameliorating social inequality, rather than simply providing better access to equal opportunity. The former is more strongly linked to a variety of socialist visions, whereas the latter is more typically associated with liberal reformism. Research on social policy struggles in the 1970s Labour Party illustrate that the traditional view was still an important part of Labour discourse and debate, if not government policy. For the continuity arguments, see Eric Shaw, "Review Essay: The Roots of New Labour in Revisionism," *Parliamentary Affairs* 60, no. 2 (2007): 363–9; Stephen Meredith, "Mr Crosland's Nightmare? New Labour and Equality in Historical Perspective," *British Journal of Politics and International Relations* 8 (2006): 238–55. For evidence of discontinuity, see Chris Rogers, "From Social Contract to 'Social Contrick': The Depoliticisation of Economic Policy-Making under Harold Wilson, 1974–75," *British Journal of Politics and International Relations* 11 (2009): 634–51; Tony Wood, "Editorial: Good Riddance to New Labour," *New Left Review* 62 (Mar.–Apr. 2010): 5–28.

123 David Denver, James Mitchell, Charles Pattie, and Hugh Bochel, *Scotland Decides: The Devolution Issue and the Scottish Referendum* (London: Frank Cass, 2000), 33.

124 Panitch and Leys, *End of Parliamentary Socialism*, 237, 250–7.

125 A number of commentators refer to this as "depoliticization statecraft." See Jim Buller and Matthew Flinders, "The Domestic Origins of Depoliticisation in the Area of British Economic Policy," *British Journal of Politics and International Relations* 7 (2005): 526–43.

126 In a move that seemed to confirm this view, few of the critics were renominated, and two were even expelled from the party. See Andrew Reynolds, "Electoral System Reform in the United Kingdom," in H. Milner, *Making Every Vote Count*, 172–3. See also John Curtice and Martin Range, "A Flawed Revolution? Britain's New European Parliament Electoral System," *Representation* 35, no. 1 (1998): 12–13. Blair's efforts to extend the central party's control over all aspects of party activity reflected his view that self-chosen activists at the local level were not often representative of typical Labour voters, and letting them have too much

influence only made the party unelectable in the past. Taking this up in a more critical way, there is some justification to the view that local branches of political parties do not have the kinds of links they once had with local communities precisely because of changes in member–party interactions referred to above. See Colin Leys, "The British Labour Party's Transition from Socialism to Capitalism," in *Are There Alternatives? Socialist Register 1996*, ed. L. Panitch, 10–14 (London: Merlin, 1996); Panitch and Leys, *End of Parliamentary Socialism*, 3–5, and chap. 10, "Disempowering Activism: The Process of Modernization," 214–36.

127 A number of commentators have highlighted the limited nature of the devolved powers, particularly in Wales and London. See Laura McAllister, "The New Politics in Wales: Rhetoric or Reality?," *Parliamentary Affairs* 53 (2000): 595–6; Peter Smith, "Beyond Our Ken," *Representation* 37, no. 3 (2000): 227–30. In addition, despite this new arena of devolved political party activity, Labour resisted any restructuring of the national party to recognize this new regionalism, which it justified as a means of protecting the party brand in competing for Westminster. See Martin Laffin and Eric Shaw, "British Devolution and the Labour Party: How a National Party Adapts to Devolution," *British Journal of Politics and International Relations* 9 (2007): 55–72.

128 John Curtice, "Forecasting and Evaluating the Consequences of Electoral Change: Scotland and Wales," *Acta Politica* 41, no. 3 (2006): 300–14; Reynolds, "Electoral System Reform in the United Kingdom," 173–4.

129 Peter Lynch, "Making Every Vote Count in Scotland: Devolution and Electoral Reform," in Milner, *Steps toward Making Every Vote Count*, 145–58; Patrick Dunleavy and Helen Margetts, "The United Kingdom: Reforming the Westminster Model," in Colomer, *Handbook of Electoral System Choice*, 296–7.

130 Dunleavy intervened in the debate over partisan versus consultative influences on the Labour government decisions on institutional choices, arguing that the process of designing the various subnational systems was complex, involved many different experts, and was subject to a check against excessive partisanship due to the fact that they had to be endorsed in public referendums. He alleged that those who suggest narrow partisan political motives behind the reforms do not connect them with any specific actors or events, unlike his careful elucidation of the specific people involved and the contexts within which they acted. He is certainly correct to underline the complexity of the process, though this needn't derail examination of the political supervision of the process or the many veto points available to government. Indeed, his account demonstrates quite convincingly the many ways in which the Labour leadership actively managed

the process of shaping these new institutions, despite the constraints. Furthermore, it is often much easier to find publicly stated rationales that focus on principle rather than power, if only because the former are more likely to gain public approval. But it would be naive to assume that the publicly stated rationales for policies are the only or even most important factors influencing their adoption. See Patrick Dunleavy, "Assessing How Far Charter 88 and the Constitutional Reform Coalition Influenced Voting System Reform in Britain," *Parliamentary Affairs* 62, no. 4 (2009): 618–44.

131 Peter Dorey, "Between Ambivalence and Antipathy: The Labour Party and Electoral Reform," *Representation* 40, no. 1 (2003): 23–6. For a good breakdown of the different currents within the Labour party caucus on the question of voting system reform, see Dunleavy, "Assessing How Far Charter 88 and the Constitutional Reform Coalition Influenced Voting System Reform," 630–40.

132 Dunleavy and Margetts, "From Majoritarian to Pluralist Democracy," 303.

133 Farrell, "United Kingdom Comes of Age," 537.

134 Thomas Carl Lundberg, "Electoral System Reviews in New Zealand, Britain and Canada: A Critical Comparison," *Government and Opposition* 42, no. 4 (2007): 478–80. One academic mocked the gap between the broad terms of reference set for the commission and its seemingly narrow, politically motivated interpretation of them, suggesting, "They may be rephrased as 'Find something which satisfies reformers just enough to count as barely acceptable to them, while comforting conservatives that it is the minimum you could offer.'" See Iain McLean, "The Jenkins Commission and the Implications of Electoral Reform for the UK Constitution," *Government and Opposition* 34, no. 2 (1999): 153.

135 The moves by Labour to create what have been dubbed "consensual models" of governing at the devolved level but maintain the executive dominant system at Westminster have mystified a number of analysts who can readily describe what they have done but not the reasons they have done it. Referred to as "biconstitutionalism" or the "Blairist constitutional paradox," the gist of the analysis is that the New Labour's various reforms do not add up to a coherent whole. But applying consensus models to dependent political arenas that political actors wish to control is an old British strategy, for instance, utilized with the application of STV by Westminster to First World War–era Ireland, as noted in chapter 4. For the "paradox" work, see Matthew Flinders, "Charter 88, New Labour and Constitutional Anomie," *Parliamentary Affairs* 62, no. 4 (2009): 645–62; Kevin Theakston, "Prime Ministers and the Constitution: Attlee to Blair," *Parliamentary Affairs* 58, no. 1 (2005): 35. Needless to say, sometimes it

takes a politician to see through political rhetoric. Some of the most scathing indictments of Labour's actions have come from former Labour leaders. Former Labour deputy leader Roy Hattersley complained in 2003 that too much of New Labour's consultative approach was manipulative and elitist, despite it populist rhetoric, and amounted to a "dialogue [that] is a monologue in disguise." See David Judge, "Whatever Happened to Parliamentary Democracy in the United Kingdom?," *Parliamentary Affairs* 57, no. 3 (2004): 698.

136 "Hain Backs Reform of Vote System," *BBC News*, 16 Mar. 2004, http://news.bbc.co.uk/go/pr/fr/-/2/hi/uk_news/politics/3517900.stm; Marie Woolf, "Government in Secret Talks with Liberal Democrats over Voting System Reform," *Independent*, 23 Dec. 2003; Dunleavy and Margetts, "From Majoritarian to Pluralist Democracy," 304; Dunleavy and Margetts, "The United Kingdom: Reforming the Westminster Model," 298.

137 John Bartle, "Labour and Liberal Democrat Relations after 7 June 2001," *Representation* 38, no. 3 (2001): 231–41.

138 After promising to hold the referendum in their first term and then not doing so, Labour continued to promise (and not deliver) some kind of referendum on the voting system in each of their two subsequent terms. See Robert Hazell, "The Continuing Dynamism of Constitutional Reform," *Parliamentary Affairs* 60, no. 1 (2007): 13. After Labour's defeat in 2010, a referendum was finally held on the voting system in May 2011, sponsored by the Conservative / Liberal Democrat coalition government. In a choice between the traditional SMP system of the United Kingdom and the majoritarian alternative vote, 68 per cent voted for the status quo. See BBC News, "Vote 2011: UK Rejects Alternative Vote," 6 May 2011, http://www.bbc.co.uk/news/uk-politics-13297573.

Chapter 8

1 Arend Lijphart, "The Demise of the Last Westminster System: Comments on the Report of New Zealand's Royal Commission on the Electoral System," *Electoral Studies* 6, no. 2 (1987): 97–103; Jonathon Boston, "Electoral Reform in New Zealand: The Report of the Royal Commission," *Electoral Studies* 6, no. 2 (1987): 105–14.

2 Norris, "Introduction," 4.

3 For one exploration of such a future, see Colin Crouch, *Post-Democracy* (London: Polity, 2004).

Select Bibliography

Unpublished Materials

Ahmed, Amel F. "Constituting the Electorate: Voting System Reform and Working Class Incorporation in France, the United Kingdom and the United States, 1867–1913." PhD dissertation, University of Pennsylvania, 2006.

Eckelberry, Robert L. "The Swedish System of Proportional Representation." PhD diss., University of Nebraska, 1964.

Hastings, Preston B. "Proportional Representation and the Weimar Constitution." PhD diss., University of North Texas, 1992.

Jansen, Harold. "The Single Transferable Vote in Alberta and Manitoba." PhD diss., University of Alberta, 1998.

Phillips, Harry Charles John. "Challenges to the Voting System in Canada, 1874–1974." PhD diss., University of Western Ontario, 1976.

Ziegler, Donald J. "Proportional Representation in the Social and Political Conflict in Germany 1871–1920." PhD diss., University of Nebraska, 1956.

Articles

Aardal, Bernt. "Electoral Systems in Norway." In Grofman and Lijphart, *Evolution of Electoral Systems in Nordic Countries*, 167–224.

Ahmed, Amel. "Reading History Forward: The Origins of Electoral Systems in European Democracies." *Comparative Political Studies* 43, nos 8–9 (2010): 1059–88. http://dx.doi.org/10.1177/0010414010370436.

Aimer, Peter. "From Westminster Plurality to Continental Proportionality: Electoral System Change in New Zealand." In *Making Every Vote Count: Reassessing Canada's Electoral System*, ed. H. Milner, 145–155. Peterborough: Broadview, 1999.

Aimer, Peter, and Raymond Miller. "Partisanship and Principle: Voters and the New Zealand Electoral Referendum of 1993." *European Journal of Political Research* 41, no. 6 (2002): 795–809. http://dx.doi.org/10.1111/1475-6765.t01-1-00032.

Alexander, Gerard. "Institutions, Path Dependence, and Democratic Consolidation." *Journal of Theoretical Politics* 13, no. 3 (2001): 249–69. http://dx.doi.org/10.1177/095169280101300302.

Allern, Elin H., and Karina Pedersen. "The Impact of Party Organisational Changes on Democracy." *West European Politics* 30, no. 1 (Jan. 2007): 68–92. http://dx.doi.org/10.1080/01402380601019688.

Anderson, John M. "Romantic Democracy." *American Quarterly* 2, no. 3 (Autumn 1950): 251–8. http://dx.doi.org/10.2307/3031341.

Andeweg, Rudy B. "Institutional Conservatism in the Netherlands: Proposals for and Resistance to Change." *West European Politics* 12, no. 1 (Jan. 1989): 42–60. http://dx.doi.org/10.1080/01402388908424722.

– "Institutional Reform in Dutch Politics: Elected Prime Ministers, Personalized PR, and Popular Veto in Comparative Perspective." *Acta Politica* 32, no. 3 (Autumn 1997): 227–57.

Andrews, Josephine T., and Robert W. Jackman. "Strategic Fools: Electoral Rule Choice under Extreme Uncertainty." *Electoral Studies* 24, no. 1 (2005): 65–84. http://dx.doi.org/10.1016/j.electstud.2004.03.002.

Arditi, Benjamin. "From Globalism to Globalization: The Politics of Resistance." *New Political Science* 26, no. 1 (Mar. 2004): 5–22. http://dx.doi.org/10.1080/0739314042000185102.

Barber, Benjamin. "The Politics of Political Science: 'Value-Free' Theory and the Wolin-Strauss Dust-up of 1963." *American Political Science Review* 100, no. 4 (Nov. 2006): 539–45. http://dx.doi.org/10.1017/S000305540606240X.

Barrow, Clyde W. "Charles A. Beard's Social Democracy: A Critique of the Populist-Progressive Style in American Political Thought." *Polity* 21, no. 2 (Winter 1988): 253–76. http://dx.doi.org/10.2307/3234806.

– "The Intellectual Origins of New Political Science." *New Political Science* 30, no. 2 (2008): 215–44. http://dx.doi.org/10.1080/07393140802082598.

Bastian, Sanil. "The Political Economy of Electoral Reform: Proportional Representation in Sri Lanka." In Bastian and Luckham, *Can Democracy Be Designed?*, 196–219.

Bastian, Sanil, and Robin Luckham. "Introduction: Can Democracy Be Designed?" In Bastian and Luckham, *Can Democracy Be Designed?*, 1–13.

Bawm, Kathleen. "The Logic of Institutional Preferences: German Electoral Law as a Social Choice Outcome." *American Journal of Political Science* 37, no. 4 (1993): 965–89. http://dx.doi.org/10.2307/2111539.

Bennett, Scott. "Political Corruption, the Fall of the Braddon Government and Hare-Clark Voting: E.T. Miles, 1899–1900." *Tasmanian Historical Research Association: Papers and Proceedings* 39, no. 4 (Dec. 1992): 155–6.

Benoit, Kenneth. "Electoral Laws as Political Consequences: Explaining the Origins and Change of Electoral Institutions." *Annual Review of Political Science* 10, no. 1 (2007): 363–90. http://dx.doi.org/10.1146/annurev.polisci .10.072805.101608.

Berns, Walter. "Voting Studies." In *Essays on the Scientific Study of Politics*, ed. Herbert J. Storing, 3–62. New York: Holt, Rhinehart and Winston, 1962.

Blais, André. "The Classification of Electoral Systems." *European Journal of Political Research* 16, no. 1 (1988): 99–110. http://dx.doi.org/10.1111/j.1475-6765 .1988.tb00143.x.

Blais, André, Agnieszka Dobrzynska, and Indridi H. Indridason. "To Adopt or Not Adopt Proportional Representation: The Politics of Institutional Choice." *British Journal of Political Science* 35, no. 1 (2004): 182–90.

Blewett, Neal. "The Franchise in the United Kingdom 1885–1918." *Past & Present* 32, no. 1 (Dec. 1965): 27–56. http://dx.doi.org/10.1093/past/32.1.27.

Bogdanor, Vernon. "Conclusion: Electoral Systems and Party Systems." In *Democracy and Elections: Electoral Systems and Their Political Consequences*, ed. V. Bogdanor and D. Butler, 247–62. Cambridge: Cambridge University Press, 1983.

– "Electoral Reform and British Politics." *Electoral Studies* 6, no. 2 (1987): 115–21. http://dx.doi.org/10.1016/0261-3794(87)90018-7.

– "Literature, Sources and Methodology for the Study of Electoral Reform in the United Kingdom." In *Political Strategies and Electoral Reforms: Origins of Voting Systems in Europe in the 19th and 20th Centuries*, ed. Serge Noiret, 335–61. Baden-Baden: Nomos Verlagsgesellschaft, 1990.

Boix, Carles. "Setting the Rules of the Game: The Choice of Electoral Systems in Advanced Democracies." *American Political Science Review* 93, no. 3 (Sept. 1999): 609–24. http://dx.doi.org/10.2307/2585577.

Bonnell, Victoria E. "The Uses of Theory, Concepts and Comparison in Historical Sociology." *Comparative Studies in Society and History* 22, no. 2 (Apr. 1980): 156–73. http://dx.doi.org/10.1017/S0010417500009270.

Boston, Jonathon. "Electoral Reform In New Zealand: The Report of the Royal Commission." *Electoral Studies* 6, no. 2 (1987): 105–14. http://dx.doi.org/10 .1016/0261-3794(87)90017-5.

Bowler, Shaun, Todd Donovan, and Jeffrey A. Karp. "Why Politicians Like Electoral Institutions: Self-Interest, Values, or Ideology." *Journal of Politics* 68, no. 2 (May 2006): 434–46. http://dx.doi.org/10.1111/j.1468-2508.2006 .00418.x.

Bromund, Ted R. "Uniting the Whole People: Proportional Representation in Great Britain, 1884–5, Reconsidered." *Historical Research* 74, no. 183 (Feb. 2001): 77–94. http://dx.doi.org/10.1111/1468-2281.00117.

Bull, Martin J., and James L. Newell. "Italian Politics and the 1992 Elections: From 'Stable Instability' to Instability and Change." *Parliamentary Affairs* 46, no. 2 (Apr. 1993): 203–27.

Butler, David. "Electoral Reform and Political Strategy in Britain." In *Political Strategies and Electoral Reforms: Origins of Voting Systems in Europe in the 19th and 20th Centuries*, ed. Serge Noiret, 451–63. Baden-Baden: Nomos Verlagsgesellschaft, 1990.

Cairns, Alan. "The Electoral System and the Party System in Canada, 1921–1965." *Canadian Journal of Political Science* 1, no. 1 (Mar. 1968): 55–80. http://dx.doi.org/10.1017/S0008423900035228.

Calvo, Ernesto. "The Competitive Road to Proportional Representation." *World Politics* 6, no. 2 (Apr. 2009): 254–95.

Cammack, Paul. "Democratization and Citizenship in Latin America." In *Democracy and Democratization*, ed. G. Parry and M. Moran, 174–95. London: Routledge, 1994.

Carothers, Thomas. "Democracy without Illusions." *Foreign Affairs (Council on Foreign Relations)* 76, no. 1 (Jan.–Feb. 1997): 85–99. http://dx.doi.org/10.2307/20047911.

Carty, R. Kenneth, André Blais, and Patrick Fournier. "When Citizens Choose to Reform SMP: The British Columbia Citizens' Assembly on Electoral Reform." In *To Keep or to Change First Past the Post*, ed. André Blais, 140–61. Oxford: Oxford University Press, 2008. http://dx.doi.org/10.1093/acprof:oso/9780199539390.003.0006.

Capoccia, Giovanni, and Daniel Ziblatt. "The Historical Turn in Democratization Studies: A New Research Agenda for Europe and Beyond." *Comparative Political Studies* 43, nos 8–9 (2010): 931–68. http://dx.doi.org/10.1177/0010414010370431.

Christensen, Raymond V. "Electoral Reform in Japan: How It Was Enacted and Changes It May Bring." *Asian Survey* 34, no. 7 (July 1994): 589–605. http://dx.doi.org/10.1525/as.1994.34.7.00p0405n.

Collier, David, and Robert Adcock. "Democracy and Dichotomies: A Pragmatic Approach to Choices about Concepts." *Annual Review of Political Science* 2, no. 1 (1999): 537–65. http://dx.doi.org/10.1146/annurev.polisci.2.1.537.

Collier, David, and Steven Levitsky. "Democracy with Adjectives: Conceptual Innovation in Comparative Research." *World Politics* 49, no. 3 (Apr. 1997): 430–51. http://dx.doi.org/10.1353/wp.1997.0009.

Colomer, Josep. "The Strategy and History of Electoral System Choice." In *Handbook of Electoral System Choice*, ed. J. Colomer, 81–109. New York: Palgrave-Macmillan, 2004. http://dx.doi.org/10.1057/9780230522749.

Commons, John R. *Proportional Representation*. 2nd ed. 1907; reprint, New York: August M. Kelley Publishers, 1967.

Corbetta, P., and A. Parisi. "The Referendum on the Electoral Law for the Senate: Another Momentous April." In *Italian Politics: A Review*. Vol. 9, *Ending the First Republic*, ed. C. Mershon and G. Pasquino, 75–92. Boulder: Westview, 1995.

Craig, David M. "High Politics and the New Political History." *Historical. Journal (Cambridge, England)* 53, no. 2 (2010): 453–75. http://dx.doi.org/10 .1017/S0018246X10000129.

Criddle, Byron. "Electoral Systems in France." *Parliamentary Affairs* 45, no. 1 (Jan. 1992): 108–16.

Curtice, John. "Forecasting and Evaluating the Consequences of Electoral Change: Scotland and Wales." *Acta Politica* 41, no. 3 (2006): 300–14. http:// dx.doi.org/10.1057/palgrave.ap.5500160.

Curtice, John, and Martin Range. "A Flawed Revolution? Britain's New European Parliament Electoral System." *Representation* 35, no. 1 (1998): 7–15. http://dx.doi.org/10.1080/00344899808523366.

Cusack, Thomas, Torben Iversen, and David Soskice. "Coevolution of Capitalism and Political Representation: The Choice of Electoral Systems." *American Political Science Review* 104, no. 2 (May 2010): 393–403. http://dx.doi.org/ 10.1017/S0003055410000134.

– "Economic Interests and the Origins of Electoral Systems." *American Political Science Review* 101, no. 3 (Aug. 2007): 373–91. http://dx.doi.org/10.1017/ S0003055407070384.

Denemark, David. "Choosing MMP in New Zealand: Explaining the 1993 Electoral Reform." In *Mixed Member Electoral System: The Best of Both Worlds?*, ed. M. Shugart and M. Wattenberg, 70–95. Oxford: Oxford University Press, 2003. http://dx.doi.org/10.1093/019925768X.003.0005.

De Sousa Santos, Boaventura. "The World Social Forum and the Global Left." *Politics & Society* 36, no. 2 (2008): 247–70.

Diamond, Larry. "Defining and Developing Democracy." In Dahl, Shapiro, and Cheibub, *Democracy Sourcebook*, 29–39.

Donovan, Mark. "The Politics of Electoral Reform in Italy." *International Political Science Review* 16, no. 1 (1995): 47–64. http://dx.doi.org/10.1177/ 019251219501600104.

– "The Referendum and the Transformation of the Party System." *Modern Italy* 1, no. 1 (1995): 53–69. http://dx.doi.org/10.1080/13532949508454758.

Dorey, Peter. "Between Ambivalence and Antipathy: The Labour Party and
Electoral Reform." *Representation* 40, no. 1 (2003): 15–28. http://dx.doi.org/
10.1080/00344890308523243.

Dunbabin, J.P.D. "Some Implications of the 1885 British Shift towards Single-
Member Constituencies: A Note." *English Historical Review* 109, no. 430
(Feb. 1994): 89–100. http://dx.doi.org/10.1093/ehr/CIX.430.89.

Dunleavy, Patrick. "Assessing How Far Charter 88 and the Constitutional
Reform Coalition Influenced Voting System Reform in Britain." *Parliamentary
Affairs* 62, no. 4 (2009): 618–44. http://dx.doi.org/10.1093/pa/gsp020.

Dunleavy, P., and H. Margetts. "From Majoritarian to Pluralist Democracy?
Electoral Reform in Britain since 1997." *Journal of Theoretical Politics* 13, no. 3
(2001): 295–319. http://dx.doi.org/10.1177/095169280101300304.

– "Understanding the Dynamics of Electoral Reform." *International Political
Science Review* 16, no. 1 (1995): 9–29. http://dx.doi.org/10.1177/0192512195
01600102.

– "The United Kingdom: Reforming the Westminster Model." In *Handbook of
Electoral System Choice*, ed. J. Colomer, 294–308. New York: Palgrave-
Macmillan, 2004.

Elklit, Jørgen. "The Best of Both Worlds? The Danish Electoral System 1915–20
in a Comparative Perspective." *Electoral Studies* 11, no. 3 (1992): 189–205.
http://dx.doi.org/10.1016/0261-3794(92)90014-W.

– "The Politics of Electoral System Development and Change: The Danish
Case." In *The Evolution of Electoral and Party Systems in the Nordic Countries*,
ed. B. Grofman and A. Lijphjart, 15–66. New York: Agathon.

Fabbrini, Sergio. "Has Italy Rejected the Referendum Path to Change? The
Failed Referenda of May 2000." *Journal of Modern Italian Studies* 6, no. 1
(Spring 2001): 38–56. http://dx.doi.org/10.1080/13545710010025907.

Farnsworth, Lee W. "Challenges to Factionalism on Japan's Liberal Democratic
Party." *Asian Survey* 6, no. 9 (Sept. 1966): 501–9. http://dx.doi.org/10.1525/
as.1966.6.9.01p0205d.

Farr, James. "Historical Concepts in Political Science: The Case of 'Revolution.'"
American Journal of Political Science 26, no. 4 (Nov. 1982): 688–708. http://
dx.doi.org/10.2307/2110968.

Farrell, David. "The United Kingdom Comes of Age: The British Electoral
Reform 'Revolution' of the 1990s." In *Mixed Member Electoral Systems: The
Best of Both Worlds?*, ed. M. Shugart and M. Wattenberg, 521–41. Oxford:
Oxford University Press, 2001.

Farrell, David, and Ian McAllister. "1902 and the Origins of the Preferential
Electoral Systems in Australia." *Australian Journal of Politics and History* 51,
no. 2 (2005): 155–67. http://dx.doi.org/10.1111/j.1467-8497.2005.00368.x.

Feuchtwanger, E.J. ""Electoral Systems: An Anglo-German Comparison, 1867–1933." *Historical Research* 65, no. 157 (June 1992): 194–200.

Flanagan, Scott, and Aie-Rei Lee. "Value Change and Democratic Reform in Japan and Korea." *Comparative Political Studies* 33, no. 5 (June 2000): 626–59. http://dx.doi.org/10.1177/0010414000033005003.

Flinders, Matthew. "Charter 88, New Labour and Constitutional Anomie." *Parliamentary Affairs* 62, no. 4 (2009): 645–62. http://dx.doi.org/10.1093/pa/gsp023.

Frears, John. "The French Electoral System in 1986: PR by Lists and Highest Average." *Parliamentary Affairs* 39, no. 4 (Oct. 1986): 489–95.

Furlong, P. "Government Stability and Electoral Systems: The Italian Example." *Parliamentary Affairs* 44, no. 1 (1991): 50–9.

Gambetta, Diego, and Steve Warner. "Italy: Lofty Ambitions and Unintended Consequences." In *Handbook of Electoral System Choice*, ed. J. Colomer, 237–52. New York: Palgrave-Macmillan, 2004.

Garner, James W. "Electoral Reform in France." *American Political Science Review* 7, no. 4 (Nov. 1913): 610–38. http://dx.doi.org/10.2307/1944310.

Goldey, David, and Phillip Williams. "France." In *Democracy and Elections: Electoral Systems and Their Political Consequences*, ed. Vernon Bogdanor and David Butler, 62–8. New York: Cambridge University Press, 1983.

Graham, B.D. "The Choice of Voting Methods in Federal Politics, 1902–1918." *Australian Journal of Politics and History* 8, no. 2 (Nov. 1962): 164–81. http://dx.doi.org/10.1111/j.1467-8497.1962.tb01039.x.

Green, Fletcher M. "Cycles of American Democracy." *Mississippi Valley Historical Review* 48, no. 1 (June 1961): 3–23. http://dx.doi.org/10.2307/1902401.

Green, Philip. "'Democracy' as a Contested Concept." In *Democracy*, ed. Philip Green, 2–18. New Jersey: Humanity Books, 1999.

Hacker, A. "Inescapable Subjective Judgments." In *The Practice of Comparative Politics*, ed. P.G. Lewis, D.C. Potter, and F.G. Castles, 214–27. London: Longman, 1978.

Hall, Peter A., and Rosemary C.R. Taylor. "Political Science and the Three New Institutionalisms." *Political Studies* 44, no. 5 (1996): 936–57. http://dx.doi.org/10.1111/j.1467-9248.1996.tb00343.x.

Hamer, David. "The Second Ballot: A New Zealand Electoral Experiment." *New Zealand Journal of History* 21, no. 1 (Apr. 1987): 97–111.

Hands, Gordon. "Roberto Michels and the Study of Political Parties." *British Journal of Political Science* 1, no. 2 (Apr. 1971): 155–72. http://dx.doi.org/10.1017/S0007123400009029.

Harris, Joseph P. "The Practical Workings of Proportional Representation in the United States and Canada." *National Municipal Review* 19, no. S5 (May 1930): S335–S83.

Hideo, Otake. "Forces for Political Reform: The Liberal Democratic Party's Young Reformers and Ozawa Ichiro." *Journal of Japanese Studies* 22, no. 2 (Summer 1996): 269–94. http://dx.doi.org/10.2307/132974.

Hodge, Carl Cavanagh. "Three Ways to Lose a Republic: The Electoral Politics of the Weimar SPD." *European History Quarterly* 17, no. 2 (1987): 165–93. http://dx.doi.org/10.1177/026569148701700203.

Hooghe, Marc, and Kris Deschouwer. "Veto Players and Electoral Reform in Belgium." *West European Politics* 34, no. 3 (2011): 626–43. http://dx.doi.org/10.1080/01402382.2011.555987.

Hopkins, Michael F. "Continuing Debate and New Approaches in Cold War History." *Historical Journal (Cambridge, England)* 50, no. 4 (2007): 913–34. http://dx.doi.org/10.1017/S0018246X07006437.

Hrebenar, Ronald J. "The Politics of Electoral Reform in Japan." *Asian Survey* 17, no. 10 (Oct. 1977): 978–96. http://dx.doi.org/10.1525/as.1977.17.10.01 p0343w.

Hughes, Colin A. "STV in Australia." In *Elections in Australia, Ireland, and Malta under the Single Transferable Vote*, ed. S. Bowler and B. Grofman, 155–77. Ann Arbor: University of Michigan Press, 2000.

Immergut, Ellen M. "Historical-Institutionalism in Political Science and the Problem of Change." In *Understanding Change: Models, Methodologies, and Metaphors*, ed. Andreas Wimmer and Reinhart Kossler, 237–59. Basingstoke: Palgrave, 2005.

Immergut, Ellen M., and Karen M. Anderson. "Historical Institutionalism and West European Politics." *West European Politics* 31, nos 1–2 (Jan.–Mar. 2008): 345–69. http://dx.doi.org/10.1080/01402380701835165.

Irvine, William. "A Review and Evaluation of Electoral System Reform Proposals." In *Institutional Reforms for Representative Government, Royal Commission on Economic Union Research*. Vol. 38, ed. Peter Aucoin, 71–98. Toronto: University of Toronto Press, 1985.

Jenson, Jane, and Frederic Merand. "Sociology, Institutionalism and the European Union." *Comparative European Politics* 8, no. 1 (2010): 74–92. http://dx.doi.org/10.1057/cep.2010.5.

Jesse, Eckhard. "Electoral Reform in West Germany: Historical, Political and Judicial Aspects." In *Political Strategies and Electoral Reforms: Origins of Voting Systems in Europe in the 19th and 20th Centuries.*, ed. Serge Noiret, 365–93. Baden-Baden: Nomos Verlagsgesellschaft, 1990.

– "The Electoral System: More Continuity than Change." In *Institutions and Institutional Change in the Federal Republic of Germany*, ed. Ludger Helms. New York: St Martin's, 2000.

– "The West German Electoral System: The Case for Reform, 1949–87." *West European Politics* 10, no. 3 (July 1987): 434–48. http://dx.doi.org/10.1080/01402388708424642.

Johnston, J. Paul, and Miriam Koene. "Learning History's Lessons Anew: The Use of STV in Canadian Municipal Elections." In *Elections in Australia, Ireland, and Malta under the Single Transferable Vote*, ed. S. Bowler and B. Grofman, 205–47. Ann Arbor: University of Michigan Press, 2000.

Jones, Mark P. "A Guide to the Electoral Systems of the Americas." *Electoral Studies* 14, no. 1 (1995): 5–21. http://dx.doi.org/10.1016/0261-3794(94)00021-Z.

Katznelson, Ira. "Reflections on History, Method, and Political Science." *Political Methodologist: Newsletter of the Political Methodology Section, American Political Science Association* 8, no. 1 (Fall 1997): 11–14.

Keeler, John T.S., and Martin A. Schain. "Institutions, Political Poker, and Regime Evolution in France." In *Presidential Institutions and Democractic Politics*, ed. Kurt von Mettenheim, 84–105. Baltimore: Johns Hopkins University Press, 1997.

Kelsen, Hans. "Foundations of Democracy." *Ethics* 66, no. 1 (Oct. 1955): 1–101. http://dx.doi.org/10.1086/291036.

Kinsey, Barbara Sgouraki, and Olga Shvetsova. "Applying the Methodology of Mechanism Design to the Choice of Electoral Systems." *Journal of Theoretical Politics* 20, no. 3 (2008): 303–27. http://dx.doi.org/10.1177/0951629808090137.

Knapp, Andrew. "Orderly Retreat: Mitterrand Chooses PR." *Electoral Studies* 4, no. 3 (1985): 255–60. http://dx.doi.org/10.1016/0261-3794(85)90018-6.

– "Proportional but Bipolar: France's Electoral System in 1986." *West European Politics* 10, no. 1 (Jan. 1987): 89–114. http://dx.doi.org/10.1080/01402388708424616.

Kolk, Henk van der. "Electoral System Change in the Netherlands: The Road from PR to PR (1917–2006)." *Representation* 43, no. 4 (2007): 271–87. http://dx.doi.org/10.1080/00344890701574914.

Kreuzer, Marcus. "Germany: Partisan Engineering of Personalized Proportional Representation." In *Handbook of Electoral System Choice*, ed. J. Colomer, 222–36. New York: Palgrave-Macmillan, 2004.

– "Historical Knowledge and Quantitative Analysis: The Case of the Origins of Proportional Representation." *American Political Science Review* 104, no. 2 (May 2010): 369–92. http://dx.doi.org/10.1017/S0003055410000122.

Krier, Dan. "Finance Capital, Neo-Liberalism and Critical Institutionalism." *Critical Sociology* 35, no. 3 (2009): 395–416. http://dx.doi.org/10.1177/0896920508101505.

Lamare, James W., and Jack Vowles. "Party Interests, Public Opinion, and Institutional Preferences: Electoral System Change in New Zealand." *Australian Journal of Political Science* 31, no. 3 (1996): 321–46. http://dx.doi.org/10.1080/10361149651085.

Lamb, Peter. "Laski on Rights and the Problem of Liberal Democratic Theory." *Politics* 19, no. 1 (1999): 15–20. http://dx.doi.org/10.1111/1467-9256.00081.

Leffler, Melvyn P. "From the Truman Doctrine to the Carter Doctrine: Lessons and Dilemmas of the Cold War." *Diplomatic History* 7, no. 4 (Fall 1983): 245–66. http://dx.doi.org/10.1111/j.1467-7709.1983.tb00394.x.

– "Inside Enemy Archives: The Cold War Reopened." *Foreign Affairs (Council on Foreign Relations)* 75, no. 4 (1996): 120–35. http://dx.doi.org/10.2307/20047663.

Lehoucq, Fabrice Edouard. "Institutional Change and Political Conflict: Evaluating Alternative Explanations of Electoral Reform in Costa Rica." *Electoral Reform* 14, no. 1 (1995): 23–45.

Lewis, John D. "The Elements of Democracy." *American Political Science Review* 34, no. 3 (June 1940): 467–80. http://dx.doi.org/10.2307/1949351.

Lewis, P.A. "Agency, Structure and Causality in Political Science: A Comment on Sibeon." *Politics* 22, no. 1 (Feb. 2002): 17–23. http://dx.doi.org/10.1111/1467-9256.00154.

Leyenaar, Monique, and Reuven Y. Hazan. "Reconceptualising Electoral Reform." *West European Politics* 34, no. 3 (2011): 437–55. http://dx.doi.org/10.1080/01402382.2011.555974.

Lijphart, Arend. "The Demise of the Last Westminster System: Comments on the Report of New Zealand's Royal Commission on the Electoral System." *Electoral Studies* 6, no. 2 (1987): 97–103. http://dx.doi.org/10.1016/0261-3794(87)90016-3.

– "The Dutch Electoral System in Comparative Perspective: Extreme Proportional Representation, Multipartism, and the Failure of Electoral Reform." *Netherlands Journal of Sociology* 14 (1978): 115–33.

Lingelbach, William E. "American Democracy and European Interpreters." *Pennsylvania Magazine of History and Biography* 61, no. 1 (Jan. 1937): 1–25.

Lippincott, Benjamin E. "The Bias of American Political Science." *Journal of Politics* 2, no. 2 (May 1940): 125–39. http://dx.doi.org/10.2307/2125249.

Lipset, Seymour Martin. "Some Social Requisites of Democracy: Economic Development and Political Legitimacy." *American Political Science Review* 53, no. 1 (Mar. 1959): 69–105. http://dx.doi.org/10.2307/1951731.

Livingston, James. "Social Theory and Historical Method in Williams's Work." *Diplomatic History* 25, no. 2 (Spring 2001): 251–74. http://dx.doi.org/10 .1111/0145-2096.00262.

Luckham, Robin, Anne Marie Goetz, and Mary Kaldor. "Democratic Institutions and Democratic Politics." In *Can Democracy Be Designed?*, ed. S. Bastian and R. Luckham, 14–59. New York: Zed Books, 2003.

Lundberg, Thomas Carl. "Electoral System Reviews in New Zealand, Britain and Canada: A Critical Comparison." *Government and Opposition* 42, no. 4 (2007): 471–90. http://dx.doi.org/10.1111/j.1477-7053.2007.00232.x.

Lutz, Georg. "Switzerland: Introducing Proportional Representation from Below." In *The Handbook of Electoral System Design*, ed. J. Colomer, 279–93. New York: Palgrave-Macmillan, 2004.

Lynch, Peter. "Making Every Vote Count in Scotland: Devolution and Electoral Reform." In *Steps toward Making Every Vote Count: Electoral Reform in Canada and Its Provinces*, ed. H. Milner, 145–58. Peterborough: Broadview, 2004.

Mahaim, Ernest. "Proportional Representation and the Debates upon the Electoral Question in Belgium." *Annals* 15, no. 3 (1900): 381–404.

Mahoney, James, and Dietrich Rueschemeyer. "Comparative Historical Analysis: Achievements and Agendas." In *Comparative Historical Analysis in the Social Sciences*, ed. J. Mahoney and D. Rueschemeyer, 3–38. Cambridge: Cambridge University Press, 2003.

Maloy, J.S. "A Genealogy of Rational Choice: Rationalism, Elitism, and Democracy." *Canadian Journal of Political Science* 41, no. 3 (Sept. 2008): 749–71. http://dx.doi.org/10.1017/S0008423908080815.

Markoff, John. "Where and When Was Democracy Invented?" *Comparative Studies in Society and History* 41, no. 4 (1999): 660–90. http://dx.doi.org/ 10.1017/S0010417599003096.

Massicotte, Louis, and André Blais. "Mixed Electoral Systems: A Conceptual and Empirical Survey." *Electoral Studies* 18, no. 3 (1999): 341–66. http:// dx.doi.org/10.1016/S0261-3794(98)00063-8.

McAdam, Doug, and Sidney Tarrow. "Ballots and Barricades: On the Reciprocal Relationship between Elections and Social Movements." *PS: Perspectives on Politics* 8, no. 2 (June 2010): 529–42. http://dx.doi.org/10.1017/ S1537592710001234.

McCarthy, Patrick. "The Referendum of 9 June." In *Italian Politics: A Review*. Vol. 7, ed. S. Hellman and G. Pasquino, 11–28. New York: Pinter Publishers, 1992.

McClosky, Herbert. "The Fallacy of Absolute Majority Rule." *Journal of Politics* 11, no. 4 (Nov. 1949): 637–54. http://dx.doi.org/10.2307/2126227.

McKee, Paul. "The Republic of Ireland." In *Democracy and Elections: Electoral Systems and Their Political Consequences*, ed. Vernon Bogdanor and David Butler, 167–89. New York: Cambridge University Press, 1983.

McLean, Iain. "The Jenkins Commission and the Implications of Electoral Reform for the UK Constitution." *Government and Opposition* 34, no. 2 (1999): 143–60. http://dx.doi.org/10.1111/j.1477-7053.1999.tb00475.x.

Medearis, John. "Schumpeter, the New Deal, and Democracy." *American Political Science Review* 91, no. 4 (Dec. 1997): 819–32. http://dx.doi.org/10.2307/2952166.

Meier, Heinz K. "The Swiss National General Strike of November 1918." In *Neutral Europe between War and Revolution 1917–23*, ed. Hans A. Schmitt, 66–86. Charlottesville: University Press of Virginia, 1988.

Melleuish, Gregory. "Bruce Smith, Edward Shann, W.K. Hancock: The Economic Critique of Democracy in Australia." *Australian Journal of Political Science* 44, no. 4 (2009): 579–95. http://dx.doi.org/10.1080/10361140903296529.

Miller, Gary J. "The Impact of Economics on Contemporary Political Science." *Journal of Economic Literature* 35, no. 3 (Sept. 1997): 1173–204.

Miller, James E. "Taking Off the Gloves: The United States and the Italian Elections of 1948." *Diplomatic History* 7, no. 1 (Winter 1983): 35–56. http://dx.doi.org/10.1111/j.1467-7709.1983.tb00381.x.

Milner, Henry. "Obstacles to Electoral Reform in Canada." *American Review of Canadian Studies* 24, no. 1 (1994): 39–55. http://dx.doi.org/10.1080/02722019409481757.

Nagel, Jack. "Social Choice in a Pluralitarian Democracy: The Politics of Market Liberalization in New Zealand." *British Journal of Political Science* 28, no. 2 (1998): 223–67. http://dx.doi.org/10.1017/S0007123498000155.

Nagel, Jack. "New Zealand: Reform by (Nearly) Immaculate Design." In *Handbook of Electoral System Choice*, ed. Josep M. Colomer, 530–43. New York: Palgrave-Macmillan, 2004.

Naville, Ernest. "PR in Switzerland." *PR Review* 1, no. 2 (Dec. 1893): 55–8.

Nelson, Joan. "The Politics of Economic Transformation: Is Third World Experience Relevant in Eastern Europe?" *World Politics* 45, no. 3 (1993): 433–63. http://dx.doi.org/10.2307/2950725.

Neumann, Robert G. "The Struggle for Electoral Reform in France." *American Political Science Review* 45, no. 3 (Sept. 1951): 741–55. http://dx.doi.org/10.2307/1951162.

Niehuss, Merith. "Historiography, Sources and Methods of Electoral and Electoral Law Analysis in Germany: 1871–1987." In *Political Strategies and Electoral Reforms: Origins of Voting Systems in Europe in the 19th and*

20th Centuries, ed. Serge Noiret, 141–61. Baden-Baden: Nomos Verlagsgesellschaft, 1990.

Noiret, S., ed. *Political Strategies and Electoral Reforms: Origins of Voting Systems in Europe in the 19th and 20th Centuries*. Baden-Baden: Nomos Verlagsgesellschaft, 1990.

Norris, Pippa. "Introduction: The Politics of Electoral Reform." *International Political Science Review* 16, no. 1 (1995): 3–8. http://dx.doi.org/10.1177/019251219501600101.

– "The Politics of Electoral Reform in Britain." *International Political Science Review* 16, no. 1 (1995): 65–78. http://dx.doi.org/10.1177/019251219501600105.

O'Mahony, Jane. "The Irish Referendum Experience." *Representation* 35, no. 4 (1998): 225–36. http://dx.doi.org/10.1080/00344899808523044.

Orliffe, Herbert. "Proportional Representation." *Canadian Forum* 22, no. 205 (Feb. 1938): 388–90.

Paley, Julia. "Toward an Anthropology of Democracy." *Annual Review of Anthropology* 31, no. 1 (2002): 469–96. http://dx.doi.org/10.1146/annurev.anthro.31.040402.085453.

Parker, Simon. "Electoral Reform and Political Change in Italy, 1991–1994." In *The New Republic: From the Fall of the Berlin Wall to Berlusconi*, ed. S. Gundle and S. Parker, 40–58. London: Routledge, 1996. http://dx.doi.org/10.4324/9780203431443_chapter_2.

Parsons, Tim. "The Community Schools Movement." *Community Issues* 2, no. 6 (Dec. 1970): 1–77.

Pasquino, Gianfranco. "A Postmortem of the Bicamerale." In *Italian Politics: A Review*. Vol. 14, *The Return of Politics*, ed. D. Hine and S. Vassallo. New York: Berghahn Books, 2000: 101–20.

– "Reforming the Italian Constitution." *Journal of Modern Italian Studies* 3, no. 1 (1998): 42–54. http://dx.doi.org/10.1080/13545719808454965.

– "That Obscure Object of Desire: A New Electoral Law for Italy." In *Political Strategies and Electoral Reforms: Origins of Voting Systems in Europe in the 19th and 20th Centuries*, ed. S. Noiret. Baden-Baden: Nomos Verlagsgesellschaft, 1990.

– "Tricks and Treats: The 2005 Italian Electoral Law and Its Consequences." *South European Society & Politics* 12, no. 1 (2007): 79–93. http://dx.doi.org/10.1080/13608740601155500.

Penadés, Alberto. "Choosing Rules for Government: The Institutional Preferences of Early Socialist Parties." In *Controlling Governments: Voters, Institutions, and Accountability*, ed. J. Maravall and I. Sanchez-Cuenca, 202–46. Cambridge: Cambridge University Press, 2008. http://dx.doi.org/10.1017/CBO9780511611414.009.

Peters, B. Guy, Jon Pierre, and Desmond S. King. "The Politics of Path Dependency: Political Conflict in Historical Institutionalism." *Journal of Politics* 67, no. 4 (Nov. 2005): 1275–300. http://dx.doi.org/10.1111/j.1468-2508.2005.00360.x.

Pierce, Roy. "France Reopens the Constitutional Debate." *American Political Science Review* 46, no. 2 (June 1952): 422–37. http://dx.doi.org/10.2307/1950838.

– "The French Election of January 1956." *Journal of Politics* 19, no. 3 (Aug. 1957): 391–422. http://dx.doi.org/10.2307/2126767.

– "French Legislative Elections: The Historical Background." In *The French National Assembly Elections of 1978*, ed. Howard R. Penniman, 1–37. Washington: American Enterprise Institute, 1980.

Pilet, Jean-Benoit, and Damien Bol. "Party Preferences and Electoral Reform: How Time in Government Affects the Likelihood of Supporting Electoral Change." *West European Politics* 34, no. 3 (2011): 568–86. http://dx.doi.org/10.1080/01402382.2011.555984.

Pilon, Dennis. "Democracy, BC-Style." In *British Columbia Politics and Government*, ed. Michael Howlett, Dennis Pilon, and Tracy Summerville, 87–108. Toronto: Emond Montgomery, 2010.

– "Explaining Voting System Reform in Canada: 1874 to 1960." *Journal of Canadian Studies/Revue d'études canadiennes* 40, no. 3 (Autumn 2006): 135–61.

– "Investigating Media as a Deliberative Space: Newspaper Opinions about Voting Systems in the 2007 Ontario Provincial Referendum." *Canadian Political Science Review* 3, no. 3 (Sept. 2009): 1–23.

Pollock, James K. "The West German Electoral Law of 1953." *American Political Science Review* 49, no. 1 (Mar. 1955): 107–30. http://dx.doi.org/10.2307/1951642.

Polosky, Janet L. "A Revolution for Socialist Reforms: The Belgian General Strike for Universal Suffrage." *Journal of Contemporary History* 27, no. 3 (1992): 449–66. http://dx.doi.org/10.1177/002200949202700304.

Pottie, David, and Shireen Hassim. "The Politics of Institutional Design in the South African Tradition." In Bastian and Luckham, *Can Democracy Be Designed?*, 60–92.

Prewitt, Kenneth. "Political Ideas and a Political Science for Policy." *Annals of the American Academy of Political and Social Science* 600, no. 1 (2005): 14–29. http://dx.doi.org/10.1177/0002716205276660.

Pryce, Roy. "The New Italian Electoral Law." *Parliamentary Affairs* 6, no. 3 (1952): 269–76.

Pugh, Martin. "Political Parties and the Campaign for Proportional Representation 1905–1914." *Parliamentary Affairs* 33, no. 3 (Summer 1980): 294–307. http://dx.doi.org/10.1093/pa/33.3.294.

Pulzer, Peter. "Germany." In *Democracy and Elections: Electoral Systems and Their Political Consequences*, ed. Vernon Bogdanor and David Butler, 84–109. New York: Cambridge University Press, 1983.

Quintal, David P. "The Theory of Electoral Systems." *Western Political Quarterly* 23, no. 4 (1970): 752–61. http://dx.doi.org/10.2307/446474.

Rahat, Gideon. "The Study of the Politics of Electoral Reform in the 1990s: Theoretical and Methodological Lessons." *Comparative Politics* 36, no. 4 (July 2004): 461–79. http://dx.doi.org/10.2307/4150171.

Rahat, Gideon, and Reuven Y. Hazan. "The Barriers to Electoral System Reform: A Synthesis of Alternative Approaches." *West European Politics* 34, no. 3 (2011): 478–94. http://dx.doi.org/10.1080/01402382.2011.555976.

Reed, S.R., and M.F. Thies. "The Causes of Electoral Reform in Japan." In *Mixed-Member Electoral Systems*, ed. M. Shugart and M. Wattenberg, 152–72. Oxford: Oxford University Press, 2003. http://dx.doi.org/10.1093/019925768X.003.0008.

Reilly, Ben, and Michael Maley. "The Single Transferable Vote and the Alternative Vote Compared." In *Elections in Australia, Ireland, and Malta under the Single Transferable Vote*, ed. S. Bowler and B. Grofman, 37–58. Ann Arbor: University of Michigan Press, 2000.

Remner, Karen L. "The Politics of Institutional Change: Electoral Reform in Latin America, 1978–2002." *Party Politics* 14, no. 1 (2008): 5–30. http://dx.doi.org/10.1177/1354068807083821.

Renwick, Alan. "Do 'Wrong Winner' Elections Trigger Electoral Reform? Lessons from New Zealand." *Representation* 45, no. 4 (2009): 357–67. http://dx.doi.org/10.1080/00344890903235256.

– "Electoral Reform in Europe since 1945." *West European Politics* 34, no. 3 (2011): 456–77. http://dx.doi.org/10.1080/01402382.2011.555975.

– "Why Did National Promise a Referendum on Electoral Reform in 1990?" *Political Science (Wellington, N.Z.)* 59, no. 1 (2007): 7–22. http://dx.doi.org/10.1177/003231870705900104.

Reynolds, Andrew. "Electoral System Reform in the United Kingdom." In *Making Every Vote Count: Reassessing Canada's Electoral System*, ed. H. Milner, 171–8. Peterborough: Broadview, 1999.

Ritter, Gerhard A. "The Electoral Systems of Imperial Germany and Their Consequences for Politics." In *Political Strategies and Electoral Reforms: Origins of Voting Systems in Europe in the 19th and 20th Centuries*, ed. Serge Noiret, 53–75. Baden-Baden: Nomos Verlagsgesellschaft, 1990.

Roberts, G.K. "The Explanation of Politics: Comparison, Strategy and Theory." In *The Practice of Comparative Politics*, 2nd ed., ed. P.G. Lewis, D.C. Potter, and F.G. Castles, 287–304. London: Longman, 1978.

Robertson, David Brian. "The Return to History and the New Institutionalism in American Political Science." *Social Science History* 17, no. 1 (Spring 1993): 1–36.

Rogers, Daniel E. "Transforming the German Party System: The United States and the Origins of Political Moderation, 1945–1949." *Journal of Modern History* 65, no. 3 (Sept. 1993): 512–41. http://dx.doi.org/10.1086/244673.

Rogowski, Ronald. "Trade and the Variety of Democratic Institutions." *International Organization* 41, no. 2 (Spring 1987): 203–23. http://dx.doi.org/10.1017/S0020818300027442.

Rosanvallon, Pierre. "The History of the Word Democracy in France." *Journal of Democracy* 6, no. 4 (1995): 140–54. http://dx.doi.org/10.1353/jod.1995.0072.

Rueschemeyer, Dietrich. "Can One or a Few Cases Yield Theoretical Gains?" In *Comparative Historical Analysis in the Social Sciences*, ed. J. Mahoney and D. Rueschemeyer, 305–36. Cambridge: Cambridge University Press, 2003.

Rustin, Michael. "Revisiting Charter 88." *Parliamentary Affairs* 62, no. 4 (2009): 568–79. http://dx.doi.org/10.1093/pa/gsp025.

Rydon, Joan. "Electoral Methods and the Australian Party System." *Australian Journal of Politics and History* 2, no. 1 (Nov. 1956): 68–83. http://dx.doi.org/10.1111/j.1467-8497.1956.tb01001.x.

Saul, John. "For Fear of Being Condemned as 'Old Fashioned': Liberal Democracy vs Popular Democracy in Sub-Saharan Africa." *Review of African Political Economy* 24, no. 73 (1997): 339–53. http://dx.doi.org/10.1080/03056249708704267.

Saunders, Robert. "The Politics of Reform and the Making of the Second Reform Act, 1848–1867." *Historical Journal (Cambridge, England)* 50, no. 3 (2007): 571–91. http://dx.doi.org/10.1017/S0018246X07006267.

Sawer, Marian. "Australia: Replacing Plurality Rule with Majority-Preferential Voting." In *Handbook of Electoral System Choice*, ed. Josep Colomer, 475–86. New York: Palgrave-Macmillan, 2004.

Scammon, Richard. "Postwar Elections and Electoral Processes." In *Governing Postwar Germany*, ed. Edward H. Litchfield, 500–33. New York: Kennikat, 1953.

Scarrow, Susan E. "Germany: The Mixed-Member System as a Political Compromise." In *Mixed-Member Electoral Systems: The Best of Both Worlds?*, ed. Matthew Soberg Shugart and Martin P. Wattenberg, 55–69. Oxford: Oxford University Press, 2003. http://dx.doi.org/10.1093/019925768X.003.0004

Seidle, F. Leslie. "The Canadian Electoral System and Proposals for Reform." In *Canadian Parties in Transition*, 2nd ed., ed. A. Brian Tanguay and Alain-G. Gagnon, 282–306. Toronto: Nelson, 1996.

Seip, Dick. "The Netherlands." In *European Electoral Systems Handbook*, ed. Geoffrey Hand, Jacques Georgel, and Christoph Sasse, 193–216. London: Butterworths, 1979.

Seton-Watson, Christopher. "Italy." In *Democracy and Elections: Electoral Systems and Their Political Consequences*, ed. Vernon Bogdanor and David Butler, 110–21. New York: Cambridge University Press, 1983.

Shepard, Walter J. "Democracy in Transition." *American Political Science Review* 29, no. 1 (Feb. 1935): 1–20. http://dx.doi.org/10.2307/1947163.

Shepsle, Kenneth A. "A Comment on Institutional Change." *Journal of Theoretical Politics* 13, no. 3 (2001): 321–5. http://dx.doi.org/10.1177/095169 280101300305.

Shin, Michael E., and John Agnew. "The Geographical Dynamics of Italian Electoral Change." *Electoral Studies* 26, no. 2 (2007): 287–302. http://dx.doi .org/10.1016/j.electstud.2006.05.002.

Shiratori, Rei. "The Politics of Electoral Reform in Japan." *International Political Science Review* 16, no. 1 (1995): 79–94. http://dx.doi.org/10.1177/01925121 9501600106.

Shugart, Matthew. "Comparative Electoral Systems Research: The Maturation of a Field and New Challenges Ahead." In *The Politics of Electoral Systems*, ed. Michael Gallagher and Paul Mitchell, 25–56. Oxford: Oxford University Press, 2005. http://dx.doi.org/10.1093/0199257566.003.0002.

Shugart, Matthew Soberg. "'Extreme' Electoral Systems and the Appeal of the Mixed-Member Alternative." In *Mixed Member Electoral Systems: The Best of Both Worlds?*, ed. M. Shugart and P. Wattenberg, 25–51. Oxford: Oxford University Press, 2001.

Skocpol, Theda, and Margaret Somers. "The Uses of Comparative History in Macrosocial Inquiry." *Comparative Studies in Society and History* 22, no. 2 (Apr. 1980): 174–97. http://dx.doi.org/10.1017/S0010417500009282.

Steinmo, Sven. "Historical Institutionalism." In *Approaches and Methodologies in the Social Sciences*, ed. Donatella Della Porta and Michael Keating, 118–38. Cambridge: Cambridge University Press, 2008.

Stockwin, J.A.A. "Japan." In *Democracy and Elections: Electoral Systems and Their Political Consequences*, ed. Vernon Bogdanor and David Butler, 209–27. New York: Cambridge University Press, 1983.

Studlar, Donley. "Will Canada Seriously Consider Electoral System Reform? Women and Aboriginals Should." In *Making Every Vote Count*, ed. H. Milner, 123–32. Peterborough: Broadview, 1999.

Sundberg, Jan. "The Electoral System of Finland: Old, and Working Well." In *The Evolution of Electoral and Party Systems in Nordic Countries*, ed. B. Grofman and A. Lijphjart, 68–9, 74. New York: Agathon, 2002.

Thayer, James R. "The Contribution of Public Opinion Polls to the Understanding of the 1953 Election to Italy, West Germany and Japan." *Public Opinion Quarterly* 19, no. 3 (Autumn 1955): 259–78. http://dx.doi.org/10.1086/266571.

Thelen, Kathleen, and Sven Steinmo. "Historical Institutionalism in Comparative Politics." In *Structuring Politics: Historical Institutionalism in Comparative Politics*, ed. S. Steinmo, K. Thelen, and F. Longstreth, 1–32. Cambridge: Cambridge University Press, 1992. http://dx.doi.org/10.1017/CBO97805 11528125.002.

Therborn, Goran. "The Rule of Capital and the Rise of Democracy." *New Left Review* 103 (May–June 1977): 3–41.

Ullrich, Hartmut. "Historiography, Sources and Methods for the Study of Electortal Laws in Italy." In *Political Strategies and Electoral Reforms: Origins of Voting Systems in Europe in the 19th and 20th Centuries*, ed. Serge Noiret, 297–334. Baden-Baden: Nomos Verlagsgesellschaft, 1990.

Vincent, John. "The Effect of Second Reform Act in Lancashire." *Historical Journal (Cambridge, England)* 11, no. 1 (1968): 84–94. http://dx.doi.org/10.1017/S0018246X00002363.

Vowles, Jack. "The Politics of Electoral Reform in New Zealand." *International Political Science Review* 16, no. 1 (1995): 95–115. http://dx.doi.org/10.1177/019251219501600107.

Wahl, Nicholas. "The French Constitution of 1958: II. The Initial Draft and Its Origins." *American Political Science Review* 53, no. 2 (June 1959): 358–82. http://dx.doi.org/10.2307/1952152.

Walker, Jack L. "A Critique of the Elitist Theory of Democracy." *American Political Science Review* 60, no. 2 (June 1966): 285–95. http://dx.doi.org/10.2307/1953356.

Walker, R.B. "Catherine Helen Spence and South Australian Politics." *Australian Journal of Politics and History* 15, no. 1 (Apr. 1969): 35–46. http://dx.doi.org/10.1111/j.1467-8497.1969.tb00938.x.

Weaver, Leon. "The Rise, Decline, and Resurrection of Proportional Representation in Local Governments in the United States." In *Electoral Laws and Their Political Consequences*, ed. B. Grofman and A. Lijphart, 139–53. New York: Agathon, 1986.

Whitehead, Laurence. "The Vexed Issue of the Meaning of Democracy." *Journal of Political Ideologies* 2, no. 2 (1997): 121–35. http://dx.doi.org/10.1080/13569319708420754.

Wolfe, Eugene L. "Japanese Electoral and Political Reform: Role of the Young Turks." *Asian Survey* 35, no. 12 (Dec. 1995): 1059–74. http://dx.doi.org/10.1525/as.1995.35.12.01p00747.

Wollheim, Richard. "Democracy." *Journal of the History of Ideas* 19, no. 2 (Apr. 1958): 225–42. http://dx.doi.org/10.2307/2707936.

Zelizer, Julian E. "What Political Science Can Learn from the New Political History." *Annual Review of Political Science* 13, no. 1 (2010): 25–36. http://dx.doi.org/10.1146/annurev.polisci.032708.120246.

Ziblatt, Daniel. "Shaping Democratic Practices and the Causes of Electoral Fraud: The Case of Nineteenth Century Germany." *American Political Science Review* 103, no. 1 (Feb. 2009): 1–21. http://dx.doi.org/10.1017/S0003055409090042.

Books

Adcock, Robert Mark Bevir, and Shannon C. Stimson, eds. *Modern Political Science: Anglo-American Exchanges since 1880*. Princeton: Princeton University Press, 2007.

Almond, Gabriel, and Sidney Verba. *The Civic Culture*. Boston: Little, Brown, 1965.

Amadae, S.M. *Rationalizing Capitalist Democracy: The Cold War Origins of Rational Choice Liberalism*. Chicago: Chicago University Press, 2003.

Andrews, G.R., and H. Chapman, eds. *The Social Construction of Democracy, 1870–1990*. New York: New York University Press, 1995.

Archibugi, Daniele, ed. *Debating Cosmopolitics*. London: Verso, 2003.

Arrow, Kenneth J. *Social Choice and Individual Values*. New York: Wiley, 1951.

Aucoin, Peter, ed. *Institutional Reforms for Representative Government, Royal Commission on Economic Union Research*. Vol. 38. Toronto: University of Toronto Press, 1985.

Barber, Kathleen. *A Right to Representation*. Columbus: Ohio State University Press, 2000.

Barrow, Logie, and Ian Bullock. *Democratic Ideas and the British Labour Movement, 1880–1914*. Cambridge: Cambridge University Press, 1996. http://dx.doi.org/10.1017/CBO9780511521287.

Bastian, S., and R. Luckham, eds. *Can Democracy Be Designed?* London: Zed Books, 2003.

Bendix, Richard. *Nation-Building and Citizenship: Studies of Our Changing Social Order*. New York: Wiley, 1964.

Benello, C. George, and Dimitrios Roussopoulos, eds. *The Case for Participatory Democracy*. New York: Viking Compass, 1971.

Bernhard, Michael. *Institutions and the Fate of Democracy*. Pittsburgh: University of Pittsburgh Press, 2005.

Beyme, Klaus von. *Parliamentary Democracy: Democratization, Destabilization, Reconsolidation, 1789–1999*. Houndsmill: Macmillan, 2000.

Blais, André, ed. *To Keep or to Change First Past the Post: The Politics of Electoral Reform*. Oxford: Oxford University Press, 2008. http://dx.doi.org/10.1093/acprof:oso/9780199539390.001.0001.

Bogdanor, Vernon. *The People and the Party System*. Cambridge: Cambridge University Press, 1981.

Bogdanor, Vernon, and David Butler, eds. *Democracy and Elections: Electoral Systems and Their Political Consequences*. Cambridge: Cambridge University Press, 1983.

Bowler, Shaun, and Bernard Grofman, eds. *Election in Australia, Ireland, and Malta under the Single Transferable Vote*. Ann Arbor: University of Michigan Press, 2000.

Brady, Alexander. *Democracy in the Dominions: A Comparative Study in Institutions*. 3rd ed. Toronto: University of Toronto Press, 1958.

Buxton, William. *Talcott Parsons and the Capitalist Nation-State: Political Sociology as a Strategic Vocation*. Toronto: University of Toronto, 1985.

Campbell, John L. *Institutional Change and Globalization*. Princeton: Princeton University Press, 2004.

Campbell, Peter. *French Electoral Systems and Elections since 1789*. 2nd ed. Hamden: Archon Books, 1965.

Carstairs, Andrew McLaren. *A Short History of Electoral Systems in Western Europe*. London: George Allen and Unwin, 1980.

Carter, April. *Direct Action and Democracy Today*. Cambridge: Polity, 2005.

Christensen, Ray. *Ending the LDP Hegemony: Party Cooperation in Japan*. Honolulu: University of Hawaii Press, 2000.

Cole, Alistair, and Peter Campbell. *French Electoral Systems and Elections since 1789*. Aldershot: Gower, 1989.

Collier, Ruth Berins. *Paths towards Democracy: The Working Class and Elites in Western Europe and South America*. Cambridge: Cambridge University Press, 1999.

Colomer, Josep M., ed. *Handbook of Electoral System Choice*. New York: Palgrave-Macmillan, 2004. http://dx.doi.org/10.1057/9780230522749.

Commons, John R. *Proportional Representation*. 2nd ed. 1907. Reprint, New York: August M. Kelley Publishers, 1967.

Cook, Terrence E., and Patrick M. Morgan, eds. *Participatory Democracy*. New York: Harper and Row, 1971.

Cowling, Maurice. *1867 Disraeli, Gladstone and Revolution: The Passing of the Second Reform Bill*. Cambridge: Cambridge University Press, 1967. http://dx.doi.org/10.1017/CBO9780511560477.

Cox, Gary W. *Making Votes Count: Strategic Coordination in the World's Electoral Systems*. Cambridge: Cambridge University Press, 1997.

Crick, Bernard. *In Defence of Politics*. 2nd ed. Chicago: University of Chicago Press, 1972.

Crouch, Colin. *Post-Democracy*. London: Polity, 2004.

Crozier, Michel, Samuel Huntington, and Joji Watanuki. *The Crisis of Democracy: Report on the Governability of Democracies to the Trilateral Commission*. New York: New York University Press, 1975.

Cunningham, Frank. *Theories of Democracy: A Critical Introduction*. New York: Routledge, 2002.

Curtis, Gerald D. *The Logic of Japanese Politics; Leaders, Institutions, and the Limits of Change*. New York: Columbia University Press, 1999.

Dahl, Robert, ed. *Political Oppositions in Western Democracies*. New Haven: Yale, 1966.

– *A Preface to Democratic Theory*. Chicago: University of Chicago Press, 1956.

Dahl, Robert A., Ian Shapiro, and Jose Antonio Cheibub, eds. *The Democracy Sourcebook*. Cambridge, MA: MIT Press, 2003.

Dahms, Harry F., ed. *No Social Science without Critical Theory*. Bingley, UK: Emerald, 2008.

Dalton, R.J., S.C. Flanagan, and P.A. Beck, eds. *Electoral Change in Advanced Industrial Democracies: Realignment or Dealignment?* New Jersey: Princeton University Press, 1984.

Denver, David, James Mitchell, Charles Pattie, and Hugh Bochel. *Scotland Decides: The Devolution Issue and the Scottish Referendum*. London: Frank Cass, 2000.

Diamond, Larry, Juan Linz, and Seymour Martin Lipset, eds. *Democracy in Developing Countries. Vol. 4: Latin America*. Boulder, CO: Lynne Rienner Publishers, 1989.

Diamond, L., and M. Plattner, eds. *The Global Resurgence of Democracy*. 2nd ed. Baltimore: Johns Hopkins University Press, 1996.

Duverger, Maurice. *Political Parties: 1954*. Reprint, New York: John Wiley and Sons, 1963.

Ebsworth, Raymond. *Restoring Democracy in Germany: The British Contribution*. New York: Praeger, 1960.

Eley, Geoff. *Forging Democracy: The History of the Left in Europe, 1850–2000*. Oxford: Oxford University Press, 2002.

Evans, P., D. Rueschemeyer, and T. Skocpol, eds. *Bringing the State Back In*. Cambridge: Cambridge University Press, 1985. http://dx.doi.org/10.1017/CBO9780511628283.

Farrell, David M. *Electoral Systems: A Comparative Introduction*. New York: Palgrave, 2001.

Farrell, David, and Ian McAllister. *The Australian Electoral System*. Sydney: University of New South Wales Press, 2006.

Finer, Herman. *The Case against PR*. London: Fabian Society, 1924.

Fung, Archon, and Erik Olin Wright, eds. *Deepening Democracy: Institutional Innovations in Empowered Participatory Governance*. London: Verso, 2003.

Gallagher, Michael, and Paul Mitchell, eds. *The Politics of Electoral Systems*. Oxford: Oxford University Press, 2005. http://dx.doi.org/10.1093/0199257566.001.0001.

Gill, Stephen. *Power and Resistance in the New World Order*. 2nd ed. Houndsmills: Palgrave Macmillan, 2008. http://dx.doi.org/10.1057/9780230584518.

Ginsberg, Benjamin. *The Consequences of Consent: Elections, Citizen Control and Popular Acquiescence*. Reading: Addison-Wesley, 1982.

Golay, John Ford. *The Founding of the Federal Republic of Germany*. Chicago: University of Chicago Press, 1958.

Goldstein, Robert J. *Political Repression in 19th Century Europe*. London: Croom Helm, 1983.

Goodwyn, Lawrence. *Democratic Promise: The Populist Moment in America*. Oxford: Oxford University Press, 1976.

Green, Philip, ed. *Democracy*. New Jersey: Humanity Books, 1993.

Green, Philip, and Sanford Levinson, eds. *Power and Community: Dissenting Essays in Political Science*. New York: Random House, 1970.

Grofman, Bernard, Sung-Chull Lee, Edwin A. Winckler, and Brian Woodall, eds. *Elections in Japan, Korea, and Taiwan under the Single Non-Transferable Vote*. Ann Arbor: University of Michigan Press, 1999.

Grofman, Bernard, and Arend Lijphart, eds. *Electoral Laws and Their Political Consequences*. New York: Agathon, 1986.

Grugel, Jean. *Democratization: A Critical Introduction*. Houndsmill: Palgrave Macmillan, 2002.

Gundle, Stephen, and Simon Parker, eds. *The New Republic: From the Fall of the Berlin Wall to Berlusconi*. London: Routledge, 1996. http://dx.doi.org/10.4324/9780203431443.

Hallett, George Jr. *Proportional Representation: The Key to Democracy*. 1940. Reprint, Westport: Hyperion, 1979.

Hand, Geoffrey, Jacques Georgel, and Christoph Sasse, eds. *European Electoral Systems Handbook*. London: Butterworths, 1979.

Hart, Jenifer. *Proportional Representation: Critics of the British Electoral System, 1820–1945*. Oxford: Clarendon, 1992.

Hay, Colin. *Political Analysis*. Houndsmill: Palgrave Macmillan, 2002.

Held, David. *Models of Democracy*. 2nd ed. Stanford: Stanford University Press, 1996.

Helleiner, Eric. *States and the Reemergence of Global Finance*. Ithaca: Cornell University Press, 1994.

Helms, Ludger, ed. *Institutions and Institutional Change in the Federal Republic of Germany*. New York: St Martin's, 2000. http://dx.doi.org/10.1057/9780333977699.

Hermans, Ferdinand A. *Democracy or Anarchy? A Study of Proportional Representation*. 1941. Reprint, New York: Johnson Reprint, 1972.

Hirschl, Ran. *Toward Juristocracy: The Origins and Consequences of the New Constitutionalism*. Cambridge, MA: Harvard University Press, 2004.

Hoag, Clarence, and George Hallett Jr. *Proportional Representation*. New York: Macmillan, 1926.

Hudson, W.J., and M.P. Sharp. *Australian Independence: Colony to Reluctant Kingdom*. Melbourne: Melbourne University Press, 1988.

Irvine, William. *Does Canada Need a New Electoral System?* Montreal and Kingston: McGill-Queen's University Press, 1979.

Isaac, Jeffrey C. *Democracy in Dark Times*. Ithaca: Cornell University Press, 1998.

Jackson, Keith, and Alan McRobie. *New Zealand Adopts Proportional Representation*. Aldershot: Ashgate, 1998.

Jones, Andrew. *The Politics of Reform 1884*. Cambridge: Cambridge University Press, 1972.

Katz, Richard. *Democracy and Elections*. New York: Oxford University Press, 1997. http://dx.doi.org/10.1093/acprof:oso/9780195044294.001.0001.

Katz, R., and P. Mair, eds. *How Parties Organize: Change and Adaptation in Party Organizations in Western Democracies*. London: Sage, 1994.

Keyssar, Alexander. *The Right to Vote: The Contested History of Democracy in the United States*. New York: Basic Books, 2000.

Kohno, Masaru. *Japan's Postwar Party Politics*. Princeton: Princeton University Press, 1997.

Kolko, Gabriel. *The Politics of War: The World and United States Foreign Policy, 1943–45*. New York: Vintage Books, 1968.

Laski, Harold. *Democracy in Crisis*. London: George Allen and Unwin, 1933.

Levin, Michael. *The Spectre of Democracy: The Rise of Modern Democracy as Seen by Its Critics*. New York: New York University Press, 1992.

Lijphart, Arend. *Electoral Systems and Party Systems: A Study of Twenty-Seven Democracies, 1945–1990*. Oxford: Oxford University Press, 1994.

– *Patterns of Democracy: Government Forms and Performance in Thirty-Six Countries*. New Haven: Yale University Press, 1999.

– *The Politics of Accommodation: Pluralism and Democracy in the Netherlands*. Berkeley: University of California Press, 1968.

Lipset, Seymour Martin. *Political Man: The Sociological Bases of Politics*. 1960; New York: Anchor Books, 1963.

Lundell, Krister. *The Origins of Electoral Systems in the Postwar Era*. New York: Routledge, 2009.

Mackie, Gerry. *Democracy Defended*. Cambridge: Cambridge University Press, 2003. http://dx.doi.org/10.1017/CBO9780511490293.

Mackie, Thomas T., and Richard Rose. *The International Almanac of Electoral History*. 2nd ed. New York: Facts on File, 1982.

Macpherson, C.B. *The Life and Times of Liberal Democracy*. Oxford: Oxford University Press, 1977.

– *The Real World of Democracy*. 1965. Toronto: CBC Enterprises, 1992.

Manin, Bernard. *The Principles of Representative Government*. Cambridge: Cambridge University Press, 1997. http://dx.doi.org/10.1017/CBO9780511659935.

Maravall, J., and I. Sanchez-Cuenca, eds. *Controlling Governments: Voters, Institutions, and Accountability*. Cambridge: Cambridge University Press, 2008.

Marshall, T.H. *Citizenship and Social Class and Other Essays*. Cambridge: Cambridge University Press, 1950.

Massicotte, Louis, André Blais, and Antoine Yoshinaka. *Establishing the Rules of the Game: Election Laws in Democracies*. Toronto: University of Toronto Press, 2004.

Merkl, Peter H. *The Origin of the West German Republic*. New York: Oxford University Press, 1963.

Mershon, Carol, and Gianfranco Pasquino, eds. *Italian Politics*. Vol. 9, *Ending the First Republic*. Boulder: Westview, 1995.

Mettenheim, Kurt von, ed. *Presidential Institutions and Democratic Politics*. Baltimore: Johns Hopkins University Press, 1997.

Miliband, Ralph. *The State in Capitalist Society*. 1969; London: Quartet Books, 1973.

Mills, C. Wright. *The Sociological Imagination*. New York: Oxford University Press, 1959.

Milner, Henry, ed. *Making Every Vote Count: Reassessing Canada's Electoral System*. Peterborough: Broadview, 1999.

– *Steps toward Making Every Vote Count: Electoral Reform in Canada and Its Provinces*. Peterborough: Broadview, 2004.

Moore, Barrington, Jr. *Social Origins of Dictatorship and Democracy: Lord and Peasant in the Making of the Modern World*. Boston: Beacon, 1966.

Myers, A.R. *Parliaments and Estates in Europe to 1789*. London: Thames and Hudson, 1975.

Newman, W.L. *Social Research Methods: Quantitative and Qualitative Methods*. 4th ed. Boston: Allyn and Bacon, 2000.

Noiret, Serge, ed. *Political Strategies and Electoral Reforms: Origins of Voting Systems in Europe in the 19th and 20th Centuries*. Baden-Baden: Nomos Verlagsgesellschaft, 1990.

Nordlinger, Eric A. *On the Autonomy of the Democratic State*. Cambridge: Harvard University Press, 1981.

Norris, Pippa. *Electoral Engineering: Voting Rules and Political Behavior*. Cambridge: Cambridge University Press, 2004. http://dx.doi.org/10.1017/CBO9780511790980.

Ostrogorski, M. *Democracy and the Organization of Political Parties*. Vol. 1. England: 1902.

Panebianco, Angelo. *Political Parties: Organization and Power*. Cambridge: Cambridge University Press, 1988.

Parry, Gerraint, and Michael Moran, eds. *Democracy and Democratization*. London: Routledge, 1994. http://dx.doi.org/10.4324/9780203198551.

Pateman, Carole. *Participation and Democratic Theory*. Cambridge: Cambridge University Press, 1970.

Pennock, J. Roland. *Democratic Political Theory*. Princeton: Princeton University Press, 1979.

Pierce, Roy. *French Politics and Political Institutions*. New York: Harper and Row, 1973.

Piven, Frances Fox. *Challenging Authority: How Ordinary People Change America*. Lanham: Rowman and Littlefield, 2006.

Pugh, Martin. *Electoral Reform in War and Peace 1906–18*. London: Routledge and Kegan Paul, 1978.

– *The Evolution of the British Electoral System, 1832–1987*. London: Historical Association, 1990.

Rae, Douglas. *The Political Consequences of Electoral Law*. New Haven: Yale University Press, 1971.

Renwick, Alan. *The Politics of Electoral Reform: Changing the Rules of Democracy*. Cambridge: Cambridge University Press, 2010.

Reynolds, Andrew. *Electoral Systems and Democratization in Southern Africa*. Oxford: Oxford University Press, 1999. http://dx.doi.org/10.1093/0198295103.001.0001.

Rokkan, Stein. *Citizens, Elections, Parties: Approaches to the Comparative Study of Processes of Development*. New York: David McKay, 1970.

Roper, Jon. *Democracy and Its Critics: Anglo-American Democratic Thought in the Nineteenth Century*. London: Unwin Hyman, 1989.

Rose, Richard, ed. *Electoral Behaviour: A Comparative Handbook*. New York: Free Press, 1974.

Rowat, Donald C. *The Ombudsman Plan: Essays on the Worldwide Spread of an Idea*. Toronto: McClelland and Stewart, 1973.

Rueschemeyer, Dietrich, Evelyne Huber Stephens, and John D. Stephens. *Capitalist Development and Democracy*. Chicago: University of Chicago Press, 1992.

Schumpeter, Joseph P. *Capitalism, Socialism and Democracy*. 1943; New York: Harper Torchbooks, 1976.

Self, Peter. *Government by the Market?* Boulder: Westview, 1993.

Seymour, Charles. *Electoral Reform in England and Wales: The Development and Operation of the Parliamentary Franchise, 1832–1885*. New Haven: Yale University Press, 1915.

Shugart, Matthew Soberg, and Martin P. Wattenberg, eds. *Mixed-Member Electoral Systems: The Best of Both Worlds?* Oxford: Oxford University Press, 2001.

Skocpol, Theda, ed. *Vision and Method in Historical Sociology*. Cambridge: Cambridge University Press, 1984.

Steinmetz, George, ed. *The Politics of Method in the Human Sciences*. Durham: Duke University Press, 2005.

Steinmo, S., K. Thelen, and F. Longstreth, eds. *Structuring Politics: Historical Institutionalism in Comparative Politics*. Cambridge: Cambridge University Press, 1992. http://dx.doi.org/10.1017/CBO9780511528125.

Storing, Herbert J., ed. *Essays on the Scientific Study of Politics*. New York: Holt, Rhinehart and Winston, 1962.

Stretton, Hugh. *The Political Sciences*. London: Routledge and Kegan Paul, 1969.

Swanson, D.L., and P. Mancini, eds. *Politics, Media and Modern Democracy: An International Study of Innovations in Electoral Campaigning and Their Political Consequences*. Westport: Praeger, 1996.

Thompson, Dorothy. *The Chartists*. London: Temple Smith, 1984.

Thompson, E.P. *Customs in Common*. New York: New Press, 1991.

– *The Poverty of Theory*. Manchester: Merlin, 1978.

Tilly, Charles. *Democracy*. Cambridge: Cambridge University Press, 2007.

Todd, Malcolm J., and Gary Taylor, eds. *Democracy and Participation: Popular Protest and New Social Movements*. London: Merlin, 2004.

Tornudd, Klaus. *The Electoral System of Finland*. London: Hugh Evelyn, 1968.

Wainwright, Hilary. *Reclaim the State: Experiments in Popular Democracy*. London: Verso, 2003.

Waligorski, Conrad. *The Political Theory of Conservative Economists*. Lawrence: University Press of Kansas, 1990.

Author Index

Subject Index

Albania, 134
alternative vote (AV), 108–9, 111, 113–16, 118, 120–1, 125, 138, 140, 142, 145–8, 288*n*194, 345*n*138
American Proportional Representation League, 122
Asquith, Herbert, 110, 112, 123, 138, 297*n*290
Australia, 30, 39, 41, 63–4, 73, 105–7, 114–20, 123–5, 140–1, 143, 146, 157, 188, 202, 231
Austria, 52, 127, 134, 269*n*10
Austro-Hungarian Empire, 84, 127, 129, 134, 158

Belgium, 19, 30, 39, 42–3, 51–2, 55, 59, 64–72, 74–5, 87, 93, 97, 101, 109, 124, 127, 129, 133–4, 143, 229
Benoist, Charles, 97
Bismarck, Otto von, 63–4, 76–7, 263*n*52, 269–70*n*10
Blair, Tony, 215, 219–23, 225, 341*n*110, 342*n*122, 342*n*126, 344*n*135
Blum, Leon, 170, 318*n*79, 321*n*99
Branting, Hjalmar, 90, 265*n*71
Briand, Aristide, 97, 279*n*115, 280*n*127

Britain. *See* United Kingdom
Broadbent, Ed, 194, 328*n*9

Canada, 8, 19, 30–1, 39, 41, 44, 53, 63, 73, 105–6, 114, 117, 122–5, 127, 140–1, 143, 145–8, 157, 188, 191–5, 224, 232
Canadian PR Society, 122
capitalism, 3, 46, 62–3, 107, 128, 134, 189, 215, 229
Chartism, 60–1
Clemenceau, Georges, 97, 279*n*115
Communist International, 129, 131
comparative historical method, 7, 19, 20, 22–6, 29
Confindustria, 162
Craxi, Bettino, 210, 313*n*34, 336*n*77
critical institutionalism, 7, 9, 26–9, 228
cultural modernization, 6–7, 12–15, 17, 23, 27
Czechoslovakia, 127, 129

de-alignment, 13, 19, 31, 190, 198–9, 200–1
De Gasperi, Alcide, 160, 162–4, 313*n*30, 313*n*32, 314*n*39

Studies in Comparative Political Economy and Public Policy